Scenographies of Perception
Sensuousness in Hegel, Novalis, Rilke, and Proust

LEGENDA

LEGENDA is the Modern Humanities Research Association's book imprint for new research in the Humanities. Founded in 1995 by Malcolm Bowie and others within the University of Oxford, Legenda has always been a collaborative publishing enterprise, directly governed by scholars. The Modern Humanities Research Association (MHRA) joined this collaboration in 1998, became half-owner in 2004, in partnership with Maney Publishing and then Routledge, and has since 2016 been sole owner. Titles range from medieval texts to contemporary cinema and form a widely comparative view of the modern humanities, including works on Arabic, Catalan, English, French, German, Greek, Italian, Portuguese, Russian, Spanish, and Yiddish literature. Editorial boards and committees of more than 60 leading academic specialists work in collaboration with bodies such as the Society for French Studies, the British Comparative Literature Association and the Association of Hispanists of Great Britain & Ireland.

The MHRA encourages and promotes advanced study and research in the field of the modern humanities, especially modern European languages and literature, including English, and also cinema. It aims to break down the barriers between scholars working in different disciplines and to maintain the unity of humanistic scholarship. The Association fulfils this purpose through the publication of journals, bibliographies, monographs, critical editions, and the MHRA Style Guide, and by making grants in support of research. Membership is open to all who work in the Humanities, whether independent or in a University post, and the participation of younger colleagues entering the field is especially welcomed.

ALSO PUBLISHED BY THE ASSOCIATION

Critical Texts
Tudor and Stuart Translations • *New Translations* • *European Translations*
MHRA Library of Medieval Welsh Literature

MHRA Bibliographies
Publications of the Modern Humanities Research Association

The Annual Bibliography of English Language & Literature
Austrian Studies
Modern Language Review
Portuguese Studies
The Slavonic and East European Review
Working Papers in the Humanities
The Yearbook of English Studies

www.mhra.org.uk
www.legendabooks.com

STUDIES IN COMPARATIVE LITERATURE

Editorial Committee
Chairs: Dr Emily Finer (University of St Andrews)
and Professor Wen-chin Ouyang (SOAS, London)

Dr Ross Forman (University of Warwick)
Professor Angus Nicholls (Queen Mary, University of London)
Dr Henriette Partzsch (University of Glasgow)
Dr Ranka Primorac (University of Southampton)

Studies in Comparative Literature are produced in close collaboration with the British Comparative Literature Association, and range widely across comparative and theoretical topics in literary and translation studies, accommodating research at the interface between different artistic media and between the humanities and the sciences.

ALSO PUBLISHED IN THIS SERIES

20. *Aestheticism and the Philosophy of Death: Walter Pater and Post-Hegelianism*, by Giles Whiteley
21. *Blake, Lavater and Physiognomy*, by Sibylle Erle
22. *Rethinking the Concept of the Grotesque: Crashaw, Baudelaire, Magritte*, by Shun-Liang Chao
23. *The Art of Comparison: How Novels and Critics Compare*, by Catherine Brown
24. *Borges and Joyce: An Infinite Conversation*, by Patricia Novillo-Corvalán
25. *Prometheus in the Nineteenth Century: From Myth to Symbol*, by Caroline Corbeau-Parsons
26. *Architecture, Travellers and Writers: Constructing Histories of Perception*, by Anne Hultzsch
27. *Comparative Literature in Britain: National Identities, Transnational Dynamics 1800-2000*, by Joep Leerssen with Elinor Shaffer
28. *The Realist Author and Sympathetic Imagination*, by Sotirios Paraschas
29. *Iris Murdoch and Elias Canetti: Intellectual Allies*, by Elaine Morley
30. *Likenesses: Translation, Illustration, Interpretation*, by Matthew Reynolds
31. *Exile and Nomadism in French and Hispanic Women's Writing*, by Kate Averis
32. *Samuel Butler against the Professionals: Rethinking Lamarckism 1860–1900*, by David Gillott
33. *Byron, Shelley, and Goethe's Faust: An Epic Connection*, by Ben Hewitt
34. *Leopardi and Shelley: Discovery, Translation and Reception*, by Daniela Cerimonia
35. *Oscar Wilde and the Simulacrum: The Truth of Masks*, by Giles Whiteley
36. *The Modern Culture of Reginald Farrer: Landscape, Literature and Buddhism*, by Michael Charlesworth
37. *Translating Myth*, edited by Ben Pestell, Pietra Palazzolo and Leon Burnett
38. *Encounters with Albion: Britain and the British in Texts by Jewish Refugees from Nazism*, by Anthony Grenville
39. *The Rhetoric of Exile: Duress and the Imagining of Force*, by Vladimir Zorić
40. *From Puppet to Cyborg: Pinocchio's Posthuman Journey*, by Georgia Panteli
41. *Utopian Identities: A Cognitive Approach to Literary Competitions*, by Clementina Osti
43. *Sublime Conclusions: Last Man Narratives from Apocalypse to Death of God*, by Robert K. Weninger
44. *Arthur Symons: Poet, Critic, Vagabond*, edited by Elisa Bizzotto and Stefano Evangelista
45. *Scenographies of Perception: Sensuousness in Hegel, Novalis, Rilke, and Proust*, by Christian Jany
46. *Reflections in the Library: Selected Literary Essays 1926–1944*, by Antal Szerb
47. *Depicting the Divine: Mikhail Bulgakov and Thomas Mann*, by Olga G. Voronina
48. *Samuel Butler and the Evolutionary Debate: Science, Literature and Unconscious Memory*, by Cristiano Turbil
49. *Death Sentences: Literature and State Killing*, edited by Birte Christ and Ève Morisi
50. *Words Like Fire: Prophecy and Apocalypse in Apollinaire, Marinetti and Pound*, by James P. Leveque

Scenographies of Perception

Sensuousness in Hegel, Novalis, Rilke, and Proust

Christian Jany

LEGENDA

Studies in Comparative Literature 45
Modern Humanities Research Association
2019

Published by Legenda
an imprint of the Modern Humanities Research Association
Salisbury House, Station Road, Cambridge CB1 2LA

ISBN 978-1-78188-509-3 (HB)
ISBN 978-1-78188-510-9 (PB)

First published 2019
Paperback edition 2021

All rights reserved. No part of this publication may be reproduced or disseminated or transmitted in any form or by any means, electronic, mechanical, photocopying, recording or otherwise, or stored in any retrieval system, or otherwise used in any manner whatsoever without written permission of the copyright owner, except in accordance with the provisions of the Copyright, Designs and Patents Act 1988, or under the terms of a licence permitting restricted copying issued in the UK by the Copyright Licensing Agency Ltd, Saffron House, 6–10 Kirby Street, London EC1N 8TS, *England, or in the USA by the Copyright Clearance Center, 222 Rosewood Drive, Danvers MA 01923. Application for the written permission of the copyright owner to reproduce any part of this publication must be made by email to legenda@mhra.org.uk.*

Disclaimer: Statements of fact and opinion contained in this book are those of the author and not of the editors or the Modern Humanities Research Association. The publisher makes no representation, express or implied, in respect of the accuracy of the material in this book and cannot accept any legal responsibility or liability for any errors or omissions that may be made.

Trademark notice: Product or corporate names may be trademarks or registered trademarks, and are used only for identification and explanation without intent to infringe.

© *Modern Humanities Research Association 2019*

Copy-Editor: Dr Nigel Hope

CONTENTS

Preface		ix
Translations and Abbreviations		xiv
Introduction: On Perception and Narration		1
Starting points		1
Aesthesis and diegesis		9
Participation and concretization		13
Perceiving diegetic worlds		16
Aesthesiologies		20
Texts and scenes		24
Scenographies		28
The task ahead		31
I The 'Story' of Perception (Hegel)		43
	1 The Dialectic Force of the Senses	45
	Hegel in the Swiss Alps	45
	Sense experience in the *Phenomenology*	47
	2 Sense-Certainty (Process)	54
	Noticing, meaning, knowing	54
	Negation, deixis, language	57
	Here and Now as abstractions, and as dialectic	63
	The (hi)story of sense-certainty	70
	3 Object Perception (Relation)	75
	Perception as determinate negation	75
	The recursivity of perception	77
	The intervention of reflection	84
	Logos as substance of reflection	90
	(Hi)stories and concepts	96
II The Language of the Senses (Novalis, Rilke, Proust)		115
	1 Reciprocity of Perception and Poetry in Novalis	117
	The poetry of perception, or, 'the art to become almighty'	117
	Difficulties with the senses	123
	'Wechselbestimmung'	130
	The perception of poetry, or, 'the blue flower'	139

2	Looking with Rilke	160
	Seeing things	160
	Exchanging imprints	163
	Anxiety and objectification	169
	Nachträglichkeit	176
	Anonymity and inexhaustibility	181
3	Listening to Proust's *Recherche*	195
	Music and memory, or, the leitmotif	195
	'Longtemps'	200
	The music of Vinteuil	209

Conclusion — 225

Bibliography — 231

Index — 249

PREFACE

This is a book about the interplay between perception and narration, aesthesis and diegesis. The most delightful manifestation of this interplay I take to be the complex forms of perception and bodily sense that arise in response to narrative scenes of perception. The unheard-of things a Rilkean poem has us see, the evocative sound pervading the overture of *À la recherche du temps perdu*, and the strange fusion of thought and feeling at the beginning of *Heinrich von Ofterdingen* are chief examples thereof. Like all perceptions, these complex literary perceptions, in which sensory and narrative processes mingle, transcend pure affect and immediate sensation. They involve cognition and understanding as well, but in 'a state of bodily possession', Stanley Corngold points out, 'associable neither with reason nor imagination alone but produced by and between their conjuncture'.[1] It is, perhaps, because of such in-betweenness that literary perceptions often feel just as puzzling and elusive as fascinating and entertaining.

The given examples, discussed at length in Part Two, derive from literary works. They refer to scenes communicated *in writing*. For that reason, my inquiry cannot concern phenomenal scenes as such, or the specific sensations and feelings individual readers or a group of readers may develop in response to literature. Instead of measuring and determining the nature of what is perceived in reading, as psychologists and neuroscientists variously do, I consider how passages of text *describe* processes of perception, scriptings of perception I call 'scenographies'.[2]

Sometimes, reading scenographies produces novel perceptions and sensations unheard of, a new sense in itself that has the power to change one's ways of looking, listening, and feeling. I am convinced that the scenographies discussed in this book have the power to do so. Therein lies their aesthetic power, in their very ability to affect not only intellect but also sensorium. Scenographies are the place where this power becomes palpable, and the interplay between aesthesis and diegesis perceptible.[3]

Although the sensuous power of literature is an irrefutable fact of experience, it is usually excluded from the study of literature as it is, strictly speaking, external to the text. Texts themselves do not 'perceive', nor 'think' or 'feel'. They contain words rather than sensations, for they are literary objects, verbal compositions. New Critics such as W. K. Wimsatt and M. C. Beardsley underscored this simple but equally irrefutable fact, while Paul de Man built an entire theory around it.[4]

It is true that literary texts and sensory experiences operate differently. They differ materially as well as conceptually, because their constitutive elements or 'matters' — sensations and words — are not the same. But are they therefore incommensurable? Is there no link between the two? Is it possible, and what could it mean, to speak of an 'interplay' between sensory and narrative processes? This theoretical crux is the starting point of my inquiry and one key question addressed in this book. The other key question, addressed primarily in Part Two, applies the crux to works of literature by asking: How do scenographies from works by Novalis, Rilke, and Proust enable and indeed provoke literary perceptions? By what literary means and strategies do these scenographies reach our sensorium, and in what sense do they contain 'sensory-perceptual dynamics'[5] within their textual structure and scenic set-up?

To illustrate the theoretical crux, the Introduction first considers two poems by Durs Grünbein, a contemporary German poet whose works often display distinctly scenic qualities. This inductive approach paves the way for theoretical reflections on the interdependence of sensory and narrative processes, aesthesis and diegesis. I hypothesize that these two processes overlap insofar as both require a reorganization of their basic elements (sensations or words), a reorganization of successive contents achieved through the generation and application of temporal schemata. These *emergent* schemata or 'stories', which we develop as readers and perceivers alike, I then define as 'aesthesiologies'. The closer definition of scenographies finally gathers these hypotheses and relates them to features of narrative.

The following Part One explicates Hegel's theory of sense perception in the *Phänomenologie des Geistes*. According to this theory, sense perception is basically a narrative activity. The process and logic of sense perception correspond to a 'story' (*Geschichte*), Hegel argues, which means perception too is characterized by a linkage of process and result, succession and relation — or, in narratological terms, of discourse and story. Hegel's theory thus specifies the interplay between words and sensations, narrative and sensory activity, aesthesis and diegesis, but it also has implications with regard to his mode of demonstration in the *Phenomenology*: Scenographies are here the essential means of understanding consciousness, since they illustrate a process, a movement, a history of conscious experience, while simultaneously communicating concepts or knowledge — the logic or, indeed, story underlying that experience.

Part Two turns to scenographies in works of literature, hence to the genre of text that speaks 'the language of the senses'.[6] I examine the distinctive logics of perception or aesthesiologies that are at work in scenographies by Novalis, Rilke, and Proust. The opening chapter explores the fundamental reciprocity of poetry and perception in texts by Novalis. In *Die Lehrlinge zu Saïs*, poetry (*Dichten*) is presented as an 'inverted usage' of the senses, while *Heinrich von Ofterdingen* poeticizes this paradigm under the sign of the 'blue flower'. The next chapter concerns scenographies of looking in works from Rilke's middle period. Looking here, however, proceeds as an anonymous exchange of glances, a paradoxical aesthesiology, which displaces origins and complicates the temporality of looking. The chapter on *À la recherche du temps perdu* examines Proust's leitmotif technique, an operatic aesthesiology that underlies several important scenographies in this novel. Thanks to his leitmotif technique, the narrator has the power not only to speak of involuntary memories but actually to trigger them with words.

Having indicated the scope and intent of this book, I should also like to situate it briefly in the scholarly landscape. 'Perception' and 'sensation' have become popular topics in literary studies, especially in the past twenty years.[7] The self-understanding of these newer studies is predominantly historical, since they reconstruct the social, cultural, technological, and political regimes of perception during a specific period. The necessary presupposition of such reconstructions is that literary texts also reflect a historically contingent discourse on perception, viz. the cross-disciplinary 'knowledge' determining the limits of what can be said, written, or thought concerning the human senses at a given point in time.

My approach is different. This book is not a history of perception in the context of nineteenth- and early twentieth-century literary culture, nor a critical history of the idea that literature appeals, or ought to appeal, to the senses. I will not demonstrate that certain literary passages conceptually overlap with contemporaneous concepts or practices of perception, thus revealing the ruling discourse of perception at the time, nor will I historicize the concepts and ideas employed in this book. Although based on historical sources, this book is firmly rooted in the present, in the present desire I share with other readers and critics to reclaim the inherent sensuousness of literature.[8]

What I have attempted, therefore, is to explain the aesthetic power of literature both theoretically and through close readings of scenographies. These readings are 'close' in the twofold sense of staying close to the text and, moreover, staying close to the kind of immersion scenographies call for. The latter point is particularly important since perceiving and understanding a scenography fundamentally means to *produce* its scene, 'to feel some of the things with some of the faculties' therein described.[9]

This is not to say that discursive backgrounds and historical contexts are irrelevant in reading scenographies, nor to deny the historicity of perception as a cognitive act shaped by culture and technology. I simply insist on the essential difference between historical knowledge *about* perception and the inherent potential of scenographies *for* perception. Considering the former as the source of the latter would simply confuse the genesis and historical context of scenographies with their aesthetic impact today, the power and appeal they currently have and, perhaps, continue to have.

Ideally, this book will form a connected whole in the eye of its reader. To some, however, its chapters may amount to no more than a series of loosely connected essays, each staking out its own domain. Either way, taken as a proper monograph or a collection of essays, I hope that each chapter will in its own way illuminate the 'strange coincidence of form, feeling, and intellect', as Coleridge once put it, defining the aesthetic — 'that something, which, confirming the inner and the outward senses, becomes a new sense in itself, to be tried by laws of its own, and acknowledging the laws of the understanding so far only as not to contradict them'.[10]

★ ★ ★ ★ ★

Writing a book is a solitary undertaking that I could not have accomplished, however, without the friendship and support of others. My thanks go to Claudia Brodsky, for her universal brilliance and her utter devotion to my work, and to Brigid Doherty, for her prudent counsel and her support in getting my dissertation over the line. I am also much indebted to Stanley Corngold for his generosity as a mentor and friend, including several critical lessons in clarity and style. Andreas Kilcher I wish to thank for providing me with the liberty to pursue my research freely, but never alone. My friend Hamish Robb I must thank for reading me often, carefully, and with musical sympathy. Additionally, Mārtiņš Mašulis and Anat Benzvi helped me to enhance my prose, for which I am grateful. Regular conversations with Klas Molde were instrumental in keeping my senses fresh and alive, while Philipp Auchter, Christian Finger, Emanuel Tandler, and Jonas Stähelin have more than once prevented me from expiring in my study. Legenda's Managing Editor, Nelson Graham, I wish to thank for running a smooth operation. It has been a pleasure publishing with Legenda, not least because of my excellent copy-editor Nigel Hope. Without his tireless and incredibly meticulous work, this book would contain flaws beyond counting. Whatever mistakes remain are entirely my own. Finally, I want to thank Kani Keita for her love and enthusiasm, 'a sense sublime | Of something far more deeply interfused'. I couldn't have written this book without her.

Zurich, April 2019

Notes to the Preface

1. Stanley Corngold, *Complex Pleasure: Forms of Feeling in German Literature* (Stanford: Stanford University Press, 1998), pp. xiv, xvi.
2. For me, the sketch after John Singer Sargent's *El Jaleo* on the cover of this book represents a wonderful example of a scenography in the medium of drawing rather than writing. Literary scenographies, however, are neither images nor sketches but text, scenes described in words, *verbal* outlines, hence scriptings of perception.
3. For a justification of the belief, shared by Schiller, Adorno, Merleau-Ponty, and many other aestheticians, that works of art have the power to extend our sensory faculties, see Hans Robert Jauß, *Ästhetische Erfahrung und literarische Hermeneutik* (Frankfurt am Main: Suhrkamp, 1982), pp. 39–40, 125–65.
4. At the same time, it was one of the most formalistically minded literary critics of the twentieth century, Northrop Frye, who wrote in *Anatomy of Criticism: Four Essays* (Princeton: Princeton University Press, 1957) that all criticism 'comes out of' experience — although, Frye continues, it 'cannot be built on it', because 'the experience of literature is, like literature itself, unable to speak' (pp. 27–28). Continuing this line of thought, one might say that criticism means, quite simply, making literature speak by explaining one's experience to others.
5. I borrow this term from Kerry McSweeney, *The Language of the Senses: Sensory-Perceptual Dynamics in Wordsworth, Coleridge, Thoreau, Whitman, and Dickinson* (Montreal: McGill-Queen's University Press, 1998). McSweeney here maintains that literature is not just an affair of 'language-talking-to-language' but based on 'sensory-perceptual acuity' (p. x). In contrast to my reader-oriented approach, however, according to which the perceptual dynamic emerges between reader and text, McSweeney considers it 'an essential attribute of a poet' (p. ix), so that it is necessarily 'blunted' by the poet's 'illness or age' (p. x). But really, is the visual force of a work such as *Paradise Lost* in any way diminished by the fact that Milton was blind when he composed it? Does sensory acuity always correlate with sensuous poetry? I would not think so.

The sensory force of literature is surely based on composition rather than the author's private sensations, on the masterly combination of words, and simultaneously on the reader's response to these words.

6. This line is taken, with a slight alteration, from William Wordsworth's 'Tintern Abbey', wherein the speaker calls himself a lover 'of all the mighty world | Of eye and ear' who is 'well pleased to recognize | In nature and the language of the sense [...] the guardian of my heart, and soul | Of all my moral being' (William Wordsworth and Samuel Taylor Coleridge, *Lyrical Ballads*, ed. by R. L. Brett and A. R. Jones (London: Routledge, 1991), p. 113). According to William Empson, 'Sense in *The Prelude*', *The Kenyon Review*, 13 (1951), 285–302, Wordsworth's peculiar usage of 'sense' here and elsewhere in his work betrays that for him, the word 'means both the process of sensing and the supreme act of imagination, and unites them by a jump' (p. 302).
7. See, for example, Jonathan Crary, *Techniques of the Observer: On Vision and Modernity in the Nineteenth Century* (Cambridge, MA: MIT Press, 1990); *Armaturen der Sinne: Literarische und technische Medien 1870 bis 1920*, ed. by Jochen Hörisch and Michael Wetzel (Munich: Fink, 1990); the 'Sensory Formations Series' edited by David Howes (London: Bloomsbury, 2005–); Mark M. Smith, *Sensing the Past: Seeing, Hearing, Smelling, Tasting, and Touching in History* (Berkeley: University of California Press, 2007); Ralph Köhnen, *Das optische Wissen: Mediologische Studien zu einer Geschichte des Sehens* (Paderborn: Fink, 2009); *A Cultural History of the Senses*, ed. by Constance Classen and others, 6 vols (London: Bloomsbury: 2014).
8. In particular, I am thinking of Peter Utz, *Das Auge und das Ohr im Text: Literarische Sinneswahrnehmung in der Goethezeit* (Munich: Fink, 1990); McSweeney; Corngold, *Complex Pleasure*; *Sensual Reading: New Approaches to Reading in its Relations to the Senses*, ed. by Michael Syrotinski and Ian Maclachlan (Lewisburg: Bucknell University Press, 2001); Susan Stewart, *Poetry and the Fate of the Senses* (Chicago: University of Chicago Press, 2002); *Wahrnehmen und Handeln: Perspektiven einer Literaturanthropologie*, ed. by Friedmar Apel and others (Bielefeld: Aisthesis, 2004); Noel Jackson, *Science and Sensation in British Romantic Poetry* (Cambridge: Cambridge University Press, 2008); Peter Mendelsund, *What We See When We Read: A Phenomenology* (New York: Vintage Books, 2014).
9. Corngold, *Complex Pleasure*, p. 15.
10. S. T. Coleridge to William Blackwood in 1821; see *Biographia Epistolaris: Being the Biographical Supplement of Coleridge's Biographia Literaria, with Additional Letters, Etc.*, ed. by Arthur Turnbull, 2 vols (London: G. Bell and Sons, 1911), II, 236–37.

TRANSLATIONS AND ABBREVIATIONS
❖

I refer throughout to the original texts. When quoting longer passages in French or German, I generally offer standard English translations, modifying these throughout in the interests of greater literalness or, in the case of theoretical and philosophical texts, simplicity. Shorter passages I quote only in translation, inserting 'the original phrase' [die ursprüngliche Wendung] in square brackets whenever in doubt about the translation. All other translations are my own.

The '*emphasis* of words' within quotations always reflects the original unless noted otherwise, as in '*Longtemps*, je me suis couché de bonne heure' (*Swann*, 3; emphasis added).

* * * * *

The following abbreviations are used for frequently cited editions:

- F J. G. Fichte, *Sämmtliche Werke*, ed. by Immanuel Hermann Fichte, 8 vols (Berlin: Veit & Comp., 1845–46)
- GW G. W. F. Hegel, *Gesammelte Werke*, ed. by Walter Jaeschke and others (Hamburg: Meiner, 1968–)
- KrV Immanuel Kant, *Kritik der reinen Vernunft*, in Kant, *Werke*, ed. by Wilhelm Weischedel, 12 vols (Frankfurt am Main: Suhrkamp, 1977), as well as Kant, *Critique of Pure Reason*, trans. and ed. by Paul Guyer and Allen W. Wood (Cambridge: Cambridge University Press, 1998)
- N Novalis, *Werke, Tagebücher und Briefe Friedrich von Hardenbergs*, ed. by Hans-Joachim Mähl and Richard H. Samuel, 3 vols (Munich: Hanser, 1978)
- PhG G. W. F. Hegel, *Phänomenologie des Geistes* (= TWA III), followed by the corresponding page number, always marked with an asterisk (*), in *Phenomenology of Spirit*, ed. by J. N. Findlay, trans. by Arnold V. Miller (Oxford: Clarendon Press, 1977)
- R Rainer Maria Rilke, *Sämtliche Werke*, ed. by Ernst Zinn, 7 vols (Frankfurt am Main: Insel, 1955–97)
- TWA G. W. F. Hegel, *Werke* ('Theorie-Werkausgabe'), ed. by Eva Moldenhauer and Karl Markus Michel, 20 vols (Frankfurt am Main: Suhrkamp, 1986)

Swann, Filles, Prisonnière, Retrouvé each refer to the respective volume in the 'folio classique' paperback edition of:

Marcel Proust, *À la recherche du temps perdu*, ed. by Jean-Yves Tadié and others, 7 vols (Paris: Gallimard, 1988–90)

and are followed by the corresponding volume and page numbers in:

Proust, *In Search of Lost Time*, trans. by C. K. Scott Moncrieff, Terence Kilmartin, and Andreas Mayor, revised by D. J. Enright, 6 vols (London: Chatto & Windus, 1992).

★ ★ ★ ★ ★

Finally, a word about orthography in Hegel's *Phänomenologie des Geistes*. Hegel was displeased with the error-ridden first edition of the *Phänomenologie* and generally thought that a 'revision [Umarbeitung] of the work' (GW IX, 476) would be necessary. But, because of his premature death in 1831, he could not revise his work beyond a certain point in the Preface. Most orthographical emendations the editors of the 'Theorie-Werkausgabe' applied to the *Phänomenologie* are, therefore, not sanctioned by Hegel. Take, as an example, '*Sichaufsichbeziehen*' (PhG 95/69★) against '*sich auf sich beziehen*' in the first edition (GW IX, 72). I think nominalizations of this kind cast a metaphysical shadow on perfectly ordinary formulations, which is why I have always compared these two editions against each other, tacitly removing the more misleading orthographic emendations.

INTRODUCTION

On Perception and Narration

Starting points

In der Provinz 2

(Auf Gotland)

Nur dies gab es auf lange Sicht hier, diesen Wellenfluß
Von Landschaft, fokussiert in einem Bussardauge, —
Die kahlen Hügel, einen Feldweg und am Rand
Die Hasenpfote im Gebüsch, vom Wind zerzaust
Ein abgenagtes Sprunggelenk, das in der Hand
So leicht wog wie ein Vogeljunges,
Das noch beweglich war, noch warm war und heraus
Sprang aus der Pfanne, blutig wie die Beute
Des Grauen Würgers auf dem Dorn der Eberesche, —
Ein kleiner Knöchel, winkend mit dem Fetzchen Fell.

Sah so der Rest von einem Hasen aus, nachdem
Der Schatten eines Flügels über ihn gekommen war,
Den Zickzacklauf ein Krallengriff, den flachen Atem
Gezielter Schnabelhieb beendet hatte? Unbequem
Muß dieser Tod gewesen sein, auf winterlicher Erde
Wehrlos verrenkt, die letzte Zuckung.
Was vom Gemetzel übrigblieb, hing in den Zweigen,
Die sich an nichts erinnern wie bestochne Zeugen.
Das Gras, längst wieder aufgerichtet, sorgt dafür,
Daß es auf lange Sicht nur dies gab hier, den Hasenfuß.

In the Provinces 2

(On Gotland)

This was all there was to see here, this
Undulating landscape assembled in a buzzard's eye —
The bare hills, a track, and at the edge of it
A rabbit's foot in the undergrowth, ruffled by the wind,
A gnawed-off ankle joint that weighed no more
In your hand than a baby bird,
Still bendable, still warm, and that leapt
Out of the socket, bloodied as the prey
Of the grey strangler on top of the rowan —
A little lump of bone, beckoning with a flap of fur.

> Was that all that was left of a rabbit after
> The shadow of a wing crossed its path,
> After its zigzag run was ended by a claw, and its panting
> Breath by a well-aimed beak? How uncomfortable
> This death must have been, helplessly splayed
> On the wintry earth, and there its last convulsion.
> The remains of the butchery perched in the boughs,
> Which do not remember anything, like bribed witnesses.
> The grass, resurrected long since then, ensures
> That this was all there was to see here, the rabbit's foot.

Durs Grünbein's poem summons a scene wherein perception and narration are closely intertwined. Like the other four thing-poems from the cycle 'In der Provinz', first published in the volume *Nach den Satiren* (1999), it depicts an encounter with an animal carcass.[1] Moving downward, from landscape to hills to trail, the observer's gaze halts on something lying sideways in a bush — the foot of a rabbit, which appears to have been gnawed off at its ankle. The observer may have taken it into her fingers at some point, observing it more closely, for we are told that it 'weighed no more | In your hand than a baby bird' and is still 'bendable'. The recognition of the rabbit's foot as gnawed off raises the obvious question: what happened here? Are these the remains of a struggle? Consequently, the observer turns away from the visible scene for a moment to imagine the rabbit's 'uncomfortable' death, surmising in the second stanza that the animal was probably killed by an attacking bird of prey, though now this foot is the only trace left of the past 'butchery'.

The poetic scene, however, is more complex because in it the actions of observing the 'gnawed-off ankle joint' and imagining the rabbit's death, which the 'buzzard'[2] symbolizes and possibly caused, do not simply succeed each other but run in parallel. Seeing something and 'seeing' a story go hand in hand in this poem. In fact, the rabbit's potential killer, the buzzard, appears already in the second line, whereas the sorry trace of the attack, the rabbit's foot, is not discovered until the fourth line, so that in a way the story precedes its object.

'This was all there was to see here, this | Undulating landscape *assembled in a buzzard's eye*'. What are we to make of this strange second line? Is the buzzard just an accidental part of the scene? Or is it, rather, that the entire scene is actually seen through this buzzard's eye? Is the scene literally shot through a bird's eye? In that case, the last line of the first stanza could be read as the continuation of the second line, in the sense that the buzzard's eye is focused on 'a little lump of bone, beckoning with a flap of fur', a reading the two dashes actually support. In any case, knowing that a bird of prey, the buzzard, is in one way or another part of the scene, the rabbit's sad story might dawn on both reader and observer before it is told in the second stanza.

The first stanza certainly alludes to this story. The comparison of the rabbit's foot to a 'baby bird' in terms of weight semantically connects the foot to the 'isotopy'[3] comprising words like 'buzzard', 'grey strangler', and 'shadow of a wing', while the ensuing comparison, 'a gnawed-off ankle [...] *bloodied as* the prey | Of the grey strangler', suggests also a causal connection between the buzzard as the predator and the rabbit as its 'bloodied' prey. In the second stanza, their causal connection is then made explicit, but in the form of a question envisioning a *possible* death struggle, wherefore it remains unclear how the rabbit was killed. Ultimately, there is no telling whether the buzzard mentioned in the second line and the rabbit's foot relate to each other at all.

The other grammatical means of associating buzzard and rabbit, and hence perception and narration, in this poem is the rhetorical parallelism connecting the first to the last line. The opening formula (*Nur dies gab es auf lange Sicht hier, diesen Wellenfluß*) recurs verbatim in the ultimate line (*Daß es auf lange Sicht nur dies gab hier, diesen Hasenfuß*), albeit in chiastic inversion because of the subordinating conjunction *daß*. This parallelism produces a perfect rhyme between *Wellenfluß* and *Hasenfuß*, thus closing the poem harmoniously, while simultaneously aligning one last time the two things and activities both observer and poem continually confound — perceiving the remains of a rabbit and 'perceiving' their story, since this *Wellenfluß*, we should remember, is seen in or through 'a buzzard's eye'.

Despite its scenic complexity (which is further augmented by the retrospective tense), the poem's language is fairly accessible, a general trait of Grünbein's poetry disdained only by those readers who seek to intuit impenetrable secrets in poems.[4] But Grünbein's oeuvre also includes poems in which it is still harder, if not impossible, to recognize one consistent scene — a difficulty of directly translating text into scene, however, that hardly diminishes the poem's sensory force. Grünbein's poem 'Unten am Schlammgrund', the first part of a three-part cycle named 'Niemands Land Stimmen' (1991), illustrates both. Due to its length, I reproduce only the first half of the first part.

1. Unten am Schlammgrund[5]

Auf den Boden gesunken
   Dieser warmen aquarischen Nacht,
                               Ströme
Von Luftblasen sprudelnd vor Augen
   (Ein glasiges Perlen, ein Tanz
     Klebriger Laichkugeln
           In Mineralwasser lichtwärts)
Müde in einer U-Bahn
                (‚Was fährt, das fährt'.)
   Unten am Schlammgrund
              der Straßen
   Schaukelnd zwischen Erinnerungsschlieren:
Ein deutscher Wachtraum.[6]
      ... irgendwas macht, daß Musik
Die du morgens gehört hast
                dir Abends noch einmal
   Hochkommt, erbrochener Schleimrest
    Von Rhapsodien in Schwarz,
      Dunkelgrau, Violett ...
(Langsame Kamerafahrt durch die Lakunen
     Eines gespaltenen Hirns).

>   Lichtpunkte, Schreie
>   und jähe Blendungen
>   auf einer
>   Unendlich schleichenden
>   Schnellen Fahrt
>   ohne das Jaulen,
>   Ohne das Heulen des Schienenwolfs.
>   Eingepfercht
>   Diesseits von Raum und Zeit
>   (Der Verwandlungen und des Pollenflugs,
>   Der Kontinentaldrift und der Erfindungen,
>   Der Hierarchiezerfälle und der Geburten)
>   Gefangen in der Geschwindigkeitsdruse,
>   ein Knäuel,
>   Umspeichelt, verdaut,
>   im Ekel zerwürgt,
>   Oder steckengeblieben in einer
>   Von diesen Speiseröhren der Stadt.
>   So dämmerst du
>   wieder einmal
>   mitten im Zwischendrin:
>
>   'In der Mitte von Nirgendwo'

           1. On the muddy ground

Sunk down to the ground
   Of this warm aquatic night,
                             streams
Of bubbles sparkling in front of the eyes
   (A glassy swirl, a dance
      Of round and sticky spawn
                      In mineral water towards the light)
Tired in a subway
                ('Whatever goes, goes'.)
   Down there on the muddy ground
                                of streets
   Toing and froing in streaks of memory:
A waking dream of Germany.
         ... something makes the music
You heard this morning
                     come back to you at night,
   Thrown-up mucus
      Of rhapsodies in black,
         Dark grey or violet ...
(Slow movement of the camera through lacunae
      Of a split brain).
Points of light, screams
                     and sudden flashes
                                     on an

>   Endlessly slow-moving
>   Fast ride
>   without the yowling,
>   Without the howling of that wolf on tracks.
>   Penned up
>   On this side of time and space
>   (Of transformations and pollen-laden air,
>   Of continental drift as of inventions,
>   Of disintegrating hierarchies and births)
>   Trapped inside the pocket of speed,
>   a tangle,
>   Salivated and digested,
>   retched up in disgust,
>   Or stuck up in
>   Some gullet of the city.
>   And so you're dozing
>   once again
>   right there in-between:
>
>   'In the middle of nowhere'

The erratic layout of this poem, reproduced as faithfully as possible, visualizes the incommensurability of the described phenomena just as much as it captures the irregularity of readerly comprehension itself. We are confronted with a disparate series of sensations, feelings, associations, events. Bubbles are sparkling towards the light, bits of music keep coming back like residual mucus, as do buzzwords of the day like 'continental drift' or 'disintegrating hierarchies', all of which seems to happen while he or she — or, still better, we — have 'sunk down to the ground'. Possibly, all these perceptions belong to a 'waking dream' that evolves over the course of a sluggish subway ride on a warm and aquatic or sultry night.

As such, however, the poetic text bears some resistance to this scenic interpretation. The disparity of the signified occurrences is certainly one major source of resistance, which manifests itself not only graphically, or in terms of layout, but also rhetorically, in the form of countless oxymoronic expressions. The other source of resistance is the eminent lack of indications regarding the syntagmatic connection within and between the lines. Apart from the merely additive use of 'and', there is not a single conjunction coordinating or subordinating the clauses, for instance, in a contrastive or a consecutive way. In addition, the deliberate omission of grammatical subjects makes it difficult to identify a chain of actions connecting the sequence of perception. The long opening period, for example, lacks a subject altogether. We cannot tell what or who has 'sunk down', and in what sense it did so, literally or figuratively. The following participle constructions carry the same ambiguity. It is not until the end of the second period that a perceiving subject is introduced: 'And so *you* are dozing | once again | right there in-between' — supposing, to be sure, this 'you' may be read as a self-apostrophe indeed.

The explicit indications regarding syntagmatic cohesion provided by the text are primarily spatial in kind: Something or somebody has sunk down (to the ground), then moves up towards something (the light), thereafter back and forth (in streaks of memory), etc. Perhaps, these spatial markers mean to delineate a course, a movement to be followed and embodied by the reader, but a paradoxical one. Like 'you', we are travelling through 'the middle of nowhere' on an 'Endlessly slow-moving | Fast ride', thereby following, as Grünbein writes later in the poem, 'the *furies of disappearance*'.[7]

At the end of 'Unten am Schlammgrund' (which is not reproduced above), the meandering movement towards disappearance reaches its consequent destination. The drowsy rider — you yourself — turns out to be, or has meanwhile turned into, an 'Imago in a no man's land', wherein the earlier perceptions fade away in 'silence, a twilight silence'. We have finally reached that uninhabited land of which the entire cycle, 'Niemands Land Stimmen', speaks in various voices.

Clearly, the strange movement towards disappearance is not a textual reality. It is not immanent to its language, but gains tangible shape and meaning only through our senses, through our faculty and activity of perception. We experience it only insofar as we insert ourselves into the literary scene and partake in the represented actions. We must bring our senses to the text to discover its scene, lending our bodies to the text to perceive its content. These *creative* acts of perception are, in my opinion, indispensable in apprehending and understanding actions like a movement the poem can only describe, but not perform in and of itself.

That literary scenes of perception should activate the readers' senses and ask for his perceptual participation seems evident enough. As it belongs to the reader, however, this perceptual activity is routinely excluded from the study of literature. It is, strictly speaking, no intrinsic textual property and would therefore seem an extraneous ingredient in literary interpretation. 'Affective fallacy' was the term that literary critics formerly used to discredit, in the name of 'objective criticism', the ostensible conflation of the literary object with its mental and specifically emotional effects on the reader.[8]

Paul de Man took the misgivings about the sensuous or, as he usually called it, 'phenomenal' dimension of reading a step further. In the name of pure literary immanence and standing, as he thought he did, on the 'irrefutable' grounds of rhetoric, de Man condemned the recourse to perception in the study of literature. A key passage from 'The Rhetoric of Blindness' expresses his view clearly:

> A literary text is not a phenomenal event that can be granted any form of positive existence, whether as a fact of nature or as an act of the mind. It leads to no transcendental perception, intuition, or knowledge but merely solicits an understanding that has to remain immanent because it poses the problem of its intelligibility in its own terms. This area of immanence is necessarily part of all critical discourse. Criticism is a metaphor for the act of reading, and this act is itself inexhaustible.[9]

'Literature', in short, 'bears little resemblance to perception'.[10]

De Man repeated this point throughout his career. In 'The Resistance to Theory', which contains the sum of his critical method, he once more chastises the 'confusion of linguistic with natural reality', as of literary descriptions with readerly perceptions. According to de Man, this 'mimetic' ideology does not enable but, on the contrary, impedes a proper understanding of literary language. 'Literature involves the voiding, rather than the affirmation, of aesthetic [i.e. sensuous] categories', he writes, so that 'we now have to recognize the necessity of a non-perceptual, linguistic' approach, consequently urging a 'rhetorical', as opposed to aesthetic or phenomenological, concept of literature that takes seriously the 'epistemological thrust of the rhetorical dimension of discourse'. Although literary texts may seem to describe phenomena, they thus pose for de Man chiefly semantic problems — problems of intelligibility, precisely, that are 'irreducible to grammar or to historically determined meaning'.[11]

De Man's 'non-perceptual' or rhetorical approach (which he considers not only 'irrefutable' but, alas, also 'unreliable' and due to 'language's impossibility to be a model language' ultimately 'defective')[12] rests on the fundamental assumption that literary texts constitute a perfectly autonomous, self-referential, and self-regulatory system absorbing and controlling the process of reading completely. De Man summarized this assumption very precisely in an interview he gave in 1983. He explained here that 'I assume, as a working hypothesis (as a working hypothesis, because I know better than that) that the text knows in an absolute way what it's doing.' In other words, literary language 'has no blind spots: it accounts at all moments for its own rhetorical mode'.[13] Thus, literature must be treated, at least for analytic purposes, as if it were an autonomous system that is, not unlike Hegel's absolute spirit, entirely transparent to itself (although one should 'know better than that').

De Man's name for this absolute system or subject of signification is 'the rhetoric' of a text, its main features being an 'actively negative relationship to grammar and to logic' and the power to lure readers with mindfully employed figures and tropes into all kinds of paradoxes, embarrassments, aberrations, and traps.[14] Since literary language 'implicitly or explicitly signifies its own rhetorical mode and prefigures its own misunderstanding as the correlative of its rhetorical nature', it necessarily represents the most sophisticated form of rhetorical deception and aporia.[15] Indeed, literature consists for de Man primarily of deceptive fictions and epistemologically challenging figures. Literature is, fundamentally, fiction and as such, contrary to popular belief, both incommensurable with the sensory world and impervious to the empirical concepts of perception. 'To stay clear of any undue phenomenalization' of literary texts and to resist 'the phenomenalism of reading [...] rooted in aesthetics' is therefore the imperative task of literary interpretation.[16]

The categorical exclusion of sensuousness, together with a visceral reaction against anything that smacks of aesthetics (a discipline rooted in *aisthēsis*, the Greek word for 'sense perception'), forms the core of de Man's theory of literature, as well as his method of reading. He repudiated the idea, espoused by Alexander Gottlieb Baumgarten, the founder of modern aesthetics, no less than Diderot, Kant, Hegel, and Adorno, that 'even the discursive arts, in order to be conceptualized as such — rather than as inartistic instances of merely communicative speech [...] — cannot be entirely abstracted from their sensuous condition'.[17]

De Man's prejudice against the senses and hence aesthetics, which may very well be the lasting legacy of his brand of deconstruction, is the antithesis to all that follows.[18] There is no such thing as the pure, unsullied immanence of literature wherein 'the text' acts all by itself, always ready to deceive its readers as if it was an all-knowing subject. It is neither possible, as de Man[19] conceded himself, nor for that matter desirable, to consider literature purely as text, since the so-called immanence of literary text is in truth *the product of reading*. We produce the strange 'inside' of literary signification, including the complex meaning of its rhetoric. We bring something to the text in order to understand its language 'from within', using our cognitive faculties to create such immanence in the first place.

Our faculty of perception is one important means of doing so. Indeed, confronted with a certain type of text, such as the two Grünbein poems, that faculty might be, contrary to de Man's belief, simply indispensable in creating and accessing the sphere of literary immanence. I therefore insist in this book on the necessity of perception in literary comprehension and, likewise, on the inherently sensuous potential of literary text. I emphasize the perceptual activity through which readers bring this potential to fruition, and I analyze the unique and in each case individual logic of perception by which certain texts appeal to our senses. The sensuous potential of literature is not automatically undone by 'the rhetoric' of the text, as de Man would have it, nor is the reader's perceptual activity fully explained by measuring physical reactions in his or her brain. Instead, one must focus on the dynamic interplay between reader and text to address these complex sensory realities of literature. Indeed, if there is a kind of sensuousness in literature, then it emerges *between* subject and object, *between* the act of reading and the evocative power of literary form.

My discussion of Grünbein's poems was meant to broach these fundamental issues. The primary goal, however, was to introduce examples of the sort of text wherein all these issues intersect — *scenographies* of perception, as I would like to call them. These scriptings of perception undoubtedly enable readerly perception, and sometimes even call for perceptual participation in order to be understood. Confronted with Grünbein's scenographies, for example, I was prompted to delve into a stream of manifold perceptions, which I then recast and orchestrated, again in writing, by selecting certain textual features over others so as to discover an inherent meaning or rather sense (*Sinn*). I thus made sense of these poems by perceiving or, at least, trying to perceive these poems as *scenes* to be heard and felt and seen — and, afterwards, also pondered and relived. This is, in a nutshell, what I mean by readerly perception, the process of interpreting descriptions and piecing them together such that you perceive their corresponding scene or scenes.

Although imaginary and subjective in appearance, these scenes are neither illusory nor fictitious. On the contrary, perceiving texts as scenes actually means, just as the German word for perception, *Wahr-nehmung*, says, to also *take their words for a truth*, regardless of their supposed fictionality or factuality. One then reads them as interesting scripts for, rather than spurious fictions of, perception. For this reason, however, readerly perception is textually determined and constrained. Unless we are hallucinating or daydreaming, our perceptual activity while reading is not an arbitrary process but largely controlled by the textual set-up, which consists of various descriptions and direct statements of fact, as well as implicit conceptual and rhetorical structures guiding our perceptual movements in other ways. This textual set-up or script of scenographies is what I meant earlier by the objective power of literary form. Establishing the exact reach of that power is a traditional, if ultimately unattainable, goal of textual analysis, an *ideal*, indeed, to which my discussion of Grünbein and, I believe, any close reading deserving of the name remains indebted.

Aesthesis and diegesis

In the preceding section, I related poetic descriptions to sensory perceptions. But on what grounds can they be related at all? Are these incommensurable opposites, as de Man so vehemently declares? Is perception just as self-contained a system as literary language is on account of de Man and, due to this radical autonomy, fundamentally impervious to linguistic description? Or is there, perhaps, an essential link between linguistic and sensory processes — various 'aesthesiologies', as I would like to call them, allowing for communication between these two distinct modes of cognition?

To consider these questions more closely, I now turn to suggestive remarks by Nietzsche and Hegel. In 1885, Nietzsche noted:

> Der Mensch ist ein Formen- und Rhythmen-bildendes Geschöpf; er ist in nichts besser geübt und es scheint daß er an nichts *mehr* Lust hat als am *Erfinden* von Gestalten. Man beobachte nur, womit sich unser Auge sofort beschäftigt sobald es nichts mehr zu sehen bekommt: es *schafft* sich Etwas zu sehen. Muthmaßlich thut im gleichen Falle unser Gehör nichts anderes: es *übt* sich. Ohne die Verwandlung der Welt in Gestalten und Rhythmen gäbe es für uns nichts 'Gleiches', also auch nichts Wiederkehrendes, also auch keine Möglichkeit der Erfahrung und Aneignung, der *Ernährung*. In allem Wahrnehmen, das heißt dem ursprünglichsten Aneignen, ist das wesentliche Geschehen ein Handeln, strenger noch: ein Formen-Aufzwingen: — von 'Eindrücken' reden nur die Oberflächlichen.[20]

> [Man is a creature that fabricates forms and rhythms; he is most skilled at and seems to enjoy nothing *more* than *inventing* shapes. Just notice what our eye does as soon as it has nothing to see anymore: it *creates* something to see for itself. Our ear is likely to do the same thing in that situation: it *trains* itself. Without the transformation of the world into shapes and rhythms, nothing would seem 'identical' to us; recurring things would not exist either, nor the possibility of experience and acquisition, of *nourishment*. In each perception, which is the most basic mode of acquisition, the critical event is a deed, or more strictly an imposition of forms — only superficial people speak of 'impressions'.]

Sensory perception, says Nietzsche, involves both a spatial (or figural) and a temporal (or rhythmic) organization of sensory signals. But this organization is for Nietzsche — in marked contrast to Kant[21] — neither passive nor based on universal rules. It is, as his wording signals, a distortive and partly idiosyncratic process, an active imposition of figures and patterns on what is usually, but also falsely, called 'impressions'. Still, through these acts of form-giving humans impose order on the Dionysian chaos of bodily sensation, thereby producing distinct feelings and recurrent perceptions that seem only in hindsight and on the basis of conceptual assumptions like causality and constancy to be caused (or, literally, im-pressed) by permanent objective properties. Perception thus becomes invention, as Nietzsche puts it, a process of rhythmic as well as figural organization or form-giving not entirely dissimilar from the work of aesthetic composition. In the words of neuropsychologist Richard L. Gregory, who describes the matter similarly, 'perception is intelligent decision-taking, from limited sensory evidence', wherefore perceptions must be considered 'predicative, never entirely certain, *hypotheses* of what may be out there'.[22]

The connection between perception and creation Nietzsche makes in this fragment is already looming in *Die Geburt der Tragödie*, where he characterizes the Apollonian principle precisely as the creative aesthetic power of humans to give shape, and hence meaning, to our *a priori* chaotic and ultimately pointless Dionysian reality. In *Ueber Wahrheit und Lüge im aussermoralischen Sinne*, composed shortly thereafter, Nietzsche claims much the same, though this time in the terminologies of Kantian epistemology and rhetoric rather than aesthetics and theatre. Seeing images and perceiving their meaning, he writes here, involve all kinds of 'metaphoric' transfers and displacements, which as such follow above all the 'legislation' [Gesetzgebung] of language.[23] Perceptions thus amount to acts of translation (from Greek *metapherein*, 'to transfer', 'to translate') without external criteria to be measured against, because

> between two absolutely different spheres, as between subject and object, there is no causality, no correctness, no expression but at most an *aesthetic response* [Verhalten], and by that I mean a suggestive transference [andeutende Uebertragung], a stammering translation [nachstammelnde Uebersetzung] into a completely foreign language.[24]

Hegel offered a view that takes the necessity of form-giving in perception a step further still. According to the *Phänomenologie des Geistes*, sense perception assumes, through reflexive organization, the form of a 'story' (*Geschichte*). Like a story, which represents the whole of its fable, *histoire*, *Handlung*, plot, or more plainly content discursively, and hence through a sequence of words, perception too represents a synchronic whole diachronically. It (quite literally) articulates a set of simultaneous objective relations or properties as a diachronic sequence of sensory events. Thought of in that way, as narrative activity, the comprehension of perceptions consequently means to identify (or, for Nietzsche, invent) the conceptual connection between these two opposite temporalities, the logic or 'plot', as Peter Brooks calls it, uniting them.[25]

Nietzsche suggests that sensory perception and, more generally, the perception of sense involves form-giving above all else, while Hegel describes this mental act of form-giving more closely as narrative in kind. Hence, sensory perception and narration — *aesthesis* and *diegesis* — belong together. This, indeed, is the theoretical idea developed in this book. I contend that aesthesis necessitates narrative or diegetic organization and, conversely, that aesthesis is integral to the comprehension of certain types of diegesis in either prose or verse. Sense perception gains shape and meaning through narration, while narrations assume force and cohesion through readerly perception. Each requires the form-giving influence of the other. The first point, the narrativity of perception, I develop in Part One by expounding Hegel's concept of perception. The second point, the sensuousness of narration, is developed primarily in Part Two by explicating distinctive logics of perception that belong to certain texts (or rather scenographies) by Novalis, Rilke, and Proust.

To do so, however, it will be necessary to define my terms more closely, and then consider their applicability. By 'aesthesis', which derives from the Greek *aisthēsis* ('sense perception'), I do not only mean the five traditional senses of perception, namely sight, hearing, taste, smell, and touch, but the whole range of sensory experience. This includes bodily states and emotions such as joy, excitement, feebleness, lethargy, pain, and sadness, which may accompany, often strangely combined, the perceptions of the five sensory organs, as well as the fundamental feeling of being situated Here and Now, at a specific time and in a concrete space. In short, aesthesis produces and often intermingles all kinds of physical sensations.[26]

'Diegesis', from the Greek *diēgeisthai* ('to set out in detail', 'to describe', 'to narrate'), has acquired a double meaning in narratology, and whenever I employ it I wish to invoke precisely that double sense. On the one hand, diegesis designates the act of narration as such, the verbal discourse by which a story is told, regardless of meter and genre. Plato develops this notion of *diēgēsis* in the third book of *The Republic*, where he characterizes literary works precisely in terms of speaking voice rather than represented content — which is what Aristotle does, of course, in defining epic as well as tragic works as representing or imitating (*mimēsis*) characters and their actions through a plausible plot (*mythos*). Though Plato criticizes the artistic practice of imitation elsewhere in *The Republic* as both dishonest and politically dangerous, in the third book he focuses primarily on the verbal, discursive form of poetry, narration, or *diēgēsis*, distinguishing three characteristic types or dictions (*lexeis*) of narration of which the imitation of foreign voices — Plato's technical definition of *mimēsis* — is but one.[27]

On the other hand, diegesis came to designate in narratology (and also in film studies) the world evoked through narration, the totality of persons, places, and occurrences represented in a narrative text. Gérard Genette introduced this key term of narratology capturing representational content. Drawing upon Anne and Etienne Souriau's earlier work on film, he defined *diégèse* precisely as 'l'univers spatio-temporel du récit',[28] subsequently using this minimal definition of literary worlds to differentiate amongst various diegetic levels or frames as well as degrees of narratorial involvement. Intra-, extra-, and metadiegetic are Genette's terms to designate the frames within which narrators speak, while hetero-, homo-, and autodiegetic mark the positions narrators can take in relation to the worlds of which they speak.

This double meaning of diegesis (which qualifies it as a speculative concept in the Hegelian sense) directly reflects the double temporality of a story mentioned earlier. The diegetic world (*diégèse* according to Genette) is the story's *synchronic* content or meaning — *what* it shows as a whole, while narration or description (*diēgēsis* according to Plato) is the *diachronic* process by which the whole story unfolds — *how* it is told sequentially. Another common way of addressing the same temporal differential, which is constitutive of stories, would be to juxtapose the duration of discursive articulation with the duration of the events thus represented. This varying discrepancy between narrative time (duration of articulation) and narrated time (duration of represented events) on the level of individual sentences, paragraphs, chapters, or entire books is a convenient and, in fact, widely accepted criterion to distinguish narrative from non-narrative ways of speaking such as argumentation and postulation, which belong to the domain of reasoning, or laudation, lamentation, exclamation, exhortation, exaggeration, and even hubris, which often characterize lyric poetry.[29]

Nietzsche and Hegel were not the only ones to recognize the narrative logic of sense perception. As such, the idea is already looming in Kant, since Kant's theory of cognition (*Erkenntnis*) consists, as Claudia Brodsky has shown, chiefly in 'a general theory of representational narration'.[30] Over the past twenty to thirty years, a body of interdisciplinary research has emerged that also empirically supports the idea that perception requires narrative action. For example, cognitive scientist Robert C. Schank and psychologist Robert P. Abelson conclude from their studies that 'stories about one's experiences, and the experiences of others, are the fundamental constituents of human memory, knowledge, and social communication', for they provide us with 'scripts' — meaning 'a set of expectations about what will happen next' — to make sense of the world.[31] Similarly, cognitive scientist Mark Turner holds that 'narrative imagining — story — is the fundamental instrument of thought. Rational capacities depend on it. It is our chief means of looking into the future, of predicating, of planning, and of explaining.' According to Turner, even the most basic acts of perception are narrative, because it is 'impossible for us to look at the world and not to see reportable stories distinguished from background'.[32]

The view that objects of perception are, as Turner puts it, surrounded by 'reportable stories' refers in many ways to James J. Gibson's 'theory of affordances', which Gibson developed in his 1979 book, *The Ecological Approach to Visual Perception*.[33] His theory basically asserts that we have meaningful object perception only insofar as we understand what the perceived object enables or 'affords' us to do. The perception of objective affordances can result from concrete interactions with the object in question, but in most cases the observer only looks at it and then *imagines* possible interactions. The identification of some thing as a cup, to give an example, essentially means to imagine or 'see' that this thing could be filled with, say, milk and then seized at its handle to take a sip from it. The observer thus incorporates the cup in an imaginary sequence of actions, which is to say, he or she invents a narrative of its possible usage, thereby *perceiving* the object. When looking at familiar things such as cups, ideas on how to use them present themselves almost instantaneously and without much conscious reflection. The observer simply recalls his or her mental script of affordances associated with a particular class of objects. Confronted with an unfamiliar object of complex detail, however, the concrete and/or imaginary exploration of the object's affordances takes longer, and is therefore a more challenging cognitive process.

Arguably, the basic idea of Gibson's theory of affordances goes back to John Dewey's seminal essay, 'The Reflex Arc Concept in Psychology', published in 1896. Against the mechanistic view that sensory stimuli and perceptual response form a 'sensori-motor circuit', Dewey here holds that perception is a 'teleological process', which means, for example, that the burn a child feels when reaching into a flame, the 'heat-pain quale', is actually anticipated by the 'seeing-of-a-light-that-means-pain-when-contact-occurs'.[34] This kind of anticipatory seeing (or rather imagining) is, I think, pretty much what Gibson means by perceiving objective affordances. At any rate, Gibson remains influential to this day since his theory gave rise to several newer theories of 'enactive' perception and 'embodied' cognition.[35]

Participation and concretization

As interesting as the psychology and neuroscience of perception may be, both currently and historically, this book is above all a contribution to literary aesthetics. Therefore, the reader's sensory involvement in *literary* narrations must be the foremost concern. How does the sensuous figure in literary texts (if, that is, it figures therein at all), and in which ways is sensuousness necessarily involved in literary reception and interpretation? The chapters on Novalis, Rilke, and Proust give specific answers to these questions, but in each of these cases the fundamental assumption is, as I stated earlier, that literary narrations (diegesis) require the reader's perceptual participation (aesthesis). Their textual discourse is accessed through readerly aesthesis and thus transformed into a diegetic world, and in lending our bodily senses and feelings to this *evolving* world, we gradually actualize the sensory potential of literary narrations by producing a series of imaginary yet sensate scenes.

Although the specific role of the senses is a contentious issue in literary theory, the need for readerly participation and imagination hardly is. Romantic authors are amongst those who have most expressly advocated these two requirements (while simultaneously insisting on the 'hallucinatory' sensuousness of literature).[36] Contemplating a draft of the final book of *Wilhelm Meisters Lehrjahre*, Friedrich Schiller gives the following advice to Goethe:

> Dem Inhalte nach, muß in dem Werk *alles* liegen, was zu seiner Erklärung nötig ist, und, der Form nach, muß es *nothwendig* darinn liegen, der innere Zusammenhang muß es mit sich bringen; aber wie fest oder locker es zusammenhängen soll, darüber muß Ihre eigenste Natur entscheiden. Dem Leser würde es freilich bequemer seyn, wenn Sie selbst ihm die Momente worauf es ankommt blank und baar zuzählten, daß er sie nur in Empfang zu nehmen brauchte; sicherlich aber hält es ihn bey dem Buche fester, und führt ihn öfter zu demselben zurück, wenn er sich selber helfen muß. Haben Sie also nur dafür gesorgt, daß er gewiß findet, wenn er mit gutem Willen und hellen Augen sucht, so ersparen Sie ihm ja das Suchen nicht. Das Resultat eines solchen Ganzen muß immer die eigene freie, nur nicht willkürliche Production

des Lesers sein, es muß eine Art von Belohnung bleiben, die nur dem Würdigen zuteil wird, indem sie dem Unwürdigen sich entziehet.

[As regards content, the work ought to contain *all* that is needed for its explanation, and as regards form, this [explanation] must *of necessity* be contained in it, the inner connection must provide it; but how closely or loosely the work should be connected must be left to your own inmost nature to decide. It would indeed be more convenient to the reader were you yourself point-blank to state to him the crucial moments, in which case he could simply receive them; assuredly, however, he would be more drawn to the book, and return more often to it, if he had to help himself. Hence, if only you make sure that he can find [explanation] if he reads in good earnest and with open eyes, then, I say, do not spare him the trouble of searching. The result of such a whole must always be the reader's own free production, yet not an arbitrary one: It must be a kind of reward that presents itself only to those deserving it, while remaining inaccessible to the undeserving ones.][37]

Goethe's (possibly unconscious) paraphrase of Schiller's eloquent observation is as dry as it is succinct. Four months later, in November 1796, Goethe remarks in a letter to Schiller 'that the reader must act productively if he wishes to partake in any [written] product'.[38]

Novalis was still more radical than Schiller and Goethe, also regarding the sensuousness of literature. But I shall save that second point for Part Two, focusing at this time on the still more fundamental concept of readerly participation. Schiller attributes considerable influence to the literary author in portraying him as the enabling and, thanks to the chosen form (which, Schiller notes elsewhere, 'should do everything'),[39] also determining, source of reading. Novalis, by contrast, maintains the priority of reading over both authorial intention and textual form. In a fragment from 1797 or 1798, which is nowadays often cited as key to the Romantic ideal of 'sympoetic' authorship, although it was never published in the *Athenäum*, Novalis notes:

Der wahre Leser muß der erweiterte Autor seyn. Er ist die höhere Instanz, die die Sache von der niedern schon vorgearbeitet erhält. Das Gefühl vermittelst dessen der Autor die Materialien seiner Schrift geschieden hat, scheidet beim Lesen wieder das Rohe und das Gebildete des Buchs — und wenn der Leser das Buch nach seiner Idee bearbeiten würde, so würde ein 2ter Leser noch mehr läutern, und so wird dadurch, daß die bearbeitete Masse immer wieder in frischtätige Gefäße kommt, die Masse endlich wesentlicher Bestandteil — Glied wirksamen Geistes. (N II, 282 #125)

[The true reader must be the extended author. He is the higher court that receives the case already prepared by the lower court. The feeling by means of which the author has chosen the materials of his work again distinguishes, in the process of reading, the raw from the refined aspects of the book — and if the reader were to edit the book according to his own idea, a second reader would refine it still more, the result being that, since the edited mass is constantly poured into fresh vessels, this mass finally becomes an inherent element — a part in the chain of this operative spirit.][40]

Literary works do not readily reveal their 'spirit', nor would it suffice to simply turn to 'the lower court', the author, to have it clarified. It is, rather, the continual formation and transformation of text through the reader that uncovers and simultaneously clarifies, refines, purges, and perfects (all meanings of *läutern*) the meaning and, indeed, being of a work. Hence, literary works are dynamic creations that, though based on texts that authors provide, essentially result from the workflow between text and reader(s). In describing this continued and ever more evolving workflow with the verbs *bearbeiten* and *bilden* ('das Gebildete des Buchs'), Novalis also makes an unmistakable reference to the programmatic idea and, according to his own words, also imperative 'mission' of the epoch: *Bildung*.[41]

The readers are the indispensable agents or 'vessels' in this self-perfecting and potentially endless process of *Bildung* through which literature at once exists and develops. As such, however, reading involves for Novalis not only mental acts of concretization such as interpretation, imagination, and contextualization, but possibly also manifest modifications and edits. In fact, Novalis claimed to be 'unable to read properly'[42] without pen and paper ready at hand, which indicates that, for him, the reception of a literary work necessarily required writerly operation such as mark-ups, excerpts, critical commentary on the margins, as well as other forms of note-taking. But sometimes even that was not sufficient to excavate the true meaning or 'spirit' of a work. Novalis then took more radical measures, undertaking a thorough re-formation or rewriting of the work in question. Such is the case of his unfinished novel *Heinrich von Ofterdingen*, which is not simply a repudiation but in truth a thoroughgoing revision and reform — a *Läuterung* — of Goethe's *Wilhelm Meisters Lehrjahre*, and therefore represents the ultimate consequence of extended authorship in the sense of Novalis.[43]

Novalis's finding that literary reception and literary authorship, or reading and writing literature, are interdependent operations was echoed by several other Romantic writers. Friedrich Schlegel, Novalis's like-minded friend, had similar thoughts about the ideal relation between author and reader, describing it as a 'relationship of inmost symphilosophy or sympoetry' whereby the reader feels tempted 'to invent the work himself'.[44] Similarly, Ludwig Tieck remarked that 'understanding a work of art in full means, in a way, to create it'.[45] In Joseph von Eichendorff's 1815 novel *Ahnung und Gegenwart*, to name a final example, it is said that true readers are 'composing' [dichten] when reading — as they must, for the author

> does not offer a complete heaven, only a ladder to heaven which he places on this pretty earth. To the dull or lazy reader who lacks the strength to climb its golden but loose bars, the book's mysterious letter will remain forever dead, so he had better dig and plough through it, instead of wasting his time with futile reading.[46]

If works of literature are conceived as requiring both readerly participation and concretization, perhaps even modification, then reading must be a free and in principle inexhaustible operation. In that exact spirit, Novalis notes (N II, 398–99 #398): '/Is not every reader a philologist?/ There is no *generally valid* reading in the usual sense. Reading is a free operation. No one can prescribe to me how and what I am to read.' The reader — even a professional reader such as a philologist — 'places the *accent* at will [willkührlich]' and ultimately 'makes of a book whatever he wants', as evidenced, Novalis adds (ibid.), by '[Friedrich] Schlegel's treatment of [Goethe's] *Meister*' in his enthusiastic review, or better still, his sympoetic commentary published in the *Athenäum*.[47] Nonetheless, Novalis does not conceive of reading literature as a totally arbitrary flight of fancy. The reader's free concretizations are also partly restricted by the text, since 'a book engenders, like *everything* else, a thousand [tausendfältige] *sensations* and *functions* — determinate or *specific* and *free* ones'.[48]

This Romantic freedom of reading, which is based on free choices and specific textual facts in equal measure, still resonates in Proust's *À la recherche du temps perdu*. After hundreds of pages spent ruminating on his life experience and what it calls for, the narrator realizes that the meaning of both ultimately depends on the desires of the reader, since in

> reality every reader is, while he is reading, the reader of his own self. The writer's work is merely a kind of optical instrument which he offers to the reader to enable him to discern what, without this book, he would perhaps never have experienced in himself. (*Retrouvé*, 217–18; VI: 273)

Just as the life of Swann provides the narrator with the 'raw material of my experiences' and thus enables him to write 'my book' (*Retrouvé* 221; VI: 278), so does Proust enable and indeed encourage his readers to use his book as a resource of experience and, possibly, aesthetic production.

Perceiving diegetic worlds

Earlier, I have called the comprehensive sphere generated by way of readerly aesthesis a diegetic 'world', scenes being coherent, if partial, manifestations thereof. This terminological choice reflects the convention to describe the sphere of literary immanence precisely as a 'fictional world' or, in Genette's formulation, a 'spatiotemporal universe' (diegesis). More specifically, however, my choice is informed by Edmund Husserl's concept of a world. Husserl elaborates on this key concept of phenomenology in his 1913 *Ideen zu einer reinen Phänomenologie und phänomenologischen Philosophie*, where he defines a world as a sphere of immersion surrounded by a '*vaguely conscious horizon of yet unspecified reality*'.[49]

The 'natural' or physical world represents for Husserl the basic example of such a sphere wherein current experience always points to an even larger network of potential, not yet actualized experiences that appear on the proverbial 'horizon'. Immersed in the physical world, we actualize these potential experiences through sensory perceptions, of course, but also, as Husserl points out, through cognitive acts like imagination, recollection, as well as logical judgements. These exploratory movements, in thought as in deed, then refer to new realities on the horizon of possible experience, to further sites and scenes waiting for exploration. In phenomenological terms, therefore, a world comprises much more than the sum of all currently perceived facts. It cannot be limited to 'all that is the case', as Wittgenstein famously said, but in fact includes also that which is possibly, though not currently, the case. Hence, in addition to its immersive reality, a world also establishes a system of references wherein the actual and the unactual, the seen and the unseen, presence and absence, experience and horizon are necessarily compounded.

Naturally, these immersive as well as referential qualities depend on consciousness. Consciousness is for Husserl the essential (though not existential, physical) locus of a world. For that reason, the world-structure applies not only to the encounter with physical phenomena. There are also ideational worlds, Husserl points out, for example 'the arithmetical world', which arises as we think in numbers and thus achieves no less presence and, indeed, reality than the physical or 'natural' world does.

To conceive also of literary and specifically diegetic worlds is, therefore, entirely consistent with Husserl's conception. Husserl himself did not elaborate a theory of literary worlds, but his student Roman Ingarden did. In *Das literarische Kunstwerk* (1931), Ingarden theorized precisely the world emerging from literary discourse — just a few years before Martin Heidegger considered the 'world' the work of art 'opens up',[50] and decades before Nelson Goodman and others came to think of storytelling as 'worldmaking'.[51] Ingarden writes that the objects represented in a literary work

> do not lie isolated and alien alongside one another but [...] form instead a uniform sphere of being. In doing so they always constitute — quite remarkably — a segment of a still largely undetermined world [...] that is, a segment whose boundaries are never sharply drawn. It is always as if a beam of light were illuminating a part of a region, the remainder of which disappears in an indeterminate cloud but is still there in its indeterminacy. For instance, if in a small poem a single object is represented in a single state or in one situation, it is still always represented as something existing in an extensive objective whole [...] We can take as an example the situation in act 1, scene 1, of Lessing's *Emilia Galotti*. There we find a prince in his study, attending to various petitions. These petitions already indicate objectivities that are to be found outside the visible room. But the room itself is apprehended from the first as a part of the princely palace. What is represented does not stop at the walls of the study but extends further, into the other rooms of the palace, into the town, etc., even though none of this is directly given to us. It is, in fact, a background.[52]

Paraphrasing the above, one might say that narrations (diegesis) of whatever type or genre show specific things by naming and describing them — a young lad named 'Heinrich', for example, or the 'black fur' of a cat. Other things and occurrences within or outside the currently described 'segment' or scene remain implicit or simply unspoken of — for example, Heinrich's Christening or the smell of the cat's fur. Such absences, however, which Ingarden termed 'indeterminacies' [Unbestimmtheitsstellen], do not designate the limit but rather the threshold or, indeed, horizon of readerly experience. They indicate a potential for further concretization through forms of perception and movement, as well as acts of representation, imagination, and deduction that are analogous, though not identical, to those sensory and cognitive actions through which we explore the phenomenal world.

In short, the way in which the literary 'sphere of objects' (meaning the diegetic world) unfolds before the reader is, as Ingarden writes, analogous to 'Husserl's doctrine of horizons'.[53] Literary narrations, too, establish an ever-expanding horizon of possibilities, a totality of partly named, partly unnamed places, persons, and things in virtually infinite connections of possible interaction, evoking such totality not through ostensive reference, as Paul Ricoeur points out, but precisely by disclosing 'possible worlds' and 'possible ways of orientating oneself in those worlds'.[54]

In considering these references to phenomenology, as well as the earlier section on participation and concretization, similar positions of reader-response theory will inevitably come to mind, Hans Robert Jauß's historicizing aesthetics of reception (*Rezeptionsästhetik*) and Wolfgang Iser's theory of aesthetic response (*Wirkungsästhetik*) as set forth in *Der Akt des Lesens* being perhaps the most notable examples. Both Jauß and Iser were of the view that readers have to concretize the literary text through selection and interpretation so as to generate literary meaning. Concretization is ineluctable because of the 'indeterminacy' of literary descriptions (as they both call it in the wake of Ingarden), which is rooted in two basic facts. On the one hand, it is impossible ever to describe an object or incident exhaustively, in complete detail, but only schematically, a point Ingarden explained at length.[55] The multiplicity of descriptions within one and the same text, on the other hand, makes it necessary to reduce semantic complexity through selection on the basis of certain interpretative assumptions. To discover textual consistency and unity of meaning, the reader must first fabricate what Roland Barthes has aptly termed an '*interested simulacrum*' of the text in question.[56]

These are widely accepted axioms of reader-oriented theories of literature, which I share, yet my approach conflicts with Iser and Jauß in one fundamental regard. I want to demonstrate the involvement of perception in the genesis of literary understanding, whereas Iser and Jauß have little to say about that. Even though they were repeatedly criticized for founding their theories of literary reception precisely on sense perception, each of them rejected this suggestion. When, for example, Stanley Fish attacked Iser for modelling literary reception on sense perception, Iser repudiated that charge vehemently, insisting that 'the world arising from the literary text (apart from the printed pages as a physical object) is accessible to the imagination but not the senses'.[57] Similarly, de Man criticized Jauß for founding 'literary understanding' upon 'sense perception' — an assumption against which, as we have seen, de Man fought his entire career — but Jauß flatly disputed de Man's charge, although the term *aisthēsis* does figure prominently in his theory of aesthetic experience.[58]

The rejection of perception is somewhat plausible in the case of Jauß, because his *Rezeptionsästhetik* concerns the collective history of literary reception, specifically the changing horizons of apprehension enabling readers to discover meaning in works of literature. Accordingly, Jauß conceives of literary experience essentially in terms of history and hermeneutics, whereas the individual act of reading and its phenomenology are not pertinent to his theory.[59] In the case of Iser, however, the rejection of sensory perception as a foundation of literary experience is hardly plausible, because Iser investigates precisely the possible impact (*Wirkung*) of literature on individual readers, the reader's 'involvement' [Verstricktsein] in the literary text being his immediate concern.[60] To investigate this kind of involvement, Iser relies in *Der Akt des Lesens* frequently on phenomenological concepts, which are, as Derrida points out, 'always' derived from a 'phenomenology of perception'.[61]

Nonetheless, Iser pays little attention to the sensory aspects of literary reception, focusing instead on the ways in which readers create semantic coherence and consistency. This gradual 'formation of meaning' [Sinnbildung] involves above all the disambiguation of semantic ambiguities and indeterminacies in the text, which Iser calls 'blanks' [Leerstellen]. These include, for example, vague or even unreliable descriptions, competing narrative perspectives and unclear focalizations, ellipses and omissions, as well as a general scarcity — or proliferation — of explanations offered by the narrator. The act of reading as described by Iser gradually eliminates the blanks through interpretative judgments and so 'realizes' the literary work, even though each realization remains necessarily partial and selective.[62]

It goes without saying that the aesthetic appearance of literary descriptions cannot be separated from its semantics, since the diegetic world originates from acts of signification — from descriptions. Hans Georg Gadamer is certainly right in calling the opposition between 'semantic' and 'phenomenological' approaches to literature a false dichotomy, since the latter necessarily depends on the former. A phenomenological approach to literature, Gadamer writes,

> means in truth only this: that we follow its language [...] calling something into being. We need only conjure up [aufzubauen] in ourselves the phenomena language shows and has us see. The interpreter must certainly isolate the semantic means employed to do so, but only to restore them to the unity of speech.[63]

Iser, by contrast, investigates primarily abstract logical relations between words and sentences, since his readings revolve around categories like consistency, unity, and determinacy of meaning (*Bedeutung*), as well as the textual repertoire restricting or extending the range of possible meaning. Iser thus focuses on the semantics of literary text, instead of analysing the sensate sense (*Sinn*) evolving in diegetic scenes, which is my ambition.[64]

At one point in *Der Akt des Lesens*, however, Iser does reflect upon the perceptual (rather than semantic and logical) aspects of reading literature, attributing here a 'visual character' [Bildcharakter] to the reader's mental representation of literary discourse. Immersed in the literary world, Iser writes, the reader effectively embodies the 'moving point of view', visualizing the story in his mind as a series of affectively charged 'images'.[65]

In emphasizing the visual, eidetic character of literary reception, Iser follows not only Husserl's lead but in fact a long-standing tradition of aesthetics and art criticism, according to which literary experience consists above all in an image or a series of images appearing before the inner eye of consciousness. As indicated by its name, the imagination represents, also in the phenomenological tradition, the source of these mental images. At once a productive and a reproductive faculty, the imagination possesses the power of obtaining and also recalling snapshots from experience and, at the same time, the power of summoning at will inner images not seen before. Iser undoubtedly subscribes to this oculocentric tradition by assimilating literary reception to the work of the imagination, the necessary consequence being, however, that readerly aesthesis is reduced to a sequence of images, and more specifically to an inner vision with distinctly cinematic characteristics, including sound.[66]

As with sensory perception, however, which is often largely *but never exclusively* visual, seeing inner images is not the only mode of literary perception. The notion of readerly aesthesis developed in this book is, therefore, more comprehensive. Instead of equating literary perception with the imagination and thus with mental images, I seek to both accommodate and appreciate the aesthetic power of literature to appeal, possibly simultaneously, to multiple senses and to generate complex mixtures of feeling, just as it happens when reading scenes about, for instance, rosy lips and tea-soaked madeleines, melancholic corners and tantalizing liquids, blue flowers with delightful faces, charming little phrases of music, or cats with a blindingly sleek black fur. What these and, in fact, all scenographies considered in this book contain is not simply images or a sequence of images but, rather, stories of perception that unfold in time and often defy visualization.

Aesthesiologies

If it is true that both perception and narration, aesthesis and diegesis, are incomprehensible without acts of form-giving and concretization, they overlap in two fundamental regards. Firstly, their constitutive elements — sensations or words — require reorganization to assume shape and meaning. This partly conscious, but largely unconscious, structuration concerns chiefly temporal relations amongst these constitutive elements, namely succession, duration, and configuration. Unfolding in time itself, this procedure of structuration then establishes, secondly, in either case a double-layered temporality that combines a diachronic process with a synchronic meaning and configuration according to an inherent logic or, indeed, story. Comprehending that story is tantamount to grasping the inner sense of either perception or narration.

The first point, the temporal structuration of either sensory or readerly experience, may be described more closely as an interplay between 'retention' and 'protention', two concepts coined by Husserl.[67] 'Retention' basically means momentary recollection of previous impressions, a lingering unconscious memory that gradually fades away. Husserl distinguishes this spontaneous 'presentation' of retained memories from voluntary acts of remembrance as deliberate 'reproductions' of past moments. The difference between these two types of memory, the one spontaneous and unconscious, the other deliberate and fully consciousness, is obviously a matter of degree. Their difference is functional and thus implies commutability. If we consciously attend to our retentions and thus bring them to mind, they become conscious memories or remembrances.

'Protention' designates the inverse operation. Proceeding in the opposite temporal direction, protention means the anticipated continuation of the current perception or activity. It is a momentary and spontaneous anticipation that directly results from the unconscious retention of what happened before. As with retention, however, spontaneous protentions will readily turn into conscious expectations as soon as we attend to them and ask ourselves what comes next, how things might continue.[68]

Taken together, retention and protention both connect and reconfigure the primary sequence of experience (a chain of either words or sensations) by creating an extended presence, rather than a succession of discrete now-points, a configuration in which past, present, and future moments permeate each other. Derrida provides a good characterization of this phase of extended presence as '*continuously compounded* with a nonpresence and nonperception' that are 'neither added to, nor do they *occasionally* accompany, the actually perceived now; they are essentially and indispensably involved in its possibility'.[69] Thanks to this largely unconscious mechanism, discrete moments appear to blend seamlessly into each other, establishing a coherent 'flow' of experience that is joined together by an inner sense of continuity.[70]

Naturally, this sense of continuity can last only for a certain *period* of time, because it is easily disrupted by unexpected developments. The interplay between retention and protention is therefore dynamic. The protentions resulting from previous retentions may be fulfilled, so that the inner 'flow' of time continues, although it is equally likely that they will be disappointed by the ensuing (sensory or verbal) occurrences. Disappointed expectations indeed constitute one typical source of disruption altering the course of experience. Imagine, for example, that the music you are currently listening to, keenly anticipating its delicious ending, were to stop all of a sudden. Such an unforeseen change no doubt disrupts the felt continuity of your musical experience, consequently shifting your attention away from the music to an altogether different object and intention, namely finding an explanation for the abrupt stop. This intention would last for a while, connecting your perceptions and filling your actions with a different kind of sense than the one perceived before — until that new sense is disrupted yet again.

Another common disruption of the inner sense of continuity involves sudden flashes of remembrance entering your mind. Such a spontaneous intervention of consciousness not only alters your conscious and unconscious, protentional expectations but may, in retrospect, even change your memory of the past. This perceptual dynamic occurs in sensory experience often in the form of déjà vu, subsequently causing a revision of both the past and present situation, but it also figures in literary texts as a prominent marker of turning points. The narrator's ingestion of the tea-soaked madeleine in *À la recherche du temps perdu*, during which a sudden, involuntary memory of childhood intervenes with enormous consequences, would be one example, the sudden recognition of Mathilde's face as identical with the face of the previously seen blue flower in *Heinrich von Ofterdingen* another.

In reconfiguring the successive elements of perception and narration alike, the interplay of retention and protention generates in either case a double-layered temporality. The logic coordinating these two temporal layers and, by extension, the interplay of retention and protention is what I want to call an *aesthesiology* — or rather aesthesiologies, since there are so many of them. This term, I should note, was first coined by Helmut Plessner, a key proponent of Philosophical Anthropology. But my usage of the term has little in common with the complicated system of 'accordances' and 'concordances' that, according to Plessner, defines the aesthesiologies of seeing, hearing, and bodily sensation.[71] My understanding is much simpler. I understand aesthesiologies basically as ways of structuring the succession of words or sensations. They represent rules or logics and hence a kind of grammar to relate the successive elements of both aesthesis and diegesis to the perceived whole. In short, aesthesiologies are *emergent* 'stories' of perception that are about temporal relations, while unfolding, through retention and protention, in time themselves.

Considering this definition of aesthesiologies as 'stories' of perception, one could also describe them as *schemata* in the Kantian sense. Kant (KrV A 137–47) defined schemata in essence as rules to order sensations in time, rules concerning the temporal relations among yet unspecified intuitions (*Anschauungen*). Schemata thus represent '*determinations of time*' [*Zeitbestimmungen*] that are '*intellectual* on the one hand and *sensuous* on the other'.[72] The latter qualification is actually important, since it clarifies, against views[73] in Kant scholarship to the contrary, that schemata are not simply concepts of concepts — rules about the application of concepts. Although their form is partly conceptual or logical — they are indeed *rules* — schemata are for Kant neither real nor intelligible if not applied to sensations.

However, in contrast to transcendental schemata such as those of substance and causality, which Kant considers *a priori* determinations of time, aesthesiologies do not precede the experience they structure. But neither are aesthesiologies purely empirical rules derived from perception (or for that matter reading) alone. Aesthesiologies are always mixtures of both thoughts and sensations, logic and experience. They are at once given and made, learned and discovered, derived and applied, received and conceived, contained within and brought to bear upon scenes of perception. In other words, aesthesiologies always possess both a concrete sequential and an abstract logical character, or a perceptual and a grammatical syntax, although the latter is intelligible only in retrospect, after perception (or reading) has taken place.

A few illustrations might help to clarify my understanding of aesthesiologies as 'stories' coordinating perceptions in time. When listening to music, for example, we apply and also embody certain aesthesiologies, and in doing so, we structure our acoustic perceptions, finally hearing the sequence of individual sounds as a coherent phrase. Some of the most elementary aesthesiologies producing tonal cohesion are crescendo and decrescendo, accelerando and ritardando, rhythmic or motific repetition, as well as a repertoire of common cadential formulae. These musical schemata are usually notated in the score and thus textually given, but in that form they are mute text. For there to be music, the schematic text of music — precisely the score — must be translated into 'moments of presence', as Scott Burnham puts it, which happens by way of performance and, no less important, through the *act of listening*.[74]

Notations like crescendo and decrescendo textually indicate local aesthesiologies, short musical 'stories', if you will, that performers present acoustically and listeners meanwhile realize perceptually — through corresponding retentions and protentions. Rondo or sonata forms represent, by contrast, musical schemata operating on a larger temporal scale. For a proper apprehension of these long 'stories', a trained ear is required, as well as a certain degree of musicological knowledge and also an excellent musical memory. On that basis, however, these musical schemata enable a very dynamic listening experience. For since these schemata structure acoustic perceptions for a longer duration, and hence on a global syntactic scale, they consequently enable you to connect larger sections of the music, thus following and projecting its 'flow'. For example, by recognizing the sonata form in and simultaneously applying it to a piece of music — both go hand in hand — you experience a phase of retentional and protentional cohesion that is syntactically more complex and also more long-lasting than the aforementioned local aesthesiologies. With the sonata form in mind, you are likely to start anticipating, in accordance with the convention, the return of the main theme as the development is drawing to a close. This expectation may be undermined by the music, however, which thus alters the retentional and protentional course of your listening experience — the 'story' you hear. The sonatas and symphonies from Beethoven's middle period are frequently singled out to illustrate this powerful dynamic of playing with listening expectations (a power that Hegelians like Adorno naturally attribute to the 'negativity' of musical progression in Beethoven).[75]

Seeing also involves schematic acts of form-giving — aesthesiologies. Or as Richard L. Gregory puts it, seeing necessitates '*rules* of grammar (syntax), and *meanings* of symbols (semantics)' on the basis of which optical signals are interpreted.[76] Though these aesthesiologies of looking are very different from acoustic aesthesiologies and their temporal extension is usually shorter, they are similarly necessary means of organizing visual impressions in time. For seeing *something*, as opposed to merely staring into space without noticing anything in particular, is never an immediate event — not even in the most elementary cases, as Hegel will teach us — but always a temporal process.

It may sometimes seem that way, but one does not actually see the entire picture at once. Looking at something, your eyes automatically break it up into bits and pieces, before this series of isolated glimpses come together again and thus constitute a comprehensible image — a picture that *shows* something. It takes time until we discern and process visual differences, different colours, for example, and distinct lines (which according to Kant visualize the continuous flow of time itself).[77] It takes time to discern geometrical shapes in a mass of colours and to distinguish between foreground and background, and still more time, as well as eye movement, to identify concrete objects and to recognize, say, the silhouette of a female body, then her facial expression, the strange gesture of her hand before her naked breast, and so forth. In short, it takes time until you have pieced together the entire image, and still more time to see what it shows to you. Aesthesiologies are the cognitive means of arranging this sequential process, the schematic 'stories' to concatenate, on the basis of retention and protention, the erratic process of seeing such that a mass of optical signals finally becomes, or rather *looks like*, a meaningful image.[78]

To appreciate fully the erratic temporality of seeing, specifically the complex process of figure recognition (or figural form-giving), imagine a gable-ended inn — let's call it the Spouter Inn — wherein a very large oil painting catches your eye. The painting is so thoroughly besmoked, and in every way defaced, that in the unequal crosslights it literally looks like chaos bewitched. Or does the unaccountable mass of shades and shadows it shows not rather seem like a blasted heath? A Hyperborean winter scene? The breaking-up of the ice-bound stream of Time? Clearly, only diligent study and a series of systematic visits will produce a clear perception of this painting. Throwing open the little window towards the back of the entrance might also help, of course. But stop; what about that long, limber, portentous, black mass of something in the picture's midst, which hovers over three blue, dim, perpendicular lines floating in a nameless yeast? Just look more closely at that thing to identify it, and all the rest will be plain. Does it not bear a faint resemblance to a gigantic fish? Even the great leviathan himself? In that case, the painting would seem to represent a half-foundered ship weltering in a great hurricane, and an exasperated whale who, purposing to spring clean over the craft, is in the enormous act of impaling himself upon its three splintered masts. The aesthesiology or 'story' of looking connecting these observations would be, precisely, the formidable idea and expectation of 'going a-whaling'.[79]

Texts and scenes

All of the preceding considerations come together in one and the same place, the scene, because the scene is the concrete and irreducible *domain* of the senses — of all senses. Within and through scenes, perceptions occur and aesthesiologies unfold. The oldest recorded meaning of the Greek *skēnē* — 'tent', and only later 'stage' — signifies in principle just that: an enclosed domain, an inside separated from an outside, moreover, that belongs to someone (namely the *dominus*) and defines a space of activity (such as living, worshipping, governance, etc.).[80]

The scene represents the referential frame of aesthesis and diegesis alike, at least if one supposes, against de Man and like-minded theorists, that diegesis is not self-referential language but at once describes and refers to a diegetic world. In either world, that of perception as of narration, experience gains shape and meaning in the context of a scene, which simply means: over time and *in situ*. The experience of hearing temporally unfolds in, and is spatially confined to, a scene of listening — for example, within the very red and in winter rather chilly auditorium of Carnegie Hall, with curious concertgoers to notice and much distracting noise around you, so that your attention easily wanders. The experience of seeing temporally unfolds in, and is spatially confined to, a scene of looking — for example, within a noisy and poorly lit bar such as the Spouter-Inn, where you might be studying an old oil painting or, perhaps more likely, the strange features of another guest. And the experience of taste unfolds in, and is confined to, a scene of eating and drinking — for example, while facing the resentful gaze of a colleague seated on the other side of the table at a fine brasserie with an art nouveau interior, so that even the sweetest things taste bitter.

Accordingly, a scene is defined not only by location and setting but also involves, in each and every case, temporal action. It combines an arrangement of person(s) and/or thing(s) with certain movements, interactions, and occurrences and thus represents a spatiotemporal unit. Understood in this way, however, as the space wherein *and* the time whereby perceptions take place, a scene has no permanent appearance but lasts only for a period of time — as long as something is perceived as happening within its confines. Just as perception depends upon the scene in which it takes place, so does the scene as action depend upon perception.

As such, narrations are not yet scenes but verbal compositions — discourse, text — and unlike sensory perceptions, narrative descriptions do not necessarily result from a phenomenal scene, nor do they deliver direct impressions thereof, not immediately and never by themselves. Surely, literary authors may often wish to *evoke* vivid scenes through narrations, as Gotthold Ephraim Lessing writes in his *Laokoon*:

> Der Poet will nicht bloß verständlich werden, seine Vorstellungen sollen nicht bloß klar und deutlich sein; hiermit begnügt sich der Prosaist. Sondern er will die Ideen, die er in uns erwecket, so lebhaft machen, daß wir in der Geschwindigkeit die wahren sinnlichen Eindrücke ihrer Gegenstände zu empfinden glauben, und in diesem Augenblicke der Täuschung, uns der Mittel, die er dazu anwendet, seiner Worte bewußt zu sein aufhören.
>
> [The poet does not merely wish to be understood, his representations should not only be clear and distinct; this is good enough for the prose writer. He seeks to render the ideas he awakens within us so vividly that we think we receive the true sensory impressions of the corresponding objects in real time, while ceasing, in this moment of illusion, to be conscious of the means he has employed — words.][81]

But whatever the author's desires and intentions, readers are not actually confronting phenomenal scenes when reading their works. They at first see only text, because these works are made up of letters, words, sentences. The common claim that literature 'thinks in scenes'[82] is therefore somewhat inaccurate, a metaphorical slippage confusing literary discourse with its representational content — the scenes therein described.

The medium in which literature operates or 'thinks' are words; or as Mallarmé phrased it: 'One does not make poems with ideas [...] but with *words*.'[83] Schiller brilliantly expands on this trivial but, as Lessing pointed out, easily forgotten fact about literary representation in his final *Kallias* letter, and he did so long before theoreticians like de Man latched onto it:

> Das Medium des Dichters sind *Worte*; also abstrakte Zeichen für Arten und Gattungen, niemals für Individuen; und deren Verhältnisse durch Regeln

> bestimmt werden, davon die *Grammatik* das System enthält. [...] Die Sache und ihr Wortausdruck sind bloß zufällig und willkürlich (wenige Fälle abgerechnet), bloß durch Übereinkunft miteinander verbunden. [...] Das darzustellende Objekt muß also, ehe es vor die Einbildungskraft gebracht und in Anschauung verwandelt wird, durch das abstrakte Gebiet der Begriffe *einen sehr weiten Umweg nehmen*, auf welchem es viel von seiner Lebendigkeit (sinnlicher Kraft) verliert. Der Dichter hat überall kein anderes Mittel, um das Besondere darzustellen, als die künstliche *Zusammensetzung des Allgemeinen*. 'Der eben jetzt vor mir stehende Leuchter fällt um' ist ein solcher individueller Fall, durch Verbindung lauter allgemeiner Zeichen ausgedrückt. [...] Die Sprache beraubt also den Gegenstand, dessen Darstellung ihr anvertraut wird, seiner Sinnlichkeit und Individualität und drückt ihm eine Eigenschaft von ihr selbst (Allgemeinheit) auf, die ihm fremd ist.

> [The poet's medium is *words*, hence abstract signs for kinds and species, but never for individuals, and their relationships are determined by rules of which our *grammar* comprises the system. [...] The connection between referent and verbal expression is merely accidental and arbitrary (except for a few cases); they are linked merely by convention. [...] To appear in the imagination and become perception again, the object of representation must *take a very long detour* through the abstract domain of concepts and thus loses much of its vividness (sensuous force). The poet has in all cases no other means of representing particulars than the artificial *composition of something universal*. 'The candleholder standing right in front of me topples over' is such an individual case, expressed through a combination of entirely universal signs. [...] Language thus deprives the object it is entrusted to represent of its sensuousness and individuality and so impresses on it a property of its own (universality) that is foreign to it.][84]

The sensory potential of literature, namely its power to evoke vivid scenes, is partly undermined by the literary medium of representation itself, words, because in order to evoke vivid scenes, Schiller points out, the writer must take 'a very long detour' through the abstract domain of language. Instead of reproducing perceptible individualities, as our sensory organs do, the writer can only use arbitrary signs to represent objects, thereby producing verbal compositions that follow the laws of grammar and thus constitute an abstract world of its own — diegesis.

It is this seeming deficiency, however, their abstract generality, that at the same time enables literary descriptions to *communicate* a process of perception and thus evoke a vivid scene. Surely, literary texts cannot make perceptions; they can only describe a process of perception. They are not self-aware entities, let alone subjects with perceptions, feelings, and thoughts; they are still objects made of letters, descriptions without interiority and depth. Yet this immediate *Unsinnlichkeit* of literary text, its objective lack of sensuousness and inner life, calls for an aesthetic response. The lack of sensory content necessitates concretization through readerly aesthesis, and by the same token ensures that reading is, and remains, a fundamentally free operation through which this blank can be filled.

Since descriptions cannot really contain perceptions but only a script thereof, including a story of how to make them, readers must take their sensory faculties to the text if they wish to create and, in a sense, revive and replay the scene previous readers (including the author)[85] have, each in their own way, retrieved from a certain description before. This relationship between description and perception, aesthesis and diegesis, is not without contradiction, but nonetheless integral to literature and works of art in general, Niklas Luhmann points out, since art solves the problem that 'consciousness cannot communicate' and 'communication cannot perceive' by making

> perception available for communication, and it does so outside the standardized forms of language [...] It cannot overcome the separation between psychic [i.e. perceptual] and social [i.e. communicative] systems. Both types of system remain operatively inaccessible to each other. *This, precisely, makes art significant.* Art can integrate perception and communication without merging or confusing these operations. Integration means nothing more than this: that different systems operate simultaneously (are synchronized) and thus constrain the degree of freedom each system contains in and of itself.[86]

Applied to literature this means that narrations (diegesis) transform perceptions (aesthesis) into an abstract discursive matter, namely text, thus making the intra-subjective or psychic process of perception available to the intersubjective or social process of communication. Only upon this twofold condition, verbal abstraction and discursive communication, can literary texts become appearance — a type of appearance, however, that will inevitably bear the 'impression', as Schiller wrote, or 'the stamp', as another aesthetician put it later, of language.[87]

These observations may seem obvious enough, but they are not at all trivial if held against the metaphysical idea, or rather fiction, flourishing in nineteenth-century art criticism in the wake of Schopenhauer and reiterated by Gilles Deleuze that 'the aim of art is to wrest the percept from perceptions of objects and the states of a perceiving subject, to wrest the affect from affections as the transition from one state to another: to extract a bloc of sensations, a pure being of sensations.'[88] This is something that works of art simply cannot do, least of all works consisting of letters. Literature does not incarnate perceptual essences, let alone the pure being of sensations, nor is it correct to say, as Deleuze does, that artists 'paint, sculpt, compose, and write with sensations'.[89] Writers like Lessing, Schiller, Mallarmé, or Proust in fact claim the opposite, foregrounding the verbal nature of their products instead. Works of art and literary works in particular cannot be 'reduced to brute sensation', Pierre Ouellet points out, because literature is 'ideas crossbred with affects, knowledge mixed with sensations; in short, it is *epistémè* married to *esthèsis* [viz. aesthesis], without any possible divorce between concept and percept'.[90] We must first do something with these works made of letters, namely read them, and only then will they, perhaps, affect our senses in turn.

The same applies to descriptions of perception, because those cannot fuse the operations of communication and perception either. Only subjects can do both, though never at exactly the same moment. Neither can descriptions contain phenomena in themselves or produce sensations in the same way as physical objects do, because despite their interdependence, of which I spoke earlier, sensory perception (aesthesis) and discursive description or narration (diegesis) are not identical processes.

Scenographies

Still, the subtitle of this book promises an investigation of sensuousness 'in' texts by Hegel, Novalis, Rilke, and Proust. How, then, and in what form could sensuousness be said to reside 'in' texts? Certainly not as phenomena, but only in the form of sceno*graphies*, scenic *descriptions* of perceptual processes which readerly aesthesis then translates into scenes (again) in an effort to obtain sensuousness from, while simultaneously applying such sensate meaning to, these scenographies.

I put 'again' here in brackets because in a reader-oriented perspective, for which I have opted throughout, it hardly matters whether the scene perceived by the reader coincides with the scene the author had imagined as she devised it on paper, because her 'original' imagination (if such a thing exists at all) is gone the moment it is written down, consumed by the universality of language. Described in words, the 'original' scene invariably loses all individuality and vividness, for writing means, as Schiller pointed out, to '*take a very long detour* through the abstract domain of concepts' and hence of language, which in its abstractness and universality nonetheless constitutes the very possibility of communicating individual experience and which Hegel for this reason praises as 'divine' (PhG 92/66*).

The term 'scenography' is not a new creation, and so its meaning varies depending on discipline and context. Deriving from the Greek *skēnographia*, 'scene painting', scenography originally meant the painted cloth hung at the back of a theatre stage, hence its backdrop. However, this 'pictorial two-dimensional scenography' is 'a far cry from' from what scenography means in the context of theatre today, namely all aspects of stage design and *mis-en-scène*.[91] More recently, this theatrical notion of scenography was picked up by architects, designers, and museum curators, who now use it to describe the art of 'making spaces talk' by arranging features like colour, sound, lighting, placement, or hanging in such a way as to guide the viewer's attention as he or she moves through an exhibition room.[92]

In literary theory, an attempt was made to establish the term 'scenography' as a basic concept to describe the *mis-en-scène* through writing, a literal interpretation of sceno-graphy not unlike my own.[93] However, fusing metaphors of theatricality and performativity with all kinds of semiological speculations, this attempt remained largely theoretical. At stake are abstract *grammatical* issues such as the 'micro-drama' of signification, the 'scene' of thought, the 'theatricality of signs', or the 'arena of words'. Literary examples — scenographies taken from literary works — are completely absent from the stage of reflection, not to mention readerly aesthesis.[94]

More tangible and also applicable is the definition of scenography provided by literary scholar Ralf Simon, who recently defined it in a study on the 'visuality of lyric text' as a 'scripting of actions' [Handlungsskript] combining a 'site' [Schauplatz] with 'profiles of interaction' [Interaktionsprofile].[95] This definition comes close to some of the things I have said, of course, and I would in principle agree with it if Simon had not conceived of scenographies in purely visual terms — as verbal 'images' referring to 'places of seeing', which is a literal translation of the German *Schauplätze* . This general limitation of scenographies to a single sense (the eye) and a single sensory medium (the image) — a limitation which I oppose and the concept of scene in fact defies — nonetheless results from Simon's theoretical framework. For since he is concerned with the 'visuality' or 'iconicity' (*Bildlichkeit*) of poetic language, he invariably conceives of scenes and their written literary representations, scenographies, as instantiations and species of 'image'.[96]

The theatrical understanding of scenographies as set-up spaces of presentation — as stages designed to show something — is certainly applicable to literary texts, because they too are often designed to show or even stage something, whatever it may be, whatever readers want it to be. Unlike theatrical scenes, however, which have a manifest appearance and scenery, literary scenes are not phenomenal but at first textual in nature; they are written-up scenes. As literary objects, therefore, scenographies would be defined best, I think, as a genre of text and, more precisely, as a style of narration (diegesis). Indeed, scenographies are a 'genre' of text insofar as they represent a *mode of writing* readers and writers have derived from, and continue to develop through, an ever-growing canon of examples, and a 'style' of narration insofar as they describe individual scenes, rather than representing entire worlds, as longer literary narrations like epics and novels do. This is why scenographies tend to be, though need not be, passages within a longer narrative text.

Another important feature of scenographies is their generic versatility. The scenographies I discussed at the beginning — two *poems* by Durs Grünbein — are written in verse, but prose texts may contain scenographic passages as well. In fact, most scenographies considered in this book are written in prose. Such scenographic passages are not exclusive to literary works. They are found in philosophical and especially in phenomenological prose as well, for example in Hegel's *Phenomenology of Spirit*, and necessarily so, for there is no phenomenological theory (from Greek *theōrein*, 'to look at') of the mind without spectatorial observation, and hence illustration, of its operations. And so, in considering a diverse range of texts and authors, the following chapters might indeed demonstrate that scenographies cut across traditional generic boundaries and thus evade, for example, the classic distinction between lyric poetry and narrative prose, as well as that between literary and philosophical writings.

Scenes consist of things and perceptions, which they arrange in space *and* time, whereas scenographies are made of descriptions — of words narrating scenes in either prose or verse. If scenographies constitute a style of narration (diegesis), however, they must consist, like all narratives, of three interconnected layers, namely descriptions and a scene thus described, as well as an inherent aesthesiology connecting these two and guiding readerly aesthesis. This tripartite structure obviously reflects the structure of narrations at large, in which a series of events pertaining to a fictional world is conveyed through narratorial discourse, with the plot or story serving as the schematic intermediary between discourse and *histoire* as interpreted by the reader.[97]

The diegetic scene as perceived by the reader shows all kinds of interactions between animate and inanimate agents within various environments, but this spatiotemporal ensemble, the scene, comes into existence through verbal descriptions. Interpreting these descriptions is not simply a lexical matter. Words do not directly translate into sensations and appearances, because their meaning depends on syntax, as well as semantics and graphic arrangement. Indeed, formal language structures such as rhetorical tropes and figures, graphic appearance and prosody, as well as word order and sentence structure, complicate the perception of diegetic scenes. To unpack the scene, interpretation and participation are therefore required — acts of concretization, however, that also simplify and homogenize the text by eliminating semantic ambiguities and indeterminacies. That is the price one must pay to recognize scenes and, by extension, sensuousness in scenographies. But, then again, is there a way of reading that could avoid such deformations? 'To read [ablesen] a text as text without interposing an interpretation' may be the philological ideal, as Nietzsche noted, adding, however, that this is 'hardly possible'.[98]

Scenographies are seldom plain descriptions of scenes, least of all scenographies that are composed with poetic intent. The same applies to the aesthesiologies connecting narration and perception, description and scene. These 'stories' we both discover in and apply to scenographies are hardly plain scripts of perception. They are shaped by writerly means and devices and thus emerge from a *poetics* of perception. In this respect, they do differ from aesthesiologies evolving in, and under the dissimilar conditions of, a phenomenal scene, which is made of physical appearances rather than poetic descriptions.

Still, in neither domain would it be possible to detach aesthesiologies from the senses because only these bring them to fruition. Aesthesiologies are real and effective only insofar as we actualize and embody them through forms of perception, and like schemata they are conceptual on the one hand and sensory on the other. In perception, these two sides are inseparable. Only in analysis must they come apart, for analysing is an act of the understanding that happens in retrospect, after perception has taken place.

Although literary aesthesiologies are experienced aesthetically, through forms of perception, they are still based on descriptions — on text. Hence, the text must bear legible traces of them and textually constrain readerly aesthesis. Just as the physical setting of a scene will shape the course of perception, so will the text of a scenography shape its perception and aesthesiology, in the following way. Inscribed in the scenographic text we recognize a potential scene (descriptions of persons, things, and actions as happening in the same location), as well as formal patterns (syntactic, rhetoric, graphic, prosodic, etc.). Taken together, these two aspects constitute the diegetic set-up and grammar of the scenography that guide and constrain our observations. They exert a certain degree of control over readerly aesthesis — never absolutely, of course, but directionally — thus influencing the aesthesiologies we develop while reading. To put it with Novalis, the text of scenographies has the power to elicit 'a thousand *sensations* and *functions*' in a reader, '*determinate* or *specific* and *free* ones' (N II 356 #205).

Granted that scenographies consist of descriptions and aesthesiological traces that together represent a scene, how do these three components relate to each other? To specify their correlation, I investigate scenographies *of perception* — scenographies of looking in Rilke, scenographies of hearing in Proust, and scenographies of sensing poetry in Novalis, as well as scenographies of sensory cognition in Hegel. These scenographies differ in many ways. Some are written in verse, others in prose; some describe concrete things, others inner visions and dreams; some were composed with poetic intent, others to illustrate philosophical concepts. What unites these scenographies beyond formal and functional differences, however, is that they all communicate sensory events and for this reason share four basic features: they describe perceptual actions and occurrences, mostly through verbs of perception like looking and seeing, seeming, listening and hearing, sensing and feeling, but not necessarily in chronological order; they indicate, however indirectly, the setting of the perceptual scene; they mark or at least imply the place of an observer (as opposed to, say, a telephone book or a statistical report, which suggest no such place); and finally, they map out a multisensory space surrounded by a larger world of possible experience.

It goes without saying that scenographies may also dramatize processes, forces, or logics that are invisible, abstract, intangible. Take, for example, *L'Éducation sentimentale*, Gustave Flaubert's famous novel about an unfulfilled love, which contains intense scenographies of desire and frustration, or *Michael Kohlhaas*, Heinrich von Kleist's novella about a horse dealer's increasingly radical quest for justice, which contains violent scenographies of power and powerlessness. Fundamentally, however, these examples are scenographies of perception, too, because the dynamic of desire would remain intangible and the force of political power invisible without a scene in which they manifest. Their power could not affect us if we did not sense and see them, however indirectly, and their story (which in the context of a scene becomes an aesthesiology) would escape us if it did not appear. Their sense would remain abstract. Consequently, every scenography is at root a scenography of perception.

The task ahead

The sensuousness of scenographies needs to be perceived to come into existence, which happens in response to text. The task ahead is, therefore, to observe 'how sensuousness emerges in the process of reading', as Peter Utz once put it.[99] For the literary critic, as opposed to the psychologist or neuroscientist, this can only mean to examine the individual textual traces that both call for and lend themselves to readerly aesthesis. How, then, is the sensuous discursively coded and narrativized in scenographies? What are the literary devices prompting readerly perception and embodiment? That is the basic question pursued in Part Two, 'The Language of the Senses'. Under scrutiny here is the sensuous force of scenographies by Novalis, Rilke, and Proust — 'the force', as Peter Brooks put it, 'that makes the connection of incidents powerful'.[100] Brooks identifies this force with the plots of desire, which is undoubtedly another potent force of cohesion, but in the case of scenographies of perception it seems only logical to suppose that this force issues from the aesthesiologies indicated by, and formed in response to, scenographies — a foreign fusion of thought and sensation in Novalis, the anonymous exchange of glances between observer and observed in Rilke, and the evocative recurrences of a certain sound in Proust's *Recherche*. The preceding part, 'The "Story" of Perception', prepares the ground for these aesthesiological readings by elaborating on Hegel's theory of perception as a story-like process in which words and sensations, concepts and perceptions, are bound together.

'Hypotheses are nets', says Novalis, 'only he who casts will catch' [nur der wird fangen, der auswirft] (N II, 434). This is the spirit in which I hope this introduction will be read. The introduced ideas — the interplay of aesthesis and diegesis, diegetic worlds, aesthesiologies, scenographies — are hypotheses to reveal new facets when cast over Hegel, Novalis, Rilke, and Proust. They provide coordinates to discern patterns and figures that might otherwise have passed me by. Novalis's saying is especially true for generic concepts such as 'the novel', 'the lyric', or for that matter 'scenographies', as the definition of literary genres is never a purely objective matter but is based on deliberate choices — on *defining* the common features of a *selection* of texts, while ignoring other texts and existent features that could have been highlighted as well. Literary genres are at once precepts and concepts, rules and results, of reading. They are hypotheses, too — nets you cast on texts to make a catch.

Notes to the Introduction

1. The cycle 'In der Provinz', first published with Suhrkamp, is included in the anthology *Limbische Akte: Gedichte* (Stuttgart: Reclam, 2011), pp. 111–12. I thank the Suhrkamp Verlag for granting permission to reproduce this poem. The English translation, which I have partly modified, is by Michael Hofmann, <https://www.poetryinternationalweb.net/pi/site/poem/item/2243> [accessed 1 April 2019].
2. Hearing this word, American readers might imagine a kind of vulture. But the common buzzard (*Buteo buteo*), which is indigenous only to Europe and parts of Asia, is in fact a hawk-like bird of prey.
3. The semiotic concept of 'isotopy' was first introduced by A. J. Greimas in his *Structural Semantics: An Attempt at a Method* (Lincoln: University of Nebraska Press, 1983) and basically designates a semantic field connected by a common meaning trait or 'seme'.
4. One such reader is Fritz J. Raddatz who, in his review 'Durs Grünbein — die dichtende Luftnummer' (*Die Welt*, 21 August 2012), criticizes Grünbein for writing 'without mystery, without secret, without amazement [Erschütterung] for its reader. They are conversation poems [Plauderpoeme] [...] readily comprehensible — like TV news. And without rigor too. But, as a fruit contains a stone, so great poetry contains an almost sacred inside, something untouchable, insoluble.' Reading this review, I cannot help but recall William Empson's dictum that 'critics have been perhaps too willing to insist that the operation of poetry is something magical, to which only their own method of incantation can be applied' (*Seven Types of Ambiguity* (New York: New Directions, 1966), p. 9).
5. Reprinted in Grünbein, *Limbische Akte*, pp. 38–43. I only reproduce pp. 38–40, and once again thank the Suhrkamp Verlag for granting permission to do so.
6. The compound *Erinnerungsschlieren* ('streaks of memory') might refer to Paul Celan's poem 'Schliere', first published in 1957. Celan here makes a similar connection between streaks and memories by comparing a 'Schliere im Auge' to a 'durchs Dunkel getragenes Zeichen, | vom Sand (oder Eis?) einer fremden | Zeit'. Considering Grünbein's biography — he grew up in Dresden — as well as the publication date of 'Niemands Land Stimmen' shortly after German reunification in 1991, one might interpret these 'streaks of memory' also historically, as an allusion to the time before reunification. The poem would thus comment upon both the individual and collective formation and transformation of memories during the so-called *Wendezeit*, picturing

that process as a 'waking dream' in which 'streaks of memory' — reminiscences of what life used to be in the GDR or the old BRD — keep inserting themselves.
7. This expression refers to both Hegel ('die *Furie* des Verschwindens', PhG 436/359*) and Hans Magnus Enzensberger, *Die Furie des Verschwindens: Gedichte* (Frankfurt am Main: Suhrkamp, 1980). It certainly resonates with the historical context of the poem, the *Wendezeit*.
8. W. K. Wimsatt and M. C. Beardsley, 'The Affective Fallacy', *The Sewanee Review*, 57 (1949), 31–55.
9. Paul de Man, *Blindness and Insight: Essays in the Rhetoric of Contemporary Criticism* (Minneapolis: University of Minnesota Press, 1983), p. 107.
10. Ibid., p. 34.
11. De Man, *The Resistance to Theory* (Minneapolis: University of Minnesota Press, 1986), pp. 3–20 (pp. 11, 10, 14, 18).
12. Ibid., p. 19. Cf. Corngold, *Complex Pleasure*, p. 20:

    Under the spell of Paul de Man, in whom a hyperawareness of recursiveness was projected into literature as its basic character, writing became an easily penetrable allegory of its own unintelligibility, one that yielded in every case one good master cognition. This is the knowledge of literature's principal opacity and violence.

13. De Man, *Resistance to Theory*, p. 118; *Blindness and Insight*, p. 139.
14. De Man, *Resistance to Theory*, p. 17.
15. De Man, *Blindness and Insight*, p. 136.
16. De Man, *Resistance to Theory*, pp. 18–19.
17. Claudia Brodsky, 'Szondi and Hegel: "The Troubled Relationship of Literary Criticism to Philosophy"', *Telos*, 140 (2007), 45–63 (pp. 45–46).
18. It is sometimes alleged, e.g. by Martin Jay, *Downcast Eyes: The Denigration of Vision in Twentieth-Century French Thought* (Berkeley: University of California Press, 1993), p. 497, and McSweeney, p. x, that the other famous deconstructionist, Jacques Derrida, discarded sense perception in a similar fashion. This impression is based on the remark Derrida made during the 1966 conference on structuralism at Baltimore that he does not 'believe that anything like perception exists' and that 'perception is interdependent with the concept of origin and of center', wherefore his critique of Western metaphysics 'strikes also at the very concept of perception' (*The Languages of Criticism and the Sciences of Man*, ed. by Richard Macksey and Eugenio Donato (Baltimore: Johns Hopkins University Press, 1970), p. 272). Reading the remark more closely, however, it becomes clear that Derrida did not mean to condemn perception *in toto* but rather a specific concept of perception, namely the 'concept of an intuition or of a given originating from the thing itself [...] *independently from language*' (ibid.; emphasis added). The narrative conception of perception on which this book relies is completely in line with this remark, because it similarly asserts that without discursive form-giving, there are no perceptions.
19. '[T]echnically correct rhetorical readings', says de Man, *Resistance to Theory*, p. 19, are immanent readings and therefore in principle 'irrefutable', but in fact also impossible because 'of language's impossibility to be a model language'.
20. Friedrich Nietzsche, *Sämtliche Werke: Kritische Studienausgabe*, ed. by Giorgio Colli and Mazzino Montinari, 15 vols (Munich: dtv, 1999), 11, 608 (NF 1885, 38[10]); cf. the similar posthumous fragments or *Nachlassfragmente* NF 1881, 11[293]; NF 1883, 24[14]; NF 1885, 2[82–95]; and NF 1885, 34 [131–32].
21. However, the Neo-Kantian concept of cognition comes closer to the quoted fragment by Nietzsche, e.g. Ernst Cassirer, *Das Erkenntnisproblem in der Philosophie und Wissenschaft der neueren Zeit*, 4 vols (Berlin: Cassirer, 1906–52), I (1906), pp. 1–3.
22. Richard L. Gregory, *Eye and Brain: The Psychology of Seeing*, Princeton Science Library, 5th edn (Princeton: Princeton University Press, 1997), p. 5, and similarly in his 'Perceptions as Hypotheses', *Philosophical Transactions of the Royal Society*, 290 (1980), 181–97. Gregory adds that his idea of perception as 'intelligent decision-taking' derives from Helmholtz's concept of perceptions as 'unconscious inferences' (*Eye and Brain*, p. 5). Helmholtz is also Nietzsche's main point of reference; see Christian Emden, 'Metapher, Wahrnehmung, Bewußtsein: Nietzsches Verschränkung von Rhetorik und Neurophysiologie', in *Text und Wissen: Technologische und*

anthropologische Aspekte, ed. by Renate Lachmann and Stefan Rieger (Tübingen: Narr, 2003), pp. 127–51, as well as Sören Reuter, 'Nietzsche und die Sinnesphysiologie und Erkenntniskritik', in *Handbuch Nietzsche und die Wissenschaften: Natur-, geistes- und sozialwissenschaftliche Kontexte*, ed. by Helmut Heit and Lisa Heller (Berlin: De Gruyter, 2014), pp. 79–106.

23. Nietzsche, II, 877.
24. Nietzsche, II, 884; cf. the related fragments NF 1872, 19[66–67], [78–79].
25. In *Reading for the Plot: Design and Intention in Narrative* (New York: Alfred A. Knopf, 1984), Peter Brooks characterizes plot as 'the design and intention' that 'shapes a story and gives it a certain direction' (p. xi), and more precisely as the 'structuring operation' and 'dynamic logic [...] which makes sense of succession and time' (p. 10). For Brooks, however, plot does not simply represent an inherent design or logical property of narrative texts but, rather, an interpretative achievement, namely 'the active interpretive work of discourse on story' (p. 27), which as such pertains 'to the reader's literary competence, his training as a reader of narrative' (p. 19). Reading a story is therefore tantamount to 'plotting' (p. xiii), as Brooks puts it, so that the resulting plot would be best described as an *evolving* logic of mediation — which is just what *Geschichte* represents in Hegel.
26. My understanding of sense perception as aesthesis is informed by phenomenologies of perception in the tradition of Husserl and Merleau-Ponty, especially Bernhard Waldenfels, *Das leibliche Selbst: Vorlesungen zur Phänomenologie des Leibes*, ed. by Regula Giuliani (Frankfurt am Main: Suhrkamp, 2000) and Gernot Böhme, *Aisthetik: Vorlesungen über Ästhetik als allgemeine Wahrnehmungslehre* (Munich: Fink, 2001), as well as Martin Seel, *Ästhetik des Erscheinens* (Frankfurt am Main: Suhrkamp, 2003). In a narrower sense, however, I refer here to Plato's understanding of *aisthēsis*, which in addition to the five senses similarly includes the affections of the body, many of which have names, Plato writes in *Theaetetus*, ed. and trans. by Harold North Fowler (Cambridge, MA: Harvard University Press, 1928), while still more 'are unnamed' (p. 57 (156b)). For a brief summary of Plato's theory of sense perception, see the entry 'Aisthesis' in *Metzler Philosophie Lexikon: Begriffe und Definitionen*, ed. by Peter Prechtl and Franz-Peter Burkard, 2nd edn (Stuttgart: Metzler, 1999), pp. 11–13. Thomas Schirren, *Aisthesis vor Platon: Eine semantisch-systematische Untersuchung zum Problem der Wahrnehmung* (Stuttgart: Teubner, 1998), has traced the changeable history of *aisthēsis* before its meaning was consolidated by Plato, who unlike pre-Socratic thinkers sought to distinguish *aisthēsis* from purely intellectual (noetic) operations such as 'attention and awareness' ['Aufmerksamkeit und Achtsamkeit'] (p. 261). Daniel Heller-Roazen, *The Inner Touch: Archaeology of a Sensation* (New York: Zone Books, 2007) similarly remarks that prior to Plato, the meaning of *aisthēsis* included 'the often-elusive power of awareness that would later be said to be that of consciousness' (p. 22). As for the heterogeneous meanings of *aisthēsis*, see also the entry 'sense/meaning' in the *Dictionary of Untranslatables: A Philosophical Lexicon*, ed. by Barbara Cassin, trans. by Steven Rendell and others (Princeton: Princeton University Press, 2014), pp. 949–52.
27. See Plato, *The Republic*, trans. by Paul Shorey (Cambridge, MA: Harvard University Press, 1930), pp. 224–30 (392c–394c), where poetry is defined as *diēgēsis*. Plato bases his distinction of narrative styles or dictions (*lexeis*) on the relation of the speaker (or writer) to the portrayed incidents and characters. Either 'the poet himself is the speaker and does not even attempt to suggest to us that anyone but himself is speaking' (393a), or the narration (*diēgēsis*) 'is effected through imitation [*mimēsis*]' (392b) of voices other than his. Plato considers the dithyramb an example of the former, simple type of description or narration (*haplē diēgēsis*), while a tragedy counts as mimetic narration in that it imitates throughout foreign or, still worse, fictitious voices. A mixture of these two pure dictions characterizes the third style of narration distinguished by Plato, an epic such as the *Iliad* being the prime example. Aristotle partly draws on these distinctions when he describes, in chapters two and three of his *Poetics*, the ways and means by which poets impart a story (*mythos*). Yet the fact remains that he chose *mimēsis* over *diēgēsis*, represented content over discursive form, to define the common essence of poetic works. With this conceptual choice, however, Aristotle follows in principle Plato's *ontological* concept of art as an imperfect and often spurious imitation (*mimēsis*) of natural appearances. The Platonic verdict against art as *mimēsis*, developed in Book Ten of *The Republic*, no doubt contrasts with the formalist or technical

understanding of poetic works as *diēgēsis* in Book Three, of which *mimēsis* is but one style. Cf. Klaus Hempfer's helpful gloss in *Handbuch Gattungstheorie*, ed. by Rüdiger Zymner (Stuttgart: Metzler, 2010), pp. 39–41. Prior to Plato, *mimēsis* did not have a moral connotation at all but may have simply meant the imitation of divine love-making, as Friedrich Kittler suggests in *Musik und Mathematik*, 2 vols (Munich: Fink, 2006–09), I.1 (2006), pp. 127–28, as well as *Philosophien der Literatur: Berliner Vorlesung 2002* (Berlin: Merve, 2013), pp. 52–59. Two slaves, for example, would imitate, or rather re-enact, the amorous play of Ariadne and Dionysus on stage so as to animate married viewers to do the same, or else encourage viewers to marry and then imitate the gods by making love. The strange line from *Heinrich von Ofterdingen*, 'die Liebe ist eine endlose Wiederholung' (N I, 338), may be an echo of this ancient notion of *mimēsis*, which Friedrich Kittler loved.

28. Gérard Genette, *Figures III* (Paris: Editions du Seuil, 1972), pp. 48 (n. 1), 280; cf. Genette, *Narrative Discourse: An Essay in Method* (Ithaca, NY: Cornell University Press, 1980), p. 94 (n. 12). For more details, see the entry 'diegesis' in both the *Reallexikon der deutschen Literaturwissenschaft*, ed. by Harald Fricke and others, 3rd edn, 3 vols (Berlin; New York: De Gruyter, 1997–2003) and the *Routledge Encyclopedia of Narrative Theory*, ed. by David Herman and others (London and New York: Routledge, 2008).

29. For example, Seymour Chatman cites the 'doubly temporal logic' as the generally established criterion of narrative, wherefore non-narrative (such as argumentative) texts would precisely lack 'an internal time sequence' (Seymour Benjamin Chatman, *Coming to Terms: The Rhetoric of Narrative in Fiction and Film* (Ithaca: Cornell University Press, 1990), p. 9). Günther Müller was the first narratologist to expand upon the double temporality of narrative; see his 'Erzählzeit und erzählte Zeit' (first published in 1948), reprinted in *Morphologische Poetik: Gesammelte Aufsätze*, ed. by Elena Müller (Tübingen: Niemeyer, 1968), pp. 269–86. For a characterization of lyric (as opposed to narrative) ways of speaking, see Jonathan Culler, *Theory of the Lyric* (Cambridge, MA: Harvard University Press, 2015), pp. 186–243, as well as Klas Molde, 'Enchantment and Embarrassment in the Lyric' (PhD, Cornell University, 2016).

30. In *The Imposition of Form: Studies in Narrative Representation and Knowledge* (Princeton: Princeton University Press, 1987), Brodsky claims that narrative representation, which she defines 'as the means by which a story is told', is 'the literary form most generally understood to foster its own logical understanding' and therefore enables a 'coherent presentation of experience' (p. 3). She derives this claim from Kant, whose 'critical limitation of knowledge to a formal knowledge of representation seems to describe a general theory of representational narration' (p. 3, n. 1), and demonstrates it in the following chapter (pp. 21–87).

31. Robert C. Schank and Robert P. Abelson, 'Knowledge and Memory: The Real Story', in *Knowledge and Memory: The Real Story*, ed. by Robert S. Wyer (Hillsdale: Erlbaum, 1995), pp. 1–85 (pp. 1, 7) <http://cogprints.org/636/> [accessed 1 April 2019].

32. Mark Turner, *The Literary Mind* (New York: Oxford University Press, 1996), pp. 4–5, 145.

33. For an introduction to James J. Gibson's theory of affordances, see Andrea Scarantino, 'Affordances Explained', *Philosophy of Science*, 70 (2003), 949–61.

34. John Dewey, 'The Reflex Arc Concept in Psychology', *Psychological Review*, 3 (1896), 357–70 (pp. 357, 365, 359–60). I thank Julian Petri for bringing this text to my attention.

35. See Alva Noë, *Action in Perception* (Cambridge, MA: MIT Press, 2004), as well as *The Routledge Handbook of Embodied Cognition*, ed. by Lawrence A. Shapiro (New York: Routledge, 2014), pp. 101–05 (on Gibson's influence).

36. According to Friedrich Kittler, *Aufschreibesysteme 1800/1900*, 4th edn (Munich: Fink, 2003), pp. 135, 138–43, Romantic literature served around 1800 as an 'hallucinatory substitute' for sensory experience and did so for the simple reason that advanced audiovisual media like phonography and film, which replicate phenomena better than words, were not available at the time.

37. Schiller and Goethe, *Der Briefwechsel: Historisch-kritische Ausgabe*, ed. by Norbert Oellers, 2 vols (Stuttgart: Reclam, 2009), I, 232–33 (Schiller to Goethe on 9 July 1796); *Correspondence between Schiller and Goethe, from 1794 to 1805*, trans. by L. Dora Schmitz, 2 vols (London: Bell, 1877), I, 197.

38. Goethe to Schiller on 19 November 1796: 'Bey diesem Aufsatz [i.e. an essay on *Wilhelm*

Meisters Lehrjahre by Schiller's friend Christian Gottlieb Körner] ist es aber auch überhaupt sehr auffallend, daß sich der Leser productiv verhalten muß wenn er an irgendeiner Production Theil nehmen will. Von den passiven Theilnahmen habe ich leider schon die betrübtesten Beyspiele wieder erlebt' (*Briefwechsel*, I, 311). As for Goethe's varying theories of perception, see Fritz Breithaupt, *Jenseits der Bilder: Goethes Politik der Wahrnehmung* (Freiburg im Breisgau: Rombach, 2000).

39. In the twenty-second letter on *Ästhetische Erziehung*, Schiller makes it clear that he believes primarily in the powers of aesthetic form: 'In a truly beautiful work of art the content should do nothing, but the form everything; for it is form alone that affects man as a whole, whereas content affects only individual powers' [In einem wahrhaft schönen Kunstwerk soll der Inhalt nichts, die Form aber alles tun; denn durch die Form allein wird auf das Ganze des Menschen, durch den Inhalt hingegen nur auf einzelne Kräfte gewirkt] (Schiller, *Sämtliche Werke*, ed. by Peter André Alt and others, 5 vols (Munich: Hanser, 2004), V, 639).

40. Novalis, *Philosophical Writings*, trans. by Margaret Mahony Stoljar (Albany: State University of New York Press, 1997), p. 45. It is unclear who decided not to publish this fragment in the *Athenäum* as part of *Blüthenstaub*, nor why it was deemed unfit for publication; see N III, 342–43. One should think, however, that Friedrich and August Wilhelm Schlegel, the editors of the *Athenäum* and self-styled 'critical dictators of Germany' (*Kritische Friedrich-Schlegel-Ausgabe*, ed. by Ernst Behler and others, 35 vols (Munich: Schöningh, 1958–), XXIV (1985), 31–32), had a hand in the decision.

41. Novalis hailed the readers of the *Athenäum* with the words: 'Wir sind auf einer Mißion: zur Bildung der Erde sind wir berufen' (N II, 241 #32).

42. Novalis to Fr. Schlegel on 10 January 1797: 'Meine Hand hat mich 8 Tage faul seyn lassen, welches mich häßlich quält — Selbst Lesen kann ich nicht recht, weil ich dabey unaufhörlich die Feder haben muß' (N I, 607–08).

43. As for Novalis's ambivalent reception of *Wilhelm Meisters Lehrjahre*, see Robert T. Ittner, 'Novalis' Attitude toward *Wilhelm Meister* with Reference to the Conception of his *Heinrich von Ofterdingen*', *The Journal of English and Germanic Philology*, 37 (1938), 542–54. On the matter of extended authorship, see also Nikolaus Wegmann and Ulrich Breuer, 'Editorial', *Athenäum: Jahrbuch der Friedrich Schlegel Gesellschaft*, 23 (2013), 9–18 (p. 12).

44. Lyceum fragment no. 112, in *Kritische Friedrich-Schlegel-Ausgabe*, II (1967), 161:

> Der synthetische Schriftsteller konstruiert und schafft sich einen Leser, wie er sein soll; er denkt sich denselben nicht ruhend und tot, sondern lebendig und entgegenwirkend. Er läßt das, was er erfunden hat, vor seinen Augen stufenweise werden, oder er lockt ihn es selbst zu erfinden. Er will keine bestimmte Wirkung auf ihn machen, sondern er tritt mit ihm in das heilige Verhältnis der innigsten Symphilosophie oder Sympoesie.

> [The synthetic writer constructs and creates a reader as he should be; he doesn't think of him as calm and dead, but as alive and critical. He allows for his invention to take shape gradually before the reader's eyes, or else he tempts him to discover it himself. He does not wish to make any particular impression on him, but enters with him into the sacred relationship of symphilosophy or sympoetry.]

Schlegel juxtaposes this Romantic ideal of 'synthetic' co-authorship with the 'analytic writer', who 'observes the reader as he is — and then calculates accordingly, employing his devices [seine Maschinen] to produce the proper effect' (ibid.). Paul de Man's theory of literary language as an acutely self-aware and always deceptive machinery seems not far from that.

45. '[D]enn ein Kunstwerk ganz verstehen, heißt, es gewissermaßen erschaffen', a line from Ludwig Tieck's 1822 novella *Die Gemälde*, in *Werke in vier Bänden*, ed. by Marianne Thalmann, 4 vols (Munich: Winkler, 1963–66), III (1965), 7–74 (p. 54).

46. Joseph von Eichendorff, *Werke in sechs Bänden*, ed. by Wolfgang Frühwald and others, 6 vols (Frankfurt am Main: Deutscher Klassiker Verlag, 1985–93), II (1985), p. 156: 'Und das sind die rechten Leser, die mit und über dem Buche dichten. Denn kein Dichter gibt einen fertigen Himmel; er stellt nur die Himmelsleiter auf von der schönen Erde. Wer, zu träge und unlustig, nicht den Mut verspürt, die goldenen, losen Sprossen zu besteigen, dem bleibt der geheimnisvolle

Buchstab ewig tot, und er täte besser, zu graben oder zu pflügen, als so mit unnützem Lesen müßig zu gehn.'
47. *Philosophical Writings*, p. 108. Novalis also names in this fragment some of the operations the reader freely executes:

   Die meisten Schriftsteller sind zugleich ihre *Leser* — indem sie schreiben — und daher entstehn in den Werken so viele Spuren des Lesers — so viele kritische Rücksichten — so manches, was dem Leser zukömmt und nicht dem Schriftsteller. Gedankenstriche — großgedruckte Worte — herausgehobne Stellen — alles dies gehört in das Gebiet des Lesers. (N II, 398–99 #398)

   [Most writers are at once their own *readers* as they write — which is why so many traces of the reader appear in their works, so many critical considerations, so much which pertains to the sphere of the reader, rather than the writer. Dashes, words in capitals, highlighted passages — all this belongs to the sphere of the reader.] (*Philosophical Writings*, p. 108)

48. N II, 356 #205; *Philosophical Writings*, p. 69. Arguably, Novalis's miscellaneous comments on literary reading anticipate the phenomenological model of literature properly introduced by Roman Ingarden and further developed by Wolfgang Iser, since Novalis too foregrounds the necessity of participation and concretization in reading works of literature.

49. The following paragraphs on Husserl paraphrase primarily §§ 27–28 of his *Ideen zu einer reinen Phänomenologie und phänomenologischen Philosophie*, viz. *Husserliana: Gesammelte Werke*, ed. by H. L. van Breda and others, 42 vols (The Hague: Nijhoff, 1950–), III.1 (1977), 56–60. Note also the passage in the *Cartesianische Meditationen* (*Husserliana*, I (1973), 94–99), where Husserl explains that the reality and evidence of both physical and ideational worlds always depends on conscious experience. As for the genesis and meaning of *Welt* as key concept of phenomenology, see *Husserl-Lexikon*, ed. by Hans-Helmuth Gander (Darmstadt: Wissenschaftliche Buchgesellschaft, 2010), pp. 308–11. Heidegger exploited the concepts of world and worldliness very thoroughly in *Sein und Zeit*, but without crediting Husserl at all. Still, the concept has had a stubborn afterlife in theory and philosophy, not least because Niklas Luhmann incorporated it into his systems theory — and unlike Heidegger with reference to Husserl; see Luhmann, *Die Gesellschaft der Gesellschaft* (Frankfurt am Main: Suhrkamp, 1997), pp. 153–54, as well as Rainer Schützeichel, *Sinn als Grundbegriff bei Niklas Luhmann* (Frankfurt am Main: Campus, 2003), pp. 32–37.

50. Martin Heidegger, *Der Ursprung des Kunstwerkes* (1935/36), in *Gesamtausgabe*, ed. by Friedrich Wilhelm von Hermann and others (Frankfurt am Main: Klostermann, 1977–), V (1977), 1–74 (pp. 27–36). The recent publication of Heidegger's so-called *Schwarze Hefte* again raises the question whether key concepts of Heidegger's philosophy of art are rooted in völkisch ideas. These notebooks contain blatantly anti-Semitic remarks and above all endless ramblings on the supposed destiny of the German people or *Volk* to overturn Western metaphysics in the name of Being. Seen in that light, the prominence of *Erde, Volk, Ursprung, Bewahrung*, and *Stiftung* in the *Kunstwerk* essay appears particularly suspect. The fact that these concepts take on an increasingly culturalist meaning in Heidegger's discourse (cf. pp. 50, 63–66) only deepens this suspicion. Perhaps, the disgruntled art critic from Thomas Bernhard's 'comedy' *Alte Meister* (Frankfurt am Main: Suhrkamp, 1985), Reger, was right in calling Heidegger a 'nationalsozialistischen Pumphosenspießer' (p. 87). See also Philippe Lacoue-Labarthe, *Heidegger, Art and Politics: The Fiction of the Political*, trans. by Chris Turner (Oxford: Blackwell, 1990), as well as Peter Trawny, *Heidegger und der Mythos der jüdischen Weltverschwörung*, 3rd edn (Frankfurt am Main: Klostermann, 2015).

51. See Nelson Goodman, *Ways of Worldmaking* (Hassocks: Harvester, 1978) and Richard J. Gerrig, *Experiencing Narrative Worlds: On the Psychological Activities of Reading* (New Haven: Yale University Press, 1993). For an introduction to more recent theories of narrative as 'worldmaking', see *Cultural Ways of Worldmaking: Media and Narratives*, ed. by Ansgar Nünning and others (Berlin: De Gruyter, 2010), pp. 191–264.

52. Roman Ingarden, *Das literarische Kunstwerk, mit einem Anhang von den Funktionen der Sprache im Theaterschauspiel* (Tübingen: Niemeyer, 1931), pp. 230–31; *The Literary Work of Art: An Investigation on the Borderlines of Ontology, Logic, and Theory of Literature*, trans. by George G.

Grabowicz (Evanston: Northwestern University Press, 1973), pp. 218–19 (translation slightly modified). Wolfgang Iser, *Der Akt des Lesens: Theorie ästhetischer Wirkung*, 2nd edn (Munich: Fink, 1984), pp. 177–83, describes this kind of unfolding as 'the moving point of view'.
53. Ingarden, *Das literarische Kunstwerk*, p. 231 (n. 1).
54. Paul Ricoeur, 'Metaphor and the Main Problem of Hermeneutics', *New Literary History*, 6 (1974), 95–110 (pp. 106). Because of his 'non-perceptual' concept of literature discussed earlier, De Man is naturally opposed to the essentially phenomenological idea that literary texts bear aesthetic worlds, and so is Remigius Bunia, *Faltungen: Fiktion, Erzählen, Medien* (Berlin: Erich Schmidt, 2007), pp. 121–33, 367–73.
55. Ingarden, *Das literarische Kunstwerk*, pp. 270–306. Cf. Wolfgang Iser, *Die Appellstruktur der Texte: Unbestimmtheit als Wirkungsbedingung literarischer Prosa* (Konstanz: UVK, 1970), translated as 'Indeterminacy and the Reader's Response in Prose Fiction', in *Aspects of Narrative: Selected Papers from the English Institute*, ed. by J. Hillis Miller (New York: Columbia University Press, 1971), pp. 1–45.
56. Roland Barthes, 'L'activité structuraliste' (1963), in *Œuvres complètes*, ed. by Eric Marty, 3 vols (Paris: Le Seuil, 1993–95), I (1993), 1328–33.
57. Stanley Fish, 'Why No One's Afraid of Wolfgang Iser', *Diacritics*, 11 (1981), 2–11 (pp. 8–11); Wolfgang Iser, 'Talk like Whales: A Reply to Stanley Fish', *Diacritics*, 11 (1981), 82–87 (p. 85). Note also *Akt des Lesens*, pp. 177–79, where Iser categorically distinguishes acts of perception from acts of reading.
58. De Man, 'Reading and History', in *Resistance to Theory*, pp. 54–72 (p. 67), which was first published as the 'Introduction' to Hans Robert Jauß's *Toward an Aesthetic of Reception*, trans. by Timothy Bahti (Minneapolis: University of Minnesota Press, 1981), and Jauß, 'Response to Paul de Man', in *Reading de Man Reading*, ed. by Lindsay Waters and Wlad Godzich (Minneapolis: University of Minnesota Press, 1989), pp. 202–08. Jauß's theory of aesthetic experience does include *aisthēsis*, but he thinks of it as a receptive act, as opposed to *poiēsis*, the creation of fictional worlds, and *catharsis*, the identification with these worlds; see Hans Robert Jauß, *Ästhetische Erfahrung und literarische Hermeneutik* (Frankfurt am Main: Suhrkamp, 1982), pp. 71–90, 125–65.
59. Hans Robert Jauß, *Literaturgeschichte als Provokation* (Frankfurt am Main: Suhrkamp, 1970), p. 127. In 'Der Leser als Instanz einer neuen Geschichte der Literatur', *Poetica*, 7 (1975), 325–44, Jauß nicely summarizes his main idea that reception history determines the horizon of all literary understanding.
60. Iser, *Akt des Lesens*, p. 214.
61. Jacques Derrida, *Speech and Phenomena, and Other Essays on Husserl's Theory of Signs* (Evanston: Northwestern University Press, 1973), p. 104.
62. Iser, *Akt des Lesens*, pp. iv–vii.
63. Hans Georg Gadamer, 'Phänomenologischer und semantischer Zugang zu Paul Celan?', in *Gesammelte Werke*, 10 vols (Tübingen: Mohr Siebeck, 1999), IX, 461–69 (p. 462).
64. The final chapter on the *Leerstellen* or 'blanks' of a story (*Akt des Lesens*, pp. 257–355) makes it clear that by filling the blanks, Iser essentially means the production of logical consistency and semantic cohesion, which as such requires a high degree of abstraction (cf. pp. 312–15, 322–27 as examples).
65. Iser, *Akt des Lesens*, pp. 219–31, as well as pp. 177–83 (concerning the 'moving point of view').
66. In line with its name, the work of the imagination was regularly likened to visual media such as paintings and the magic lantern, especially in Romanticism. Although newer audiovisual media such as cinema and TV may have superseded them by now, the paradigm of the imagination as a kind of 'vision' remains intact. The constant rise of PC games may alter this paradigm in significant ways, since unlike viewers, gamers do not only receive pictures and sounds but also have to respond to them, manually interacting with the game's audiovisual interface through devices like mouse, keyboard, controller, or direct touch on screen. Still, in PC games, too, the imaginary world consists of a sequence of audiovisual images. For a historical survey of how visual media and paradigms have shaped the literary imagination, see Ralph Köhnen, *Das optische Wissen*.

67. See Husserl's *Phänomenologie des inneren Zeitbewußtseins* (*Husserliana*, X (1966)), but also the later *Bernauer Manuskripte* (*Husserliana*, XXXIII (2001), 3–49), in which Husserl conceives of the dynamic 'entwinement' [Ineinander] or 'complexion' of retention and protention still more radically. For a quick introduction, see the entries 'Retention' and 'Protention' in the *Wörterbuch der phänomenologischen Begriffe*, ed. by Helmuth Vetter (Hamburg: Meiner, 2004), as well as Dan Zahavi, *Subjectivity and Selfhood: Investigating the First-Person Perspective* (Cambridge, MA: MIT Press, 2005), pp. 49–73.
68. Husserl generally struggles, not only in his analyses of time-consciousness, with distinguishing deliberate from spontaneous acts of consciousness, as well as active from passive syntheses. Note e.g. *Husserliana*, XI (1966), 357–61, where Husserl represents sensory receptivity — traditionally associated with passivity — as a species of spontaneity. In another passage, he describes receptivity in general as the '*lowest degree of activity*' (*Husserliana* IV (1952), 213). Clearly, in considering only *acts* of consciousness, complete passivity is as unthinkable to Husserl as it was to Fichte. Understood as total cognitive inaction, therefore, passivity has no real place in the 'life of the ego' [Ichleben], Husserl concludes, because such inaction pertains for him to a moment 'anterior to the act of receiving' (XI, 361) and, hence, consciousness. As for the active/passive crux in Husserl, see Hans Blumenberg, *Zu den Sachen und zurück*, ed. by Manfred Sommer (Frankfurt: Suhrkamp, 2002), pp. 189–23, who demonstrates the instability of this division with regard to Husserl's conceptions of intentionality and time-consciousness.
69. Derrida, *Speech and Phenomena*, p. 64.
70. The conception of sense (*Sinn*) as identical intention over time or felt continuity Husserl articulated perhaps most clearly in *Husserliana*, XXXIII (2001), 289–98, 352–56.
71. In *Die Einheit der Sinne: Grundlinien einer Ästhesiologie des Geistes* (1923), reprinted in *Gesammelte Schriften*, ed. by Günter Dux and others, 10 vols (Frankfurt am Main: Suhrkamp, 2003), III, 7–315, Plessner investigates the 'modalities' in which the senses communicate with the mind, and the mind with the senses. Of these 'modalities' he identifies three distinctive types, one pertaining to seeing, the other to hearing, and the third to the remaining bodily senses. In each case, Plessner notes formal correspondences, or 'concordances' as he calls them, between the mode of sensation and cognition, between, for example, the directedness of the gaze and the purposiveness of a conceptual schema. Additionally, he introduces the concept of 'accordance', which signifies an inherent affinity of sensory matter and mind, sensation and understanding. Absolute music and geometry are for Plessner the concrete manifestations of such 'accordance' between matter and mind, which explains their immediate, pre-conceptual intelligibility. Plessner finally connects his system of 'concordances' and 'accordances' to corporeal movements of expression. The schematic comprehension of visual perceptions, for example, finds its suitable expression in targeted action, while bodily feeling leads, by way of syntagmatic comprehension, to verbalization. The 'aesthesiology of the mind' thus comprises for Plessner always both comprehension of sensations ('Vergeistigung des Sinnlichen', p. 221) and sensory expression of such comprehension ('Versinnlichung des Geistes', ibid.).
72. In the German original, Kant defines a schema as the mediating link between concepts and intuitions, as a 'vermittelnde Vorstellung [...] einerseits *intellektuell*, andererseits *sinnlich*' (KrV A 138). Schemata assume this mediating function in that they represent '*Zeitbestimmungen*', which means, more specifically, rules concerning 'die *Zeitreihe*, den *Zeitinhalt*, die *Zeitordnung*, endlich den *Zeitinbegriff* in Ansehung aller möglichen Gegenstände' (KrV A 145). The four aspects of time Kant distinguishes here are, in other words, the succession, the content, and the relation of events in time, as well as their frequency (e.g. never, once, sometimes, always). According to Kant, these four aspects of time match up with the four categories of quantity, quality, relation, and modality. In combining temporal patterns with these logical categories, schemata enable us to recognize regularities in phenomena. The schema of necessity, for example, combines the frequency of always with the category of existence, while the schema of causality correlates the temporal pattern of before/after with the categories of cause and effect (KrV A 144–45). For a lucid summary of Kant's concept of 'schematism', see Thomas Khurana, 'Kant, Heidegger und das Verhältnis von Repräsentation und Abstraktion', *Zeitschrift für Ästhetik und allgemeine Kunstwissenschaft*, 58 (2013), 203–24 (pp. 203–11).

73. See e.g. G. J. Warnock, 'Concepts and Schematism', *Analysis*, 9 (1948), 77–82 (p. 80) and Jonathan Bennett, *Kant's Analytic* (Cambridge: Cambridge University Press, 1966), p. 146.
74. Scott G. Burnham, *Beethoven: Hero* (Princeton: Princeton University Press, 1995), pp. 162–68. In contrast to his earlier claim that Beethoven's music itself projects 'the voice and authority of a narrator but also the compelling sweep of an enacted narrative' (p. 146), Burnham in this passage clarifies that it is, in fact, the listener who carries all this out. It is 'our presence', he writes (pp. 165–66), our perceptual activity, that invests Beethoven's music with a 'heroic' sweep, since music is not only happening to but always *within* the listener.
75. In *Beethoven: Philosophie der Musik: Fragmente und Texte*, ed. by Rolf Tiedemann (Frankfurt am Main: Suhrkamp, 2004), Adorno describes, for instance, the beginning of Beethoven's Waldstein sonata as a movement of negation (pp. 90–91).
76. Gregory, *Eye and Brain*, p. 5.
77. But only 'insofar as we trace' them with the eye: '[...] daß wir die Zeit, die doch gar kein Gegenstand äußerer Anschauung ist, uns nicht anders vorstellig machen können, als unter dem Bilde einer Linie, so fern wir sie ziehen' (KrV B 156).
78. Merlin Donald, 'Art and Cognitive Evolution', in *The Artful Mind: Cognitive Science and the Riddle of Human Creativity*, ed. by Mark Turner (New York: Oxford University Press, 2006), pp. 3–20 (pp. 10–11), similarly emphasizes the temporal nature of visual perception.
79. The described scene is not my own but taken verbatim from the third chapter of Herman Melville's *Moby Dick*, ed. by Tony Tanner (Oxford: Oxford University Press, 2008), pp. 9–10.
80. As for the etymology of scene and its diverse usages over time, see Heiko Christians, 'Inszenieren', in *Historisches Wörterbuch des Mediengebrauchs*, ed. by Heiko Christians and others (Cologne: Böhlau, 2015), pp. 297–321.
81. Gotthold Ephraim Lessing, *Laokoon; Briefe, Antiquarischen Inhalts*, ed. by Wilfried Barner (Frankfurt am Main: Deutscher Klassiker Verlag, 2007), p. 124.
82. Peter von Matt, *Sieben Küsse: Glück und Unglück in der Literatur* (Munich: Hanser, 2017), pp. 13–15.
83. 'Ce n'est point avec des idées, mon cher Degas, que l'on fait des vers. C'est avec des *mots*.' Mallarmé to Edgar Degas during a conversation witnessed by Paul Valéry, 'Poésie et pensée abstraite' (1939), in *Œuvres*, ed. by Jean Hytier, 2 vols (Paris: Gallimard, 1957–60), I (1957), 1314–39 (p. 1324).
84. Schiller to Körner on 28 February 1793; *Sämtliche Werke*, V, 431–32. As for Schiller's 'semiotics' of perception, see Sabine M. Schneider, *Die schwierige Sprache des Schönen: Moritz' und Schillers Semiotik der Sinnlichkeit* (Würzburg: Königshausen & Neumann, 1998).
85. For 'writing means: reading oneself' (Max Frisch, *Tagebuch 1946–1949* (Frankfurt am Main: Suhrkamp, 1985), p. 19).
86. Niklas Luhmann, *Die Kunst der Gesellschaft* (Frankfurt am Main: Suhrkamp, 1995), pp. 82–83; *Art as a Social System*, trans. by Eva M. Knodt (Stanford: Stanford University Press, 2000), pp. 47–48.
87. Theodor A. Meyer, *Das Stilgesetz der Poesie* (Leipzig: Hirzel, 1901), p. 8, remarks 'daß die Sprache allem, was durch sie hindurchgeht, auch dem Sinnlichen ihren eigenen Stempel aufdrückt'. Meyer was brought to my attention by Adorno, who quotes him in his essay on Eichendorff, in *Noten zur Literatur*, ed. by Tiedemann Rolf (Frankfurt am Main: Suhrkamp, 1981), pp. 69–94 (pp. 82–83).
88. Gilles Deleuze and Félix Guattari, *What Is Philosophy?* (New York: Columbia University Press, 1994), p. 167. This metaphysical conception of art is rooted in Deleuze's earlier *Proust and Signs: The Complete Text*, trans. by Richard Howard (Minneapolis: University of Minnesota Press, 2000), where he similarly claims (pp. 39–51) that Proust, or rather his narrator, aspires to capture the essence of things with his book.
89. Deleuze and Guattari, p. 166.
90. Pierre Ouellet, 'The I's Eye: Perception and Mental Imagery in Literature', trans. by Larry Marks, *SubStance*, 22 (1993), 64–73 (pp. 65–66).
91. Joslin McKinney and Philip Butterworth, *The Cambridge Introduction to Scenography* (Cambridge: Cambridge University Press, 2009), p. 1. See also Oscar Gross Brockett, Margaret Mitchell, and

Linda Hardberger, *Making the Scene: A History of Stage Design and Technology in Europe and the United States* (Austin: University of Texas Press, 2010).
92. For an introduction by practitioners, see Atelier Brückner, *Scenography: Making Spaces Talk/ Szenografie: Narrative Räume* (Ludwigsburg: Avedition, 2011), pp. 18–23. For a theoretical introduction, see *Inszenierung und Ereignis: Beiträge zur Theorie und Praxis der Szenografie*, ed. by Ralf Bohn and Heiner Wilharm (Bielefeld: transcript, 2009), pp. 9–43.
93. *Szenographien: Theatralität als Kategorie der Literaturwissenschaft*, ed. by Gerhard Neumann and others (Freiburg im Breisgau: Rombach, 2000); the introduction by Neumann and the contributions by Gerald Wildgruber are particularly abstract.
94. The project was continued in *Inszenierte Welt: Theatralität als Argument literarischer Texte*, ed. by Ethel Matala de Mazza and Clemens Pornschlegel (Freiburg im Breisgau: Rombach, 2003), yet the earlier theory of scenographies as 'micro-dramas' of signification has virtually no bearing on this second and concluding volume. Speaking of literature and theatricality, an older school of criticism comes to mind as well, namely Kenneth Burke's *A Grammar of Motives* (Berkeley: University of California Press, 1969). Burke here develops the method of 'dramatism', which understands literature in terms of social theatre and more specifically as consisting of scenes of interpersonal interaction. The fundamental point Burke misses, however, is that literary scenes do not always and by necessity work like social encounters, for they are made *of text*. They represent verbal rather than social constructs, sceno*graphies*.
95. These and the following quotations refer to Ralf Simon, *Die Bildlichkeit des lyrischen Textes: Studien zu Hölderlin, Brentano, Eichendorff, Heine, Mörike, George und Rilke* (Munich: Fink, 2011), p. 53, as well as his *Der poetische Text als Bildkritik* (Munich: Fink, 2009), pp. 256–57.
96. I discuss Simon's theory of poetic 'images' at length in my dissertation, 'Scenographies of Perception: Recasting the Sensuous in Hegel, Novalis, Rilke, Proust' (Princeton University, 2015), pp. 44–48, pointing out inconsistencies, as well as my disagreements with him.
97. See Brooks, pp. 3–36.
98. Nietzsche, XIII, 460 (NF 1888, 15[90]).
99. Utz, p. 17.
100. Brooks, p. 282.

PART I

The 'Story' of Perception (Hegel)

§1. *The Dialectic Force of the Senses*

Am seidenen Strang | Dialektik hängt alles, wonach wir Träumer verlangen.[1]

[By that thin thread of | Dialectics hangs everything we dreamers long for.]

Hegel in the Swiss Alps

In July 1796, Hegel went on a week-long hike through the Bernese Alps. This trip, for which he teamed up with three fellow tutors from Germany teaching at Berne, gave rise to perhaps his finest literary achievement, the so-called *Bericht über eine Alpenwanderung*.[2] Hegel had been working for several years in Berne, serving as tutor to the children of local patricians, the Steigers. It seems he wanted to, or felt he should, seize the last chance to enjoy the magnificent landscape surrounding Berne before leaving for Stuttgart and Frankfurt. Christoph Meiners's *Briefe über die Schweiz*, a popular volume at that time and part of the Steigers' library, encouraged these plans.

Meiners praises above all the 'irresistible magic' of Berne and its surroundings, and the travelling party used Meiners's book as their guide.[3] But unlike Meiners, and all the other lovers of the Swiss Alps, from Rousseau to Goethe, Wordsworth, and beyond, Hegel found the Alpine landscape quite boring. The much-vaunted mountains and glaciers were especially disappointing to him. In his *Bericht*, composed during or shortly after the trip and possibly intended for publication, he writes that the Eiger and the Jungfrau, the two main summits of the Bernese Alps, left no impression on him, least of all 'feelings of greatness and sublimity' (384). Hegel was more fascinated by local customs and culture, which he discusses in some detail, but as such the Swiss mountains amount to little more than 'bleak desserts' of stone (391).

What is it, exactly, that Hegel found so boring and dissatisfying about the Alpine landscape? His description of the Grindelwald glaciers suggests an answer. Looking at these formations causes your mind to go blank. They give rise to a *'new kind of seeing'*, Hegel writes, *'which does not occupy the mind any further'* (385). Far from seeing 'something lovely', the only, and rather profane, thing to notice is the 'filthy [kothige] street' formed by meltwater trickling downhill (385). In general, the problem was that

> Weder das Auge noch die Einbildungskraft findet auf diesen formlosen Massen irgend einen Punct, auf dem jenes mit Wohlgefallen ruhen, oder wo diese Beschäftigung oder ein Spiel finden könnte. Der Mineralog allein findet Stoff, über die Revolutionen dieser Gebirge unzureichende Muthmaßungen zu wagen. Die Vernunft findet in dem Gedanken der Dauer dieser Berge oder in der Art von Erhabenheit die man ihnen zuschreibt, nichts, das ihr imponirt, das ihr Staunen und Bewunderung abnöthigte. Der Anblick dieser ewig todten Massen gab mir nichts als die einförmige und in die Länge langweilige Vorstellung: *es ist so*. (391–92)

> [Neither eye nor imagination finds a single point on these formless masses where the former could rest with pleasure, or the latter could find cause for occupation or play. Only the mineralogist discovers features that invite his inadequate conjectures on the revolutions of these mountains. The thought of their permanence or the kind of sublimity attributed to them does not impress reason or prompt its wonder and admiration. Looking at these eternally dead masses I just had the monotonous and after a while boring idea: *it is so.*]

Mountains are dead masses of stone, and unlike local customs and cuisine, on which Hegel elaborates frequently and with interest, their very appearance does not provide much to think about. Hegel thus criticizes especially those tales and writers that romanticize and even mythologize the Alps, a view on nature that struck the young Hegel as outdated and 'ludicrous'.[4] The only proper way for the human understanding to relate to natural phenomena is to describe them scientifically, as mineralogists do, for example, however inadequately. Their philosophical significance consists, nonetheless, in little more than the illustration of blind necessity. Watching the 'eternally pointless' [ewig wirkungslosen] motion of waves crashing against the rocks, he remarks earlier, gives you an idea 'of nature's must-do' [vom *Müssen* der Natur] (390), but that is all.

The shortage of intellectual stimulation during his journey is the general cause of Hegel's boredom, but a more subtle, aesthetic problem looms in his *Bericht* as well. It concerns the uniform rigidity of these mountains — the it-is-so-and-not-otherwise of their appearance. Hegel expands on the issue in comparing the dynamic of a waterfall (a natural spectacle he for once calls 'majestic') to the static nature of a painting. Looking at the actual waterfall, he writes, affords a charming sight because of its tumbling waves,

> die den Blick des Zuschauers beständig mit sich niederziehen und die er doch nie fixiren, nie verfolgen kann, denn ihr Bild, ihre Gestalt, lös't sich alle Augenblicke auf, wird in jedem Moment von einem neuen verdrängt, und *in diesem Falle sieht er ewig das gleiche Bild, und sieht zugleich, daß es nie dasselbe ist.*
>
> [which continuously pull the spectator's gaze downward and which he can never fix or trace, since their image or shape vanishes in an instant, with the new replacing the old one at every moment, *in which case he sees forever the same image but at the same that it is never the same.*] (388)

Hegel is fascinated by the interplay between continuity and change, or identity and difference, the waterfall places before the eyes. By contrast, a painting depicting the waterfall would show the same image at all moments:

> *Die sinnliche Gegenwart des Gemäldes* erlaubt der Einbildungskraft nicht, den vorgestellten Gegenstand auszudehnen, sondern sie faßt ihn so auf, wie er sich dem Gesicht darstellt. [...] im besten Gemälde [muß] das Anziehendste, das Wesentlichste eines solchen Schauspiels fehlen: das ewige Leben, die gewaltige Regsamkeit in demselben. Ein Gemälde kann nur einen Theil des ganzen Eindrucks geben, nämlich die Gleichheit des Bildes, die es in bestimmten Umrissen und Partieen geben muß; hingegen der andere Theil des Eindrucks, die ewige, unaufhaltbare Veränderung jeder Partie, die ewige Auflösung jeder Welle, jedes Schaumes, die das Auge immer mit sich hernieder zieht, die keine

Terze lang ihm die gleiche Richtung des Blicks erlaubt: all diese Macht, all dies
Leben geht gänzlich verloren. (388–89)

[*The sensuous presence of the painting* does not allow for the imagination to expand
on the represented object. The imagination apprehends it just as it appears to
the eye. [...] the most attractive and essential aspects of such a spectacle must be
missing even in the best painting: its eternal life and massive bustle. A painting
can show only one aspect of the whole impression, namely the identity of the
image, which it must render through explicit contours and parts, while the
other aspect of the impression — the eternal and ineluctable change of each
part, the eternal undoing of each wave and whitecap pulling the eye downward
at all times and not letting it stay focused for more than a brief interval — is
totally lost in all its power and life.]

The panorama of the Alps disappoints for the same reason. Just like a painting, which Hegel characterizes in ways recalling Lessing's *Laokoon*,[5] it exhibits permanence without perceptible, indeed without conceivable, change or 'play' [Spiel], as the earlier quote reads (391–92). All there is to see is unmoved and unmoving permanence, a selfsame image, precisely, rather than an ever-changing spectacle or, literally, *Schau-spiel*.

Hegel's *Bericht* thus indicates two philosophical problems of lasting significance. On the one hand, it brings to light the schism between the physical world and the realm of spirit or *Geist* Hegel will belabour for a long time. In fact, it took Hegel several years to reach the conclusion that philosophical thinking about nature amounts to more than a 'theoretical fancy' [eine theoretische Müßigkeit] that is 'not without reason' of little interest to the younger minds.[6] On the other hand, the *Bericht* casts a first light on the inherent dynamic between identity and difference that Hegel attributes to sensory perception. Bearing in mind the older meaning of aesthetics as — in Hegel's own words (TWA XIII, 13) — 'the science of the sensuous, of *sensation*' [die Wissenschaft des Sinnes, des *Empfindens*], one might think that he elaborates on the dynamic of perception in his *Aesthetics*. But perception (or aesthesis) plays no important role in Hegel's object-oriented '*philosophy of beautiful art*' (TWA XIII, 13), the proper subject of these lectures as he clarifies at the very beginning. It is, instead, in the inaugural chapters of the 1807 *Phänomenologie des Geistes* [*Phenomenology of Spirit*] where Hegel fleshes out the dynamic of perception and, with it, the dialectic of consciousness.

Sense experience in the *Phenomenology*

Essentially, the two opening chapters of the *Phenomenology*, on 'sense-certainty' [sinnliche Gewissheit] and 'perception' [Wahrnehmung], serve to demonstrate the deficiencies or 'untruth' of knowledge obtained through the senses. Sense-certainty — the certainty of having something in front of the eye, right here, right now — at first feels like the richest truth of all, because it seems to reflect the object's being without any losses, reproducing it, so to speak, like a photograph. Upon reflection, however, sense-certainty turns out to be the 'poorest' and 'most abstract' way of knowing something, because if you stop feeling and start to think about it for just a moment, this certainty hardly means anything. 'All it says', writes Hegel, 'is this: *it is*' (PhG 82/58★) — a conclusion that recalls the nearly identical phrase from Hegel's *Bericht*, 'it is so', which therefore seems to represent the earliest description of sense-certainty, including its shortcomings. What sense-certainty really knows is an empty truism that applies to just about anything, be it a house, a tree, the night, or for that matter a supposedly magnificent glacier. The essential content or knowledge of sense-certainty that 'this' exists here and now is therefore utterly universal and its inherent concept, existence or being as such, is the most general of all.

Although more specific with regard to the object's properties, the knowledge obtained through perception proper is in a certain way even more spurious. Sensory perception — which Hegel defines as a cognitive activity, in contrast to the kind of receptivity on which sense-certainty is based — purports to take in the whole truth of the object. What perception truly creates, however, is nothing but 'contradiction' and, still worse, 'deception' [Täuschung]. The 'contradiction' of perception concerns, roughly speaking, the appearance of the perceived object as 'both one and many, discrete and continuous, at the same time'.[7] The *Phenomenology* renders this 'contradiction' of perception in terms of a dialectic between 'One' [Eins] and 'Also' [Auch]. In perception, consciousness can solve this conflict only by means of 'sophistry', the opportunistic distinction of partial 'regards' [Rücksichten] that do not, however, come together as a whole (PhG 105–07/77–79★). This argumentative tactic of perception underlies for Hegel most appeals to 'so-called common sense' [der wahrnehmende, oft so genannte gesunde Menschenverstand] (PhG 105/77★), yet it also pervades proper philosophy as a whole. In the 1830 *Enzyklopädie der philosophischen Wissenschaften*, Hegel writes that 'Kantian philosophy', as well as 'the ordinary sciences', remains bound to the standpoint of 'perception', including its sophistic method of drawing convenient distinctions without ever confronting their shallow and often contradictory nature.[8]

At first, all of this sounds quite abstruse. Many readers might consider Hegel's assertions as to the nature of both sense-certainty and perception a grotesque violation of sound reason and common sense, if not 'bombastical nonsense [...] bordering on madness', the conceit of 'a mere swaggerer and charlatan', or even more plainly 'a brain-damaging [geistesverderbliche] and stupefying [...] pseudo-philosophy'.[9] For Hegel, however, the contradictions within sense-certainty and perception only indicate the necessity to confront them logically, that is to say, to think them through discursively and then rectify them conceptually. To find their true conceptual basis, the 'unconditioned universality' [unbedingte Allgemeine] (PhG 107/79★) upon which indubitable knowledge must be founded, consciousness turns to the world of the understanding (*Verstand*). But once the understanding has also failed to solve the conflicts of perception as of sense-certainty, consciousness discovers the universal foundation of knowledge to be that which it has been all along — self-consciousness. Hegel expresses this point, the a priori reflexive nature of all knowledge and cognition, most clearly in his 1822 lecture on the philosophy of subjective spirit, stressing that '*there is no consciousness without self-consciousness*'.[10]

In the *Phenomenology*, Hegel establishes the invariably reflexive nature of consciousness early on, though he attributes this to Kant and Fichte rather than considering it his own insight. Kant first brought it to light, at least according to Hegel's account, in calling the 'transcendental unity of apperception' the 'highest principle' of all cognition. Fichte then radicalized this point in positing that self-consciousness (which he simply calls 'I') produces cognizance not just in principle but truly in fact.[11] Hegel names Fichte in the quoted passage from his 1822 lecture as a source of inspiration. His debt to Kant he acknowledges in the second book of the *Wissenschaft der Logik*, the so-called *Begriffslogik*, praising the idea of the 'transcendental unity of apperception' as Kant's 'deepest and most accurate insight'. The exact scope of this debt has been determined by Robert Pippin, who interprets Hegel's speculative idealism as a radical completion of Kant's transcendentalism and his concept of apperception in particular, whereas others regard the foundational role of apperception as a toxic inherence and indeed the original sin of German idealism as a whole.[12]

In discovering its fundamentally self-reflexive nature at the end of the *Phenomenology's* third chapter, consciousness finally understands that perception cannot succeed without reflection or self-consciousness. The 1802 essay *Glauben und Wissen* contains perhaps the first explicit formulation of this position. Hegel here notes that the 'spontaneity and absolute synthetic activity' of self-consciousness must be taken as 'the principle of sensuousness' (TWA II: 305), thereby criticizing Kant's fundamental distinction between intuition and concept, or sensuous receptivity and cognitive spontaneity. In the slightly earlier *Differenzschrift*, Hegel makes essentially the same point, but the scope of the argument is even more ambitious. A philosophical system, he claims here, is coherent and true beyond doubt only insofar as it describes 'the totality of empirical consciousness as the objective totality of self-consciousness' (TWA II, 55).[13] This expression already indicates the fundamental claim of the *Phenomenology* that the logical structure of self-consciousness is key to philosophy because it represents 'the domicile [das einheimische Reich] of truth' (PhG 138/104★), a domicile he then explores in great detail, successively revealing the various shapes of consciousness it encompasses.

If self-consciousness is the key to understanding all forms of consciousness, sensuousness too cannot be thought of as a self-sufficient faculty devoid of spontaneity, nor can it suffice to explain the apperceptive or reflexive unity of the mind metaphorically, which is what Kant did in describing the synthetic powers of the understanding as 'an art hidden in the depths of the human soul, whose true operations [Handgriffe] we will hardly ever decipher' (KrV A 141).[14] Instead, the reflexivity of the mind must be studied in all its manifestations and the criteria of each explained in their own right, starting with sense-certainty (which does not yet recognize itself as a product of self-consciousness, of course). Striving to overcome the dichotomy between concepts and intuitions, as well as phenomena and noumena, its 'speculative goal', Robert Pippin sums up, 'can only be a knowledge by reflective subjectivity *of its own* criteria of knowledge, and hence of objectivity'.[15] The structure of self-consciousness meets this demand by uniting opposites without contradiction and, moreover, according to criteria of its own making (cf. PhG 137/104★).

At a later point, in the 1822 lectures on subjective spirit, Hegel sums up the speculative insight of the *Phenomenology*: all knowledge and indeed the truth itself comes into being through a process of self-determination. According to Heinrich Gustav Hotho's lecture notes, Hegel said

> Der Geist ist ewiger Proceß, ewige Bewegung. Das Wissen hat den Punkt[,] sich die Voraussetzung seiner selbst zu machen [...] Der Weg zum Ziel, der selbst ein absolutes Moment des Geistes ist, dieser stellt sich am endlichen Geist dar [...] Man hört oft sprechen, daß es Thatsachen des Bewußtseins gäbe, und daß diese das Erste des Geistes wären. Auf dem Standpunkt des Bewußtseins ist diß in Wahrheit der Fall, aber der Geist muß die Thatsachen des Bewußtseins erklären, zeigen, daß der Inhalt der Thatsachen Thaten des Geistes sind, keine Sachen, die dem Geist nur gegeben wären. Die Stufen des Geistes sind also die Bestimmungen des Objects so, daß diese Bestimmungen durch den Geist gesetzt werden. (GW XXV.1, 119–20)[16]

> [Spirit is eternal process, eternal movement. Knowledge has as its goal the creation of its own premises [...] The path to this goal, which is itself an absolute moment of spirit, can be observed in our finite spirit [i.e. the mind] [...] It is often said that there are facts of consciousness and that these are the origin of the mind. That is true on the level of consciousness, but the mind must explain the facts of consciousness, showing that the content of these facts are products of the mind, as opposed to things that are merely given to the mind. The various shapes of the mind are therefore specifications of the object such that these specifications are established by the mind.]

These remarks may suffice to introduce the general project of the *Phenomenology*. Regarding this project, the two chapters dealing with sensory experience have only a transitional function. They initiate the long quest towards knowledge through self-determination, but do so, Pippin writes, in a 'rather murky' fashion and without 'begging significant questions' on the whole.[17]

Such murkiness is not due to the dialectician's inability to talk plainly. In fact, the clarity of Hegel's journalistic writings and some of his prefaces suggests the opposite, as does the elegance of his private letters. Therefore, the obscurity of Hegel's style must be rooted in systematic difficulties, one of which appears to be the constant vacillation between epistemology and ontology. The first chapter of the *Phenomenology* is exemplary in this regard, since it relates the ontological nature of time and space with the epistemological problem of intending or 'meaning' the Here and Now. This vacillation — or 'dialectic' — between ontological and epistemological claims, or between in-itself and appearance-for-consciousness, is nonetheless inevitable because the *Phenomenology* strives to establish the point in which these two claims coincide without discrepancy and contradiction. Hegel's various names for this point of non-contradiction and reconciliation are 'absolute knowledge', 'scientific concept' [wissenschaftlicher Begriff], and more plainly 'truth'.[18]

At any rate, taken as a section on their own, the two first chapters of the *Phenomenology* develop, in my view, an interesting theory of sense perception, although in a somewhat convoluted language. The stakes of these initial chapters are much higher than Hegel conveys in those moments when he belittles sense-certainty and perception. The sheer amount of critical commentary on these two chapters, including studies in book length, just underscores their significance.[19]

What first comes to light in those two first chapters concerning sensory experience is nothing less than the *Phenomenology*'s entire method of development through progressive self-doubt, also known as 'self-perfecting scepticism' [sich vollbringende[r] Skeptizismus] (PhG 72/50★). The phenomenological method must be sceptical because, according to Hegel, the 'pathway of *doubt*' (PhG 72/49★) is the natural tendency of consciousness in its quest for true knowledge.[20] In retrospect, however, he concedes that this sceptical method is rooted in the '*dialectic movement*' intrinsic to both sense-certainty and perception (PhG 160/123★). In one of his later lectures on subjective spirit, Hegel even remarked that '*sensation [Empfindung]* contains the *whole of reason*, the *entire matter of spirit*. All representations, thoughts, and concepts [...] come out of this sentient intelligence [aus der empfindenden Intelligenz]'.[21]

Because of its self-perfecting tendency, the sceptical or dialectic movement of consciousness over time produces increasingly self-conscious forms of knowledge, such as reason and moral introspection, and even philosophical reasoning, yet these formations of self-consciousness, too, are derived from 'the world of sensation and perception' [der sinnlichen und wahrgenommenen Welt] (PhG 138/105★). Consequently, sense-certainty and perception do not simply pave the way for self-conscious knowledge but are in fact embodied forms of self-consciousness, while simultaneously exemplifying the key concepts of dialectics itself, namely negation, opposition, and determinate negation or sublation. According to the *Phenomenology*, it is the force of the sensuous that establishes and impels these dialectical operations, which is why the fundamental conflicts of sense-certainty and perception return throughout 'until absolute knowledge is attained'.[22]

To prove this point, it will be necessary to grapple with two interconnected issues. On the one hand, one must explain the supposed deficiencies of sense-certainty and perception, which are by no means evident. It will take considerable conceptual effort — *Arbeit des Begriffs*, as Hegel calls it — to understand the claim that sense-certainty is undermined by the utter disjunction between seeing and meaning, or sensation and intention. It will be similarly difficult to fathom the 'contradiction' between objective unity and diversity in perception, an either/or that arises because perception seeks to produce, as Charles Taylor puts it, 'a stable static image of the thing'.[23]

The other issue to grapple with concerns Hegel's mode of presentation: the ways in which he imparts the dialectic of sensory experience. This issue may seem obvious, since the expression of ideas always raises the question of their adequate representation. In Hegel's case, however, the issue is complicated by his understanding of language as logos, by which he means both speech and reason, the medium to impart and the concept to solve philosophical problems. Thinking means speaking, so that language is not only the instrument but truly the medium of knowledge. All there is can be said, and hence understood, because the world is logical. According to Hegel, therefore, language does not merely re-present things and thoughts but contains their true essence, knowledge, or, in a more emphatic expression, spirit.

This logical conception of both being and truth, which in a technical sense is not wrongly described as 'logocentrism', pervades Hegel's theory of the senses as well. Sense-certainty and perception speak; they are language, just like the other forms of consciousness considered in the *Phenomenology*, whether they know it or not. They are defined by discursive, and ultimately narrative, acts of speech, which coincide with acts of cognition. Sense-certainty and perception tell *stories* — those stories of aesthesis and diegesis identified in the Introduction as aesthesiologies and powerfully recast by Novalis, Rilke, and Proust.

The observation and representation (*Darstellung*) of the stories of both sense-certainty and perception are the task of the *phenomenologist*, Hegel. He describes the operations and relations by which consciousness determines its cognitions, thus producing knowledge. To that end, Hegel writes up scenes — scenographies — introducing the various shapes of, and illustrating the basic concepts of, consciousness. In the case of sense-certainty and perception, these concepts include time and space (which Hegel regards as ontological, as opposed to purely phenomenological, realities), individuality and universality, existence and essence, as well as intention, negation, opposition, and relation through reflection. It is this odd entwinement of scene and concept, illustration and explanation, that needs clarification, the key question being, of course, how these two relate in each chapter of the *Phenomenology*, how Hegel's scenographies relate to the concepts they are meant to illustrate.

The intentions of Hegel the *philosopher*, by contrast, belaboured above all in the preface to the *Phenomenology*, are all too clear. The lesson the reader ought to take from the initial chapters is simply this: the concept of substance and specifically substantial thinghood, at which sense perception naturally aims, proves unfit to reconcile the inherent contradictions of sensory experience and indeed of all conscious experience. What is needed instead is a more dynamic concept or structure[24] that can accommodate both the processual and the relational aspects of sensation and perception. This realization then leads, according to Hegel's narrative, to a concept of objecthood produced through self-conscious discourse and identified by the 'story' so defined. Hegel's name for this complex logical formation and relation is 'subject'. Although Hegel derives this concept of objecthood from sensory experience, it remains in effect throughout the *Phenomenology*, serving to define not only living matter and individual experience in both its freedoms and limitations, but also increasingly abstract, interpersonal structures such as family, state, art, religion, and finally truth itself.

Demonstrating the fundamental flaw of substantial thinghood — namely its dualistic nature as *either* a unit *or* a bundle of qualities, at which perception must stare like one of those ambiguous images, continually vacillating between the one and the other figure — is imperative with regard to Hegel's general project. For indeed, if substantial thinghood could reconcile this either/or and thus meet the epistemic requirement of non-contradiction, consciousness would have no reason to recognize the 'I' and, at last, the intersubjective relation called 'spirit' as the determining origin and form of knowledge. Then a metaphysics of substance would prevail, according to which the world is divided into causally interacting substances that are either simple or compounded, and there would be no compelling reason to break with it. In a word, Hegel could not declare, as he does (PhG 22–29/9–14★), that truth must be understood 'as subject'.[25]

§2. Sense-Certainty (Process)

> Die Natur kommt auf dem kürzesten Weg zu ihrem Ziel. Dies ist richtig; aber der Weg des Geistes ist die Vermittlung, der Umweg.[26]
>
> Nature takes the shortest path to reach its goal, that is correct; but spirit takes the path of mediation, and hence a detour.

Noticing, meaning, knowing

In the first chapter of the *Phenomenology*, entitled 'Sense-Certainty, or, the This and Meaning' [Die sinnliche Gewißheit oder das Diese und das Meinen], Hegel examines the most immediate form of conscious knowledge: the moment when consciousness becomes aware of a particular thing, state, or object and thus notices its presence — its existence right here and right now. This awareness establishes a direct connection between my consciousness (*Ich*) and the noticed thing (*Sache*):

> [W]eder Ich noch die Sache hat darin die Bedeutung einer mannigfaltigen Vermittlung, Ich nicht die Bedeutung eines mannigfaltigen Vorstellens oder Denkens, noch die Sache die Bedeutung mannigfaltiger Beschaffenheiten, sondern die Sache *ist*; und sie *ist*, nur weil sie *ist*; sie *ist*, dies ist dem sinnlichen Wissen das Wesentliche, und dieses reine Sein oder diese einfache Unmittelbarkeit macht ihre *Wahrheit* aus. (PhG 82)
>
> [In it, neither the I nor the thing has the meaning of complex mediation. The I does not represent a manifold way of imagining or thinking, nor does the thing represent something that has many diverse qualities. On the contrary, the thing *is*, and it *is* merely because it *is*. It *is*: that is the essential point of sensory knowledge, and this pure being or simple immediacy constitutes its *truth*.] (58–59*)

It is this immediate relationship between a receptive subject and the noticed thing Hegel names sense-certainty — a relationship, to be sure, that already in this early definition appears dangerously tautological: 'it *is* merely because it *is*'. In any case, sense-certainty directly results from sensory presentation, while sensory intention or 'meaning' (*das Meinen*) — the keeping of one's eyes and ears on the noticed thing — is the way to confirm and retain the certainty that *this* thing exists, here and now.

Meinen is a key term of the chapter on sense-certainty, along with *das Diese*, 'the This', and deictic or indexical markers such as 'here', 'now', and 'I'. In German, the verb *meinen* has basically two meanings. On the one hand, *meinen* signifies the mental and possibly gestural act of 'meaning' something, for which reason *das Meinen*, and in certain contexts also *die Meinung*, designate the 'intention' connecting a subject to the object it intends. On the other hand, *meinen* means 'to opine', and *Meinung* in most cases 'opinion'. In the sense-certainty chapter, Hegel plays with this double meaning to introduce doubts as to the veracity and credibility of sense-certainty. For upon closer inspection, my sensory intention (*Meinung*) might indeed turn out to be mere opinion (again *Meinung*), a kind of knowledge with little, if any, connection to the intended object, in which case sense-certainty would seem mistaken on both objective and subjective grounds: neither would I *know* the object (for I only *mean* it), nor would it be certain that I acquire direct knowledge by intending the object (for intending is a subjective procedure according to subjective criteria). In pointing out this discrepancy, Hegel in fact follows Kant's lead, who defined the act of meaning something precisely as 'taking something to be true with the consciousness that it is subjectively as well as objectively insufficient' (KrV A 822).

Sense-certainty emerges within the blink of an eye. You open your eyes and ears, immediately noticing 'this' here — that thing over there. Behaving in this passive and purely receptive way, you seem to obtain a direct record of the noticed thing, which Hegel calls 'the This', an odd locution for an as yet unspecified particular (*ein Einzelnes*)[27] that goes back to Aristotle's *Metaphysics*, where it is termed *tode ti*, 'some this'. The seeming passivity of the act suggests to consciousness that it apprehends the pure presence of the object 'without any abstraction from its unique specificity or pure particularity', as Robert Stern puts it, thereby producing 'the most important kind of knowledge, which is of things as concrete, singular entities'.[28] As immediate and purely receptive 'apprehension' [Auffassen], sense-certainty seems to do without 'comprehension' [Begreifen] and would thus ensure the perfect concreteness and non-conceptuality of the obtained knowledge (PhG 82/58★).

Hegel will demonstrate, however, that the knowledge of sense-certainty is neither immediate nor concrete but thoroughly abstract and dependent on both logical and verbal concepts. To do so, he must first disprove the seeming immediacy of sense-certainty, which puts him in direct opposition to Kant's definition of sensuousness (*Sinnlichkeit*) as an 'immediate' relation of 'receptivity', or in an alternative formulation, as a receptive faculty bearing the 'character of passivity', which he contrasts with the spontaneity of the understanding (*Verstand*) — a problematic dichotomy, as Kant realized himself.[29]

In refuting the immediate passivity of sensation, Hegel in fact radicalizes the other famous assertion of Kant, according to which 'intuitions [Anschauungen] without concepts [Begriffe] are blind' — an assertion, however, Kant immediately qualifies, and in a way retracts, by adding that 'one must not mix up their roles' and 'separate them carefully from each other'.[30] Against this strict separation between concepts and intuitions, as well as receptivity and spontaneity, Hegel develops a concept of sensuousness in which these two modes of cognition permeate each other.

What, then, does sense-certainty truly *know*? The direct connection sense-certainty establishes between perceiver and perceived content suggests that in the shape of sense-certainty, consciousness knows the object 'completely and entirely' [in seiner ganzen Vollständigkeit] (PhG 82/58★). Yet this connection at the same time introduces a fundamental distinction: the difference between the noticing *subject* and the noticed *object*, or in more general terms, the difference between the 'being-for-consciousness' and the 'being-in-itself' (PhG 78). In recognizing this 'main difference' [Hauptverschiedenheit] (PhG 83/59★) obtaining in all experience, consciousness has and, indeed, *becomes* knowledge. For according to Hegel, knowledge consists always of two discrepant facets, the one representing the object's ontological being and the other the subjective cognition thereof. Consequently, acquiring knowledge means, according to Hegel, processing and conceptually reconciling these discrepancies. Knowledge results from this comparison between the ontology or *An-sich* and the epistemology or appearance of the cognized object, which in the *Phenomenology* is often staged as a veritable contest between these two sides.

Consciousness is the site where this contest takes place, the stage on which the discrepant truth claims meet and the relationship between 'being-in-itself' and 'being-for-consciousness' is determined. The question is not, however, which truth claim takes precedence over the other. What consciousness aims at instead is to unite both claims in such a way that their difference, and hence the 'double nature' of truth, is at once preserved and reconciled. In the case of sense-certainty, the comparison concerns the difference between the concrete and mind-independent individuality of the noticed object called *das Diese* on the one hand, and the universal form by which it is intended through sensation on the other. To truly know *das Diese*, instead of only meaning it, would therefore mean to develop a kind of relationship that reconciles their categorial discrepancy.

Hegel specifies this method of knowledge production through 'comparison' [Vergleichung] and 'examination' [Prüfung] on the basis of a self-defined 'set of criteria' [Maßstab] in the Introduction (PhG 75–80/52–56★). The way towards true knowledge involves not only one but many such comparisons — after all, consciousness follows the 'pathway of *doubt*' (PhG 72/49★) — which in turn give rise to new internal disagreements and contradictions, to more self-estrangement and diremption. Such forms of 'oppositional doubling' [entgegensetzende Verdopplung] (PhG 23/10★) inhere not only in consciousness but, in fact, in reason itself, for the truth is never 'an *original* unity' but a result produced and completed through negation and 'reflection in otherness' (PhG 23/10★). Even so-called 'absolute' spirit — the unlimited and unconditional truth, or, God — remains subject to this double nature of truth. 'Absolute' spirit, too, must divide itself and become twofold, for in order to be something rather than nothing — which is to say, empty abstraction — it has to *materialize*, has to take on manifest form and expression, which it does according to Hegel in the shape of world history.[31]

The method of consciousness for progressing on its path towards true knowledge is to sublate (*aufheben*) its internal discrepancies — *aufheben* in the threefold meaning of cancelling, surpassing, and yet preserving that Hegel briefly glosses in the chapter on object perception (PhG 94/68★), but which he may have initially discovered in Schiller's eighteenth letter on the *Ästhetische Erziehung des Menschen*.[32] Only as the knowledge of consciousness is finally elevated to 'absolute' knowledge — to philosophical concepts purged of contradictions and discrepancies — are all preceding struggles and conflicts of consciousness sublated in the threefold sense of the term, which is to say, not only cancelled out and elevated but at the same time preserved (*aufbewahrt*). Such, at least, is the promise of the *Phenomenology* as a 'ladder' (PhG 29/14★) taking its readers up to the plane of purely conceptual thinking or 'absolute' knowledge.

To analyse the knowledge of sense-certainty, or its epistemic content, Hegel has devised a number of scenographies illustrating its operations. Each of these short scenographies represents an artificial set-up designed to isolate specific parameters of sense-certainty. In the first phase (PhG 83–86/59–61★), sense-certainty figures as immediate *Ein-fall*, as passive 'in-come' or intake of objective presence into consciousness. The struggling hero of the *Phenomenology*, consciousness, then registers the naked being of 'this' thing over there, but without intentional activity. In the second phase (PhG 86–87/61–62★), Hegel shifts attention to the act of noticing. It is 'I' — my consciousness — that directs its senses at something, thus noticing it. Therefore, the existence of the noticed thing appears to depend primarily on my sensory intention. As a result of this, consciousness becomes aware of the key difference on which sense-certainty and all the other forms of conscious knowledge depend, namely the contrast between the apprehending subject and the apprehended object, or the subjective mode and the objective content of cognition. As before, however, sense-certainty seems to be the immediate product of pure sensation without intellection. This changes in the third phase (PhG 87–90/62–65★), which abandons the claim of sense-certainty to immediacy by relating its two facets, noticing subject ('I') and noticed particular ('this'), through a temporal movement. The final scenographies are precisely designed to demonstrate the temporal nature of sense-certainty — the fact that its constitutive acts of noticing and retaining actually take time. For that reason, Hegel concludes that sense-certainty is not a passive relationship 'but the simple story [*Geschichte*] of its movement' (PhG 90/64★), hence a diachronic process.[33]

Negation, deixis, language

To show 'an actual [*wirkliche*] sense-certainty' (PhG 83/59★), Hegel comes up with a first example, a scenography staging the attempts of consciousness at taking a permanent record of a particular in an entirely passive way. As the knowledge of sense-certainty — the certainty that 'this' thing exists here and now — is utterly universal, however, specific sensations and objective properties do not play a role in this and all other scenographies of sense-certainty. Although sensations 'tag along' with sense-certainty — Hegel's exact term is *beiherspielen* (PhG 83), derived from *Beispiel*[34] — and thus exemplify what it knows, they do not affect its knowledge, belonging instead to the domain of sensory perception, which Hegel examines in the following chapter. Consequently, there is a noticeable discrepancy between the universally applicable knowledge of sense-certainty that something *exists* and the concrete thing this knowledge refers to — *this* tree, for example, which in its concreteness instantiates the concept of existence.

To specify further the structure of sense-certainty, Hegel literally addresses himself to consciousness, thus staging a scene in which consciousness plays the role of sense-certainty. We readers are invited to observe the dramatic spectacle under his guidance:

> *Sie* [die sinnliche Gewissheit] ist also selbst zu fragen: *Was ist das Diese?* Nehmen wir es in der gedoppelten Gestalt seines Seins, als das *Jetzt* und als das *Hier*, so wird die Dialektik, die es an ihm hat, eine so verständliche Form erhalten, als es selbst ist. Auf die Frage: *was ist das Jetzt?* antworten wir also zum Beispiel: *das Jetzt ist die Nacht*. Um die Wahrheit dieser sinnlichen Gewißheit zu prüfen, ist ein einfacher Versuch hinreichend. Wir schreiben diese Wahrheit auf; eine Wahrheit kann durch Aufschreiben nicht verlieren; ebensowenig dadurch, daß wir sie aufbewahren. Sehen wir *Jetzt*,[35] diesen *Mittag*, die aufgeschriebene Wahrheit wieder an, so werden wir sagen müssen, daß sie schal geworden ist. (PhG 84)
>
> [Sense-certainty itself has thus to be asked: *What is the This?* If we take the This in the twofold shape of its being, as the *Now* and as the *Here*, its inherent dialectic will take a form as intelligible as the This itself is. To the question, *What is the Now?* we reply, for example, *The Now is night-time*. To test the truth of this sense-certainty, a simple experiment will suffice. We write down this truth; a truth cannot lose anything by being written down, and just as little by our preserving it. If we look again at the written truth — *Now, at noon* — we shall have to say that it has turned stale.] (59–60★)[36]

Hegel's first example of sense-certainty is grammatically flawed, but the oddities and mistakes are carefully put in place. Standard grammar dictates that the sentence, *das Jetzt ist die Nacht*, should read, *jetzt ist Nacht*. 'The Now', by contrast, is not and never night-time, not even during the night, since the nominalized Now expresses a universal concept, whereas night or night-time designates a concrete empirical state to which one can only refer. This, clearly, is a mix-up of categories. The question, *Was ist das Diese?* performs the same type of nominalization, similarly transforming a demonstrative pronoun into an ontological concept. In fact, the entire chapter is predicated upon this little ruse to nominalize both demonstratives and indexicals, a small but decisive grammatical manipulation that precludes their adverbial or pronominal, and hence their referential, usage.

What these nominalizations bring to light, however, is the double nature of sense-certainty as producing particular reference or meaning through universally applicable concepts. Hegel wants to stress precisely this interdependence between the noticed particular — 'this' — and the universal concept whereby it is intended — the conceptual This or thisness. Language covers both these dimensions, the conceptual and the referential, in that it provides universally applicable, and therefore possibly referential, concepts in the form of indexicals like 'this', 'here', 'now', 'I', and it is for this reason Hegel eventually concludes that the very act of apprehending something necessarily involves language and specifically indexicals. Or as Hegel puts it later, 'the sensuous This' can only be intended or meant, but it '*cannot be reached by language*' directly (PhG 91–92/66★). If this is true, however, sense-certainty is not immediate and purely receptive but indirect, mediate knowledge of particulars, whereas the content that directly 'belongs to consciousness' is language (ibid.).

In addition to calling attention to the role of language in sensory apprehension, the first example also introduces a metaphysical argument, which Hegel then develops in the ensuing comment. He challenges the positive understanding of time as unbroken continuity, suggesting instead that it is impossible to take in any individual 'now', because time has no positive existence as such but is, in fact, pure negativity. 'The Now does indeed maintain itself [erhält sich wohl]', Hegel writes, 'but as something that is not night-time' and, consequently, 'as something *negative*', indeed as a 'non-being' [Nichtseiendes] (PhG 84/60★). It is night-time 'now' only because something else is not at this very moment, for instance, the time of day. The present moment, 'now', is thus defined by way of negation:

> Dieses sich erhaltende Jetzt ist daher nicht ein unmittelbares; sondern ein vermitteltes, denn es ist als ein bleibendes und sich erhaltendes *dadurch* bestimmt, daß anderes [...] nicht ist. Dabei ist es [...] gleichgültig gegen das, was noch bei ihm herspielt; sowenig die Nacht und der Tag sein Sein ist, ebensowohl ist es auch Tag und Nacht [...] Ein solches einfaches [Jetzt], das durch Negation ist, weder dieses noch jenes, ein *nicht dieses* [Jetzt], und ebenso gleichgültig, auch dieses wie jenes zu sein, nennen wir ein *allgemeines* [Jetzt]; das allgemeine [Jetzt] ist also in der Tat das wahre [Jetzt] der sinnlichen Gewißheit. (PhG 84–85)[37]

> [This self-maintaining Now is therefore not immediate but mediated; for it is determined as a permanent and self-maintaining Now *through* the fact that something else [...] is not. It is therefore [...] indifferent to whatever tags along with it; just as little as Night and Day are its being, just as much also is it Day and Night [...] A simple [Now] of this kind, which is through negation, neither This nor That, a *not-This*, and with equal indifference This as well as That — such a thing we call a *general* [Now]. The general [Now] is therefore the true [Now] of sense-certainty.] (60★)

If it is true that the present 'now' endures because of negation, or a series of negations, it would be more appropriate to call nowness a negative universal. The same applies to any 'here'-point, of course, a negativity of location Hegel demonstrates in an analogous way. He again evokes a short scene in which '*the Here* is, for example, *the tree*' (PhG 85/60★). But it turns out the tree can stand 'here' only in not standing over 'there', where a house is standing. Spatial location is not positively given but likewise defined by negation, so that hereness, just like nowness, constitutes a negative universal. Hegel returns to both points, the negativity of Here and Now as constitutive aspects of particular existence, in the third part of sense-certainty.

Prior to that, Hegel makes a fundamental remark concerning the role of language in sensory experience. The sensory apprehension of particulars implicitly relies upon linguistic universals:

> Als ein Allgemeines *sprechen* wir auch das Sinnliche *aus*; was wir sagen, ist: *Dieses*, d.h. das *allgemeine Diese*, oder: *es ist*; d.h. das *Sein überhaupt*. Wir *stellen* uns dabei freilich nicht das allgemeine Diese oder das Sein überhaupt *vor*, aber wir *sprechen* das Allgemeine *aus*; oder wir sprechen schlechthin nicht, wie wir es in dieser sinnlichen Gewißheit *meinen*. Die Sprache aber ist, wie wir sehen, das Wahrhaftere; in ihr widerlegen wir selbst unmittelbar unsere *Meinung*; und da das Allgemeine das Wahre der sinnlichen Gewißheit ist und die Sprache nur dieses Wahre ausdrückt, so ist es gar nicht möglich, daß wir ein sinnliches Sein, das wir *meinen*, je sagen können. (PhG 85)

> [It is in universal terms that we *utter* sensuous facts. What we say is: *This*, i.e. the *universal This*; or, *it is*, i.e. *Being in general*. In doing so, however, we do not *envisage* the universal This or Being in general, but we *utter* the universal. We do not strictly say what we *mean* by this sense-certainty. But language, as we see, is closer to the truth; in it, we ourselves directly refute our own *meaning*, and since the universal is the truth of sense-certainty and language expresses this truth alone, it is just not possible for us ever to say a sensuous being that we only *mean*.] (60★)

The verbalization of sense-certainty lays bare its essential generality, for in expressing the individual content or meaning of sense-certainty — the particular thing it claims to know, but actually only refers to — one necessarily calls upon utterly universal signs like this, that, here, now, you, I, etc. The way in which these deictic signifiers operate in fact mirrors the negative universality of sense-certainty, because just like sense-certainty, their meaning or reference depends on context, and thus on negation and exclusion — on what they do not mean — *although* they are, and in order to function must be, free of any particular meaning and context. For that reason, sense-certainty as conceived by Hegel contains nothing but deixis. It is essentially a deictic '*sign*', Hegel notes in an earlier fragment[38] describing language as the primal 'power' [Potenz] of man, or a mute intention in which Here and Now figure only as 'citations', as Derrida[39] put it. Incidentally, Derrida's observation is confirmed by the fact that 'this', 'here', and 'now' are normally put in quotation marks in English translations of the sense-certainty chapter, although in the German original they are not (which is why I have again excised them from the English).

Hegel rephrases the insight into the abstract universality of sense-certainty because of its deictic nature in the *Enzyklopädie* of 1830:

> Übrigens wenn für das Sinnliche die Bestimmungen *der Einzelheit und des Außereinander* angegeben worden, so kann noch hinzugefügt werden, daß auch diese selbst wieder Gedanken und Allgemeine sind [...] Indem die *Sprache* das Werk des Gedankens ist, so kann auch in ihr nichts gesagt werden, was nicht allgemein ist. Was ich nur *meine*, ist *mein*, gehört mir als diesem besonderen Individuum an; wenn aber die Sprache nur Allgemeines ausdrückt, so kann ich nicht sagen, was ich nur *meine*. Und das *Unsagbare*, Gefühl, Empfindung, ist nicht das Vortrefflichste, Wahrste, sondern das Unbedeutendste, Unwahrste. Wenn ich sage: 'das *Einzelne*', '*dieses* Einzelne', 'Hier', 'Jetzt', so sind dies alles Allgemeinheiten; *Alles* und *Jedes* ist ein Einzelnes, Dieses, auch wenn es sinnlich ist, Hier, Jetzt. Ebenso wenn ich sage: 'Ich'; *meine* ich Mich als *diesen* alle anderen Ausschließenden; aber was ich sage, Ich, ist eben jeder. [TWA VIII, 74 (§ 20)]

> [Incidentally, when it was said that the determinations of the sensory are those of *individuality and being-outside-of-one-another*, it can also be added that the latter, too, are in turn thoughts and universals themselves [...] Given that *language* is the product of thought, nothing that is not universal can be expressed in it either. What I only *mean*, is *mine*, belonging to me as this particular individual. If, however, language expresses only what is universal, then I cannot say what I *mean* only. And the *ineffable*, feeling, sentiment, are not what is most exquisite and true, but instead the most insignificant and untrue. When I say

'the *individual*', '*this* individual', 'here', 'now', then these are all universalities. *Anything* and *everything* is an individual, a this, even when it is sensory, just as much as a here, now. Similarly, when I say 'I' I *mean* to refer to myself as *this* one individual, excluding everyone else. But what I say (namely 'I') is precisely each and every one.]⁴⁰

Verbalization reveals the structural identity of deixis and sense-certainty, namely that they both refer to particulars through utterly abstract universals. Or in the phrase of Friedrich Schiller quoted in the Introduction, sense-certainty, too, must take a '*detour* through the abstract domain of concepts' to demonstrate what it particularly means, thereby losing 'much of its vividness (sensuous force)' — actually all of it. And in revealing this correlation between deixis and sense-certainty, as that between universal concepts and particular reference, language is, the above passage (PhG 85/60★) unequivocally states, 'closer to the truth' than sense-certainty or any other immediately given sensory fact.

This wager may be puzzling at first, perhaps even alarming given the 'post-factual' inclinations of certain politicians and political commentators of our time. It has been suggested that Hegel's preoccupation with language is indicative of the theological underpinning of his philosophy. Echoing Hegel's remark that in aiming at absolute truth or God, philosophy is 'essentially rational theology and continued worship [Gottesdienst] in the service of Truth' (TWA XIII, 139), Karl Löwith, for example, claims that his philosophy is at root '*philosophical theology*' built upon 'Christian logos'.⁴¹ There is some truth to that, not least because in the *Phenomenology*, Hegel identifies 'the divine nature' [die göttliche Natur] with 'speech' [Sprechen] (PhG 92/66★), thus recalling the famous first sentence from the prologue to the Gospel of John, according to which God and logos are one, as well the biblical creation myth, according to which God has created the world through a series of speech acts, bringing forth elements, plants, and animals by calling upon them, one by one.

But this Christian rhetoric is only the vehicle to express a more radical point. For in stating that language — logos — 'is closer to the truth', Hegel expresses the most fundamental premise of his philosophical system as a whole. The premise, explained best in the second preface to the *Wissenschaft der Logik* (TWA v, 20–30), is that knowledge does not exist outside of language, not even in sense-certainty, the most elementary form of knowledge. Without the universal concept of language, signification, and specifically deictic signifiers, which generalize the concept of signification insofar as they can signify anyone or anything, the certainty that 'this' particular exists, 'here' and 'now', does not exist. It is for this profane reason that Hegel considers language or logos the foundation of knowledge.

If language is the 'divine' measure of knowledge, as Hegel claims, it necessarily follows that knowledge is propositional. A claim about a certain thing or matter is true to the extent that it can be coherently expressed and justified in the form of propositions. The truth thus proposed, however, is not simply a reproduction of perceived facts but both a discursive artefact and a conceptual construct. The material form of truth is discourse and its essential content are concepts — conceptual knowledge; which is tantamount to saying that *truth is logical*.

George di Giovanni clarifies this Hegelian proposition, expounded primarily in the *Wissenschaft der Logik*, in stating that for Hegel, the truth of a certain matter or object, and hence knowledge,

> is only to be found in the discourse about it, so that any opaqueness as to what that object is, or whether it is at all, must be resolved from within the original discourse itself by developing it according to rules internal to it. There is no exit from language. This is the central point of Hegel's position and the meaning of his repeated claim that the content of discourse is generated by its form.[42]

Hotho's record of Hegel's 1822 lectures on subjective spirit contains perhaps the most succinct expression of this dialectic between the discursive form and conceptual content of truth. The comprehension of content, Hegel remarks here, means 'to determine its form [...] what content is, it is through form'.[43] And such determination must happen in language, because in it form truly determines content. Language provides both the formal means (words, syntax, grammar) of communicating and the essential contents (meanings, concepts) of understanding the matters of thought and experience. Therefore, language is not only the discursive form but at the same time the essential content or 'substance' of spirit (PhG 376–78/308–09★), as Hegel puts it, the one thing that truly 'belongs to consciousness' (PhG 91–92/66★). It is the 'first, immediate, and natural form in which spirit appears', Theodor Bodammer writes, because in it 'the contents of spirit are "objectified"', which is to say, expressed and determined.[44] Language thus becomes, as Novalis once phrased it, the 'gentle measure and outline [Grundriß] of all things' (N II: 438).[45]

The form or medium to determine the content of truth is language, whence it follows that 'the so-called ineffable is nothing but the untrue, the irrational, mere opinion [bloß Gemeinte]' (PhG 92/66★). This is the fundamental premise of Hegel's philosophy, which remains intact throughout his entire work.[46]

Hegel's radically linguistic (and only in that sense logocentric) conception of truth has an important implication: Truth takes an intersubjective shape. Thoroughly condemning the reveries of introspection and intuition — the night, as he calls it, 'in which all cows are black' (PhG 22/9★) — as well as the empty rigour of transcendental deductions, Hegel places the criteria of truth between (at least) two subjects. Truth, he says, originates in, and evolves from, the '*I* that is *We* and the *We* that is *I*' [Ich, das Wir, und Wir, das Ich ist] (PhG 145/110★). This expression announces the basic 'concept *of spirit*' (ibid.), but also the discursive procedure whereby the matters of truth are at once constituted and negotiated. Neither given by nature nor inherent to one single mind, the criteria of knowledge are revealed and determined *by way of dialogue*.

The key consequences of this intersubjective or dialogic concept of truth Hegel spells out at the end of the preface to the *Phenomenology*, writing that 'verbalization' [das Aussprechen] is the solely valid method of philosophy (PhG 61/40★) and 'agreement with others' — the explication and reconciliation of differences and discrepancies — the solely valid measure of knowledge and indeed the 'root of humanity' (PhG 64/43★). Hegel thus replaces the traditional foundation of knowledge, the subject–object relation, with a relation connecting (at least) two subjects, and if this dialogic relationship 'is developed enough to produce, in the medium of language, mutual recognition — a "We", as Hegel writes — it may justly be called spirit'.[47] Truth is the product of intersubjective discourse and for this reason and in this very sense a logical, *dia*logical result. That is the essential meaning of Hegel's repeated claims that true or 'absolute' knowledge results from self-determination, and at the same time the gist of his notorious claim that truth is 'essentially a *result*', or a whole that 'only in the *end* is what it truly is' (PhG 24/11*).

The *Phenomenology* reflects this intersubjective, dialogical conception of truth by representing concepts through scenographies. What Hegel's 1796 poem 'Eleusius' only envisions but does not actually describe, 'The scene of reciprocal observation' [Des wechselseitigen Ausspähens Scene] (TWA 1, 230), becomes a reality in the *Phenomenology*.[48] The internal developments and reflections consciousness undergoes as it strives for true knowledge are put on the phenomenological stage, on which 'natural consciousness' — the hero of the book — embodies the pure but also naïve will to knowledge. The reader assumes the role of the spectator, watching the various manifestations of knowledge emerge and perish on stage until true knowledge is attained and the *Bildungsweg* of consciousness complete. In choosing such a theatrical set-up to elucidate concepts — a set-up some scholars[49] have likened to Goethe's *Faust* — Hegel is as faithful to the etymology of the word 'theory' as one could be, since the Greek *theōria* derives from the verb *theaomai* ('to look on, gaze at, behold'), while *theōros* means the 'spectator' of a public spectacle such as a play. The third party involved in these phenomenological scenes of knowledge is the author and philosophical narrator, Hegel, who arranges and controls these scenes by telling and explaining them, and by occasionally framing them with proleptic as well as retrospective definitions. These definitions and explanations are meant to ensure that 'we', the phenomenological spectators, come to informed conclusions as we observe the phenomenological scene before 'us' — the actions, errors, and mistakes of our struggling hero, consciousness. The narrator then often addresses his reader-spectators in a conspiratorial manner, reminding them of what counts as truth 'for us', as opposed to those notions consciousness pursues on stage. It is by way of such carefully devised scenographies that concepts are both portrayed (*dargestellt*) and conveyed in the *Phenomenology*, especially in the chapters on sense-certainty and perception.[50]

Here and Now as abstractions, and as dialectic

If sense-certainty does not apprehend 'the This' in its concreteness but only the 'empty or indifferent Now and Here', then it is nothing but 'abstraction', which means a 'purely universal' knowledge referring to the apprehended object through 'negation and mediation' (PhG 85–86/61*). But is it not the case, still, that one can at least intend precisely *this* and no other sense datum? It would be captured in that *I* am sensing it. My meaning would seem to determine the content of sense-certainty, the 'immediacy of my *seeing, hearing*, and so on', and 'the vanishing of the individual Now and Here [das Verschwinden des einzelnen Jetzt und Hier] that we mean' would seem to be 'prevented by the fact that *I* hold them fast. *The Now is day because I see it*, and *the Here is a tree* for the same reason' (PhG 86/61*).

However, anyone can contradict 'my' intention and the certainty 'I' derive from it. While one person sees a tree 'here', another might mean that house 'here', behind the tree. Both identifications of 'here' are equally valid since they are based on the same method of 'authentication [Beglaubigung], namely the immediacy of seeing, and the certainty [Sicherheit] and assurance concerning their knowledge; but the one truth vanishes in the other' (PhG 86/61*). What is obtained in this way is a private impression, an opinion (*Meinung*), really, but certainly not an objective truth, a certainty shared by everyone. Moreover, a purely subjective definition of sense-certainty qua intention is not as unequivocal and self-contained as it seems, for it, too, rests upon utterly abstract or universal forms, namely the deictic pronouns 'I' and 'my'. What 'I' sense and mean is precisely defined by what 'I' do not sense and mean, hence through negation. Again the inevitability of abstraction subverts the seeming immediacy and specificity of 'my' sense-certainty:

> Was darin nicht verschwindet, ist *Ich*, als *allgemeines* [Ich], dessen Sehen weder ein Sehen des Baums noch dieses Hauses, sondern ein einfaches Sehen ist, das, durch die Negation dieses Hauses usf. vermittelt, darin ebenso einfach und gleichgültig gegen das, was noch beiherspielt, gegen das Haus, den Baum ist. Ich ist nur allgemeines, wie *Jetzt, Hier oder Dieses* überhaupt; ich meine wohl einen *einzelnen* Ich, aber so wenig ich das, was ich bei Jetzt, Hier meine, sagen kann, sowenig bei Ich. (PhG 86–87)

> [What does not disappear in all this is the *I* as *universal*, whose seeing is neither a seeing of the tree nor of this house, but is a simple seeing which, though mediated by the negation of this house, etc., is all the same simple and indifferent to whatever figures in it, to the house, the tree, etc. The *I* is merely universal like *Now*, *Here*, or *This* in general; I do indeed mean an *individual* I, but I can no more say what I mean in the case of I than I can in the case of Now and Here.] (62*)

Even the bare noticing of particulars depends on universal concepts, namely indexicals, and thus on language, a grounding of experience in concepts that a radically nominalist world-view necessarily overlooks. Such is the key lesson philosophical commentators take from this second phase of sense-certainty.[51]

Reading it as pertaining to a theory of sensuousness, however, to 'aesthetics' in the older sense of the word, one notices that Hegel covertly introduces another issue: time. Noticing something is not an instantaneous event but takes time, and one must also *retain* the noticed sense datum. Indeed, 'the vanishing of the individual Now and Here that we mean is prevented by the fact that *I hold them fast*' (PhG 86/61*; emphasis added). Hegel thus shifts attention to the diachronic process by which sense-certainty is acquired and retained — a process, 'we' have seen, that is neither purely receptive, and hence caused by the object, nor purely subjective, and hence purely defined by 'my' intention. The *lasting* essence of sense-certainty is

weder in dem Gegenstande noch in dem Ich und die Unmittelbarkeit weder
eine Unmittelbarkeit des einen noch des anderen [...]; denn an beiden ist das,
was Ich meine, vielmehr ein Unwesentliches, und der Gegenstand und Ich
sind Allgemeine, in welchen dasjenige Jetzt und Hier und Ich, das ich meine,
nicht bestehen bleibt oder *ist*. Wir kommen hierdurch dahin, das *Ganze* der
sinnlichen Gewißheit selbst als ihr *Wesen* zu setzen, nicht mehr nur ein Moment
derselben, wie in den beiden Fällen geschehen ist, worin zuerst der dem Ich
entgegengesetzte Gegenstand, dann Ich ihre Realität sein sollte. Es ist also nur
die ganze sinnliche Gewißheit selbst, welche an ihr als *Unmittelbarkeit* festhält
und hierdurch alle Entgegensetzung, die im vorherigen stattfand, aus sich
ausschließt. (PhG 87)

[neither in the object nor in the I, and its immediacy is neither an immediacy
of the one nor of the other; for in both, what I mean is rather something
unessential, and the object and the I are universals in which that Now and
Here and I which I mean do not have a continuing being, or *are* not. Thus we
reach the stage where we have to posit the *whole* of sense-certainty itself as its
essence, and no longer only one of its moments, as happened in the two cases
where first the object as against the I, and then the I, were supposed to be its
reality. Thus it is only sense-certainty as a whole which stands firm within itself
as *immediacy* and consequently excludes from itself all the opposition which has
hitherto obtained.] (62★)

Hegel segues into the chapter's third phase. Despite the previous lessons about the
negative universality of 'this', 'here', 'now', and 'I', of which all are defined by
negation and abstraction, our actor on the phenomenological stage, sense-certainty,
is still foolish enough to uphold its claim to immediacy. Stubbornly attending to *this*
one thing over 'there', the tree, without turning away or, for that matter, considering
the fact that someone else might see 'the Here as not a tree [Nichtbaum]', sense-
certainty seeks finally to establish an 'immediate' and 'self-identical relationship'
that evades negativity (PhG 87–88/62–63★).

Naturally, the negative universals upon which any such relationship depends,
namely deictic signs, undermine this desire. Negation prevails in the context of a
synthetic conception of sense-certainty as well. Although 'we', the phenomenological
spectators, have by now understood that sense-certainty is, as Terry Pinkard puts it,
always already 'mediated (inferential) knowledge' and hence an 'abstraction from
our awareness of things', consciousness has yet to learn the lesson.[52] The narrator
therefore asks 'us' to step onto the stage and confront sense-certainty head-on. The
scene is comical. Because our stubborn hero will no longer attend to anything but
a certain Here and Now — the 'this' it has singled out –

treten wir zu ihr hinzu und lassen uns das Jetzt zeigen, das behauptet wird.
Zeigen müssen wir es uns lassen, denn die Wahrheit dieser unmittelbaren
Beziehung ist die Wahrheit *dieses* Ich, der sich auf ein *Jetzt* oder ein *Hier*
einschränkt. Würden wir *nachher* diese Wahrheit vornehmen oder *entfernt* davon
stehen, so hätte sie gar keine Bedeutung; denn wir höben die Unmittelbarkeit
auf, die ihr wesentlich ist. Wir müssen daher in denselben Punkt der Zeit oder
des Raums eintreten, sie uns zeigen, d.h. uns zu demselben diesen Ich, welches
das gewiß Wissende ist, machen lassen. Sehen wir also, wie das Unmittelbare
beschaffen ist, das uns aufgezeigt wird. (PhG 88)

> [we will approach to ask that sense-certainty indicate the Now to us which it asserts. Such *indication* is necessary since the truth of this immediate relation is the truth of *this*, I which confines itself to one *Now* or one *Here*. Were we to examine this truth *afterwards*, or stand *at a distance* from it, it would have no meaning; for that would do away with the immediacy which is essential to it. We must therefore enter the same point in time or space and have them pointed out to us, i.e. become the very same I which is the one who knows with certainty. Let us see how that immediate is constituted that is pointed out to us.] (63★)

And so the scene unfolds:

> Es wird das *Jetzt* gezeigt, *dieses Jetzt. Jetzt*; es hat schon aufgehört zu sein, indem es gezeigt wird; das *Jetzt*, das *ist*, ist ein anderes als das gezeigte, und wir sehen, daß das Jetzt eben dieses ist, indem es ist, schon nicht mehr zu sein. Das Jetzt, wie es uns gezeigt wird, ist es ein *gewesenes*, und dies ist seine Wahrheit; es hat nicht die Wahrheit des Seins. Es ist also doch dies wahr, daß es gewesen ist. Aber was *gewesen* ist, ist in der Tat *kein Wesen*; *es ist nicht*, und um das Sein war es zu tun. (PhG 88)

> [The *Now* is pointed out, *this Now. Now*; it has already ceased to be as it is presently indicated. The *Now* that *is*, is another Now than the one indicated, and we see that, in being 'now', the Now is precisely this: no more. The Now, as it is pointed out to us, is a Now that *has been*, and this is its truth; it does not have the truth of being. This much is true, therefore, that it has been. That which *has been*, however, is *no being*; *it is not* — and being was precisely the point in question.] (63★)

Hegel's scenography situates the perception of the present moment within a self-negating sequence, as opposed to a selfsame continuity that simply endures. Hegel thus combines the ontological negativity of nowness, which came to light at the beginning of the chapter, with the acts of indicating and retaining a specific point in time — the intention of *this* particular 'now'. The lesson to be learned from this exercise is, of course, that such presence is through negation and difference, which underscores the fact that Hegel is, as Derrida puts it, 'also the thinker of irreducible difference'.[53] The intended 'now' — call it t_0 — has neither positive existence nor permanent identity in itself. Instead, the intended moment t_0 is always something '*that has been*', as Hegel mentioned before, a 'non-being' [Nichtseiendes] (PhG 84/60★) identified through negation, which is to say, by distinguishing a moment before (t_{-1}) and a moment after (t_1).

Similarly, the retention of 'now' requires a series of negations, indeed a growing network of oppositions: $t_0 \neq t_{-1}$; $t_0 \neq t_1$; $t_0 \neq t_2$; $t_0 \neq t_3$; ... It is because of this very network, however, that any specific moment of presence interlaces past, present, and future moments. The intended moment, 'now', is and persists precisely not as a singular point or isolated event but rather as 'a movement which contains various moments', hence as a 'result, or a plurality of Nows all taken together' [eine Vielheit von Jetzt zusammengefaßt] whose individuality or thisness endures through negation (PhG 89/64★). According to Hegel, therefore, it is not in spite of but because of negativity and abstraction that consciousness is able to notice and hold on to a particular point in time without losing or forgetting it in the face of 'otherness' [Anderssein] (ibid.) — those other moments that have passed since.

In an 1805 manuscript containing both a philosophy of nature and a philosophy of spirit, Hegel stresses the same point.[54] In the section describing the nature of time and space, Hegel defines, in accordance with the *Phenomenology*, a single point in time — the Now — as 'utterly exclusive or negating *others* [...] its concept therefore contains negation; indeed, it is negation as such and hence that other [Now] which it negates'.[55] Because of such negativity, the Now is not a discrete point — speaking of discrete temporal moments means to speak of *'pure abstractions'*, Hegel states — but necessarily relates to the future, its 'negative moment', as well as to the past, its 'pure result, or the truth of time. [...] The Now is only the synthesis [die Einheit] of these dimensions.'[56] Pre-empting criticisms of this radically negative concept of time, Hegel even asserts that 'this negativity is the absolute concept itself, infinity, the pure being-for-itself [...] Negativity is therefore the greatest power of all being, and hence the true way of investigating being is to consider it in its time, i.e. in its concept, which contains only vanishing moments.'[57]

The summary contained in the *Encyclopedia* of 1830 is not as grand in its wording, but more comprehensive in scope. Hegel here defines time and specifically the Now — the point in which all three dimensions of time intersect — as an 'abstract' but 'negative' being:

> Die Zeit, als die negative Einheit des Außersichseins, ist gleichfalls ein schlechthin Abstraktes, Ideelles. — Sie ist das Sein, das, indem es *ist, nicht* ist, und indem es *nicht* ist, *ist*, das *angeschaute* Werden [...] Die Zeit ist wie der Raum eine *reine Form* der *Sinnlichkeit* oder des *Anschauens*, das unsinnliche Sinnliche [...] die abstrakt *sich auf sich beziehende* Negativität, und in dieser Abstraktion ist noch kein reeller Unterschied. [...] Die Dimensionen der Zeit, die *Gegenwart, Zukunft* und *Vergangenheit*, sind das *Werden* der Äußerlichkeit als solches und dessen Auflösung in die Unterschiede des Seins [...] Das unmittelbare Verschwinden dieser Unterschiede in die *Einzelheit* ist die Gegenwart als *Jetzt*, welches als die Einzelheit *ausschließend* und zugleich schlechthin *kontinuierlich* in die anderen Momente, selbst nur dies Verschwinden seines Seins in Nichts und das Nichts in sein Sein ist. [...] Übrigens kommt es in der Natur, wo die Zeit *Jetzt* ist, nicht zum *bestehenden* Unterschiede von jenen Dimensionen; sie sind notwendig nur in der subjektiven Vorstellung, in der *Erinnerung* und in der *Furcht* oder *Hoffnung*. (TWA IX, 48–49, 51–52; §§ 258, 259)

> [Time, as the negative unity of being external to self, is also purely abstract and of an ideal nature. It is the being which, in that it *is*, is *not*, and in that it is *not, is*. It is *intuited* becoming [...] Time, like space, is a *pure form* of *sensibility* or *intuition;* it is the insensible factor in sensibility [...] abstract negativity *relating itself to itself*, and in this abstraction there is as yet no difference of a real nature. [...] The *present, future*, and *past*, the dimensions of time, constitute the *becoming* of externality as such, and its dissolution into the differences of being [...] The immediate disappearance of these differences into *singularity* is the present as *Now*, which as a singularity is exclusive, but at the same time continuously passes into the other moments, and so it is merely this disappearance of its being into nothing, and of nothing into its being. [...] Incidentally, in nature, where time is always *Now*, these dimensions do not constitute *existent* differences, for

> they are only necessary in subjective representation, in *memory*, and in *fear* or *hope*.][58]

This negative conception of time and presence partly resembles Husserl's concept of time-consciousness, according to which the present 'now' exists only in relation to the continuous flow of retention and protention.[59] Derrida, by contrast, was well aware of Hegel's concept of time, defining the present 'now' similarly as a 'non-presence' — Hegel wrote: 'non-being' — that is necessarily compounded with past (retentional) and future (protentional) moments and for this reason results from *différance*.[60]

Other contexts in which to understand Hegel's concept of time better and to situate it in the philosophical history of time include Kant's Transcendental Aesthetics, according to which 'time is nothing' in and of itself (KrV A 34), a formless void inside the subject that can be represented only through 'analogies' such as 'a line continuing to infinity' (KrV A 33), as well as the *Confessions* of Augustine of Hippo. Augustine was perhaps the first to stress the radical negativity of time, which he then contrasted with the divine gift of consciousness to perceive time positively, namely as duration, and thus connect the otherwise diverging dimensions of time.[61] The conception of time Aristotle develops in his *Physics* had a powerful influence on Hegel as well. Indeed, Hegel enormously admired this work for its 'speculative' grasp of nature, 'which surpasses the concepts of today' (TWA ixx, 173), although it would be an exaggeration to say, as Heidegger does in his otherwise competent recapitulation of Hegel's concept of time, that the latter 'has been drawn *directly* from the "Physics" of *Aristotle*'.[62] Finally, Bergson should be mentioned as an instructive contrast, because in criticizing differential concepts of time as the setting-apart of the 'organic' unity and indifferent 'multiplicity' of temporal duration, he represents the direct opponent of Hegel, whose definition of time as the 'negative unity of being *external* to self' spatializes time in precisely the way Bergson criticizes.[63]

The scenography immediately following the indication of 'now' serves to demonstrate that the identification of a specific point in space, 'here', is likewise based on negation and abstraction. Our protagonist, sense-certainty, targets a specific 'here', which she then points out in front of 'us', the observing phenomenologists. But the intended spatial location turns out to be, again, 'a *negative* This' (PhG 90/64★), a coordinate defined solely by its relation to what it is not, namely other points. The chosen 'here' is located to the right, but not the left, not above but below the tree; it is '*not this* Here, but a Before and Behind, an Above and Below, a Right and Left. The Above is itself similarly this manifold otherness [Anderssein] of above, below, etc. The Here, which was supposed to have been pointed out, vanishes in other Heres, but these likewise vanish' (PhG 89/64★). Consequently, the indication of a particular location, 'here', involves 'a complex space of possible demonstrations'.[64] It is defined by, and retained through, a network of differences and juxtapositions and thus implies, as Hegel puts it, 'a movement from the intended [gemeinten] Here through many Heres into the universal Here which is a simple plurality of Heres' (PhG 90/64★).

Although the network defining the intended location represents a synchronic 'complex' [Komplexion] (PhG 90/64*), as Hegel calls it, or an *'ensemble* [*Zusammen*] of many *Heres*' (PhG 92/66*), the identification of the chosen 'here' necessitates the exact opposite, the temporal differentiation and sequential explication, the *un*folding of this synchronic 'complex'. To know what 'here' is, it is necessary to relate the intended point to other points above and below, to the right and to the left, and so on, which is done through manual and verbal, deictic gestures. As a result of this process of demonstration, the synchronic network determining the location of 'here' precisely loses its integrity and dissolves into a series of differences.

Taken by themselves, 'here' and 'now' are utter abstractions, negative universals without concrete, positive existence. Only if the one is expressed through the other will they mean something definite, rather than nothing in particular. Thus, the *explicans* of space is time, and that of time space. This is the fundamental dialectic between time and space suggested by these two final scenographies of sense-certainty. The concrete manifestations of time and space, Here and Now, are not separate but interdependent elements of perception. Consequently, the identification of a specific point in space implies temporalization — that is to say, the *explication* of a synchronic 'complex' of Heres, which takes time. Conversely, the indication of a single moment in time would necessitate spatialization — that is to say, the mental demarcation of a point, and hence of a preceding and succeeding segment, on an otherwise unbroken *line* symbolizing the continuous passage of time.

Kant had already indicated this dialectic between time and space — long before Derrida reformulated it in the name of 'writing'.[65] In his First Critique, Kant writes that time can neither be seen nor thought of 'except under the image of a line, insofar as we draw it', whereas the perception of spatial figures always entails the temporal action of visually tracing or 'describing' [beschreiben] their outer limits and, therefore, a translation of spatial relations into 'succession' (KrV B 154–56). What Kant notes only in passing, Hegel places at the centre of his philosophy of nature. In the 1805 Jena Philosophy of Nature, Hegel proposes (GW VIII, 4–14) — by way of a somewhat labyrinthine deduction — that time 'comes out' of space and also represents the negative force separating space into three dimensions. In his 1819 lectures on the philosophy of nature, Hegel then stated their dialectic more plainly. According to one of his students, Hegel described the 'inner dialectic of space as the transition [das Übergehen] into time', and 'conversely time as a transition into space', so that 'the one is the product of the other' and 'conceptually contains the other'. This holds true, Hegel added, according to another student, even though 'we keep them separate in our thoughts [in unserer Vorstellung]', thus failing to notice their interdependence.[66] In the *Enzyklopädie* of 1830, the condensation of it all, Hegel finally writes that space is not only, as Kant suggests, pure and unlimited extension or 'continuity without difference' but also heterogeneity — a complex of *different* places — and therefore intrinsically connected to the process of self-negation and differentiation in which time originates. Similarly, he continues, time is not only a series of self-negating now-points or pure negativity but in its totality also continuity — an unbroken chain of *interconnected* moments — and therefore corresponds to 'the undifferentiated separateness' [das ununterschiedene Außereinander] of space in the abstract.⁶⁷

The (hi)story of sense-certainty

Having demonstrated the abstract generality of Here and Now as the existential markers of 'the This', Hegel finally expresses the true concept of sense-certainty:

> Es erhellt, daß die Dialektik der sinnlichen Gewißheit nichts anderes als die einfache Geschichte ihrer Bewegung oder ihrer Erfahrung und die sinnliche Gewißheit selbst nichts anderes als nur diese Geschichte ist. Das natürliche Bewußtsein geht deswegen auch zu diesem Resultat, was an ihr das Wahre ist, immer selbst fort und macht die Erfahrung darüber, aber vergißt es nur ebenso immer wieder und fängt die Bewegung von vorne an. (PhG 90)

> [It is clear that the dialectic of sense-certainty is nothing else but the simple story of its movement or of its experience, and sense-certainty itself is nothing else but this story. Natural consciousness, too, proceeds towards this result, which is its essential truth, and experiences it, but also forgets it time and again, starting the movement all over again.] (64*)

According to this speculative conclusion, which sums up the preceding notions and replaces them with a more reflected understanding, sense-certainty contains the story or history (*Geschichte*) of a dialectic movement. But in what sense could sense-certainty be said to consist in 'movement'? What does it mean that the content produced by this 'movement' takes the form of a 'story'? And finally, why does the 'movement' start over and over again, thus turning into a 'dialectic'? These three key terms surely need clarification.

As to the first term, 'movement', its meaning is easy to comprehend in light of the earlier findings. Above all, Hegel has shown that abstraction is necessary to specify the meaning or content of sense-certainty. Abstraction means negation: The apprehended 'this' is known as a *particular* 'this' by explicating what it is not; it is a 'here' that is not 'here', nor over 'there', and simultaneously a 'now' that is not 'now', nor 'thereafter' or 'before'. The result of such explication, which takes place in language and specifically through deictic gestures, is an unfolding sequence of differences that defines the particular meaning of sense-certainty. According to Hegel, this logical movement of negation corresponds to the self-negating movement of time itself — temporal succession, diachrony. It is the process of time that impels the 'movement' of sense-certainty, as well as all other forms of experience considered in the *Phenomenology*, because 'time is the negative in sensuousness [im Sinnlichen]' (TWA XII, 103) itself. Consequently, the perceptual schema or aesthesiology of sense-certainty is negativity, the negative articulation — one might even say disarticulation — of the immediately and positively felt certainty that something is through deictic demonstration.

Additionally, sense-certainty involves 'movement' in yet another sense. In capturing a certain 'this', its existence Here *and* Now, sense-certainty effectively coordinates these two fundamentals of being. Indeed, contrary to Hegel's purely analytic distinction between Here and Now, which abstracts from the synthetic being or 'the twofold shape' [der gedoppelten Gestalt] of 'the This' (PhG 84/59*), sense-certainty always deals with spatial and temporal being *at once*. Movement represents for Hegel the link between these two theoretically separate, but in reality inseparable, aspects of being, because movement is the real process translating time into space, and space into time, and for this reason also the concept connecting them. 'Movement', Hegel writes in the Jena philosophy of nature of 1805, represents 'the reality of time and space', because it is 'the immediate synthesis of time and space, yet a synthesis that involves absolute mediation [...] [movement] is time that really exists through space, or space that has been truly differentiated through time'.[68]

Obscure as the quote may sound, Hegel here simply adopts the view of modern mechanics and analytic geometry, according to which motion is precisely a relation between time and space to be observed empirically and calculated numerically.[69] Incidentally, Kant adopts the same view in noting (KrV A 41), prior to Hegel, that 'motion' [Bewegung] represents the concept 'uniting both elements', time and space, although for Kant motion represents neither a transcendental form of intuition (like time and space) nor a transcendental schema of the understanding (like temporal succession) but instead an empirical concept derived from perception. Since, however, the categorical distinction between empirical and transcendental concepts is suspended in the *Phenomenology* and indeed throughout the Hegelian system, time, space, and movement are altogether *real* concepts, facts of nature *and* cognition.

Wilhelm Purpus, a late nineteenth-century philologist working as a Gymnasium teacher at Nuremberg (just as Hegel did before becoming Professor at Heidelberg), explains the meaning of 'movement' in the sense-certainty chapter by drawing on a different source. Unaware of the 1805 Jena Philosophy of Nature, which credits Zeno only in passing (GW VIII, 16) for having discovered the dialectic between Here and Now, Purpus refers to Hegel's later *Vorlesungen über die Geschichte der Philosophie* instead.[70] But here, too, Hegel claims that the 'originator' [Anfänger] (TWA xviii, 295) of dialectical thought, Zeno, regarded movement as the synthesis of time and space, summarizing Zeno's — or rather his own — position as follows:

> Das Wesen der Zeit und des Raums ist die Bewegung [...] Als Einheit der Negativität und Kontinuität ist die Bewegung als Begriff, als Gedanke ausgesprochen; an ihnen aber eben ist also weder die Kontinuität noch die Punktualität als das Wesen zu setzen. Für die Vorstellung sind diese beiden Momente selbst unzertrennlich. [...] Die Bewegung ist das Unendliche als Einheit dieser Entgegengesetzten der Zeit und des Raums. (TWA xviii, 310)
>
> [Movement is the essence of time and space [...] Conceptually speaking, or as an idea, movement is the synthesis of negativity and continuity, and so neither continuity nor punctiformity can be posited as its essence. These two moments cannot be represented separately. [...] Movement is the infinite as synthesis of these opposed elements, time and space.]

The meaning of the second key term from Hegel's speculative conclusion, *Geschichte*, is perhaps less obvious. What could it mean, exactly, to describe the knowledge of sense-certainty as a 'story' that is subject to an inherent 'dialectic' of negation and forgetting? Although sense-certainty appears to connect 'my' sensory intention to the objective being of a particular, it turns out that sense-certainty is not an instantaneous impression but essentially a 'result', as the conclusion states, the result of a process of negation and abstraction.

This processual, and hence temporal, nature of sense-certainty illuminates in what sense it is a 'story'. For like a narrative story, which discursively represents, and thus gradually unfolds, an interconnected complex of places, persons, and occurrences — a narrative world, the 'story' of sense-certainty, too, consists of two opposite temporal layers: a *diachronic process* and a *synchronic result* or *meaning*. More specifically, sense-certainty involves a diachronic movement of negation that, in differentiating among a totality of heres and nows, produces a complex of negative coordinates — a series of not-heres and not-nows — through which 'the This' is positively defined in terms of time and place.

Because of its double meaning, the 'story' of sense-certainty represents a 'speculative' concept — a word or phrase, as Hegel defines it in the *Wissenschaft der Logik* (TWA v, 114), that unites two opposite meanings and thus 'sublates' (*aufheben*) their opposition, at once preserving and suspending it, and luckily enough for philosophers, he adds in the same passage, 'the German language has several such words'. *Geschichte* is one of them, and so is English 'story', because both designate a diachronic process or a sequence of events — *a* story — and at the same time the meaning or result of this sequence — *the* story as a whole. Insofar as *a* story refers to fictional events, we are used to calling it narration or narrative. Insofar as it refers to real events, we call it history. But regardless of reference, we still suppose that there is another story hidden within the communicated chain of events — their inner logic and motivation, *the* story of what happened.

It is not at all trivial but profoundly symptomatic that narratology is haunted by the speculative ambiguity of 'story' to this day. To eradicate this ambiguity, choices are made. Some narratologists define the inner connection or motivation of events as 'the story' of a narrative, juxtaposing it with its articulation through narrative discourse, whereas others use the term in the opposite sense, defining story as the discursive form in which events are told and their inner connection is gradually revealed. Seymour Chatman, for example, defines story in the former sense, while Mieke Bal understands it in the latter sense.[71]

To underscore the ambiguity of the term, instead of eradicating it, one might say that every story is a (hi)story, since it combines a diachronic process (history) with a synchronic meaning (*the* story as a whole). Diachronic explication and development — history — is necessary for the overall meaning — *the* story — to come to light, even though this emergent whole shapes the historical development from the beginning. Every story thus contains a 'temporal dialectic', as Paul Ricoeur put it, specifically a tension between linear succession and synchronic configuration.[72]

The (hi)story of sense-certainty is — third and last term from Hegel's conclusion — subject to a 'dialectic' of forgetting: 'It is clear that the dialectic of sense-certainty is nothing else but the simple story of its movement [...] Natural consciousness, too, proceeds toward this result, which is its essential truth [...] but also forgets it time and again, starting the movement all over' (PhG 90/64★). Unable to arrive at a positive result, namely the determinate knowledge of *what* the noticed 'this' is, sense-certainty must continue its forgetful movement of negation and abstraction, for this is the only way in which it perceives particulars thus far. The eminent negativity and confusion of this process, or its forgetfulness, in fact represent the core of a 'dialectic'. For according to Hegel's succinct formula (GW x.2, 830), a 'dialectic' entails just that, 'the dynamization and confusion' [die Bewegung und Verwirrung] of abstract distinctions and oppositions. Dialectics thus represents the 'negative' side of reason, Hegel writes in the first preface to the *Wissenschaft der Logik*, insofar as it 'dissolves the determinations of the understanding into nothing' (TWA v, 16). The counterpart to dialectics is speculation, which Hegel describes as the 'positive' side of reason and the proper outcome of philosophical discourse insofar as it replaces (or 'sublates') the dialectical vacillation and confusion with better, synthetic concepts that reveal 'the *universal*, comprehending the particular [das Besondere] therein' (ibid.).[73]

Given its definition as 'dynamization and confusion', Hegel cannot think of dialectics as a safe method to miraculously proceed from 'thesis' and 'antithesis' to some higher 'synthesis' — terms, Walter Kaufmann points out, Hegel hardly ever uses.[74] On the contrary, dialectical thinking is the radical undoing of presumed stabilities and certainties, including method itself, turning all of that 'into nothing', as Hegel said, into endless loops and circles; which is why, for Hegel, dialectics without speculation amounts to little more than sophistry, to a philosophy without truth.

To deserve the title, the 'dialectic' of sense-certainty must also dynamize and confuse certain preconceived notions. This happens in three ways, the scenographies of sense-certainty taught 'us'. The *first* dialectical confusion consists in the fact that even the most immediate form of sensory apprehension relies upon negation and abstraction to specify and retain the apprehended this-here-now. The *second* dialectical confusion consists in the proposition that the existence of 'this' depends on 'my' intending it, though consciousness has yet to find a way to transform this connection into a lasting relationship, instead of forgetting it time and again. The *third* dialectical confusion concerns the relationship between Here and Now. Although separate in theory, time and space have turned out to be, in practice, inseparable elements of perception, with the one explicating the other.

Operating as sense-certainty, consciousness cannot yet fathom these dialectical results. The immediately felt certainty that 'this' thing exists right 'here' and right 'now' vanishes within the blink of an eye. Consciousness has to reassure itself of its existence at each and every moment, over and over again. In its current shape, consciousness does not yet know how to 'preserve' or 'store up' — one meaning of *aufheben* ('to sublate') — the perceived certainty, nor the (hi)story behind it.

This impasse incites consciousness to act by 'elevating' itself — another meaning of *aufheben* — from sense-certainty to the level of perception (*Wahrnehmung*). On this advanced standpoint, consciousness discovers the self-evident solution to the dialectic of sense-certainty: the substantiality of material things. Things are, as Hegel puts it, 'the truth of perception' (PhG 96/69*), because they are the causes of perception — causes sense-certainty merely noticed without perceiving them. Specifically, things unite within one and the same place a complex of heres and nows and thus form *permanent* wholes — substantial units with certain properties that remain the same over time and regardless of what 'I' sense and mean. For that reason, material things are not affected by the first dialectical confusion of sense-certainty, the dialectic of Here and Now. The second dialectical confusion, the unstable deictic nature of 'the This', doesn't concerns them either, because things *reify* 'the This' in the form of substances with permanent properties. Finally, and most importantly, material things seem unaffected by negation and abstraction — the first dialectical confusion of sense-certainty — in that they have permanent and independent existence in themselves, an apparent positivity or determinacy that would revoke the negativity of sense-certainty. Thus, the substantiality of things embodies and preserves the (hi)story of sense-certainty while simultaneously 'cancelling' — the third meaning of *aufheben* as a speculative term — its three dialectical confusions.

Strictly speaking, however, 'no shape of consciousness turns directly into the following shape'.[75] Speculation and sublation are not transitions taking place within the diegetic scene but operations of thought performed by 'us', the phenomenological spectators. 'We' are asked by the narrator to identify the contradictions of sense-certainty, and then asked to *descry*[76] their speculative solution: perception.

§3. Object Perception (Relation)

Der Weg zum Konkreten erfordert den Umweg über die Abstraktion.[77]

[To reach the concrete one must take a detour through abstraction.]

Perception as determinate negation

'Immediate certainty does not take in the truth [das Wahre], for its truth [Wahrheit] is the universal, even though it wants to take in the *This*' (PhG 93/67★). That phrase, which opens the *Phenomenology*'s second chapter, 'Perception, or, the Thing and Deception' [Die Wahrnehmung oder das Ding und die Täuschung], provides the immediate reason why sense-certainty must eventually transform into 'perception' — the perception of material objects and their properties. For although sense-certainty *notices that* something exists 'here' and 'now', it fails to *perceive what* it is. Sense-certainty cannot grasp the essence of the apprehended object as defined by its sensory properties. Essence or whatness remains peripheral to existence or thatness in sense-certainty, because in it properties merely 'tag along' (*beiherspielen*) with the noticed particular, illustrating that it exists.

It is, therefore, this most universal 'principle' of all, pure being or sheer existence, that 'has *arisen* for us' through sense-certainty (PhG 93/67★). The transition from sense-certainty to perception thus corresponds to the conceptual transition from sheer existence (thatness) to essence (whatness). Unlike 'us', however, the heroine of the second chapter, perception, is not yet aware of principles such as universality or existence, nor does she understand the conceptual operations on which both depend, negation and abstraction. Similarly, perception does not comprehend but only presupposes the determinations of being (quality, quantity, and measure) as well as the two key categories of reflection (identity and difference) — logical concepts Hegel belabours in the *Wissenschaft der Logik* over hundreds of pages.[78]

What perception can do, however, is to discriminate among sensations and ascribe these to one or several things as properties. This is possible because contrary to sense-certainty, perception knows and actively employs negation: 'The wealth of sensory knowledge belongs to perception, not to immediate certainty, wherein it was a peripheral aspect [das Beiherspielende]; for only perception contains *negation*, that is, difference or variety [Mannigfaltigkeit], within its own essence' (PhG 94/67★). Perception has the ability to make distinctions and can therefore identify 'this' complex of heres and nows as a '*thing with many properties*' (PhG 94/67★).

Perception thus understands the basic form and critical operation of all knowledge, difference (*Unterschied*) and differentiation (*Unterscheidung*), which are emphatically described as '*the determinate foundation* [Urgrund] *of all activity and self-movement*' in the *Wissenschaft der Logik* (TWA VI, 47). In contrast to the common notion that 'something is what it is', Hegel claims, also in the perception chapter, that something is determined by what it is not, hence through negation. The process of perception fully actualizes this concept of determination in that it identifies a property by way of negation and contrast. The perception of 'a *distinctive, determinate* property' [eine *unterschiedene, bestimmte* Eigenschaft] is for Hegel the result of opposing an at first indeterminate perception to a 'not-this', which does not, however, amount to nothing 'but rather to a determinate nothing [bestimmtes Nichts], or, *a nothing with content [ein Nichts von einem Inhalte]*' — to a nothing that has been '*sublated*' (PhG 94/68★). Consequently, perception follows the logic of determinate negation, while the kind of '*sublation*' [das *Aufheben*] thus accomplished involves, as Hegel puts it, 'both *negation* and *preservation*' [ein *Negieren* und ein *Aufbewahren* zugleich] (ibid.).[79]

Perception as conceived by Hegel means determinate negation, wherefore perception, too, 'depends on a correct understanding of the status and significance of negativity' (TWA IV, 434).[80] To illustrate this proposition, consider the following. A grain you immediately notice as 'this' sensation on your tongue is determined by, first, contrasting it in thought or in action with the different tastes of other things. You thus abstract from the particular character (*Besonderheit*) of the initial taste, defining it in negative terms instead, which is to say, in relation to other(s). To establish the positive identity of the noticed taste — *what* it is — these contrasts are, next, negated again and thus cancelled out (*aufgehoben*): 'This' grain, you conclude, is not a 'not-this'; it tastes as it does precisely because it does *not* taste like 'not-this'. This double negation — not a not-this — does not amount to nothing, to pick up Hegel's phrase, but to '*a nothing with content*'. You now ascribe the taste to a substance as one of its properties, thereby creating a new, determinate content that both cancels and preserves — sublates — the contrasts on which your perceptual judgment is based. Naturally, the perceptual judgment happens in a short time. What comes to mind is the positive result, not the negative process, of perception. Still, recognizing, for example, 'this' taste on your tongue as the kind of *sharpness* belonging to a grain of *salt* at the same time implies a knowledge of what it is not, for example, the kind of *sweetness* belonging to a cube of *sugar* or the *sour* taste characterizing *vinegar*. This is, in a nutshell, the (hi)story of perception.

Assuming that object perception enacts the logic of determinate negation, what about the perceptual object? How does the object relate to the act of perception? As the triple dialectic of sense-certainty suggests, and the chapter title, 'Perception, or, the Thing and Deception [Täuschung]', indicates, consciousness is operating under the assumption that *things* are the truth of perception. Their physical nature seems to determine the structure of perception. At the same time, the chapter title hints at the possibility that this assumption may be a misconception (*Täuschung*) predicated upon the false belief that material things are indeed the appropriate measure of knowledge.

To assess the epistemic structure and consistency of perception, Hegel isolates the agents constituting a scene of perception, namely the perceptual object and the perceiving subject, considering them at first separately. In addition to these physical agents, Hegel distinguishes the inherent concepts of perception, namely 'One' [Eins] and 'Also' [Auch], which more or less correspond to the physical attributes of a thing as either one coherent entity or a bundle of many properties.

Having defined these terms, the philosophical narrator, Hegel, stages three scenes of perception to demonstrate their scope — and their limitations.

The recursivity of perception

Like all other forms of knowledge, Hegel understands perception (*Wahrnehmung*) as a relation: Perception connects 'the object' to the 'act of perceiving' [das Wahrnehmen] by means of the senses (PhG 93/67★). The act of perceiving, the subjective end of this relationship, involves above all the registration as well as the successive 'discrimination' [Unterscheidung] and 'unfolding' [Entfaltung] of perceptible qualities, a perceptual procedure Hegel also describes as the 'movement of pointing out' [Bewegung des Aufzeigens] (ibid.), its result being the differentiation of the stream of sensations into distinct perceptions.

If perceiving means chiefly differentiation, the determining source of perception — the thing or the object — must contain the perceived qualities all at once, simultaneously. Indeed, the thing is the physical medium and permanent locus of these qualities, their synthetic unity or 'togetherness' [Zusammengefaßtsein] (PhG 93/67★). Recalling the concepts of sense-certainty, which are preserved and incorporated in perception, the thing of perception could be described as a *substantial* 'this' — as a permanent ensemble or 'togetherness' not only of heres and nows but also of various properties. This concept of thinghood no doubt reflects the common notion of *'concrete individual things'* as 'bearers of properties, which are capable of persisting identically through time while undergoing *qualitative*, and in many cases also *compositional*, change' and collectively 'constitute the basic furniture of the world'.[81]

In relating acts of perceiving to the composition of the object, perception creates knowledge, the knowledge of perception, which concerns sensory variety and objective unity in equal measure. Whether these numeric as well as temporal opposites can be coordinated without contradiction is the major crux of perception. 'For us', the philosophical narrator and his well-informed readers, it is clear that 'both are essential' to perception (PhG 93/67★). Neither aspect may take precedence over the other in perception precisely because its source, the object, displays both physical unity and a variety of properties.

Perceptual consciousness, by contrast, regards the object only as an either/or, Hegel stipulates, perceiving it as either *one* thing or *a cluster* of sensory properties. And so, since they seem 'opposed to each other' in perception, 'only one can be the essential moment in the relation, and the distinction of essential and unessential moment must be shared between them. One of them, the object, defined as onefold being [als das Einfache bestimmt], is the essence regardless of whether it is perceived or not, whereas the act of perceiving, as a movement, is the unessential moment, the unstable factor [das Unbeständige]' (PhG 93/67★), since in discovering manifold sensory differences, the act of perceiving contradicts the object's 'onefold' unity.

Having thus defined the natures of the perceptual object and the perceiving subject, Hegel elaborates on the logic of their relation by introducing the functions of 'Also' [Auch] and 'One' [Eins]. What do these terms determining the logic of perception stand for, and what is their operational effect in a relationship — which means, in practice, a scene — of perception? It would be a mistake to translate them into the purely numeric concepts of 'many' and 'single'. Similarly reductive would it be to interpret them as 'plurality' (the thing as a bundle of many properties) and 'unity' (the thing as a single unit). If Hegel had meant to address primarily the quantitative-numeric logic of perception, he could have chosen more specific terms — precisely the pairs unity/plurality (*Einheit/Vielheit*) and single/many (*eins/viele*). The quantitative crux no doubt plays a role in object perception, but it does not exhaust the matter. Also and One have a more complex meaning, because the quantitative immediately correlates with the qualitative dimension of perception. They are, therefore, also means of relating the diachronically perceived diversity of things (sensory properties) to their permanent synchronic identity (objective unity), thereby addressing the conflicting *temporalities* of perception.[82]

Additionally, Also and One are tangible reflections of the thoughts of '*universality and individuality*' [*Allgemeinheit* und *Einzelheit*], Hegel writes (PhG 106/78★), which first came to light with sense-certainty. The lexical similarity between the *Eins* of perception and the *Einzelheit* characterizing 'the This' in sense-certainty underscores this conceptual continuity — even though in perception, *Einzelheit* as well as *Einheit*, 'unity', which is another cognate of the numeral *ein*, are understood in terms of *Besonderheit*, as depending upon 'particular' qualities or properties. But perception, too, cannot yet fathom 'thoughts', as Hegel points out at the beginning of the third chapter (PhG 107/79★), so that the One and the Also of perception represent ideas *in action*. They are cognitive operations as well as logical attributes or determinations of objects, but never explicit concepts, because the latter belong to the domain of abstract thinking, rather than perception, which originates in the understanding, the shape of consciousness succeeding perception.

At first sight, the One of perception seems to belong to the successive discrimination of qualities 'one by one', hence to the act of perceiving, while the Also appears to reflect the togetherness (*Zusammengefaßtsein*) of properties constituting objective identity and unity. As we shall see, however, the relation between these terms and agents of perception is much more confusing or dialectical. The subject perceives this *one* quality here and now, separate from others, but thereafter *also* this, *also* that, and another *as well*. Meanwhile the object remains this *one* thing, but in being *one and the same*, it *also* contains qualities — this one here, *also* that one, *as well as* another, simultaneously. Evidently, the One and the Also are essential determinations of both the act and the object of perception.

The fact that perception constantly turns the one into the other determination, vacillating between them, further complicates the matter. One and Also are, in other words, dialectical terms of perception. Successively perceived qualities or Ones give rise to sequences that in combination constitute the object's set of properties or its simultaneous Also. Successivity (the One by One) thus turns into simultaneity (Also), at least conceptually. Conversely, the object's characteristic identity and unity turns into a chain of differences and thus into a sequence of Ones as soon as it is examined. Undivided simultaneity (Also) thus turns into successive qualities (One).

Hegel first relates the Also to the perceptual object, thus identifying the Also with 'thinghood' [Dingheit] as such, meaning the universal substrate of every thing. In contrast to 'this', 'here', and 'now', which are abstract universals without specific meaning, the Also of thinghood designates a specific or 'positive universality' (PhG 95/*69) as it permanently joins together a number of perceptible qualities (or 'thises') within one and the same place. Consequently, the Also of thinghood, which Lambert Wiesing[83] considers Hegel's most original contribution to the philosophy of perception, represents the universal *medium* wherein various qualities coexist simultaneously and without affecting each other:

> Die einfache sich selbst gleiche Allgemeinheit selbst aber ist wieder von diesen ihren Bestimmtheiten unterschieden und *frei*; sie ist das reine sich auf sich beziehen oder das *Medium*, worin diese Bestimmtheiten alle sind, sich also in ihr als in einer *einfachen* Einheit *durchdringen*, ohne sich aber *zu berühren*; denn eben durch die Teilnahme an dieser Allgemeinheit sind sie gleichgültig für sich. — Dies abstrakte allgemeine Medium [...] ist nichts anderes als das *Hier* und *Jetzt*, wie es sich erwiesen hat, nämlich als ein *einfaches zusammen* von vielen [Hier und Jetzt] [...] Dieses *Auch* ist also das reine Allgemeine selbst oder das Medium, die sie so zusammenfassende *Dingheit*. (PhG 94–95)

> [The simple, self-identical universality is itself distinct and *free* from its specific qualities. It is the pure state of self-relation, or the *medium* in which all these specificities are, and in which as a *simple* unity they therefore *permeate* each other, but without *coming into contact*; for it is precisely through participation in this universality that they exist by themselves, indifferently. — This abstract universal medium [...] is nothing else than what *Here* and *Now* have proved themselves to be, viz. a *simple ensemble* of many [Heres and Nows] [...] This *Also* is the pure universal itself; it is the medium, the *thinghood* keeping them together.] (68*)

Connected and coordinated by the Also, thinghood subsists regardless of the differences it contains. It is the universal substrate of material bodies and as such a supposedly simple or, literally, onefold (*einfach*) unit whose manifold sensory qualities affect neither each other, nor the medium containing them. In logical terms, the Also of thinghood stands for self-identity and pure self-relation — the absence of relation to other(s). These logical determinations find expression, Hegel clarifies later (PhG 97/71*), in the thing's 'continuity' or permanence on the one hand and in its being a self-sufficient '*community*' [*Gemeinschaft*] of sensory qualities on the other. Indeed, a thing can be called self-identical only insofar as its set of properties remains the same over time, and its substrate is a *simple* unity without external relationships only insofar as it is universally indifferent, or 'distinct and *free* from its specific qualities'.

To illustrate the Also of thinghood and how it is perceived, Hegel asks us to consider a grain of salt:

> Dies Salz ist einfaches Hier und zugleich vielfach; es ist weiß und *auch* scharf, *auch* kubisch gestaltet, *auch* von bestimmter Schwere usw. Alle diese vielen Eigenschaften sind in einem einfachen *Hier*, worin sie sich also durchdringen; keine hat ein anderes Hier als die andere, sondern jede ist allenthalben in

> demselben, worin die andere ist; und zugleich, ohne durch verschiedene Hier geschieden zu sein, affizieren sie sich in dieser Durchdringung nicht; das Weiße affiziert oder verändert das Kubische nicht, beide nicht das Scharfe usw., sondern da jede selbst einfaches *sich auf sich beziehen* ist, läßt sie die anderen ruhig und bezieht sich nur durch das gleichgültige *Auch* auf sie. (PhG 95)
>
> [This salt is a simple *Here*, and at the same time manifold; it is white and *also* tart, *also* cubical in shape, *also* of a specific gravity, etc. All these many properties are in one simple *Here*, in which they interpenetrate; none has a different Here from the others, but each is contained within the same place where the others are. And, at the same time, without being separated by different Heres, they do not affect each other in this interpenetration. The whiteness does not affect or change the cubical shape, and neither affects the tart taste, etc.; on the contrary, since each is in a simple *state of self-relation* it leaves the others alone, relating to these only through the indifferent *Also*.] (68–69★)

Hegel's grain of salt is self-identical and indifferent insofar as its various properties (white, tart, cubic, etc.) are permanently gathered in one and the same place. It is, in other words, a simultaneous Also whose composition never changes but statically and independently endures. Just as any other thing this grain of salt is, therefore, a *substance*.

This characterization, as well as the earlier definition of the Also of thinghood as identity devoid of difference, recall the passage from the preface to the *Phenomenology* in which Hegel defines the 'permanence or substance' of a thing precisely as 'self-identity', immediately adding that in case of 'disparity', the thing would 'break up'.[84] The perception of thinghood thus marks the first encounter with substance as both an independent physical reality (permanence) and a logical relation (self-identity).

Considering the overall intent of the *Phenomenology* to think substance as subject, this encounter must reveal the shortcoming of substantiality as a criterion of truth. The quote from the preface already indicates these shortcomings, namely, the fundamental incompatibility of substance with notions of difference and disparity. For although the accidents or particular properties of substances are manifold, the very category of substance traditionally represents the simple and indifferent substrate of all things. In contrast to empiricist repudiations of substance, however, according to which — in the phrase of David Hume[85] — the 'continu'd existence' of an object is a 'fiction' of the human mind, Hegel does not deny the permanence of substances but in fact believes in their reality. To avoid Hume's sceptical conclusion, Hegel will therefore reinterpret things as complex *subjects of relationships* characterized by both identity and disparity. How to reconcile these opposites is the logical crux of perception.

Disparity is based on difference, the other key determination of perception. The term Hegel uses to account for the experience of difference in perception is 'the One' [das Eins], which is tantamount to 'the *moment of negation*' (PhG 96/69★). Negation is inherent to perception to the extent that the perceptual object is internally differentiated — it has various properties — and also distinguished from other things. The Also of thinghood may be universally indifferent, but the specific set of qualities therein contained is not. In fact, the concrete identity or particularity of a thing — its characteristic set of properties — depends on the exact opposite, difference and distinction:

> Nämlich wenn die vielen bestimmten Eigenschaften schlechterdings gleichgültig wären und sich durchaus nur auf sich selbst bezögen, so wären sie keine *bestimmten*, denn sie sind dies nur, insofern sie sich *unterscheiden* und sich *auf andere* als entgegengesetzte *beziehen*. Nach dieser Entgegensetzung aber können sie nicht in der einfachen Einheit ihres Mediums zusammen sein, die ihnen ebenso wesentlich ist als die Negation; die Unterscheidung derselben, insofern sie nicht eine gleichgültige, sondern ausschließende, Anderes negierende ist, fällt also außer diesem einfachen Medium; und dieses ist daher nicht nur ein *Auch*, gleichgültige Einheit, sondern auch *Eins, ausschließende Einheit*. — Das Eins ist das *Moment der Negation*, wie es selbst auf eine einfache Weise sich auf sich bezieht und Anderes ausschließt und wodurch die *Dingheit* als *Ding* bestimmt ist. (PhG 95–96)

> [If the many specific properties were strictly indifferent to one another and indeed pure self-relation, they would not be *specific*; for they are specific properties only in so far as they *differentiate* themselves from one another and *relate to others* as to their opposites. Being opposed to one another, however, they cannot be together in the simple unity of their medium, which is just as essential to them as negation. The distinction of properties thus falls outside of this simple medium in so far as this distinction is not indifferent but exclusive and so negates others; and the medium, therefore, is not merely an *Also*, an indifferent unity, but a *One* as well, a *unit excluding others*. — The One is the *moment of negation*; that is, a simple way of relating to self while excluding others, as well as the means of identifying *thinghood* as a *thing*.] (69★)

The One means negation of other(s) through exclusion, thereby producing differences and contrasts. Such contrasts between exclusive Ones inform perception in two ways. On the one hand, an individual property is perceived as a One. We notice, for example, the contrast between the green leaf and the red berries next to it. In fact, these colours cannot coexist without affecting each other, because if combined, the leaf would look yellow to the eye. This One — greenness — thus excludes the other One — redness. Such rules of exclusion restrict the possible combination of properties in a thing. On the other hand, the entire thing is One insofar as it differs from another thing or One. The leaf is this One thing because, in being green and flat, also smooth and thin, lightweight, bitter as well, the leaf clearly differs from that other One, the round red berries next to it, which are also firm, sweet, and fragrant as well. Exclusive oneness thus determines a thing's characteristic identity or particularity — *what* it is.

The *Wissenschaft der Logik* rehashes the idea that the One is essential to both the distinction of individual properties and the thing as a whole. Like properties, the thing is defined by exclusion and contrast and thus represents a '*negative unit*', or in spatial terms, a 'punctiform' One separated from and distinguished against the other Ones around it. The antithesis to such exclusivity is, of course, the universal inclusivity of 'an indifferent manifold of permanence' for which the Also stands in the *Phenomenology*, and the *Wissenschaft der Logik* as well.[86]

The definition of the One as the 'moment of negation' recalls Hegel's basic definition of subjectivity, the antithesis of substantiality. In the preface to the *Phenomenology*, Hegel identifies 'subject' precisely with the movement of *'negativity'* that divides the simple identity of substance into opposites and so necessitates reflection and mediation (PhG 23/10*). Thus, in dealing with the conflict between One and Also, perception also grapples, if unwittingly, with the most fundamental issue of the *Phenomenology*, the necessity to think substance as subject, and conversely, subject as substance.[87] This, indeed, is the experience of perception, that self-identical permanence is based on difference, and difference on connection and reflection. Thinghood (Also, substance) cannot be without negation and difference (One, subject), because otherwise the thing of perception would not be that unified and persistent community of properties for which we *take* it.

Despite their different effects, namely exclusion as against inclusion, Hegel has, in fact, defined both One and Also as types of 'unity' or 'oneness' [Einheit]. This is no terminological lapse on his part but, on the contrary, an indication of their mutual dependency. With this observation, we enter the *dialectic* of perception, which — to recall Hegel's shorthand — 'dynamizes and confuses' the at first self-evident difference between One and Also. In order to be a particular One, the perceptual object must be an Also, and in order to be a particular Also, it must be One. Indeed, perceived as this One unit excluding others, the thing of perception still depends on the Also of thinghood, because it is this particular One only in contrast to another thing bearing a different set of properties — a different Also. Conversely, the Also of thinghood is an indifferent and simple ensemble (*einfaches Zusammen*) only in theory, but practically depends on internal differentiation, hence on the One, because otherwise it would not be a simultaneous *ensemble* of properties — for example, white, also cubic, also tart, crunchy as well, all at the same time.

The dialectic is, therefore, that perception is equally justified in apprehending the thing as a One or as an Also, and because of this dialectic paradox or antinomy, the process of perception turns into a *recursion*. By that I mean 'the repeated application of a rule, definition, or procedure to successive results', or more plainly a routine requiring 'many successive executions'.[88] Perception represents a recursive routine insofar as it turns each immediate One into Also, and each Also again into distinct Ones, constantly vacillating between these two. And so, unable to generate a third output that would end (or sublate) the recursion, perception must go *in circles*, which is precisely the shortcoming Hegel singles out. Perception, he writes, is a 'cycle' — literally a 'going in circles' [Kreislauf] — that never comes to a conclusion (PhG 98/71*).[89]

Defenders of clear-cut distinctions will object to Hegel's terminological design, while Hegel scholars like Robert Stern will plead in his defence that dialectical concepts are necessary for a 'fundamentally holistic' understanding of objects.[90] Kant scholars, to add a third intermediary party, will perhaps point to the category of 'community' or *Wechselwirkung* as a conceptual solution to the dialectic of object perception.[91] Or one might simply say, paraphrasing Novalis, that there is a sphere of knowledge 'in which *each proof is a circle* — or an error — in which nothing is demonstrable' (N II, 622 #634). At any rate, One and Also presuppose each other in the process of perception.

Hegel himself recapitulates the interconnected meaning of the terms in writing that 'the Thing as the truth of perception [...] is (a) an indifferent, passive universality, the *Also* of the many properties or rather *matters*; (b) negation [...] or the *One*, the exclusion of opposite properties' (PhG 96/69*). Thus, the Also designates the indifferent substrate underlying every thing, or the universal medium of properties, whereas the One stands for the particularity of a thing as made up of this specific, as opposed to another, set of properties. These two interdependent aspects come together in the perception of properties:

> γ) die vielen Eigenschaften selbst, die Beziehung der zwei ersten Momente; die Negation, wie sie sich auf das gleichgültige Element bezieht und sich darin als eine Menge von Unterschieden ausbreitet; der Punkt der Einzelheit in dem Medium des Bestehens in die Vielheit ausstrahlend. Nach der Seite, daß diese Unterschiede [d.h. Eigenschaften] dem gleichgültigen Medium angehören, sind sie selbst allgemein, beziehen sich nur auf sich und affizieren sich nicht; nach der Seite aber, daß sie der negativen Einheit angehören, sind sie zugleich ausschließend, haben aber diese entgegengesetzte Beziehung notwendig an Eigenschaften, die aus *ihrem Auch* entfernt sind. Die sinnliche Allgemeinheit, oder die *unmittelbare* Einheit des Seins und des Negativen, ist erst so *Eigenschaft*, insofern das Eins und die reine Allgemeinheit aus ihr entwickelt und voneinander unterschieden sind und sie diese miteinander zusammenschließt; diese Beziehung derselben auf die reinen wesentlichen Momente [des Auch und Eins] vollendet erst das *Ding* [der Wahrnehmung]. (PhG 96)

> [(c) the many *properties* themselves, the relation of the first two moments; or negation as it relates to the indifferent element and therein expands into a host of differences; the individual point of individuality in the medium of permanence radiating forth into plurality. In so far as these differences belong to the indifferent medium they are themselves universal, they are related only to themselves and do not affect one another. But in so far as they belong to the negative unit they at the same time exclude others; this contrastive relation they necessarily have to properties that are removed from *their Also*. The sensuous universality, or the *immediate* unity of being and the negative, is thus a *property* only in so far as the One and the pure universality are developed from it, distinguished from each other, and joined together by it; this relation of the property to the pure essential moments finally completes the *thing* [of perception].] (69–70*)

Although abstract and obscure, the passage contains two salient points: to perceive the nature of things, one must determine their properties, and this happens by way of determinate negation. At first, the thing appears as this-here-now with as yet undifferentiated qualities; this is the brief phase of sense-certainty or 'sensuous universality' during which 'the One and the pure universality' — the Also — emerge. Next, the initial simplicity of this-here-now is negated by perception, which alternately perceives its object as *either* an Also of qualities *or* One distinctive unit; this is the phase during which the two 'pure essential moments' of the perceptual object, Also and One, are 'distinguished from each other' through recursive acts of perception. In fact, the better part of the perception chapter deals with this dialectic of perception, demonstrating it, as before, in scenographic form. Finally, the opposition of One and Also is annulled (or sublated) by recognizing properties to be necessarily both universal and specific, indifferent and distinct, independent and dependent, included in some but excluded from other things; this is the phase concluding the perception chapter, where the One and the Also of perception are 'joined together' by the understanding through *explanation*.

The demands of perception are thus quite high. Consciousness, we have been told, needs to develop a relationship that successfully combines the diachronic with the synchronic aspects of perception, or the sequence of distinct sensations with the thing's unity and togetherness. To do so, consciousness needs to reconcile One and Also logically and thus overcome the antinomy of perception. To put it in Kantian terms, consciousness needs to grasp the community (*Gemeinschaft*) of substance and accidents as reciprocity (*Wechselwirkung*) and thus develop a conception of objecthood allowing for reciprocal coordination, rather than simple causation. For indeed, the thing consists of 'nothing but reciprocal relations [Wechselbeziehung]', Hegel writes in the *Wissenschaft der Logik* (TWA VI, 137).[92]

The intervention of reflection

To scrutinize the content of perception, its knowledge, Hegel returns to a dramatic mode of presentation. During the first scenography of perception, consciousness is just as passive as it is in the mode of sense-certainty, being once more 'pure apprehension' [reines Auffassen] (PhG 96/70*). The reason for this passivity is the fear that 'if consciousness itself did anything in perception [bei diesem Nehmen], it would by such adding or subtraction alter the truth [das Wahre]' of the object (PhG 96–97/70*). Objective being (*das Wahre*, as Hegel calls it) takes precedence over the passive act of perceiving (*das Nehmen*), since the object exists and remains identical to itself 'regardless [gleichgültig] of whether it is perceived or not' (PhG 93/67*), whereas the perceiving consciousness is 'the changeable and inessential' element in a scene of perception (PhG 97/70*). This realist commitment to the object's autonomous existence remains in effect throughout the entire chapter. If contradictions or discrepancies occur in perception, they must have been, therefore, caused by consciousness.

In fact, perceptual consciousness is itself aware of the 'possibility of misperception' [Möglichkeit der Täuschung], Hegel writes, meaning the possibly false 'connection [Beziehen] of the diverse moments of its apprehension to one another. If a discrepancy [Ungleichheit] makes itself felt in the course of this comparison, then this is not an untruth of the object — which is identical to itself — but an untruth in perceiving it' (PhG 97/70*). Accordingly, the 'criterion of truth' against which the perceiving subject measures its knowledge is the absence of discrepancy — 'self-identity' [Sichselbstgleichheit] (ibd.) — as it relates the One to the Also of perception. The material object displays the criterion of self-identity in the form of permanent physical unity or 'togetherness' [Zusammengefaßtsein], as Hegel called it earlier

(PhG 93/67*), and through a composition of properties persisting identically over time.

On that basis, the first scenography of perception unfolds. The narrator invites us to participate directly in the perceptions of consciousness ('I'), presenting its experience for the sake of illustration in slow motion: 'The object which I apprehend presents itself as *purely One [rein Einer]*' — as a singular this-here-now. Meanwhile, 'I also perceive in it a property which is *universal*, and which thereby transcends the singular One [Einzelheit]. The first being of the objective essence as a One was therefore not its true being. Since the object is what is true, the untruth falls in me; my apprehension was not correct' (PhG 97/70*). Consciousness thus negates the singular One, perceiving the object instead as an abstract Also — a 'community' combining multiple but as yet unspecified qualities. Yet it turns out this perception is also inaccurate, since

> Ich nehme nun ferner die Eigenschaft wahr als *bestimmte*, Anderem *entgegengesetzte* und es ausschließende. Ich faßte das gegenständliche Wesen also in der Tat nicht richtig auf, als ich es als eine *Gemeinschaft* mit anderen oder als die Kontinuität bestimmte, und muß vielmehr um der *Bestimmtheit* der Eigenschaft willen die Kontinuität trennen und es als ausschließendes Eins setzen. (PhG 97)
>
> [I now further perceive the property to be *determinate, opposed* to others and excluding them. Thus I did not in fact apprehend the objective essence correctly when I defined it as a *community* with others, or as a continuity; on account of the *specificity* [Bestimmtheit] of the property, I must break up [trennen] the continuity and posit the objective essence as an exclusive One [als ausschließendes Eins].] (71*)

That perception, however, does not hold true either, since the object clearly possesses multiple properties that 'do not affect one another but are mutually indifferent', for which reason the object appears again as an Also, only this time in the more specific sense of a 'universal *common medium* containing many properties as sensuous *universalities*, each existing on its own account and, being *specific*, excluding the others' (PhG 98/71*).

The thing thus becomes the site of a struggle between inclusion and exclusion, Also and One, but consciousness has yet to find ways to relate these opposites. As of now, it can grasp the thing only as an either/or. Either the thing appears to consciousness as an indifferent plurality, as a medium of 'pure self-relation' that 'no longer possesses the character of negativity' (PhG 98/71*); or it appears to be an exclusive unit made up of just a '*single property*' (ibid.), instead of forming a community of coexisting properties. If both perceptions were true, this would violate the stipulated criterion of truth, according to which the object must remain the same at all times and regardless of whether it is perceived or not. And so, even though accurate in certain regards, the perceptions of consciousness remain perspectival, partial truths that do not account for the object's synthetic togetherness.

Unable to solve the either/or, consciousness relapses into sense-certainty. It is 'thrown back to the beginning and drawn once again into the same cycle [Kreislauf]' (PhG 98/71*) of intending something as 'this' singular One, instead of perceiving what it is. 'For us', Hegel notes, this regression is hardly surprising because it only illustrates the recursive nature of perception implicit in the conceptual design of 'the object and the attitude [Verhalten] of consciousness towards it' (PhG 97/70★). For consciousness, however, the failure to reconcile the either/or triggers a realization that is absolutely crucial not only for perception but truly for all forms of conscious knowledge. Consciousness now realizes that it cannot remain passively focused on the object but must instead 'return into itself', using reflection to reconcile its contradictory perceptions:

> Es hat nämlich die Erfahrung über das Wahrnehmen gemacht, daß das Resultat und das Wahre desselben seine Auflösung oder die Reflexion in sich selbst aus dem Wahren ist. Es hat sich hiermit für das Bewußtsein bestimmt, wie sein Wahrnehmen wesentlich beschaffen ist, nämlich nicht ein einfaches reines Auffassen, sondern *in seinem Auffassen* zugleich aus dem Wahren [i.e. dem Gegenstand] *heraus in sich reflektiert* zu sein. Diese Rückkehr des Bewußtseins in sich selbst, die sich in das reine Auffassen unmittelbar — denn sie hat sich als dem Wahrnehmen wesentlich gezeigt — *einmischt*, verändert das Wahre. (PhG 98)

> [It has experienced in perception that the outcome and the truth of perception is its dissolution, or is reflection out of the True and into itself. Thus it becomes quite definite for consciousness how its perceiving is essentially constituted, viz. that it is not a simple pure apprehension, but *in its apprehension* is at the same time *reflected out of the true* [i.e. the object] *and into itself.* This return of consciousness into itself — which is immediately *mingled* with the pure apprehension [of the object], for this return has proven to be essential to perception — alters the truth.] (71–72★)

Hegel's message is clear: Perception is already entwined with reflection, which must 'intervene' — another possible translation of *sich einmischen* — to stop the regressive cycle of perception and thus avoid a relapse into sense-certainty. What that practically means, and to what extent the 'return into oneself' alters the perceptual object, Hegel explains immediately thereafter:

> Diese Rückkehr des Bewußtseins in sich selbst [...] verändert das Wahre. Das Bewußtsein erkennt diese Seite zugleich als die seinige und nimmt sie auf sich, wodurch es also den wahren Gegenstand rein erhalten wird. — Es ist hiermit jetzt, wie es bei der sinnlichen Gewißheit geschah, an dem Wahrnehmen die Seite vorhanden, daß das Bewußtsein in sich zurückgedrängt wird, aber zunächst nicht in dem Sinne, in welchem dies bei jener der Fall war, als ob in es die *Wahrheit* des Wahrnehmens fiele; sondern vielmehr erkennt es, daß die *Unwahrheit*, die darin vorkommt, in es fällt. Durch diese Erkenntnis aber ist es zugleich fähig, sie aufzuheben; es unterscheidet sein Auffassen des Wahren von der Unwahrheit seines Wahrnehmens, korrigiert diese, und insofern es diese Berichtigung selbst vornimmt, fällt allerdings die Wahrheit, als Wahrheit des *Wahrnehmens*, in dasselbe. Das Verhalten des Bewußtseins, das nunmehr zu betrachten ist, ist also so beschaffen, daß es nicht mehr bloß wahrnimmt, sondern auch seiner Reflexion in sich bewußt ist und diese von der einfachen Auffassung selbst abtrennt. (PhG 98–99)

> [This return of consciousness into itself [...] alters the truth. Consciousness at

once recognizes this aspect as its own and takes responsibility for it; by doing so it will preserve the true object in its purity. This being so, we have now in the case of perception the same as happened in the case of sense-certainty, the aspect of consciousness being driven back into itself; but not, in the first instance, in the sense in which this happened in sense-certainty, i.e. not as if the *truth* of perception fell in consciousness. On the contrary, consciousness recognizes that it is the *untruth* occurring in perception that falls within it. But by this very recognition it is able at once to sublate this untruth; it distinguishes its apprehension of the truth from the untruth of its perceptions, corrects them, and since it undertakes to make this correction itself, the truth, qua truth of *perception*, falls of course *within consciousness*. The behaviour of consciousness which we have now to consider is thus so constituted that consciousness no longer merely perceives, but is also conscious of its reflection into itself, and separates this from simple apprehension proper.] (72★)

Reflection basically means internal differentiation. In the context of perception, reflection means the ability to distinguish between my cognitive acts and their passive target, sense impressions. This reflexive awareness of one's own cognitive activity is traditionally termed apperception, or more plainly self-consciousness, as indicated, for example, by Kant's remark: 'Consciousness of one's self (apperception)' (KrV B 68).[93] Unlike sense-certainty, perception has a reflexive awareness of its cognitions, including its shortcomings. It can reflect upon the consistency of its perceptions by comparing them with the supposed reality or in-itself of the object. If consciousness thus notices inconsistencies, it can act upon them by self-correcting its misperceptions. In doing so, perception in fact 'alters the truth', Hegel writes, but knowingly or self-consciously so.

At the end of the *Phenomenology*'s third chapter, on 'force and the understanding', Hegel restates the necessity of reflection in unequivocal terms: 'Consciousness of an other, of an object in general, is itself necessarily *self-consciousness*, self-reflection [Reflektiertsein in sich], consciousness of self in its otherness' (PhG 135/102★). Perception, too, is a formation of self-consciousness and thus a configuration of reflection.

The important epistemological consequence of this insight is a virtual duplication of both the perceiving subject and the perceived object. For upon reflection, either element can be considered in two fundamentally different ways, either in relation to itself (being-for-itself) or in relation to others (being-for-other). This reflexive doubling of both subject and object seriously complicates perception — a complication Hegel will consider in the second and the third scenographies of perception.

Hegel's insistence on the necessity of reflection in sense perception not only contradicts passivist notions of perception. It is also at odds with empiricist and phenomenalist theories of perception, because Hegel still upholds the realist commitment that the truth of perception is determined by the object, not the subject. He rejects, as Kenneth Westphal puts it, 'the uncritical assumption that only a passive kind of cognition can be reconciled with realism', combining 'for the first and almost the only time in the history of philosophy [...] realism about the objects of knowledge with an activist account of knowledge'.[94]

Therefore, perception is not dealing, as Kant would have it, with appearances but presumes to apprehend the true being of an object, although in contradictory and necessarily perspectival ways. Surely, the act of perception will influence the ways in which an object appears, as either One or Also, depending on perspective, and is therefore 'reflected out of the true', as Hegel put it. But, by the same token, consciousness also knows its perceptions to be artefacts of the mind. As it is self-conscious, or reflected in itself, consciousness knows that 'the *untruth*' — the either/or disparity contradicting the object's steadfast selfsameness — 'falls in me' and that 'my apprehension was not correct' (PhG 97/70*). And so, removing the either/or from the object by way of reflection and taking it upon itself instead, consciousness is able to defend and preserve the integrity of the object. One might therefore say, if somewhat paradoxically, that reflection is a means of safeguarding the realism of perception.

In the so-called Jena Philosophy of Spirit, the second part of the 1805 manuscript quoted earlier, Hegel further develops the idea that object perception requires reflection. By reflection Hegel means above all '*attention* as the first necessary activity', as well as mental operations such as '*fixation*, abstraction, extraction, exertion, and the overcoming of the vague aspects of sensation'.[95] In separating sensory impressions from their cognitive processing, these more or less deliberate reflections influence the appearance of the object and thus introduce a measure of arbitrariness into perception. Hegel illustrates this point with strong imagery, contrasting the active and reflexive side of perception, which 'goes back into itself', with the receptive 'night' of the human soul, in which images suddenly appear and disappear as in 'phantasmagoric spectacles'.

> Im Anschauen ist das angeschaute in mir, — denn *ich* schaue ja an — es ist *meine* Anschauung. Aus diesem Anschauen tritt der Geist heraus und schaut sein Anschauen an, d. h. den Gegenstand als den *seinen*; den Gegenstand [hat der Geist] aufgehoben als *seyenden*, das *Bild*. [...] er ergänzt diß durch [...] die Negativität, Abtrennung des Ansich, und geht in sich zurük — und sein erstes Selbst [die Anschauung] ist ihm Gegenstand [...] Diß Bild gehört ihm an, er ist im Besitz desselben, er ist Herr darüber; es ist in seinem *Schatze* aufbewahrt, in seiner *Nacht* [...] Der Mensch ist diese Nacht, diß leere Nichts, das alles in ihrer Einfachheit enthält — ein Reichthum unendlich vieler Vorstellungen, Bilder, deren keines ihm gerade einfällt —, oder die nicht als gegenwärtige sind. Diß die Nacht, das Innre der Natur, das hier existirt — *reines Selbst*, — [wie] in phantasmagorischen Vorstellungen ist es rings um Nacht, hier schießt dann ein blutig Kopf, — dort eine andere weisse Gestalt plözlich hervor, und verschwinden ebenso — Diese Nacht erblickt man wenn man dem Menschen ins Auge blickt — in eine Nacht hinein, die *furchtbar* wird, — es hängt die Nacht der Welt hier einem entgegen. (GW VIII, 186–87)

> [When I look at something, what I look at is inside me — for *I* am the one who looks; it is *my* intuition. The mind steps out of this intuition, and looks at its intuition — i.e. it looks at the object as its own; the object is cancelled as a being [and becomes] *image* [...] the mind adds to this act [...] negativity, separation from the in-itself, going back into itself, [so that] its first self [intuition] becomes its object [...] This image belongs to the mind. The mind is in possession of

the image, is master of it. It is stored in its *treasury*, in its *night* [...] Man is this night, this empty nothing which contains everything in its simplicity — a wealth of infinitely many representations, images, none of which he currently remembers, or none of which presently appear. This [is] the night, the interior of nature, existing here — *pure Self* — [just as] in phantasmagoric spectacles[96] it is night everywhere: here a bloody head suddenly shoots up and there another white shape, only to disappear as suddenly. We see this night when we look a human being in the eye, looking into a night which turns *terrifying* — the night of the world hangs out toward us.][97]

But, Hegel continues,

> Ich ist die Form [des Bildes] nicht nur als einfaches Selbst, sondern als Bewegung; die *Beziehung* der Theile des Bildes, — die Form, *Beziehung* als die seinige setzen; — insofern sie einen *Theil* des *Inhalts* ausmacht — verändert sie dieselbe [Beziehung] — *Für sich* ist hier die freye *Willkühr* — Bilder zu zerreissen und sie auf die ungebundste Weise zu verknüpfen. — Läßt [Ich] sich bey seinem Hervorziehen der Bilder nach der *empfangnen* Beziehung gehen, so steht es unter der Herrschafft der sogenannten *Ideen*association — ein englisches Wort, denn diese nennen noch heutigstags, das blosse Bild von einem Hund z. B., eine *Idee*. Die Gesetze dieser Ideenassociation heissen weiter nichts, als die passive Ordnung der Vorstellung [...] Diese Willkühr ist die leere Freyheit [der Anschauung], denn ihr Inhalt ist nach einander, sie liegt bloß in der Form, und geht nur diese an. (GW VIII, 187–88)

> [The I is the form [of the image] not only as simple self but also as movement. It relates the parts of the image to one another; it is the form to posit [their] *relation* as its own, and insofar as [form] represents a *part* of the *content* it alters this relation. [The I] *for itself* is here free arbitrariness — [able] to dismember images and to reconnect them in the most dissociated manner. If the self, in its drawing forth of images, follows the *received* relation, then it is under the sway of the so-called association of *ideas* — an English expression referring, even today, to the mere image of, say, a dog as an *idea*. The laws of this association of ideas refer to nothing more than the passive order of the representation [...] This arbitrariness is the empty freedom [of sensory intuition], for its content is sequential, [whereas] arbitrariness lies solely in the form and concerns form alone.][98]

Thus, the selections of the observer determine the perceived object, for example, the seen image. She produces the intelligible form of perception by ordering and connecting a series of sensations according to certain arbitrary criteria, which happens through form-giving acts of reflection like attention, concentration, differentiation, and comparison.

Historically, this concept of perception reflects the general tendency of Romanticism to emphasize the import of the subject. In *Techniques of the Observer*, Jonathan Crary has shown that subjectivist theories of visual perception became dominant 'during the first few decades of the nineteenth century', variously emphasizing 'the productivity of the observer' and thus endowing him 'with a new perceptual autonomy'.[99] Considering the quoted passage from Hegel's Jena Philosophy of Spirit, as well as writings by Fichte and remarks by Novalis and Friedrich Schlegel, one would have to add, however, that the subjectivist reinterpretation of perception was well under way by the turn of the eighteenth century. In fact, these writings (to which I will return in the next chapter, on Novalis) delineate a historical nexus Crary overlooked in his influential book.[100]

But whatever its historical context, the curious and unique term of the quoted passage — 'free arbitrariness' [freye Willkühr] — concerns not at all the sensory 'content' of perception, Hegel specifies at the end, because this content is 'sequentially' given through the 'passive order' of sensation. Arbitrary is only the form of perception, reflection, which consists of the purely formal — and in that sense 'empty' — freedom to relate the received impressions to one another, a relationship it then justly claims 'as its own' product.

Logos as substance of reflection

According to the Jena Philosophy of Spirit, perception depends on yet another element that originates neither in physical sensation, nor in subjective reflection and the 'empty freedom' attached to it. This element is language. It is the *'name-giving power'* of language as logos, Hegel writes (GW VIII, 189), through which perception comes to completion, because put in words and names, subjective perceptions and objective determinations are united, forming a synthesis. The external object as well as my perceptions are sublated (in the threefold sense) through the signs of language. Hegel develops this point on the following pages:

> [Die Sprache] gibt [dem Ding] einen Namen, und spricht diß als das *Seyn* des Gegenstandes aus; was ist diß? Antworten wir, es *ist* ein Löwe, Esel u.s.f. [...] d. h. es ist gar nicht ein gelbes, Füsse und so fort habendes, ein eignes selbstständiges, sondern ein *Nahme*, ein Ton meiner Stimme; [es ist] etwas ganz anderes, als es in der Anschauung ist, und diß sein wahres *Seyn*. [...] Durch den Nahmen ist also der Gegenstand als *seyend* aus dem Ich heraus gebohren. — Diß ist die erste *Schöpferkrafft*, die der Geist ausübt; Adam gab allen Dingen einen Nahmen, diß ist das Majestätsrecht und erste Besitzergreiffung der ganzen Natur, oder das Schaffen derselben aus dem Geiste; λογος [d. h.] Vernunft[,] *Wesen* des Dings und Rede, *Sache* und *Sage*, Kategorie. Der Mensch spricht zu dem Dinge als dem *seinigen*, und diß ist das *Seyn* des Gegenstandes. Geist verhält sich zu sich selbst; — er sagt zum Esel, du bist ein innres und diß Innre ist Ich und dein Seyn ist ein Ton, den ich willkührlich erfunden — *Esel* ist ein Ton, der ganz etwas anderes ist, als das sinnliche Seyn selbst; insofern wir ihn sehen, auch fühlen, oder hören sind wir es selbst, unmittelbar eins mit ihm, erfüllt; zurüktretend aber als Nahme, ist er ein geistiges — etwas ganz anderes. Die Welt, die Natur ist nicht mehr ein Reich von Bildern, innerlich aufgehobne, die kein Seyn haben, sondern ein Reich der Nahmen. (GW VIII, 189–90)

> [[Language] gives [the thing] a name and expresses this as the *being* of the object. What is this? We answer, It *is* a lion, a donkey, etc. [...] Thus it is not merely a yellow thing having feet, etc., independently and of its own, but instead a *name*, a sound made by my voice; [it is] something entirely different from what it looks like in appearance — and this is its true *being*. [...] By means of the name the object has been born out of the I [and has emerged] as *being*. This is the primal *creativity* exercised by spirit. Adam gave a name to all things, which is the right of the sovereign and the primal seizure of all nature, or the creation of nature

out of spirit: Logos [meaning] reason, the *essence* of a thing as of speech, the *matter* itself and its *utterance*, category. Man speaks to the thing as *his*, and this is the *being* of the object. Spirit relates itself to itself: it says to the donkey, You are an internal entity, which is I; your being is a sound which I have arbitrarily invented. The sound, 'donkey', is altogether different from the sensate entity. Insofar as we see it, and also feel or hear it, we are that entity itself, immediately one with it and fulfilled. Coming back as a name, however, it is something spiritual, altogether different. The world, nature, is no longer a realm of internally preserved *images* without being but instead a realm of names.][101]

As a process of differentiation and reflection, perception determines the thing by unfolding its essence — properties — through a series of sensations. The corresponding name, by contrast, does something perception itself cannot do because of its sequential nature: the name synthesizes the perceptual process. Suppose, with Hegel, that 'this' thing in front of us is yellow and brown, has feet as well, also a fuzzy mane, and several other features. By saying its arbitrary name, 'lion', we abstract from these individual perceptions, indeed from sensory realities altogether, yet at the same time preserving and conveying them through that sign, all at once. Therefore, calling a thing by its name means to express its permanent relational structure — the connection between its particular identity (One) and its internal diversity (Also) that are in themselves universal and independent properties.

Names restore the original unity of objects, which the process of perception must break up into different impressions, because in *externalizing im*pressions through articulation, we objectify them as properties, and in calling their synchronic relationship or togetherness by its name, 'lion', we identify the object as a whole, making it One *again*. Such identity is not the thing as we actually see it, however, but as we *know* it: by its name. We now use nouns and adjectives — signs — to describe the thing and its characteristic properties. We employ logos, thus exercising our foremost power and freedom as humans. For in names, Hegel concludes the quoted passage, 'we first overcome sensory *intuition* [das *Anschauen*], [i.e.] the animal existence, as well as space and time. The seen image is now gone, has disappeared; its totality is [...] raised out of feeling into the higher sense of spirit' (GW VIII, 190–91). The seen image is shaped by arbitrary acts of reflection, yet the synthetic being of the object, its truth, is grasped in words — and thus becomes verbal meaning. Like sense-certainty, therefore, perception is bound up with language as logos, which means for Hegel not simply reason but, more fundamentally, 'the *essence* of a thing as of speech, the *matter* itself and its *utterance* [*Sage*]' (GW VIII, 190).[102]

Hegel adheres to this line of reasoning in the *Phenomenology* as well, defending throughout the necessity of articulation in perception. At the beginning of the third chapter, which moves from perception to the understanding, Hegel even radicalizes the point. Although perceptual consciousness does not yet realize, as 'we' do, that its perceptions are bound up with apperception and, ultimately, with words and concepts (PhG 107–08/80–79★), it nonetheless notices 'that the content held to be true in perception belongs, in fact, only to the form and is dissolved in the form's unity' (PhG 109/80★). The form reorganizing sensory impressions is reflexive differentiation, Hegel told us, but the higher unity of this form belongs to language, to linguistic expression. For language is the universal medium of subjectivity — the *'spiritual substance'* and 'objectivity' [Gegenständlichkeit], as Hegel puts it later, of consciousness 'in its purity' and hence 'the coming into existence of self-consciousness as such' (PhG 376–77/308–09★).

Indeed, negation and reflection may be the inner processes of subjectivity, in perception no less than any other form of consciousness, but the relationships formed in and through language are the objective shape and permanent substance of subjectivity. In anticipation of the chapters to follow, I should add that Hegel finds little difficulty in establishing relationships towards objects or other humans through the signs of language. He firmly believes in the 'name-giving power' of language, which distinguishes him from literary authors, who tend to have a less robust relationship with language. Rilke, for example, struggles with the transition from perceptions to names, and from names back to perceptions, as we shall see in Part Two.

If reflection and articulation are integral parts of perception, the 'independence [Selbständigkeit] of the thing' is effectively 'eradicated' [vertilgt] (PhG 109/81★). This conclusion, drawn by Hegel himself, seems to suggest that perception is entirely subjective and unlimited in its power of perceiving — or rather imagining — whatever it wants. Fichte has often been understood in this way, not least because he wrote, in the original *Wissenschaftslehre* of 1794/95, that his philosophy boils down to the fundamental insight that 'all reality [...] is produced solely through the imagination [Einbildungskraft]' (F I, 227). On that view (which I develop in more detail in the next chapter on Novalis), perceptions — the most immediate manifestations of reality — are not really caused by external bodies but represent instead *'higher determinations of actual sensations'* through the 'inner sense', the ego, which has the sole power to posit reality.[103]

Because of his realist commitment, Hegel rejects a subjectivist concept of perception. The second scenography of perception (PhG 99–101/72–74★) serves precisely the purpose of rebutting the idea that One and Also are not physically real and mind-independent attributes of objects but only subjective imaginings — fictions and deceptions, as Hume would say, of the human mind. Hegel thus attacks the sceptical idea, shared by Locke and Hume no less than by Fichte, that the thing assumes unity and a permanent identity only in the eye of the observer.[104]

According to Hume, objects do not have 'continu'd existence [...] distinct from the mind and perception', although 'we may easily indulge our inclination to that supposition', thereby 'feigning a continu'd being'.[105] Neither does Hume believe in the substantial unity of things, as we 'have no idea of substance, distinct from that of a collection of particular qualities'. In reality, the object of perception thus consists of 'a heap or collection of different perceptions, united together by certain relations, and suppos'd, tho' falsely, to be endow'd with a perfect simplicity and identity'.[106] Hume thus radicalizes the doubts of John Locke, claiming certainty, however, where Locke had expressed only uncertainty:

> [W]e neither have nor can have [the idea of *substance*] by sensation or reflection [...] we have no such *clear* idea at all; and therefore signify nothing by the

word *substance* but only an uncertain supposition of we know not what, i.e. of something whereof we have no [particular distinct positive] idea, which we take to be the *substratum*, or support, of those ideas we do know.¹⁰⁷

If substance was nothing but a fiction of the mind, consciousness would posit unity where there is, in reality, only 'a collection [Sammlung] of free matters', as Hegel puts it, held together by 'an enclosing surface' (PhG 101/74★). The object's identity and unity or '*oneness*' [*Einssein*] would be merely 'imagined' [vorgestellt] (ibid.). Conversely, the thing's identity — its characteristic set of *permanent* properties — would be an illusion. The thing would be 'white only to *our* eyes, *also* tart but to *our* tongue, *also* cubical to our touch, etc. We get the entire diversity [gänzliche Verschiedenheit] of these aspects not from the thing but from ourselves, though they are divided for us since the eye is quite distinct from the tongue, etc. We are the universal medium in which such moments are kept apart and exist each on its own', preserving, by that supposition, the thing's 'self-identity' [Sichselbstgleichheit] (PhG 99–100/72★).

Hegel presents no elaborate argument to squash these sceptical notions. To rectify them, he simply reminds us of the fallibility of perception and so turns scepticism on its feet. Contradictory perceptions do not warrant doubts as to the reality and substantiality of objects but should, on the contrary, raise questions as to the adequacy of our perceptions. Although it might at times *appear* illogical, reality is not in fact riddled with contradictions, paradoxes, dichotomies, antinomies, and so forth. Hegel contends, on the contrary, that all shortcomings of this kind originate in the domain of thought, and here they must be solved in language and with concepts, hence discursively, and then measured against reality, in which 'reason *searches* and *finds* itself' (PhG 577/480★). For reality is logical, and the logical real — 'Was vernünftig ist, das ist wirklich; und was wirklich ist, das ist vernünftig' — a motto that, for Hegel, sums up the only proper '*attitude of philosophy toward reality*' (TWA VII, 24). Inferring truths, or for that matter paradoxes, from perceptions, however, as Hume does in his repudiation of substance, means to turn the world upside down. It means, in other words, to mistake the subjective representations of the mind for objective reality, a distorted view of the world Hegel attacks in the third chapter of the *Phenomenology*.

This, however, is the reflexive knowledge of consciousness, that the seeming contradictions of perception may be misperceptions of its own, wherefore consciousness self-critically watches and possibly corrects itself. On that basis, and against appearances to the contrary, which it reflexively distinguishes from objective reality, consciousness can rescue its sound conviction that things are '*in and for themselves determinate*' (PhG 100/73★) and that 'the thing', not the subject, is the '*universal medium*' and '*permanent bearer* [das Bestehen] of the many diverse and independent properties' (PhG 100–01/73★). Because of this conviction, consciousness changes its view of the perceptual object, perceiving it no longer as an either/or, but determining instead that 'the *Also*, or the indifferent difference [der gleichgültige Unterschied], falls as much within the thing as does the *oneness* [*Einssein*]' (PhG 102/74★). The thing is neither a simple unit nor an indifferent manifold but a combination of both. Finally, consciousness has recognized the reciprocity of these determinations as well.

The observations concluding this second and opening the third scenography of perception are crucial, because they introduce a relational concept of objecthood. As before, when consciousness 'turned back into itself', reflection is the key to overcoming the either/or of perception:

> Sehen wir zurück [...] so ergibt sich, daß [das Bewußtsein] abwechslungsweise ebenso wohl sich selbst als auch das Ding zu beidem macht, zum reinen, vielheitslosen *Eins* wie zu einem in selbständige Materien aufgelösten *Auch*. Das Bewußtsein findet also durch diese Vergleichung, daß nicht nur *sein* Nehmen des Wahren die *Verschiedenheit des Auffassens* und *des in sich Zurückgehens* an ihm hat, sondern daß vielmehr das Wahre selbst, das Ding, sich auf diese gedoppelte Weise zeigt. Es ist hiermit die Erfahrung vorhanden, daß das Ding sich *für das auffassende Bewußtsein* auf eine bestimmte Weise *darstellt*, aber *zugleich* aus der Weise, in der es sich darbietet, *heraus* und *in sich reflektiert ist* oder an ihm selbst eine entgegengesetzte Wahrheit hat. [...] Das Ding ist *Eins*, in sich reflektiert; es ist *für sich*, aber es ist auch *für ein Anderes*; und zwar ist es ein *anderes* für sich, als *es* für Anderes ist. (PhG 101–02)

> [If we look back [...] we see that consciousness alternately makes itself, as well as the Thing, into both a pure, many-less *One* and an *Also* that resolves itself into independent matters. Consciousness thus finds through this comparison that not only *its* perceptions of the thing contain the *contrast* between *apprehension* and *turning back into itself*, but rather that the truth itself — the thing — reveals itself in this twofold way. Our experience, then, is this, that the thing *manifests itself for* perceptual *consciousness* in a specific way, but is *at the same time reflected out of* this way of manifesting itself and [pushed] *back into itself*; in other words, it holds an opposite truth inside. [...] The thing is a *One*, reflected in itself; it is *for itself*, yet it is also *for an other*; that is, it is in itself *different* from what *it is for* others.] (74★)

At first, reflection intervened in the subjective process of perception. The perceiver divided himself through acts of reflection, while simultaneously relating to another, external entity in the mode of either sense-certainty or sensory perception. Now reflection seizes the object of perception as well. For 'experience' — or rather Hegel's scenographies — has shown that the object is internally divided, or reflected into itself, as it necessarily combines One and Also. At the same time, the object is reflected into another in that its properties are determinate only in relation to other things. Through reflection, therefore, perception turns things or substances into 'subjects' — into entities that are reflected in themselves and at the same time dependent on others.

As a configuration of reflection that originates in, without being restricted to, human consciousness, 'subject' always consists of two distinct and internally divided vectors of relation, namely *self-relation* (or being-for-itself) and *relation-to-other* (or being-for-another). Seized by reflection, the object of perception takes on the same double nature. It now exists in a 'twofold way', Hegel writes, the one being intrinsic, self-identical, and self-determined or autonomous, the other extrinsic, disparate, determined by other objects or and heteronomous. The object of perception thus represents a reflexive unity, indeed a community in which 'contradictory extremes' coexist 'not merely *alongside each other*' but in reciprocity with each other. Since the set of properties embodying such community is determinate only in comparison to other things, however, the object is necessarily 'burdened with opposition itself' [mit dem Gegensatze überhaupt behaftet] (PhG 104–05/77★).

In a way, this reflexive concept of objecthood replays the earlier dialectic between One and Also, though there is one crucial difference. Hegel now conceives of both subjects and objects in strictly relational terms, consisting in each case of two opposite modes of reflection connecting in total four relata. As a result, the numeric and temporal contradictions that had previously preoccupied perception are suspended. Henceforth, consciousness will comprehend itself, as well as its perceptible or historical and imperceptible or theoretical objects, as a network of relationships to be explored and determined on the circuitous paths of reflection. Circuitous these paths must be since Spirit — Hegel's truth — always 'takes the path of mediation, and hence a detour' (TWA XVIII, 55).

In differentiating a 'mode of being for itself' from a mode of 'relating to others' (PhG 109/80★), perception manages to preserve objective unity and identity through reflection. This double reflection is not unique to perception but rather the foundation of spirit itself, which is why it represents, as Hegel puts it, 'the unconditioned absolute universality' (PhG 104/77★). The original form and basic experience of such 'absolute' universality is subjectivity, or more succinctly 'I', which first surfaces, however, in perception. Indeed, it is perceptual consciousness that begins to organize its contents through acts of reflection like negation and distinction, selection, comparison and contrast, finally uniting the results of each operation through signification. 'For us', therefore, the object of perception 'is developed [geworden] through the movement of consciousness in such a way that its development [Werden] is entwined with consciousness, and the reflection is the same on both sides, or, there is only *one* reflection' (PhG 108/79★). And the medium in which this *one* reflection takes place is, for Hegel, logos. The signs of language, or logos, constitute the substance of both subject and object, because they are 'the *essence* of a thing as of speech, the *matter* itself and its *utterance*'. At the same time, logos is categorially different from either and for this reason has the power of objectifying, through signs and as meanings, the contradictory yet coexistent reflections defining them separately and in relation to each other.

In the final chapter of the *Phenomenology*, Hegel recalls the incorporation of substance or thinghood into the proper domain of spirit, reflection, emphasizing here that '*the thing is I*; in this infinite judgement the thing is indeed sublated; in itself it is nothing; it has meaning only in a relation [im Verhältnisse], only *through the I* and *its connection* with it [Beziehung auf dasselbe]' (PhG 577/481★). This 'infinite judgement' should be taken literally. The things of perception, Hegel has told us, are interwoven with the form-giving reflections of consciousness and thus belong to 'a relation' in which logos is the foundation and ultimate measure. Perceptual objects are formed and transformed by the reflexive actions and, ultimately, the intersubjective language of consciousness, which relates percepts to objects through signs and concepts.[108] Therefore, the structured whole or *system* of sense-certainty is deixis performed through utterly universal signs; the system of perception consists of nouns and adjectives designating things and their qualities; the system of the understanding comprises categories and rules explaining observations; the system of self-consciousness consists of relations expressed in terms of reflection; and the system of spirit, finally, coincides with logos itself — the discursive form *and* conceptual content of thought.

(Hi)stories and concepts

At the end of the *Phenomenology*'s third chapter, Hegel tells us that the faculty of the understanding (*Verstand*) lies in its power to explain things. This power of explanation, however, which produces comprehension in the first place rather than proceeding from it, rests on a narrative usage of language:

> Es ist also nur die *eigene* Notwendigkeit, was der Verstand ausspricht; einen Unterschied [nämlich Kraft vs. Gesetz], den er also nur so macht, daß er es zugleich ausdrückt, daß der Unterschied kein *Unterschied der Sache selbst* sei. Diese Notwendigkeit, die nur im Worte liegt, ist hiermit die Hererzählung der Momente, die den Kreis derselben ausmachen; sie werden zwar unterschieden, ihr Unterschied aber [wird] zugleich, kein Unterschied der Sache selbst zu sein, ausgedrückt und daher selbst sogleich wieder aufgehoben; diese Bewegung heißt *Erklären*. (PhG 125)

> [It is, therefore, only its *own* necessity that is asserted by the understanding; that is, it draws a distinction [viz. force vs law] in such a way as to convey, at the same time, that this distinction is no *distinction of the thing itself.* This necessity, which is merely verbal, is thus the narration of the moments constituting the cycle of the necessity. The moments are indeed distinguished, but, at the same time, their difference is said to be not a difference of the thing itself, and consequently their difference is immediately cancelled again. This movement is called *explanation*.] (94★)

A process of reflection taking place in language, explanation provides the means to reconcile the contradictions of perception. Considering — or rather recounting, telling, narrating (*hererzählen*) — something in language, you can draw distinctions such as One/Also, thing/properties, substance/accidents while simultaneously knowing, and perhaps also saying, that these are merely logical, rather than physical, differences. You thus assert differences you regard *only in a manner of speaking* as corresponding to the object. Explaining objects and their properties in such a self-conscious way, however, the noted differences are at once asserted and retracted — sublated. You know them to reflect your perceptions and are for that reason conscious of their limitations and possible imperfections.

Hegel opens the chapter on perception with an explanation of this kind. He introduces a conceptual opposition whose reality he immediately calls into question. He differentiates between the Also of thinghood and the exclusive Oneness of things, to which he later adds the distinction between reflection-in-itself and reflection-in-other, explaining at the same time that these opposites in fact presuppose each other and thus constitute a dialectic unity.

The scenographies that follow put these concepts into practice, demonstrating to 'us', however, that in perception, as opposed to conception and reflection, the thing appears throughout as an either/or. Because of the invariably diachronic and sequential nature of perception, the thing presents itself either as 'this' simple, undivided unit; or as a set of qualities to be perceived one by one; but never as both at the same time. It is simply impossible to *see* these opposite aspects at once, and so their coexistence can only be *said*. Only an explanation can say, and thus make us understand, that the thing consists of these opposites while simultaneously acknowledging that they are 'no distinction of the thing itself'. For we know, or at least have good reason to believe, that the thing is not somehow at odds with itself but stands united and identical through time. That both these perceptions of identity and difference should be true reflections of the object may constitute a paradox of experience, but it is nonetheless a perfectly coherent thing to say. Our explanation thus reunites what the process of perception must divide, reflexively preserving the perceived opposites through signs.

In the end, consciousness itself realizes that the difference between objective unity and diversity, One and Also, is 'a distinction *existing in words only*' (PhG 104/76*; emphasis added). This is the precise moment when consciousness starts to *understand*, and only in a manner of speaking sees, that 'the origin of the unity and order of appearances', to borrow Robert Pippin's phrase, 'is not some beyond [...] but the self-conscious activity of the understanding' called explanation.[109]

This statement applies not just to object perception but to all forms of cognition. For Hegel, explanation constitutes the self-conscious origin of comprehension as such. Therefore, and in contrast to thinkers like Spinoza, Goethe, Fichte, or Schelling, who envisioned an intuitive understanding issuing directly and positively from perception or similarly immediate modes of discovery, Hegel is a fundamentally discursive thinker whose concept of apperception is founded upon negation, difference, distinction, and above all logos. The truth, he writes in a key passage of the *Phenomenology* (PhG 24/11*), is not simply there to see but, rather, the '*result*' of a process — the process of discrimination and reflection taking place in language and through concepts. If perception could by itself produce complete and self-evident cognitions, however, 'images' of sorts containing an intuitive percept of the whole, the dialectic 'labour of the concept' would be little more than scholastic baggage, if not, as Goethe once complained, a dangerous 'sickness' turning 'falsehoods into truths, and truths into falsehoods'.[110] Then, all the truth seeker would have to do would be to look patiently at phenomena for the truth to appear, intuitively pursuing this truth, as Goethe phrased it in his *Farbenlehre*, 'to the point at which [phenomena] simply appear and are and where there is nothing left in them to explain'.[111] But, Hegel explains in his *Aesthetics*, such 'sensory contemplation' [sinnige Beschauung] of objects does not yield true understanding but only a 'vague notion [Ahnung] thereof' (TWA XIII, 173–74). Without reflection and explanation, perception simply relapses into sense-certainty, pretending once again to notice everything about the object, but actually knowing only this, that 'it' exists.[112]

Still in the third chapter of the *Phenomenology*, Hegel continues his explanation of explanation. 'The reason why explaining affords so much self-satisfaction', he writes here, 'is just because in it consciousness is, so to speak, communing directly with itself [in unmittelbarem Selbstgespräche mit sich], enjoying only itself; although it seems to be busy with something else, it is in fact occupied only with itself' (PhG 134 /101★). What is it that makes this soliloquy of explanation so satisfying? The answer, Hegel characteristically suggests, does not lie in the self, let alone a single self, but only in the form by which subjects explain things to each other. This form establishing objectivity qua subjectivity is logical explanation, or in other words, comprehension through concepts:

> Das *Begreifen* eines Gegenstandes besteht in der Tat in nichts anderem, als daß Ich denselben sich *zu eigen* macht, ihn durchdringt und ihn in *seine eigene Form* [...] bringt. [...] das Denken hebt seine *Unmittelbarkeit*, mit der er zunächst vor uns kommt, auf und macht so [...] sein *Anundfürsichsein* oder seine *Objektivität*. Diese Objektivität hat der Gegenstand somit im *Begriffe*, und dieser ist die *Einheit des Selbstbewußtseins*, in die er aufgenommen worden [...] das Ich selbst. (TWA VI, 255)
>
> [In point of fact, the *comprehension* of an object consists in nothing else than in the I making it *its own*, in pervading it and bringing it into *its own form* [...] Thought sublates the *immediacy* with which it first comes before us and thus creates [...] its *being-in-and-for-itself* or its *objectivity*. This is an objectivity the object consequently attains in *conceptual comprehension*, which simply means the *unity of self-consciousness* into which it has been assumed [...] the I itself.]¹¹³

In the *Phenomenology*, Hegel states the matter even more concisely, writing that to attain true knowledge, 'consciousness must know the object as itself' (PhG 576/480★). This is not to say that knowledge is '*merely subjective*', nor does it say that the 'reality' of objects — their objectivity — could be '*pulled out*' [herausklauben] of one's head (TWA VI, 256).¹¹⁴ It simply means that subjectivity and objectivity share the same basis, logical reflection, which is tantamount to the concept of 'the I itself'.

The most elementary way in which consciousness knows the object as itself is sense-certainty, and this certainty consists of 'nothing else but the story of its movement or experience' (PhG 90/64★) — which means, logically speaking, deixis. Like every story, the deictic 'story' of sense-certainty combines two temporal layers as well, the one diachronic, sequential, and transitory, the other synchronic, relational, and in theory complete in itself. It is a sequential process or experience — *a* history — that as such contains and develops an immanent logic or concept — *the* story connecting the individual parts and motivating the historical process as a whole. The term '(hi)story' means to indicate this correlation, but without obscuring the critical fact that these two layers, though correlated, do not coincide in practice.

The initial chapters of the *Phenomenology* underscore this critical point. Sensory knowledge is here portrayed as based on the fundamental correlation — and inevitable discrepancy — between becoming and being, negation and relation, process and result, experience and concept. Sense-certainty seemed like an immediate and complete result, the direct knowledge of particulars, yet it turned out to depend on a process of negation and to contain nothing but abstract generality. Similarly, the object of perception seemed like a simple unit, yet its very unity and identity turned out to be not only entwined with but actually identical to the process of differentiation and reflection constituting the self-conscious act of perception. The fact that 'sense-certainty' as well as 'perception' signify at once a sensorial process and the resulting knowledge, and hence the relationship of both, further underscores the point that there are no pure results of cognition. Human knowledge cannot be subtracted from the process of its formation; or as Hegel puts it, 'the issue is not exhausted by its *purpose*, but by *working* it *out*, nor is the *result* the *actual* whole, but rather the result together with the process through which it came about' [Denn die Sache ist nicht in ihrem *Zwecke* erschöpft, sondern in ihrer *Ausführung*, noch ist das *Resultat* das *wirkliche* Ganze, sondern es zusammen mit seinem Werden] (PhG 13/2★).[115] Hence, consciousness cannot escape the diachrony of comprehension — its historical nature — and so resists a purely synchronic, taxonomic representation.[116]

This being so, the knowledge of consciousness 'cannot be described from a sideways-on or third-person point of view' but 'must in a sense be re-enacted, as if from the point of view of the experiencing subject', and hence as 'a kind of dramatic exercise'.[117] According to Hegel, the *Phenomenology* does just that: it portrays (*darstellen*) the formation of knowledge or *das erscheinende Wissen* — the ways in which knowledge variously emerges within consciousness (PhG 72/49★). Hegel narrates the development of consciousness into intersubjective and fully self-determining spirit in order to explain the concepts corresponding to this development. He tells (hi)stories of sense-certainty, perception, understanding, desire, scientific observation, artistic creation, and finally philosophical reason itself, thereby giving an exposition of the concept of spirit in its full range.

A narration of this kind is probably not what Kant had in mind when he designated 'the history of pure reason [...] a place [Stelle] left open in the system and to be filled in the future' (KrV A 852). Still, judging from the *Phenomenology*, as well as Hegel's countless lectures on the histories of art, religion, philosophy, or the state, there can be little doubt that Hegel sought to close this gap of the Kantian system as well. 'We' are complicit in this, because 'we' are supposed to extract the concepts from the phenomenological scene. It is our part as readers of the *Phenomenology* to follow the (hi)stories of consciousness closely, especially the dramatic — or rather scenographic — illustrations, and then abstract the underlying stories from these in accordance with Hegel's comments.

To tell the (hi)stories of consciousness takes time, the time of narration, and so does their comprehension. For that reason, the concepts represented in the *Phenomenology* cannot be separated from their diachronic medium — from the histories through which they appear. In the final chapter of the *Phenomenology*, concerning the possibility of knowing 'the absolute', meaning that which is without condition and limit and, therefore, entirely self-determined, Hegel takes this point even further. '*Time*', he writes here, 'is the *concept* itself that *exists* [der *Begriff* selbst, der *da ist*] and that presents itself to consciousness as empty intuition; for this reason, spirit necessarily appears in time [...] nothing is *known* that is not in *experience*' (PhG 584–85/487★). Hence, spirit exists only insofar as it appears and for this reason depends on time as the inner sense of consciousness and ineluctable form of all human comprehension.

But, Hegel continues, '[spirit] appears in time just so long as it has not *grasped* its pure concept, i.e. has not erased time [...] Time, therefore, appears as the destiny and necessity of spirit that is not yet complete within itself' (PhG 584–85/487★). To overcome this first and final threshold of human comprehension and thus attain 'absolute' knowledge, which, although reflected in itself like self-consciousness, is no longer human, Hegel developed a system of purely logical concepts. The precise scope and meaning of these concepts transcending subjective consciousness are expounded in the *Wissenschaft der Logik*, of course, but the *Phenomenology* establishes their fundamental nature: Concepts are 'absolute' only insofar as they 'sublate' their 'temporal form' (PhG 584/487★); that is, they must neutralize the time of comprehension by incorporating this process into their meaning. Supposing this final sublation were possible, these concepts would become timeless — and also speculative — in the sense that they express several, and possibly contradictory, aspects *at once*. Thus, in contrast to phenomenological concepts, which are narrative and historical, 'absolute' concepts are, or at least ought to be, ideational syntheses that are complete and determinate in themselves, logical totalities encompassing the process which brought them to light and expressing the meaning of this process without having recourse to scenic illustrations. According to Hegel, the truth about the world lies precisely in concepts of this all-encompassing and non-narrative kind:

> Anschauung oder Sein sind wohl der Natur nach das Erste oder die Bedingung für den Begriff, aber sie sind darum nicht das an und für sich Unbedingte; im Begriffe hebt sich vielmehr ihre Realität und damit zugleich der Schein auf, den sie als das bedingende Reelle hatten. Wenn es nicht um die *Wahrheit*, sondern nur um die *Historie* zu tun ist, wie es im Vorstellen und dem erscheinenden Denken zugehe, so kann man allerdings bei der Erzählung stehenbleiben, daß wir mit Gefühlen und Anschauungen anfangen und der Verstand aus dem Mannigfaltigen derselben eine Allgemeinheit oder ein Abstraktes herausziehe [...] Aber die Philosophie soll keine Erzählung dessen sein, was geschieht, sondern eine Erkenntnis dessen, was *wahr* darin ist, und aus dem Wahren soll sie ferner das begreifen, was in der Erzählung als ein bloßes Geschehen erscheint. (TWA VI, 260)

> [Sensory intuition or being are no doubt first in the order of nature, or are the condition for the concept, but they are not unconditioned in and for themselves; on the contrary, in the concept their reality is sublated and, consequently, so is also the appearance that they had of being the conditioning reality. If it is not the *truth* which is at issue but only the *history* of how representation operates and thought appears, then we might as well stick to the narration that we begin with feelings and intuitions and that our intellect then extracts something universal or an abstraction from this manifold [...] But philosophy ought not to be a narration of what happens, but the knowledge of what is *true* in it, and

knowing this truth, it further ought to comprehend that which in narration appears to be merely a series of events.]¹¹⁸

Although its systematic purpose is to prove the possibility of knowing the truth in an absolute way, the *Phenomenology* does not actually develop the 'absolute' concepts necessary to express the truth. It instead contains what Hegel criticizes in the quoted passage: (hi)stories of 'how representation operates and thought appears'.

For Hegel, these (hi)stories are sublated in the concepts of philosophy, and their various contradictions speculatively resolved. Knowledge thus returns to the kind of relationship in which it first originated, sense-certainty, but this time assuming the positive and truly universal shape of a well-defined conceptual system, a synchronic ensemble wherein each part immediately refers to the whole. The truth of this system, Hegel promises, is 'not only *in itself* completely identical with *certainty* [*Gewißheit*], but also has the *shape* of self-certainty' (PhG 582/485★), and in it, 'the wounds of the spirit heal without leaving scars' (PhG 492/407★).

But one might wonder, still, whether the (hi)stories of knowledge can ever be sublated in full, whether the difference, as well as the interval, between process and result can be eliminated and conceptually reconciled, and whether the self-certainty of Hegel's system — which is indeed *speculative* — is able to replace narrative demonstration with one final 'reconciliatory YEA' (PhG 494/409★) that puts an end to all division and contradiction. For without demonstration, and hence as pure disembodied thoughts outside time, concepts have neither reality nor tangible meaning, as Hegel concedes himself: 'nothing is *known* that is not in *experience*' (PhG 585/487★).

The principal means of demonstrating the (hi)stories of *human* knowledge are scenographies. Although the chapters of the *Phenomenology* usually open in an 'argumentative'¹¹⁹ style, the introduced concerns and concepts achieve significance only through scenographies. Readerly aesthesis is required to bring these demonstrations to life. *We* must translate Hegel's (hi)stories into tangible scenes to be in a position to grasp their meaning. *We* must stage his illustrations of sense-certainty and perception, of the understanding, of reason and desire, and of all the other forms of consciousness to extract their concepts. We thus connect concept and experience, story and history, process and result — not once and for all, as in the 'absolute' concepts of Hegelian philosophy, but paradoxically and recursively, as in the dialectic of perception.

Notes to Part I

1. Grünbein, *Koloß im Nebel: Gedichte* (Berlin: Suhrkamp Verlag, 2012), p. 42.
2. GW I, 381–98. All subsequent quotations from the *Bericht einer Alpenwanderung*, which is an editorial title, refer to this edition. The autograph has meanwhile disappeared, but the editors hold that it was reliably preserved through Rosenkranz's *G. W. F. Hegel's Leben* (Berlin: Duncker und Humblot, 1844), wherein it was published for the first time. I thank Emanuel Tandler for bringing this small gem to my attention.
3. Christoph Meiners, *Briefe über die Schweiz: Zweiter Theil* (Berlin: Spener, 1785), p. 1.
4. Particularly 'ludicrous' [abgeschmackt] Hegel finds the myths surrounding the Gotthard passage, especially the so-called Teufelsbrücke, adding wryly that the urge for mythic explanations

amongst the locals is readily understood considering the 'childish sense of these herdsmen [Hirtenvölker]' (GW I, 396).

5. Lessing here writes that, in showing 'never more than one single instant [Augenblick]', a painting necessarily constrains the 'free play' of the beholder's imagination, unless the depicted moment is chosen wisely (*Laokoon*, p. 32).

6. GW x.2, 827. Hegel makes this remark in a 'private report' or *Privatgutachten* (GW x.2, 823–32) concerning the 'teaching of philosophy at the Gymnasium level' [den Vortrag der philosophischen Vorbereitungswissenschaften auf Gymnasien], written in October 1812 and addressed to his friend and superior F. I. Niethammer. The optical experiments with Goethe during his time at Jena may have also contributed to Hegel's developing interest in nature. Later, Hegel and his students were instrumental in disseminating Goethe's theory of colours, thus assisting Goethe, as he wrote not without irony to Zelter in October 1821, in securing a 'triumph even in that domain' (*Hegel in Berichten seiner Zeitgenossen*, ed. by Günther Nicolin (Hamburg: Meiner, 1970), p. 229 #354).

7. Stephen Houlgate, *Hegel's Phenomenology of Spirit: A Reader's Guide* (New York: Bloomsbury, 2013), p. 51.

8. *Enzyklopädie der philosophischen Wissenschaften im Grundrisse* (1830), §§ 420–21, which I quote throughout after TWA.

9. Schopenhauer in his finest English prose to his publisher Francis Haywood in 1829 (*Hegel in Berichten seiner Zeitgenossen*, p. 408 #621), as well as *Die Welt als Wille und Vorstellung*, in *Werke in zehn Bänden* (Zurich: Diogenes, 1977), IV, 520.

10. GW xxv.1, 108. This text reproduces Hotho's record or *Mitschrift*, but similar statements can be adduced from later records, namely from Griesheim's record of Hegel's 1825 lecture on subjective spirit (GW xxv.1, 417–25). Note also § 413 in the *Enzyklopädie* of 1830, where consciousness is defined from the beginning as self-reflexive, specifically as 'die unendliche Beziehung des Geistes auf sich, aber als *subjective*'.

11. As for the 'synthetic unity of apperception', see KrV B 132–47, apperception being Kant's term for self-consciousness, 'the consciousness of oneself' (B 68). In the chapter on Novalis, I elaborate on Fichte's theory of consciousness as *Thathandlung*.

12. Robert Pippin, *Hegel's Idealism: The Satisfactions of Self-Consciousness* (Cambridge; New York: Cambridge University Press, 1989) details Kant's influence on Hegel, which concerns above all Kant's idea of a 'transcendental unity of apperception'. The case against theories of consciousness based on reflection (viz. apperception) was made by Dieter Henrich, e.g. in 'Selbstbewusstsein: Kritische Einleitung in eine Theorie', in *Hermeneutik und Dialektik*, ed. by Rüdiger Bubner and others (Tübingen: Mohr, 1970), pp. 257–84 (p. 268), and also by students of his, notably Manfred Frank, *Präreflexives Selbstbewusstsein: Vier Vorlesungen* (Stuttgart: Reclam, 2015).

13. Pippin, *Hegel's Idealism*, p. 69, brought this passage to my attention. As for Hegel's sustained critique of the concept/intuition dualism, see *Hegel's Idealism*, pp. 25–31, 85–88, 106–08, and 125–27.

14. Kant here talks about the 'schematism of the understanding', viz. the power to synthesize concepts with intuitions, in which the unity of apperception announces itself: 'From this it is clear that the schematism of the understanding [...] comes down to nothing other than the unity of all the manifold of intuition [die Einheit alles Mannigfaltigen der Anschauung] [...] and thus indirectly to the unity of apperception' (KrV A 145).

15. Pippin, *Hegel's Idealism*, pp. 114–15.

16. Cf. §§ 440–43 in the *Enzyklopädie* of 1830.

17. Pippin, *Hegel's Idealism*, pp. 121, 126.

18. As for the complex introductory mission of the *Phenomenology*, see TWA 5, 17–18, and § 36 in Hegel's first *Enzyklopädie der philosophischen Wissenschaften im Grundriss* (Heidelberg: Oßwald, 1817), pp. 30–31, as well as Stephen Houlgate, 'G. W. F. Hegel', in *The Blackwell Guide to the Modern Philosophers: From Descartes to Nietzsche*, ed. by Steven M. Emmanuel (Malden: Blackwell, 2000), pp. 278–305, and Walter Jaeschke, *Hegel-Handbuch: Leben — Werk — Schule*, 3rd edn (Stuttgart: Metzler, 2016), pp. 161–66.

19. See Matthias Kettner, *Hegels 'sinnliche Gewissheit': Diskursanalytischer Kommentar* (Frankfurt am

Main: Campus, 1990); Brady Bowman, *Sinnliche Gewissheit: Zur systematischen Vorgeschichte eines Problems des deutschen Idealismus* (Berlin: Akademie Verlag, 2003); and Kenneth R. Westphal, *Hegel, Hume und die Identität wahrnehmbarer Dinge: Historisch-kritische Analyse zum Kapitel Wahrnehmung in der Phänomenologie von 1807* (Frankfurt am Main: Klostermann, 1998). Further commentaries on which I rely include Wilhelm Purpus, *Zur Dialektik des Bewusstseins nach Hegel: Ein Beitrag zur Würdigung der 'Phänomenologie des Geistes'* (Berlin: Trowitzsch, 1908); Charles Taylor, 'The Opening Arguments of the *Phenomenology*', in *Hegel: A Collection of Critical Essays*, ed. by Alasdair MacIntyre (Garden City: Anchor Books, 1972), pp. 151–87; Kenneth R. Westphal, 'Hegel and Hume on Perception and Concept-Empiricism', *Journal of the History of Philosophy*, 36 (1998), 99–123; Anton Friedrich Koch, 'Sinnliche Gewißheit und Wahrnehmung: Die beiden ersten Kapitel der *Phänomenologie des Geistes*', in *Hegels Phänomenologie des Geistes: Ein kooperativer Kommentar zu einem Schlüsselwerk der Moderne*, ed. by Klaus Vieweg and Wolfgang Welsch (Frankfurt am Main: Suhrkamp, 2008), pp. 135–52; Houlgate, *Hegel's Phenomenology of Spirit*, pp. 31–83; and Robert Stern, *The Routledge Guide Book to Hegel's Phenomenology of Spirit*, 2nd edn (New York: Routledge, 2013), pp. 54–84.
20. Interestingly, Hegel's phenomenological method resembles the blend of scepticism Wilhelm Traugott Krug, his preferred punching bag during the Jena period, advocates in his *Entwurf eines neuen Organon's der Philosophie, oder, Versuch über die Prinzipien der philosophischen Enkenntniss* (Meissen: Erbstein, 1801). Hegel was well aware of this work. In 1802, he published a mocking review of Krug's philosophy in the *Kritisches Journal der Philosophie* (TWA II, 188–207), not yet knowing that in just a few of years he, too, would preach scepticism in order to achieve what Krug, on his account, failed to achieve, the philosophical education of the public by way of portraying 'the facts of consciousness' (TWA II, 206).
21. *Enzyklopädie* of 1830, *Zusatz* to § 447 (TWA x, 248).
22. Ryosuke Ohashi, 'Die Tragweite des Sinnlichen', in *Hegels Phänomenologie des Geistes*, pp. 115–34 (p. 115).
23. Taylor, 'The Opening Arguments of the *Phenomenology*', p. 173. Taylor is certainly right in saying that the clash 'between the two dimensions of a thing, as particular (*ausschließendes Eins*) and as ensemble of properties', need not be called a contradiction but could be regarded instead 'as two ways of presenting the same object' (ibid.). In any case, Hegel is not so much interested in the opposition as in the interdependence of these aspects, which Taylor (pp. 172–73) acknowledges.
24. The term 'structure' I understand in the sense of Jan Mukarovsky's 1940 article 'Structuralism in Aesthetics and in the Study of Literature', in *Kapitel aus der Poetik* (Frankfurt am Main: Suhrkamp, 1967), pp. 7–33, where it is defined as a dynamic interplay of distinct functional elements, as opposed to a stable 'summative totality' (p. 11). It seems fair to say that this concept of a structure is synonymous with what Hegel calls a dialectic.
25. Notice, however, that Hegel also claims the inverse, that subject must assume 'substantiality' — stability and permanence — to *be* the one and only *lasting* truth, an aspect Kant's and Fichte's epistemologies must lack, Hegel argues, because these 'subjective idealisms' merely focus on the subjective conditions of cognition. Jaeschke, *Hegel-Handbuch*, pp. 182–83, illuminates the programmatic but cryptic passage PhG 22–29/9–14★, in particular the meanings of 'subject' and 'subjectivity' in the *Phenomenology*.
26. TWA XVIII, 55.
27. Some Hegel translators render *einzeln, Einzelnes, Einzelheit* as 'individual', 'individuality' in English, while others employ 'single', 'singular', 'singularity'. *Das Besondere, Besonderheit* — an individuality recognized as belonging to a specific kind or class — is usually rendered in English as 'particular' and 'particularity', which as such already bears the mark of universality (*das Allgemeine*). Unlike perception, however, which recognizes this threefold distinctions, sense-certainty lacks the ability to differentiate between a thing's individual existence (thatness) and its particular essence (whatness), or the set of properties defining this thing against others. According to Hegel, sense-certainty only grasps the binary contrast between universals (e.g. hereness and nowness) and their opposite, everything that is not universal, which in this dual juxtaposition are traditionally termed particulars, rather than individuals or singulars. I shall

follow this tradition in calling 'the This' mostly a particular, although Hegel thinks of it not as *Besonderes* but as *Einzelnes*. As for the Hegelian triad *einzeln/besonders/allgemein*, see Michael J. Inwood, *A Hegel Dictionary* (Oxford: Blackwell, 1992), pp. 302–05, as well as Glenn Alexander Magee, *The Hegel Dictionary* (London; New York: Continuum, 2010), pp. 254–55.

28. Stern, *The Routledge Guide Book to Hegel's Phenomenology*, p. 55. The fact that Stern vacillates here between particularity and singularity in characterizing 'the This' illustrates the terminological difficulty mentioned in the preceding note.

29. See KrV A 19, as well as § 7, 'Von der Sinnlichkeit im Gegensatz mit dem Verstande', in Kant's *Anthropologie in pragmatischer Hinsicht* (*Gesammelte Schriften* (Akademieausgabe), 29 vols (Berlin: Reimer; De Gruyter, 1902–), VII (1907), 140–43). Note also KrV A 48, where Kant similarly defines sensuousness as 'the *receptivity* of our soul [unseres Gemüts]', as opposed to the ability of the understanding to spontaneously 'produce representations'. At first, the division between sensuousness and understanding, sensory receptivity and conceptual spontaneity, seems both intuitive and natural, but Kant quickly runs into difficulties, which become apparent when he talks about the apprehension of spatial shapes and figures. If it is true that the a priori form of space is as such infinite and sensuousness a purely receptive faculty, how then is it possible for us to see distinct shapes? How can the eye produce such synthesis and recognition *although* it by definition lacks spontaneity? The footnote on B 160–61 brings this paradox to light. Kant here notes that recognizing individual shapes hinges on a '*synthetic grasp* of the manifold' [*Zusammenfassung* des Mannigfaltigen] that as such does 'not belong to the senses' but 'precedes all conceptual activity' [allem Begriffe vorhergehe]. The same paradox can be observed in A 24 and B 136 (fn.). Consequently, and contrary to his narrow definition of sensuousness as pure receptivity, Kant realizes that sensory intuition involves a measure of spontaneity as well. A solution is offered in the Third Critique, where Kant (*Werke*, x, B 28) ascribes the preconceptual synthesis of the sensory manifold to 'the *imagination*'. KrV A 78–79 similarly states that the sensory manifold is synthesized 'through the imagination' — the reserve force Kant tends to call upon whenever the other faculties end up in a jam. However, neither passage specifies the complicity between sensuousness and imagination in the process of perception. As for the 'synthesis of the manifold' problem in Kant's First Critique, see Béatrice Longuenesse, *Kant and the Capacity to Judge: Sensibility and Discursivity in the Transcendental Analytic of the Critique of Pure Reason* (Princeton: Princeton University Press, 1998), pp. 214–29. Hegel did not elaborate on these passages, but they certainly deepen the suspicion against the Kantian dichotomy between concepts and intuitions, receptivity and spontaneity. Interestingly, neuroscientists are dealing with a similar crux, the so-called 'binding-problem', which concerns the question of how 'the brain' is able to organize spontaneously or 'bind' together different sensory aspects 'such as color, motion, location, and object identity', although these are 'processed in separate brain regions' (Adina L. Roskies, 'The Binding Problem', *Neuron* 24 (1999), 7–9 (p. 9)).

30. KrV A 51–52/B 75–76:

> Ohne Sinnlichkeit würde uns kein Gegenstand gegeben, und ohne Verstand keiner gedacht werden. Gedanken ohne Inhalt sind leer, Anschauungen ohne Begriffe sind blind. [...] *Deswegen darf man aber doch nicht ihren Anteil vermischen, sondern man hat große Ursache, jedes von dem andern sorgfältig abzusondern, und zu unterscheiden.* Daher unterscheiden wir die Wissenschaft der Regeln der Sinnlichkeit überhaupt, d.i. Ästhetik, von der Wissenschaft der Verstandesregeln überhaupt, d.i. der Logik. (emphasis added)

Westphal, *Hegel, Hume und die Identität wahrnehmbarer Dinge*, p. 70, also highlights the point I am making, but forgets to mention Hegel's fundamental disagreement with Kant's passivist understanding of sensuousness.

31. Jaeschke, *Hegel-Handbuch*, pp. 350–53, underscores this important point. As a first introduction to Hegel's concept of knowledge, see Koch, 'Sinnliche Gewißheit und Wahrnehmung', pp. 135–38, as well as *Handbuch Deutscher Idealismus*, ed. by Hans-Jörg Sandkühler (Stuttgart: Metzler, 2005), pp. 72–78. Overall, however, Hegel envisions one final 'reconciliatory YEA' (PhG 494/409*) sublating all contradiction and opposition. Hegel regarded this 'speculative' synthesis of differences as the 'positive' or 'reasonable' and also indubitable result of his philosophy (see §§

79–82 in the *Enzyklopädie* of 1830, as well TWA V, 16–17), a totalizing, if not totalitarian, stance frequently criticized by thinkers who reject the very notion of a philosophical system. But Hegel would not be Hegel if he did not also claim the exact opposite, that difference, not identity, is '*the determinate foundation of all activity and self-movement*' (TWA VI, 47). Such is the struggle between the negativity and the positivity of knowledge in Hegel, as that between contradiction and closure, dialectics and speculation.

32. Hegel elaborates on the meaning of *aufheben* in the *Wissenschaft der Logik*, calling it here 'one of the most important concepts of philosophy' (TWA V, 113). The idea that Hegel's use of *aufheben* was inspired by Schiller I take from Walter Kaufmann, *Hegel: A Reinterpretation* (Garden City: Anchor Books, 1966), pp. 52–53, and William Desmond, 'Art, Philosophy and Concreteness in Hegel', *The Owl of Minerva*, 16 (1985), 131–46 (p. 132 n. 3). The idea can be supported with Schiller's eighteenth letter on *Ästhetische Erziehung* (*Sämtliche Werke*, V, 624–27). Schiller calls beauty here 'an intermediary state' connecting 'two states *that are opposed to one another*', namely sensation and intellection, such that 'both states completely disappear in a third one and no trace remains of their division'. Beauty is this third state reconciling the intellect with the senses in 'pure aesthetic unity'. Additionally, Hegel seems to have appropriated Schiller's notions of alienation (*Entfremdung*) and mediation (*Vermittlung*). Despite such continuities, to which Hegel alludes in his *Aesthetics* (TWA XIII, 89–91), there are also crucial differences separating Schiller from Hegel. For example, Schiller argued, just like Kant, 'that the idea of freedom has to be *read into* appearances' (Frederick Beiser, *Schiller as Philosopher* (Oxford, Oxford University Press, 2005), p. 11), whereas Hegel regarded it as the absolute and very real essence of history. Only in his theory of beauty does Schiller come close to undermining the Kantian dichotomy between noumena and phenomena in that he defines beauty in both the *Kallias* letters and the *Ästhetische Erziehung* as 'Freiheit in der Erscheinung', a freedom appearing in and through art (cf. *Sämtliche Werke* V, 400, 409–26, as well as 644 n.).

33. Bowman, *Sinnliche Gewissheit*, pp. 236–37, provides a schematic overview on the sense-certainty chapter, similarly distinguishing three phases of sense-certainty. Koch, 'Sinnliche Gewißheit und Wahrnehmung', p. 141, also distinguishes three phases, associating each with a specific conceptual standpoint: the first phase with objectivist realism, the second with subjectivist idealism, and the third with neutral monism.

34. As for the significance of *Beispiel* and *beiherspielen* in Hegel, see Andrzej Warminski, 'Reading for Example: "Sense-Certainty" in Hegel's *Phenomenology of Spirit*', *Diacritics*, 11 (1981), 83–95 (pp. 91–94), as well as 'Pre-Positional By-Play', *Glyph*, 3 (1978), 98–117, but also Nathan Todd Andersen's critical response in 'Example, Experiment and Experience in Hegel's *Phenomenology of Spirit*' (PhD, The Pennsylvania State University, 2000), pp. 99–119.

35. This word is rendered in the Theorie-Werkausgabe (TWA) as a lower-case *jetzt*, but I am following the original print (GW IX, 64), which has *Jetzt*, or rather *Itzt*.

36. Kittler, *Aufschreibesysteme 1800/1900*, pp. 200–06, has a provocative discussion of this first example of sense-certainty, suggesting that it is an unconscious replay of motherly alphabetization.

37. The Theorie-Werkausgabe (TWA) nominalizes most adjectives in this sentence (e.g. *Einfaches*, *Allgemeines*, etc.), as though they were self-sufficient concepts. But I read these words as attributive to the omitted noun *Jetzt*, a reading that is confirmed by the lower-case spelling of these adjectives in the first edition (GW IX, 65).

38. GW VI, pp. 282–96 (pp. 286, 282). In relating 'singularity as such' [Einzelnheit als solche] to the 'universal, empty [...] concepts' (p. 283) of time and space under the sign of language, this fragment, composed in 1803 or 1804, no doubt anticipates the *Phenomenology* chapter on sense-certainty.

39. Jacques Derrida, *Glas*, trans. John P. Leavey and Richard Rand (Lincoln: University of Nebraska Press, 1986), p. 1. In a sense, however, every sign is a citation, namely a citation of the particular meaning or referent which it is supposed to represent.

40. *Encyclopedia of the Philosophical Sciences in Basic Outline: Part*, trans. and ed. by Klaus Brinkmann and Daniel O. Dahlstrom (Cambridge: Cambridge University Press, 2010–), I, 52–53 (translation slightly modified).

41. Karl Löwith, *Von Hegel zu Nietzsche: Der revolutionäre Bruch im Denken des neunzehnten*

Jahrhunderts (Hamburg: Meiner, 1995), p. 30. In 'Hegel's Begriff der Erfahrung', Heidegger similarly criticizes the 'onto-theological' essence of Hegel's philosophy (*Gesamtausgabe*, v (1977), 195). Regarding the proximity between theology and philosophy because of their common quest for God or eternal, metaphysical Truth, see § 85 in the *Enzyklopädie* of 1830, but also note the critical differences pointed out in the second and third preface to the *Enzyklopädie* (TWA viii, 22–32, 33–38).

42. George di Giovanni, 'Introduction', in G. W. F. Hegel, *The Science of Logic*, trans. and ed. by George di Giovanni (Cambridge: Cambridge University Press, 2010), pp. xi–lxii (p. xxxiv).
43. GW xxv.1, 16–17: 'Inhalt ist Formbestimmung und diese ist ihm wesentlich; was er ist, ist er durch sie.' Hegel was not the only one to stress the dialectic between form and content at his time. For example, Goethe similarly remarked: 'Gehalt bringt die Form mit; Form ist nie ohne Gehalt'; see *Goethe-Handbuch*, ed. by Bernd Witte and others, 4 vols (Stuttgart: Metzler, 1996), iv.1, 342 (concerning Goethe's notion of 'Gehalt').
44. Theodor Bodammer, *Hegels Deutung der Sprache: Interpretationen zu Hegels Äußerungen über die Sprache* (Hamburg: Meiner, 1969), pp. 239–40.
45. The expression refers to 'mathematical formulas', hence the language of mathematics, but Novalis immediately clarifies that 'the same applies to language as well' (N ii, 438).
46. As for the role of language in, and impact on, Hegel's thought, see John McCumber, *The Company of Words: Hegel, Language, and Systematic Philosophy* (Evanston: Northwestern University Press, 1993); John Durham Peters, '"The Root of Humanity": Hegel on Language and Communication', in *Figuring the Self: Subject, Absolute, and Others in Classical German Philosophy*, ed. by David E. Klemm and Günter Zöller (Albany: State University of New York Press, 1997), pp. 227–44; and Jere O'Neill Surber, ed., *Hegel and Language* (Albany: SUNY Press, 2006). Note also Adorno's 'Skoteinos oder Wie zu lesen sei', in *Zur Metakritik der Erkenntnistheorie/Drei Studien zu Hegel*, ed. by Rolf Tiedemann (Frankfurt am Main: Suhrkamp, 1970), pp. 336–75. Adorno here shows that the traditional philosophical ideal of a strictly descriptive terminology is constantly undermined by Hegel's dialectical method, since this method dynamizes static definitions and intentionally confuses distinctions.
47. Kittler, *Philosophien der Literatur*, p. 183.
48. I thank Sebastien Fanzun for bringing this passage to my attention.
49. Kaufmann, pp. 134–37, identifies Faust with consciousness's striving for true knowledge and Mephistopheles — 'der Geist, der stets verneint' — with the principle of negativity. Two students of Hegel, Karl Friedrich Göschel (1781–1861) and Hermann Friedrich Wilhelm Hinrichs (1794–1861), were in fact the first scholars to liken Goethe's *Faust* to Hegel's *Phenomenology*, interpreting the former through the lens of the latter text; see Friedrich A. Kittler, *Philosophien der Literatur*, pp. 199–209, and Klaus Weimar, *Geschichte der deutschen Literaturwissenschaft bis zum Ende des 19. Jahrhunderts* (Munich: Fink, 1989), pp. 375–83. Vesa Oittinen, 'Mephisto und die List der Vernunft', *Deutsche Zeitschrift für Philosophie*, 39 (1991), 825–38, makes an interesting connection between Mephisto and dialectical progress. For a contrasting view, see Hermann Patsch, '" ... ach! Philosophie": Fichte, Schelling und Hegel über Goethes *Faust*. Ein Fragment', *Jahrbuch des Freien Deutschen Hochstifts* (2015), 80–122 (pp. 113–22). Patsch thinks that such comparisons lack philological substance (p. 119).
50. Warminski, 'Reading for Example', pp. 86–88, and Kittler, *Philosophien der Literatur*, pp. 168–69, similarly emphasize the scenic character of the *Phenomenology*.
51. See Kettner, *Hegels 'sinnliche Gewißheit'*, pp. 9, 205–66; Koch, 'Sinnliche Gewißheit und Wahrnehmung', pp. 139–45; and Willem A. de Vries, 'Sense-Certainty and the "This-Such"', in *Hegel's Phenomenology of Spirit: A Critical Guide* (Cambridge: Cambridge University Press, 2008), pp. 63–75. In 'Hegel's Phenomenological Method and Analysis of Consciousness', in *The Blackwell Guide to Hegel's 'Phenomenology of Spirit'* (Oxford: Wiley-Blackwell, 2009), pp. 1–36, Kenneth R. Westphal even claims that Hegel anticipates 'recent semantic theory', according to which 'neither ostensive designation nor singular cognitive reference are possible' without drawing on universal concepts (p. 7).
52. Terry P. Pinkard, *Hegel's Phenomenology: The Sociality of Reason* (Cambridge: Cambridge University Press, 1994), p. 27.

53. Jacques Derrida, *Of Grammatology*, trans. by Gayatri Chakravorty Spivak (Baltimore: Johns Hopkins University Press, 1976), p. 26.
54. This manuscript, part of the so called *Jenaer Systementwürfe III* (GW VIII), was presumably written down in the autumn of 1805 and served at least once as the basis for a lecture course in the summer of 1806. Thus chronologically, it represents the closest intertext to the *Phenomenology*. There is some uncertainty, however, as to when Hegel stopped working on the manuscript, including revisions and marginal notes; see the editorial comments (GW VIII, 314–19, 348–61). It seems possible that Hegel kept using the manuscript for his teaching until he became a full Professor of Philosophy at Heidelberg, which was in 1816. At any rate, with the appearance of the first *Enzyklopädie* in 1817 the manuscript became finally obsolete. As for the genetic importance of this manuscript, see H. S. Harris, 'Hegel's Intellectual Development to 1807', in *The Cambridge Companion to Hegel*, ed. by Frederick C. Beiser (Cambridge: Cambridge University Press, 1993), pp. 25–51 (pp. 38–51), and Otto Pöggeler, 'Hegels Jenaer Systemkonzeption', *Philosophisches Jahrbuch*, 71 (1963), 268–318.
55. GW VIII, 11: 'denn das *Eins* [der Zeit] ist [...] schlechthin ausschliessend, das heißt *anderes negirend* [...] in seinem Begriff ist daher absolut das Negiren, d. h. es ist an sich selbst negiren, es ist diß Andre, welches von ihm negirt wird.'
56. GW VIII, 11, 12–13.
57. GW VIII, 13: 'diese Negativität ist der absolute Begriff selbst, das Unendliche, das reine Selbst des Fürsich seyns [...] Sie ist um deßwillen die höchste Macht alles Seyenden, und die wahre Betrachtungsart alles Seyenden ist deswegen es in seiner Zeit, d. h. in seinem Begriffe, worin alles nur als verschwindendes Moment ist, zu betrachten'.
58. *Hegel's Philosophy of Nature*, trans. and ed. by Michael John Petry, 3 vols (London: Allen and Unwin, 1970), I, 229–30, 233. In the Introduction to his *Ästhetik*, Hegel cites music as the essential representation of time's inner 'negativity' (TWA XIII, 121), yet he hardly ever explains this claim and eventually loses sight of it, defining music instead as the epitome of Romantic subjectivity. It was Adorno who brought Hegel's initial characterization to life in describing the musical process precisely as 'immanent negation' or self-negation (*Beethoven*, pp. 34–51), which he finds epitomized in works from Beethoven's middle period such as the Waldstein sonata (ibid., pp. 90–91) and his third symphony, the *Eroica* (ibid., p. 105).
59. Husserl never mentions Hegel when he writes about time-consciousness, nor does he consider him in the *Ideen*, although he too conceives of particulars here as ' "*Dies da!*" oder pure, syntaktisch formlose individuelle Einzelheit' that Aristotle had called *tode ti* (*Husserliana*, III.2, 28). As for the conceptual parallels between Husserl and Hegel, see Smail Rapic, 'Husserls Untersuchungen zur Selbstzeitigung der Subjektivität auf dem Hintergrund der Zeittheorien Kants und Hegels', in *Husserl und die klassische deutsche Philosophie*, ed. by Faustino Fabbianelli and Sebastian Luft (Cham: Springer, 2014), pp. 149–60.
60. Derrida, *Speech and Phenomena*, pp. 60–69; 84–88. Derrida's dialogue with Hegel as both a precursor and an antipode is extensive; see *Hegel after Derrida*, ed. by Stuart Barnett (London; New York: Routledge, 1998).
61. In his *Confessions*, trans. William Watts, 2 vols (London: Heinemann, 1912), Augustine writes that time 'is tending not to be' (II, 239) and that the present moment represents a purely negative unit that 'takes not up any space' (II, 245): *praesens autem nullum habet spatium*. It is only in our souls or minds (*in anima*) that we are able to perceive temporal extension and, therefore, 'a present time of past things; a present time of present things; and a present time of future things' (II, 253). Yet this ability is not, as in Hegel, the profane result of negation but rather a divine gift, which as such affords a glimpse into the eternal, unchangeable, all-encompassing Now of God himself, that never-ending heavenly presence in which the mind's 'dissolution amid the changing times' (II, 281) shall be redeemed.
62. Heidegger, *Sein und Zeit* (Tübingen: Niemeyer, 1967), pp. 432–33. The similarities Heidegger points out between Aristotle and Hegel are nonetheless striking. As for Hegel's Aristotclianism, see Nicolai Hartmann's still unsurpassed lecture 'Aristoteles und Hegel', *Beiträge zur Philosophie des deutschen Idealismus*, 3 (1923), 1–36.
63. Cf. Henri Bergson, *Essai sur les données immédiates de la conscience* (Paris: Presses Universitaires de

France, 1991), p. 170: 'Qu'est-ce que la durée au-dedans de nous? Une multiplicité qualitative, sans ressemblance avec le nombre; un développement organique qui n'est pourtant pas une quantité croissante; une hétérogénéité pure au sein de laquelle il n'y a pas de qualités distinctes. Bref, les moments de la durée interne ne sont pas extérieurs les uns aux autres.' 'Simultaneity' is another, less paradoxical term Bergson uses to capture the 'confused multiplicity' (p. 96) and 'organic' cohesion of indifferent moments that constitute the duration of time as he sees it. Yet simultaneity, too, means for him an undifferentiated multiplicity, an ensemble of many that permeate each other, instead of being next to each other — in short, an indivisible whole that resembles the 'solidary' organization of 'a living being' (p. 75). In fact, Bergson's ideas of multiplicity and simultaneity overlap with what Hegel calls 'the Also' of thinghood, or the 'indifferent unity' [gleichgültige Einheit] of substance (PhG 95/69*), and therefore prompt the same critical question Hegel is asking as he examines perception: is it possible to perceive heterogeneity without the concepts of negation and difference? If Gilles Deleuze is right in saying that Bergson thinks of temporal duration as 'substance itself' and understands its intrinsic heterogeneity 'independently of all forms of negation' (*Bergsonism*, trans. Barbara Habberjam and Hugh Tomlinson (New York: Zone Books, 1991), p. 37, 46), then the overlap is not at all coincidental.
64. De Vries, p. 73.
65. See Derrida, *Speech and Phenomena*, pp. 85–87, and *Margins of Philosophy*, trans. by Alan Bass (Chicago: University of Chicago Press, 1982), pp. 52–56. According to Martin Hägglund, *Radical Atheism: Derrida and the Time of Life* (Stanford: Stanford University Press, 2008), pp. 71–73, the 'coimplication of temporalization and spatialization' — viz. the 'becoming-space of time' and, conversely, 'the becoming-time of space' — represents the essence of Derrida's concept of 'arche-writing' or 'espacement'.
66. Hegel, *Vorlesungen über die Philosophie der Natur, Berlin 1819/1820: Nachgeschrieben von Johann Rudolf Ringier*, ed. by Martin Bondeli and Hoo Nam Seelmann (Hamburg: Meiner, 2002), pp. 19, 21, as well as p. 205 (record of Gottfried Bernhardy, who later became a professor of philology at Berlin and Halle).
67. See §§ 254–62 in the *Enzyklopädie* of 1830, esp. § 260, as well as §§ 197–203 in the first edition. In contrast to the sense-certainty chapter, Hegel begins in the *Enzyklopädie* not with a consideration of time or 'the Now' but instead with a discussion of space. For a systematic explication of Hegel's concepts of time and space, see Brigitte Falkenburg, *Die Form der Materie: Zur Metaphysik der Natur bei Kant und Hegel* (Frankfurt am Main: Athenäum, 1987), pp. 184–239.
68. GW VIII, 14, 18: 'Ihr Wesen ist die unmittelbare Einheit der Zeit und des Raumes zu seyn, welche Einheit eben die absolute Vermittlung an ihr hat [...] sie [Bewegung] ist die durch den Raum reale, bestehende Zeit, oder der durch die Zeit erst wahrhafft unterschiedne Raum.'
69. The concept of movement as a functional relation between time and space became dominant in the wake of Galilei and Descartes; see the entry 'Bewegung' in *Historisches Wörterbuch der Philosophie*, ed. by Joachim Ritter and others, 13 vols (1971), I, 872–76.
70. Purpus, p. 34. Unfortunately, Purpus's citations of Hegel are often corrupted and truncated, although he called himself the 'Alexandrian' philologist (p. 17) of Hegel's work.
71. Seymour Chatman, *Story and Discourse: Narrative Structure in Fiction and Film* (Ithaca: Cornell University Press, 1978), p. 26; Mieke Bal, *Narratology: Introduction to the Theory of Narrative* (Toronto: University of Toronto Press, 1997), pp. 7–8. It goes without saying that 'narrative' and 'narration' carry the same ambiguity as 'story' does.
72. Paul Ricoeur, 'Narrative Time', *Critical Inquiry*, 7 (1980), 169–90 (pp. 178–80). Siegfried Kracauer addresses the same 'dialectic' or 'antinomy' — he uses both terms — between diachronic and synchronic time, or historical development and historical period, in his last unfinished book, *History: The Last Things before the Last*, ed. by Paul Oskar Kristeller (Oxford: Oxford University Press, 1969), pp. 152–63.
73. Regarding philosophical speculation, see also § 81 in the *Enzyklopädie* of 1830.
74. Kaufmann, pp. 168, 175.
75. Houlgate, *Hegel's Phenomenology of Spirit*, p. 26.
76. 'Speculation' derives from Latin *speculat-* ('observed from a vantage point'), going back to

the verb *speculari* ('to spy, espy, descry', related to German *spähen*), and ultimately to *specula* ('watchtower') and *specere* ('to look, regard'). Thus, speculation basically means to be on the watch, regarding a problem closely in hopes of descrying its solution, namely a speculative concept serving as *tertium comparationis*.

77. Niklas Luhmann, *Liebe als Passion: Zur Codierung von Intimität* (Frankfurt am Main: Suhrkamp, 1982), p. 10.
78. A conceptual leap made possible by the fact that in contrast to the *Logic*, the *Phenomenology* simply 'presupposes' the existence of spatiotemporal things (Koch, 'Sinnliche Gewißheit und Wahrnehmung', p. 145).
79. The 'pittsburghegelianasaurus big beast pragmatist', as Robert Brandom was dubbed on the web, similarly interprets the perception chapter from the *Phenomenology* as exemplifying the 'fine structure of Hegelian negation'; see Brandom, 'Understanding the Object/Property Structure in Terms of Negation: An Introduction to Hegelian Logic and Metaphysics', 19 October 2014, <http://www.pitt.edu/~brandom/downloads/UOSTN%2014-10-19%20b.docx> [accessed 1 April 2019]. Moreover, Hegel's understanding of perception as differentiation resembles the concept of perception developed by Niklas Luhman in *Die Kunst der Gesellschaft*, pp. 13–91. Luhmann here defines perception as the 'actualization of distinctions (or "forms")', which are stabilized and reproduced through verbal articulation and communication (p. 27). Although Luhmann mentions Hegel when talking about differentiation (cf. pp. 52, 56 n. 71, 72–73), he does not refer to Hegel's reflexive concept of perception as involving both external difference (reflection-in-other) and internal unity (reflection-in-itself). Given the emphatic declaration from the *Wissenschaft der Logik* (TWA VI, 47), as well as similar claims in the *Phenomenology*, about the necessity of difference and diremption, it is puzzling that Luhmann, perhaps against his better judgement (cf. Luhmann, p. 43 n. 44), charges Hegel with attempting to undo difference in favour of simplicity and 'immediacy' (p. 73). This charge clearly oversimplifies Hegel's concept of identity as 'negation of negation' (TWA VI, 45), which in fact includes negation and difference. For a classic introduction to Hegel's concept of reflection, see Dieter Henrich, *Hegel im Kontext* (Berlin: Suhrkamp, 1971), pp. 95–156 (pp. 133–34). Regarding the parallels between Luhmann and Hegel, see Lutz Ellrich, 'Entgeistertes Beobachten: Desinformierende Mitteilungen über Luhmanns allzu verständliche Kommunikation mit Hegel', in *Die Logik der Systeme: Zur Kritik der systemtheoretischen Soziologie Niklas Luhmanns*, ed. by Peter-Ulrich Luhmann and Gerhard Wagner (Konstanz: UVK, 2000), pp. 73–126.
80. Hegel, *Heidelberg Writings: Journal Publications*, trans. and ed. by Brady Bowman and Allen Speight (Cambridge: Cambridge University Press, 2009), p. 8. Hegel makes this assertion in an 1816 review of F. H. Jacobi's philosophical works, where he criticizes Spinoza's concept of substance as eradicating difference and individuality, a criticism Hegel had indicated as early as 1801 in the so-called *Differenzschrift* (TWA II, 36) and fully developed in his lectures on the history of philosophy (TWA XX, 157–97). Although Hegel does not mention him by name in the *Phenomenology* chapter on perception, he certainly had Spinoza in mind when he discusses the indifferent 'Also' [Auch] of 'thinghood' — substance.
81. E. J. Lowe, 'Substance and Identity', in *Substanz: Neue Überlegungen zu einer klassischen Kategorie des Seienden*, ed. by Käthe Trettin (Frankfurt am Main: Klostermann, 2005), pp. 33–51 (p. 33).
82. Stern, *Routledge Guide Book to Hegel's Phenomenology*, pp. 62–71, is a representative example of the pervasive tendency in Hegel scholarship to understand One and Also as purely numeric concepts. Westphal, *Hegel, Hume und die Identität wahrnehmbarer Dinge*, pp. 97–118, by contrast, was the first to recognize the significance of diachrony and synchrony for Hegel's concept of object perception. My own reading is indebted to his study.
83. Lambert Wiesing, 'Einleitung', in *Philosophie der Wahrnehmung: Modelle und Reflexionen*, ed. by Lambert Wiesing (Frankfurt am Main: Suhrkamp, 2002), pp. 9–64 (pp. 53–54).
84. PhG 53/33*: 'Das Bestehen oder die Substanz eines Daseins ist die Sichselbstgleichheit; denn seine Ungleichheit mit sich wäre seine Auflösung'.
85. David Hume, *Treatise of Human Nature: A Critical Edition*, ed. by Mary J. Norton and David Fate Norton, 2 vols (Oxford: Oxford University Press, 2007), I, 136 (1.4.2.36). Pippin, *Hegel's Idealism*, pp. 126–27, reads the chapter on perception as a repudiation of 'associationism', be it empiricist

or rationalist in kind, while Westphal, *Hegel, Hume und die Identität wahrnehmbarer Dinge* focuses specifically on Hegel's implicit dialogue with Hume.
86. See TWA VI, 133–47; the direct quotations on pp. 140, 143, 141.
87. PhG 23–31/9–15*. As for the reciprocity of substance and subject in Hegel, see Henrich, *Hegel im Kontext*, pp. 95–99.
88. 'Recursive' as defined in the *Oxford Dictionary of English*, 3rd edn (Oxford: Oxford University Press, 2010).
89. Calling perception a recursive routine finds support in Anton Friedrich Koch's 2009 lectures on 'Hegel's Science of Logic' at Emory University <http://www.philosophie.uni-hd.de/imperia/md/content/fakultaeten/phil/philosophischesseminar2/koch/emory09.pdf> [accessed 1 April 2019]. Koch here describes Hegel's concept of consciousness as a 'recursive' 'computing device' (p. 13), more specifically as an 'input/output device for categorical forms' (p. 16). In 'Sinnliche Gewißheit und Wahrnehmung', pp. 135–39, Koch explains the operations of consciousness in similar terms.
90. Robert Stern, *Hegel, Kant and the Structure of the Object* (London: Routledge, 1990), p. vii. Unfortunately, Stern only glosses the chapters on sense-certainty and perception in his book (pp. 44–45), focusing instead on the *Wissenschaft der Logik* and Hegel's philosophy of nature.
91. See KrV B 111–13, as well as the 'Third Analogy of Experience' (KrV B 256–62) expanding on the 'principle of simultaneity, according to the law of reciprocity, or community'.
92. This phrase appears in a section titled 'Die Wechselwirkung der Dinge' (TWA VI, 137–39) — an unmistakable reference to Kant, specifically KrV B 111–13, B 256–62.
93. However, it was Leibniz who first introduced the term of apperception in the sense of self-consciousness; see Manfred Frank, *Ansichten der Subjektivität* (Berlin: Suhrkamp, 2012), pp. 10–11, as well as the entry 'Apperzeption' in the *Historisches Wörterbuch der Philosophie*, wherein a marginalia by Kant is cited that comes even closer to Hegel: 'To be aware of a representation means to know that you yourself are having it, viz., to distinguish it from other representations' [Sich einer Vorstellung bewust seyn, ist, wißen, daß man diese Vorstellung hat; d.h.: diese Vorstellung von den andern unterscheiden]. As for the different concepts of apperception in Kant and Hegel, see Pippin, *Hegel's Idealism*, esp. pp. 132–34.
94. Westphal, 'Hegel and Hume on Perception', p. 111.
95. GW VIII, 194–95: '*Aufmerksamkeit* ist die erste nothwendige Thätigkeit [...] *Fixiren*, Abstrahiren, herausnehmen, Anstrengung[,] Überwindung des unbestimmten der Empfindung'; cf. *Hegel and the Human Spirit: A Translation of the Jena Lectures on the Philosophy of Spirit (1805–06)*, trans. and ed. by Leo Rauch (Detroit: Wayne State University Press, 1983), pp. 93–94.
96. The 'phantasmagoric' scenery summoned by Hegel calls to mind magic lantern spectacles entertaining audiences across Europe at the turn of the eighteenth century. Johann Georg Schröpfer (1738–74), a pioneer of the industry with a telling name, and Etienne-Gaspard Robert (1736–1837), a contemporary of Hegel and the inventor of what became known precisely as 'phantasmagoria' (images projected on fumes so that they seem like moving apparitions), are names that come to mind in this context. Friedrich Kittler has demonstrated the deep fascination of Romantic writers, including Idealist philosophers, with optical media and the magic lantern in particular; see his 'Die Laterna magica der Literatur: Schillers und Hoffmanns Medienstrategien', *Athenäum: Jahrbuch für Romantik*, 4 (1994), 219–37, and *Optische Medien: Berliner Vorlesung 1999* (Berlin: Merve, 2002), pp. 114–20. In *Ghostly Apparitions: German Idealism, the Gothic Novel, and Optical Media* (New York: Zone Books, 2013), Stefan Andriopoulos takes up Kittler's cue, as he admits himself (p. 16 n. 22), and discusses 'the various surreptitious or overt adaptations of the ghostly and the magic lantern in the work of Kant, Hegel, and Schopenhauer' (p. 15). Regarding the quoted passage, Andriopoulos notes that it is 'Hegel's only conspicuous reference to the magic lantern and the visual medium of the phantasmagoria' (p. 67). I disagree, however, with Andriopoulos's claim (pp. 68–69) that 'the conclusion of Hegel's *Phenomenology* abandons "the labor of the concept"' by representing the development of consciousness as a 'gallery of images', because the usage of such (visual) metaphors is inevitable when explaining the meaning of concepts. In fact, key philosophical concepts like theory, speculation, and even concept itself are originally metaphors, metaphoric names for 'looking' at something

closely, 'espying' a possible solution, and 'grasping' meaning, and I am not sure that there is a non-metaphorical way of describing these abstract cognitive operations. To put this more radically, with Nietzsche, there is no mode of comprehension that could do without metaphoric translations.
97. *Hegel and the Human Spirit*, pp. 86–87.
98. Ibid., p. 87. What Hegel writes about 'the so-called association of *ideas*' betrays a rather superficial grasp of associationism on his part as late as 1805, and therefore casts some doubt on Westphal's claim that Hegel 'reached his results [in the *Phenomenology* chapter on perception] through an exacting reconsideration of a crucial section from Hume's *Treatise*' ('Hegel and Hume on Perception', p. 123). At any rate, Westphal never discusses this passage from the Jena Philosophy of Spirit.
99. Crary, pp. 6, 9, 79.
100. Specifically, I am thinking of Fichte's *Die Bestimmung des Menschen* (F II, 167–319 (pp. 228–29)), as well as fragments by Novalis (e.g. N II, 123 #301, 302) and philosophical lectures Friedrich Schlegel held at the University of Cologne between 1804 and 1806, wherein the seen 'image' of an object is called 'a creation [Hervorbringung] of the I' and thus 'a first step towards freedom' (*Kritische Friedrich-Schlegel-Ausgabe*, XII (1964), 344). Additionally, one might think of Schiller's claim, found in the twenty-sixth letter on *Ästhetische Erziehung*, that 'the object of eye and ear is a form we create' (*Sämtliche Werke*, V, 657). At one point in *Techniques of the Observer*, Crary (p. 99) does identify Hegel as an early proponent of 'subjective vision'. The quoted passage from the Jena Philosophy of Spirit (GW VIII, 186–88) suggests as much, of course, but the phrase Crary adduces from the *Phenomenology*'s preface to justify his claim — 'Dagegen muß behauptet werden, daß die Wahrheit nicht eine ausgeprägte Münze ist, die fertig gegeben und so eingestrichen werden kann' (PhG 40) — hardly does. In fact, there is no evidence that Hegel is here 'making a sweeping repudiation' of 'the Lockean notion of ideas "imprinting" themselves on passive minds', as Crary (p. 99) claims. As for the epistemic shift around 1800, from mechanistic models of perception to concepts emphasizing subjective activity, see Caroline Welsh, *Hirnhöhlenpoetiken: Theorien zur Wahrnehmung in Wissenschaft, Ästhetik und Literatur um 1800* (Freiburg im Breisgau: Rombach, 2003), esp. pp. 139–53 (on Schiller).
101. *Hegel and the Human Spirit*, pp. 89–90. Cf. Hegel's similar remarks on the sublation of perception through verbal expression in a slightly earlier Jena fragment (GW VI, 287–97).
102. Although Hegel took Friedrich Schlegel for a charlatan — an 'essentially *critical*' (as opposed to philosophical) mind thirsting for 'distinction' (TWA XIII, 92) — Schlegel makes nonetheless similar claims about the role of language in perception. In the aforementioned Cologne lectures on philosophy, Schlegel remarks that in 'generalizing' the perceived contents, 'the word' liberates perception from 'the tyranny of [external] things' and so increases subjective 'freedom and discretion [Spielraum]' (*Kritische Friedrich-Schlegel-Ausgabe*, XII (1964), 344). Thus for Schlegel, too, it is language that completes the transformation of passive sensations into coherent, if selective, perceptual relations. For a careful examination of their odd relationship, see Ernst Behler, 'Friedrich Schlegel und Hegel', *Hegel-Studien*, 2 (1963), 203–50.
103. Fichte expresses this view in *Die Bestimmung des Menschen* (1800), a philosophical dialogue meant to explain and popularize his ideas:

> Sehen, Schmecken u. s. w sind ja nicht selbst wirkliche Empfindungen, denn ich sehe oder schmecke nie schlechtweg, wie du schon vorhin bemerkt hast, sondern sehe immer roth oder grün u.s.w., schmecke immer süss oder bitter u.s.w. Sehen, Schmecken und dergleichen, sind nur *höhere Bestimmungen wirklicher Empfindungen*, sind Klassen, denen ich die letzteren, jedoch nicht willkürlich, sondern durch die unmittelbare Empfindung selbst geleitet, unterordne. Ich sehe sonach in ihnen überall keine *äusseren Sinne, sondern nur besondere Bestimmungen des Objects, des inneren Sinnes*, meiner Affectionen. (F II, 214–15)

> [Sight, taste, and so forth, are not indeed in themselves actual sensations, for I never see or feel absolutely, as you have previously remarked, but always see red or green, taste sweet or bitter, etc. Sight, taste, and the like, are *only higher definitions of actual sensations*; they are classes to which I refer these latter, not by arbitrary arrangement, but guided by the immediate

sensation itself. I see in them therefore not external senses, *but only particular definitions of the objects of the inward sense*, of my own states or affections.] (Fichte, *The Vocation of Man*, trans. by William Smith (London: Chapman, 1848), pp. 71–72)

Fichte here also notes that sensations are neither 'extended' nor placed 'next to each other in space' but always and only 'simple entities [...] following successively' (F II, 211).

104. Fichte had studied Hume early on and took important lessons from his sceptical philosophy, as Frederick C. Beiser points out in *German Idealism: The Struggle against Subjectivism, 1781–1801* (Cambridge, MA: Harvard University Press, 2002), p. 223 n. 1. In the *Wissenschaftslehre*, Fichte then praises Hume as 'one of the greatest thinkers of our age', for the simple reason that Hume's teachings would be 'identical' to his own (F I, 227).
105. Hume, I, 125–26 (1.4.2.2), 138 (1.4.2.40).
106. Hume, I, 16 (1.1.6.1), 137 (1.4.2.39).
107. Locke, *Essay Concerning Human Understanding*, ed. by Alexander Campbell Fraser, 2 vols (Oxford: Clarendon Press, 1894), I, 107–08 (1.iii.19).
108. Although he is not referenced, Donald Davidson's essay 'Seeing through Language', *Royal Institute of Philosophy Supplement*, 42 (1997), 15–28, calls to mind Hegel's concept of perception. Davidson here holds, like Hegel, that language is a necessary 'mode of perception' connecting percepts and concepts (p. 22). Specific similarities include Davidson's critique of the 'scepticism about the power of language to capture what is real' (p. 18), which recalls Hegel's logocentric attitude towards reality, as well as Davidson's discussion of 'ostension' and the critical 'difference between belief and truth' (pp. 25–27), which recalls Hegel's treatment of indexicals in sense-certainty. Davidson was awarded the Hegel-Preis in 1991.
109. Pippin, *Hegel's Idealism*, p. 139.
110. Goethe to Hegel according to J. P. Eckermann, 18 October 1827; Eckermann, *Gespräche mit Goethe in den letzten Jahren seines Lebens*, ed. by Christoph Michel and Hans Grüters (Berlin: Deutscher Klassiker Verlag, 2011), p. 648.
111. Johann Wolfgang von Goethe, *Werke* (Hamburger Ausgabe), ed. by Erich Trunz, 14 vols (Munich: Beck, 1981), XIII, 327.
112. For a contrasting view, see Eckart Förster, *The Twenty-Five Years of Philosophy: A Systematic Reconstruction*, trans. by Brady Bowman (Cambridge, MA: Harvard University Press, 2012). Förster (p. 372) thinks that in the *Phenomenology*, Hegel has effectively

provided philosophical justification for *scientia intuitiva*, i.e. for the form of cognition that Spinoza had demanded without being able to formulate it in methodologically adequate terms, and whose methodology Goethe was the first to work out, yet without being able to provide philosophical justification.

113. *The Science of Logic*, pp. 515–16.
114. Ibid., p. 516.
115. Hegel later rephrases this proposition:

Das Wahre ist das Ganze. Das Ganze aber ist nur das durch seine Entwicklung sich vollendende Wesen. Es ist von dem Absoluten zu sagen, daß es wesentlich *Resultat*, daß es erst am *Ende* das ist, was es in Wahrheit ist; und hierin eben besteht seine Natur, Wirkliches, Subjekt oder Sichselbstwerden zu sein. (PhG 24/11*)

[The truth is the whole, yet the whole is nothing other than the completion of its essence through development. Of the absolute it must be said that it is essentially a *result*, that only in the *end* it is what it truly is. This, precisely, defines its nature as being actual and subject, its self-becoming.]

116. Similarly, Primin Stekeler-Weithofer, *Hegels 'Phänomenologie des Geistes': Ein dialogischer Kommentar*, 2 vols (Hamburg: Meiner, 2014), I, 151, identifies 'the diachronic constitution of knowledge' as Hegel's key issue, which escapes the 'purely formal or synchronic opposition of thesis and antithesis' or similar taxonomies.
117. Robert Pippin, 'The Status of Literature in Hegel's *Phenomenology of Spirit*: On the Lives of Concepts', in *Inventions of the Imagination: Romanticism and Beyond*, ed. by Richard T. Gray (Seattle: University of Washington Press, 2011), pp. 102–20 (p. 106).

118. *The Science of Logic*, p. 519.
119. Chatman (*Coming to Terms*, pp. 10–15) defines an 'argumentative' discourse as, first, driven by consequential reasoning and, second, lacking the double temporality of narrations.

PART II

The Language of the Senses
(Novalis, Rilke, Proust)

§1. *Reciprocity of Perception and Poetry in Novalis*

Das *Abstracte soll versinnlicht*, und das *Sinnliche abstract* werden.[1]

[The *abstract shall be made sensuous*, and the *sensuous abstract*.]

The poetry of perception, or, 'the art to become almighty'

In 1798, Novalis sums up his philosophy. 'Poetry', he writes, 'is the truly absolute reality. This is the core of my philosophy. More poetry means more truth.'[2] But this 'truly absolute reality', poetry, has a double nature. It represents the essence of the natural world, but at the same time the form of cognition itself. For 'poetry-making' [das Dichten] — a synonym for poetry (*Poesie*) — is 'the mind's inherent way of acting', the arch-poet Klingsohr explains in *Heinrich von Ofterdingen* (N I, 335). And to underscore his point, he asks, 'Does not every man strive and compose at every moment?'[3]

This twofold definition of poetry (meaning both *die Poesie* and *das Dichten*) bears directly upon Novalis's concept of sense perception or aesthesis. Neither passive nor purely receptive, sensory perception involves formative acts of *poiēsis* (Greek for 'making, creating') which resemble the acts poets perform with words. Perceiving, to put it concisely, means to *make* perceptions. This connection between perception and *poiēsis* holds also in reverse: Making poetry depends on acts of perception as well. Poetic composition requires, no less than prosaic cognition, the 'willful, active, and productive use' of our senses, as Novalis remarks at the end of his life:

> Dichtkunst ist wohl nur — willkührlicher, thätiger produktiver Gebrauch unserer Organe — und vielleicht wäre Denken selbst nicht viel etwas anders — und Denken und Dichten also einerley. Denn im Denken wenden ja die Sinne den Reichthum ihrer Eindrücke zu einer neuen Art von Eindrücken an — und was daraus entsteht, nennen wir einen Gedanken. (N II, 759–60 #56)

> [The art of poetry is probably just a wilful, active, and productive use of our organs — and perhaps thought itself would be hardly different — and hence thinking and poetry the same. For in thinking, the senses turn the wealth of their impressions into a new type of impression — the result of which is called a thought.]

Thinking and poetry are identical because both are rooted in the same source, sensuousness. Both involve acts of perception transforming the 'wealth' of the senses into a 'new type of impression', namely into 'thoughts' — whether these are poetic or prosaic in kind.

The interrelation between sense perception and poetry Novalis thus proposes (and current research in neuroscience seems to support)[4] can be paraphrased with a pithy note by Friedrich Schlegel. This note is itself a striking instance of what Novalis once called the 'inner symorganization and symevolution' between Schlegel's and his own way of thinking.[5] Schlegel notes in 1798 that 'all poetic images are literally true; all of our sensations, feelings, and perceptions are poetry'.[6] It is this exact link between perception and poetry I will trace throughout Novalis's theoretical and literary works.

The unfinished prose work *Die Lehrlinge zu Saïs* offers an excellent introduction to the significance of perception for poetry in Novalis. The task of the apprentices in this work is to learn to recognize and decipher the 'wondrous figures' [wunderliche Figuren] that 'seem to belong to the great figural script [Chiffernschrift] one discovers [erblickt] everywhere' (N I, 201). This *Chiffernschrift*[7] may be discerned in animate as well as in inanimate objects, in clouds and crystals as well as in plants and animals, and even in 'strange conjunctures of chance' (N I, 201). The perception and comprehension, or the seeing and deciphering, of this 'wondrous script' [Wunderschrift] of nature is what the apprentices aspire to learn from their 'teacher' [Lehrer] (N I, 201). Inspired by their teacher's exemplary development — who already 'as a child' felt the urge 'to train, occupy, and fill his senses' [der Trieb die Sinne zu üben, zu beschäftigen, zu erfüllen] (N I, 202) — the apprentices, too, seek to sharpen their senses.

Die Lehrlinge zu Saïs thus tells a 'Sinnengeschichte', as Peter Utz put it, a story of and about the senses.[8] Like other texts by Novalis, it represents perception as an act of creation (*poiēsis*), and more specifically 'as an act of reading' the *Chiffernschrift* of nature.[9] Perception ought to become a creative faculty, or, as Novalis paradoxically names it in a fragment, 'active receptivity'.[10] At the same time, it is a story about an apprenticeship in perception, which Friedmar Apel aptly describes as a 'training of vision' [Sehschulung] based on the

> insight that the existence of sensory organs and objects does not yet ensure perception. Rather, perception depends on interest, imagination, and attention. This insight informs the investigations of looking [Blickforschung] in the *Lehrlinge* and simultaneously constitutes the principle for a culture of vision and perception in general.[11]

The apprentices' training of the senses includes the development of strategies as well as exercises enhancing both the acuity and creativity of all sensory faculties. The ultimate goal of such exercises (which are, in fact, not without historical precedent)[12] is to make the 'wondrous script' of nature 'visible and intelligible' (N I, 202). To achieve this goal, however, the apprentices must cultivate a new type of vision. They must transform the ways in which they perceive and interact with the world completely. Their teacher has completed this transformation, the result of which is described as follows:

> Nun fand er überall Bekanntes wieder, nur wunderlich gemischt, gepaart, und also ordneten sich selbst in ihm oft seltsame Dinge. Er merkte bald auf die Verbindungen in allem, auf Begegnungen, Zusammentreffungen. Nun sah er bald nichts mehr allein. — In große bunte Bilder drängten sich die Wahrnehmungen seiner Sinne: er hörte, sah, tastete und dachte zugleich. Er freute sich, Fremdlinge zusammen zu bringen. Bald waren ihm die Sterne Menschen, bald die Menschen Sterne, die Steine Thiere, die Wolken Pflanzen,

er spielte mit den Kräften und Erscheinungen, er wußte wo und wie er dies und jenes finden, und erscheinen lassen konnte, und griff so selbst in den Saiten nach Tönen und Gängen umher. (N I, 202)

[He found familiarity everywhere, but oddly commingled and combined, so that a strange order of things emerged for him. Soon he paid attention to the connections that are everywhere, to meetings and concurrences. He stopped seeing things in isolation. — The perceptions of his senses crowded together in massive, colorful images: he heard, saw, touched, and thought simultaneously. He delighted in joining together foreign entities. Soon the stars were people to him, and the people stars, the stones became animals, and the clouds plants; he toyed with forces and appearances; he knew how and where to find this or that and make it appear, thus plucking notes and runs from the strings.][13]

Having acquired this new mode of perception, the teacher sees and understands the universal network — the 'wondrous script' — connecting all things, beings, and incidents. For him, perception no longer consists of passive impressions. His senses now actively reveal to him the complementarity of all things in the form of synesthetic 'images' or simultaneous 'concurrences' that are at once visible and intelligible to the mind. His trained sensorium not only recognizes but, in fact, produces unity, so that the 'fragmentation' of perception into five distinct senses, as a late fragment by Novalis calls it, is overcome and the world made whole again.[14] In short, the teacher has learned to perceive the world as an artist, as a poet.

Perceiving as the poets do, the teacher also possesses the power to modify his perceptions at will. He becomes a creator of perceptions; he can 'toy' freely with 'appearances', the passage reads, blending distinct sensations together and employing the perceptions they produce as disposable sensory signs. These signs he then combines to 'make things appear' at will or to create synesthetic 'images'. Indeed, the poet of the senses, the teacher explains at the end of the *Lehrlinge*, has the ability to arrange 'the appearances of nature' through deliberate perceptions 'in easily comprehensible and nicely illuminated compositions' [in leicht faßliche und treffend beleuchtete Gemählde zu ordnen] (N I, 231). It is this creative ability, together with the intellectual ability to communicate his observations through 'known concepts [Begriffe] and experiences', that make him a 'true prophet [Verkündiger] of nature' (N I, 231). The teacher possesses all these abilities and has therefore mastered the method of presentation Novalis describes in a contemporaneous fragment as *Plastisirungsmethode* (N II 457 #47) — the ability to think with the senses while sensing with the intellect, thus thinking and sensing simultaneously. He follows the maxim, 'The *abstract shall be made sensuous*, and the *sensuous abstract*' (N II, 533 #331).

Several fragments of 1798, written roughly during the time Novalis was working on the *Lehrlinge*, envision a similar transformation of sense perception. Following these fragments, the teacher could be described as someone who uses his body as an 'almighty' instrument that can 'do everything':

Kunst allmächtig zu werden — Kunst unsern Willen total zu realisiren. Wir müssen den Körper, wie die Seele in unsere Gewalt bekommen. Der Körper ist das Werckzeug zur Bildung und Modification der Welt — Wir müssen

> unsern Körper zum *allfähigen* Organ auszubilden suchen. Modification unsers Werckzeugs ist Modification der Welt. (N II, 376 #256)
>
> [The art to become almighty — the art to realize our will totally. We must manage to take control of the body as well as the soul. The body is the instrument to form and modify the world — We must seek to develop our body into an organ that can *do everything*. Modifying our instrument means modifying the world.]

This power to 'modify' the world through the deliberate use of the bodily organs is what Novalis calls 'magic', which for him precisely designates 'the art to use the sensory world [Sinnenwelt] at will [willkührlich]' (N II, 335 #109). Indeed, for Novalis, magician is just another name for poet: '*The magician is a poet*' (N II, 380 #286). Thanks to the magic 'faculty to modify the impression' and 'to direct sensory excitability [Reitzbarkeit] at will' (N II, 367 #235), the poet — or magician — can freely poeticize and enchant the world.

Controlling his senses like an instrument, the poet-magician can even 'force' them to '*produce* the shape [Gestalt] he demands [...] he will see, hear, and feel whatever, however, and in whichever connection he wants' (N II, 373 #247).[15] He is able to concatenate sensations with the same degree of freedom by which he combines concepts. He thus composes perceptions in the same way poets compose their texts, freely imagining the outcome and then arranging his sensations accordingly, like words in a poem. He has become the consummate poet, which means he can use 'things and words like keys', producing powerful poetry merely through the 'active association of ideas' (N II, 692 #935). In his case, therefore, the imagination does truly '*replace* all senses', as Novalis famously claimed, not least because this inner sense 'is already very much under the control of our will', in contrast to the outer senses, which are subject to 'mechanical laws' (N II, 423 #479).

The active and deliberate, or poetic, use of the senses that all these fragments demand, and the teacher attained, is described as 'inverted' in another fragment of 1798:

> Wie der Mahler mit ganz andern Augen, als der gemeine Mensch die sichtbaren Gegenstände sieht — so erfährt auch der Dichter die Begebenheiten der äußren und innern Welt auf eine sehr verschiedne Weise vom gewöhnlichen Menschen. Nirgends aber ist es auffallender, daß es nur der Geist ist, der die Gegenstände, die Veränderungen des Stoffs poëtisirt, und daß das Schöne, der Gegenstand der Kunst uns nicht gegeben wird oder in den Erscheinungen schon fertig liegt — als in der Musik. Alle Töne, die die Natur hervorbringt sind rauh — und geistlos — nur der musikalischen Seele dünkt oft das Rauschen des Waldes — das Pfeifen des Windes, der Gesang der Nachtigall, das Plätschern des Bachs melodisch und bedeutsam. Der Musiker nimmt das Wesen seiner Kunst aus sich — auch nicht der leiseste Verdacht von Nachahmung kann ihn treffen. Den Mahler scheint die sichtbare Natur überall vorzuarbeiten — durchaus sein unerreichbares Muster zu seyn — Eigentlich ist aber die Kunst des Mahlers so unabhängig, so ganz a priori entstanden, als die Kunst des Musikers. Der Mahler bedient sich nur einer unendlich schwereren *Zeichensprache*, als der Musiker — der Mahler mahlt eigentlich mit dem Auge — Seine Kunst ist die Kunst regelmäßig, und Schön zu sehn. Sehn ist hier ganz activ — durchaus

bildende Thätigkeit. Sein Bild ist nur seine Chiffer — sein Ausdruck — Sein Werckzeug der Reproduktion. [...] Der Musiker hört eigentlich auch active — Er hört heraus. Freylich ist dieser umgekehrte Gebrauch der Sinne den Meisten ein Geheimniß, aber jeder Künstler wird es sich mehr oder minder deutlich bewußt seyn. (N II, 362–63 #226)

[As the painter sees visible objects with quite different eyes from those of the common person — so too the poet experiences the events of the outer and the inner world very differently from the ordinary person. But nowhere is it more striking than in music that it is only the spirit that poeticizes the objects and the changes of the material, and that the beautiful, the subject of art, is not given to us nor can it be found ready in phenomena. All sounds produced by nature are rough — and empty of spirit. Only the musical soul often finds the rustling of the forest — the whistling of the wind, the song of the nightingale, the babbling of the brook melodious and meaningful. The musician takes the essence of his art from within himself — not even the slightest suspicion of imitation can apply to him. To the painter, visible nature seems everywhere to be doing his preliminary work — to be entirely his unattainable model. But really the painter's art has arisen just as independently, quite as a priori, as the musician's. Only the painter uses an infinitely more difficult *symbolic language* than the musician — the painter really paints with his eyes — his art is the art of seeing with order and beauty. Here seeing is quite active — indeed a formative activity. His image is only his cipher — his expression — his reproducing tool. [...] Really the musician too hears actively — he extracts by hearing. For most people this inverted use of the senses is certainly a mystery, but every artist will be more or less clearly aware of it.][16]

This use of the senses is deemed 'inverted' by Novalis because it transforms passive sensory reception into creative acts. The musician does not merely receive sounds but rather 'poeticizes' them with his ear, while the painter 'paints with his eyes' rather than reproducing visual impressions. Silvio Vietta hails this notion of 'inverted' perception as the 'Copernican turn' towards a modernist aesthetics of expression, and with good reason.[17] But Novalis goes still further, claiming that this transformation of reproductive sensations into poetic perceptions is possible not only for artists. In principle, the fragment continues, each human perception consists in the active use of the senses:

Fast jeder Mensch ist in geringen Grad schon Künstler — Er sieht in der That heraus und nicht herein — Er fühlt heraus und nicht herein. Der Hauptunterschied ist der; der Künstler hat den Keim des selbstbildenden Lebens in seinen Organen belebt — die Reitzbarkeit der selben *für den Geist* erhöht und ist mithin im Stande Ideen nach Belieben — ohne äußre Sollicitation — durch sie heraus zu strömen — Sie, als Werckzeuge, zu *beliebigen* Modifikationen der wircklichen Welt zu gebrauchen [...]. (N II, 363 #226)

[Almost every person is to a small degree already an artist. In fact he sees actively and not passively — he feels actively and not passively. The main difference is this: the artist has vivified the germ of self-formative life in his organs — he has raised the excitability of these *for the spirit* and is thereby able to allow ideas to flow out of them at will — without external prompting — to use them as tools for *deliberate* modifications of the real world.][18]

At the close of the fragment, Novalis finally equates this active mode of perception precisely with 'poetry' as the 'active sense of feeling' [Thätiger Sinn des Gefühls] (N II, 364 #226).

It is this inherently poetic potential of the human senses, their spontaneity and magical power of creation, that the apprentices must first cultivate in order to decipher the *Chiffernschrift* of nature and then, having found their personal *Zeichensprache* or style, compose poetic ciphers themselves. Like their teacher, they gradually transform their senses into an 'instrument of speech' [Sprachwerkzeug] (cf. N II, 377 #264). To decipher the script of nature, they must learn to perceive poetically, using their senses as though they could be read and spoken like a verbal language. Just as a poet must practice and perfect his literary abilities (the choice of words and rhetorical figures, metre, rhyme, etc.) to acquire a style that is both individual and suitable to the chosen subjects, so must the student of nature learn to control her instrument, the sensory faculties, through deliberate exercise and reflection so as to unleash, finally, the creativity of her senses.[19] Novalis thus envisions a manner of perception analogous to the composition of poetry, Friedmar Apel writes, since both are described as involving both intentional and creative acts of 'selection, reduction, and combination'.[20]

The teacher never discloses exactly what became of him once he fully mastered the inverted (or magical) use of the senses. He wants his apprentices to 'pursue their own path' instead (N I, 204). As recounted in the second part, these differ with regard to the specific field of inquiry, but still aim at the same goal: the unleashing of the poetry of the senses. For example, one apprentice seeks to manipulate perception and cognition through controlled acts of 'attention' [Aufmerksamkeit] so as to create 'a new type of perception' wherein 'sensing and thinking' [empfinden und denken] coincide (N I, 219–20). He envisions a 'creative perception of the world' in which 'making and knowing' [Hervorbringen und Wissen] stand in 'the most marvellous reciprocity [Wechselverbindung]' (N I, 225).[21] Several unidentified apprentices similarly align thinking and feeling by concluding that 'thinking is just a dream made of feelings [ein Traum des Fühlens], feelings [Fühlen] that have died, a feeble life in pale grey' (N I, 219).

In the apprentices' endeavours to transform the senses into a creative faculty, poetry provides both the means and the language to bring about this change. The structure of the second part, 'Die Natur', in fact reflects the privileged role of poetry, since it consists not of doctrines but of poetic speeches and tales. Occasionally, the teacher adds an illustrative story of his own, or he comments on the recounted tales, as happens at the end of the *Lehrlinge* (N I, 231–33). This textual structure is perfectly consistent with the narrator's remark at the beginning of the second part that the 'art of poetry' has been 'the preferred instrument [das liebste Werkzeug] of all genuine friends of nature' since ancient times (N II, 206). 'Tales and poems' [Mährchen und Gedichte] (N II, 206) are described as the means of renewing and transforming human perception, and the story of Hyacinth and Rosenblüthe (N II, 214–18) exemplifies how this might work. This tale about two young lovers is told by a 'lively fellow' [muntrer Gespiele] because he wants to renew 'the spirit [Geist] that inserts itself into all your senses with a thousand colours' (N II, 214) — the spirit of love and desire. In recounting the tale, the 'lively fellow' thus instils erotic desire in his peers, especially in those who never felt such longing before. And so, cultivating their senses through tales and exercises, the apprentices may one day become what their teacher already is, magicians and prophets of nature.

Difficulties with the senses

Novalis's idea that perception involves acts of poetry (*Dichten*) resonates with the vision of poetry to which the Jena Romantics generally subscribed. They considered poetry a progressive *Universalpoesie*, to use Friedrich Schlegel's famous term, a universal language with the power not only to absorb scientific discourses and social practices but also to substitute for bodily sensations and feelings. Poetry (*Dichtung*) thus constitutes the universal medium or language of translation in Early Romanticism, as Friedrich Kittler has shown, while the composition of poetry (*Dichten*) is tantamount to the operation of translation itself.[22] Though not entirely pleased with Schlegel's far-reaching (and by now canonical) definition of Romantic poetry in the *Athenäum*, Novalis too represented poetry in various contexts as a translational operation.[23] He also applied, we have seen, that notion of poetry to sense perception, so that perception is much less a matter of physical causation as it involves poetic translation — selective acts of combination and interpretation that translate, for example, sonic waves into audible tones, a spectrum of light into visible shapes, or chemical substances into flavours. The *Lehrlinge* exemplifies this poetic approach to the senses like no other literary work by Novalis or any of his contemporaries.

However, this historical framework cannot solve the conceptual difficulties that arise if the logic of poetry is applied to perception, and the logic of perception to poetry. Their identification blurs basic categories of experience: passivity and activity, receptivity and creativity, imitation and production, and even that between reading and writing. How does one disentangle these categories we know, precisely as a matter of experience, to be distinct? Novalis is aware of these difficulties. In fact, a long and complex note from the *Fichte-Studien* associating sense perception with the imagination — and hence the faculty of poetry — contains the remark: 'Now the difficulty is to explain the senses' (N II, 183 #568).

Novalis identifies two basic issues complicating perception. Historically, sense perception is complicated by the rising consumption of print media around 1800, a medial situation Novalis portrays with quite a bit of irony in the first of his *Dialogen* (N II, 426–29). In this dialogue, two speakers, A and B, debate 'the harmful [nachtheiligen] consequences of reading' (N II, 427), specifically the concern that the 'onslaught of letters' [Last Buchstaben] (N II, 426) — the ever-growing quantity of print literature — may soon supplant first-hand experience gained through the five senses. The final stage of this development is envisioned as a world made up entirely of 'ciphers' [Chifferwelt] and 'woodcarvings' [Druckerstock][24] (N II, 428), printed and distributed en masse, with the fatal result that 'we end up seeing only books, but no longer things, and that we have as good as lost our 5 bodily senses' (N II, 428). However, these concerns regarding the 'book plague' [Bücherseuche] (N II, 426) at the same time betray an eminently modern disposition, the addiction to print media. B indeed defends this 'modern luxury' (N II, 427) against A's concerns. On B's account, the threat is not at all the ever-growing quantity of printed letters but, if anything, 'the inevitable weakness of our nature' (N II, 428).[25]

The increasing importance of printed letters debated by speakers A and B inevitably highlights the apparent antithesis, first-hand sensory experience. Novalis shared this interest in the human senses with like-minded Jena Romantics such as Schelling and Johann Wilhelm Ritter, and also with Schiller and Goethe. All these authors partook in the epistemic re-evaluation of the human senses and organs that was taking place in Germany and elsewhere in Europe around 1800. The emerging sciences of biology, physiology, and neurology gradually replaced older mechanistic paradigms with more dynamic models of the human body, so that it became indeed more difficult 'to explain the senses'. The impact of this anthropological shift on Novalis's text has been investigated in several studies.[26]

The many fragments arranged under subject headings such as 'physiology' and 'anthropology' in *Das Allgemeine Brouillon* clearly indicate that Novalis was aware of the ongoing redefinition of the human body and its organs. He also understood the epochal consequences — long before Foucault noted, at the end of *The Order of Things*, 'that man is a recent invention'.[27] In a *Blüthenstaub* fragment, Novalis notes: 'To describe humans [Menschen] has been impossible until now because we have not known what man as such [ein Mensch] is' (N II, 281 #108). For Novalis, 'man as such' is a recent scientific invention culminating around 1800. Another fragment seems to radicalize this insight into the historical novelty of the collective singular, 'man as such', by claiming, 'Being human is an art' [Mensch werden ist eine Kunst] (N II, 348 #153). As a category, 'man' remains necessarily relative, a historical concept open to new definitions and redefinitions, so that the dynamic form of life it stands for is perhaps best described as 'an art'.

Those epistemic shifts, together with the massive expansion of print media, mark the historical condition complicating the poetry of perception. The other and most immediate reason for Novalis to note the 'difficulty to explain the senses' (N II, 183 #568) is a philosophical one pertaining to what he calls *Wechselbestimmung*. This concept, as well as the note, are found in the *Fichte-Studien* — several notebooks filled with notations and excerpts constituting a 'laborious examination of Fichte's philosophy', as Novalis called them in retrospect (N I, 721). These notebooks are also striking illustrations of Novalis's incessant urge to annotate — the need to have 'at all times the quill to hand'[28] when reading — and hence typical by-products of the new print media culture.

Novalis's relationship to Fichte is complex and often studied.[29] Hans Jürgen Balmes (N III, 283–84) reports that Novalis never attended a lecture of Fichte's, but intensely studied three publications by Fichte: the 1794 essay *Ueber den Begriff der Wissenschaftslehre*, the *Grundlage der gesammten Wissenschaftslehre*, and the *Grundriss des Eigenthümlichen der Wissenschaftslehre in Rücksicht auf das theoretische Vermögen*.

The latter two works were published serially between 1794 and 1795 on the basis of Fichte's weekly lectures at the University of Jena. Incidentally, Novalis's father, Heinrich Erasmus von Hardenberg, financially supported Fichte from 1774 until 1784.

In the next section, I detail Novalis's appropriation of *Wechselbestimmung*, 'reciprocal determination', and how it bears on both his theory and poetry of perception. To do so, however, I must clarify the concept's original meaning. It directly follows from Fichte's basic theorem of *Tathandlung*, the first and foundational act of cognition developed in the *Grundlage der gesammten Wissenschaftslehre* of 1794. At once the primordial deed and absolute origin of consciousness, the *Tathandlung* is herein explained as consisting, in fact, of *two* interconnected actions. First, the *Tathandlung* of consciousness affects the categorical opposition between 'me' [Ich] and all that is 'not me' [Nicht-Ich], or 'ego' and 'non-ego'. Thanks to this transcendental opposition (*Entgegensetzung*), subject and object — the empirical instantiations of ego and non-ego — can be distinguished in experience. Such posings-against or, in the literal sense, *oppositions* are at the same time the condition of possibility for self-determination and self-knowledge. Novalis succinctly summarizes this Fichtean insight into the necessarily oppositional structure of self-consciousness: 'The ego is effective and determines itself only *by way of opposition* [nur im *Entgegengesetzten*]' (N II, 181 #566).

But, in order to pose any such oppositions in the first place, the ego must already be conceived as a transcendental origin and, more precisely, as an agent capable of positing (*setzen*) itself and simultaneously its opposite. The act of self-positing — which Fichte must present for reasons of causality as the 'first, absolutely unconditional principle [Grundsatz]' (F I, 91) — is the other, correlated action of which the *Tathandlung* consists. In effecting its own existence, however, the ego must precede not only all actual, empirical consciousness and cognizance but, taken as the determining ground and primordial cause, opposition itself.

Given the non-demonstrability of this monist proposition, which Fichte concedes at the very beginning of the 1794 *Wissenschaftslehre*, he must pretend to search for its justification. Fichte's disclaimer of non-demonstrability reads: 'Our task is to *discover* the primordial, absolutely unconditioned principle of all human knowledge. If it is to be an absolutely primary principle, however, it can be neither *demonstrated* nor *defined*' [Wir haben den absolut ersten, schlechthin unbedingten Grundsatz alles menschlichen Wissens *aufzusuchen*. *Beweisen* oder *bestimmen* lässt er sich nicht, wenn er absolut-erster Grundsatz seyn soll] (F I, 91). What Fichte actually does, however, is to *posit* the logical necessity of the ego's priority and primordial activity, rather than discovering it. He thus employs the very procedure on which his philosophy is founded, precisely the act of positing (*Setzen*), and he does so in self-affirming and circular[30] propositions, or *Setzungen*, such as 'The explanatory foundation [Erklärungsgrund] of all facts of empirical consciousness is that, prior to all acts of positing within the ego, the ego itself has to be posited [dass vor allem Setzen im Ich vorher das Ich selbst gesetzt sey]' (F I, 95). Fichte then goes on to simplify his monist proposition, noting more plainly that 'the ego posits itself' (F I, 97), and then hammers the point home by underscoring that '*the ego posits its own being originally* [*ursprünglich*] *and unconditionally* [*schlechthin*]' (F I, 98).

In juxtaposition, these three formulations from the opening section of the 1794 *Wissenschaftslehre* betray a seemingly small but, in truth, decisive discrepancy that pervades Fichte's thinking as a whole. The first formulation stipulates, with a peculiar and hardly translatable turn of phrase, that the ego 'has to be posited' prior to all other acts of positing. Owing to the passive sentence construction, it remains unclear who or what would perform this foundational act of positing 'within', but not by, the ego. The original cause of the ego's existence remains — as it must — groundless, even though this first deed is supposed to ground all further acts of consciousness. The second and third examples eliminate precisely this uncertainty in presenting the ego as the original subject and cause of all positings. This oscillation between ground and groundlessness, between the ego as the first cause or first effect, is characteristic of Fichte's conception of *Tathandlung* in the *Wissenschaftslehre* of 1794. At moments, Fichte seems to ground all acts of positing and opposing in the ego alone, while suggesting at other moments that the ego emerges from some prior opposition.[31]

This inseparable, but also paradoxical, concurrence of an ego that posits itself with a prior demarcation of opposition, these reciprocal actions of positing (*Setzen*)[32] and being posited through opposition (*Entgegensetzen*)[33] constitute the *Tathandlung*. In it, *Setzen* and *Entgegensetzen* are two equally constitutive actions determining each other. Accordingly, they stand in a relation of reciprocity or *Wechselbestimmung*, which also means they cannot occur in sequence but only at one and the same time. Fichte underscored this point with vehemence. In a 'crystal clear report'[34] meant to 'force the reader to understand', Fichte writes that it would be a 'grave misunderstanding' to think of the *Tathandlung* as a gradually unfolding sequence of events, as if it were some kind of 'narrative' [*Erzählung*]. Rather, the *Tathandlung* designates an 'organic whole' wherein each part exists 'simultaneously' (F II, 398–99). Dieter Henrich concisely captures this paradoxical duality of the Fichtean *Tathandlung*:

> The unpublished and earliest form of the *Wissenschaftslehre* teaches us that Fichte built his theory on two discoveries [...] at first, he understood that the foundational act of consciousness cannot involve relations and distinctions [ein Beziehen und Unterscheiden]. Prior to these, opposition itself [ein Entgegensetzen] must be effected, which then makes distinctions possible. This is indeed Fichte's pivotal thesis: that consciousness can be understood only in terms of opposition [...] Fichte's second discovery was that the original opposition itself required a synthetic ground [Einheitsgrund], which he could only see in the absolute faculty of self-consciousness [i.e. the ego] to encompass all opposites [alles Entgegengesetzte].[35]

The dual *Tathandlung* happens — and has to happen — simultaneously, but the knowledge it subsequently produces is, according to Fichte, strictly diachronic. Subjectivity (viz. knowledge of myself) is accessible only during self-observation and consists of a sequence of moments. Similarly, observing objects is a diachronic process, so that its reality issues from a cluster of momentary perceptions rather than from permanent substances. The object is known only insofar as I attend to it or recall a memory thereof, but it has for Fichte no reality outside this diachronic experience of consciousness.[36] This strict separation of a timeless cause, the *Tathandlung*, from its diachronic effects, the knowledge of myself and external objects, means, paradoxically, that it is 'only the product but never the action' itself we can grasp, Novalis correctly observes.[37] Or as Henrich puts it, subjectivity and objectivity depend on something that necessarily 'escapes our view'. The invisible agent *and* imperceptible process Fichte calls *Ich* fills this blind spot, enabling such recognition through the dual acts of *Setzen* and *Entgegensetzen*, but only after the fact.[38]

Though Fichte's theory of consciousness greatly influenced Novalis, it would be a mistake to read Novalis as a philosopher. For by philosophical standards, Novalis's fragments are self-contradictory, if not absurd caricatures of Fichte. Similarly, a philosophical comparison with Schelling and Hegel makes Novalis appear a failed idealist, a thinker whose theory lacks systematic closure. Manfred Frank, perhaps the most prolific philosophical interpreter of Novalis, inadvertently reveals this impasse in describing the philosophical aim of Novalis, indeed of Jena Romanticism in general, as 'a whole [...] that can never be grasped as such'. Their philosophy thus lacks, Frank continues, the 'crowning closure' of a philosophical system. But nonetheless, with or without system, the 'tendency towards the absolute' represents for Frank the dominant 'feeling' [Lebensgefühl] of Novalis and the other Romantics.[39] Frank's assessment echoes that of Theodor Haering, who was the first to identify 'the problem of the absolute' as the 'foundational aporia' in Novalis.[40]

It seems somewhat schizophrenic, however, that Novalis would go after the so-called absolute, the whole, the holy, etc. trying to 'undo all divisions in poetry'[41] and heal the contradictions of the world, as scholars keep claiming, *although* he had concluded that such perfect harmony and unity can, in fact, never be grasped. If both were true, as Frank and his followers indeed claim, then Novalis's so-called philosophy would be both mad and vacuous. Of course, it might also be that philosophical interpreters of Romanticism have themselves concocted a romantic myth, according to which Novalis and his contemporaries were either too ignorant or too sentimental to accept the functional divisions and ever-growing heterogeneity of modern life.

Recent philosophical interpretations seek to place Novalis more affirmatively in the context of German Idealism than Frank does. Typically, these readings point to how Novalis and Friedrich Schlegel replay and develop Kantian, Jacobian, Reinholdian, and Fichtean themes — for example, the problem of reflection or the idea of a so-called 'Romantic Absolute', as current scholarship terms it.[42] If the later idealisms of Schelling and Hegel are taken as the point of reference instead, the typical claim is — to cite Frederick Beiser *pars pro toto* — that Novalis:

> formulated some of the basic themes of absolute idealism. That the absolute is the divine logos, the identity of the subjective and objective; that the ideal and the real are only parts of a single living whole; that thinking lapses into falsehood and contradiction in abstracting parts from the whole; that unity is not possible without difference; and, finally, that only art has the power to

perceive the absolute — these themes are found in Novalis' notebooks as early as 1796.[43]

But even so, Beiser concludes, Novalis fails as a philosopher. His theoretical fragments 'only very crudely' and in a rather 'sketchy' and 'inchoate way [...] anticipate the more elaborate and systematic ideas of Schelling and Hegel'.[44] Friedrich Strack remarks bluntly, though not incorrectly: 'Novalis never developed a concise theory of self-consciousness, let alone one that could surpass Fichte.'[45]

Thus, instead of examining the ways in which Novalis fails to surpass the philosophies he studied, it seems more appropriate to ask how he succeeds in poeticizing them, eclectically and idiosyncratically appropriating them for his poetic production, at times even erroneously so. Nowhere does Novalis express the expectation to find 'the absolute', or more plainly the truth, by studying Fichte and other philosophers. His domain is literary writing, and his vocation poetry, while philosophy was just a source of inspiration, albeit an important one. In this he resembles Jean Paul, who read contemporary philosophers 'not at all for the sake of truth' but hoping for inspiration instead.[46] If Novalis can be considered to have had a philosophical ambition, this ambition would seem to consist instead in the desire to demonstrate the primacy of poetry for philosophy, as evidenced by the following fragment:

> Die Poësie ist der Held der Philosophie. Die Phil[osophie] erhebt die Poësie zum Grundsatz. Sie lehrt uns den Werth der Poësie kennen. Phil[osophie] ist *die Theorie* der *Poësie*. Sie zeigt uns was die Poësie sey, daß sie Eins und alles sey. (N II, 380 #280)
>
> [Poetry is the hero of philosophy. Philosophy raises poetry to the status of a principle. It teaches us to recognize the worth of poetry. Philosophy is *the theory* of *poetry*. It shows us what poetry ought to be, that it ought to be one and all.][47]

Fichte's philosophy offers to Novalis just such a conception of poetry, since it presents the imagination, the essential organ of poetry, precisely as the source of all reality: 'The doctrine of this book', Fichte declares in the *Wissenschaftslehre*, 'is that all reality [...] comes into being solely through the imagination'.[48] Novalis took this Fichtean doctrine to heart, word for word: 'Poetry is the truly absolute reality. This is the core of my philosophy. More poetry means more truth' (N II, 420 #471).

For Novalis, philosophy was a source rather than an end in itself, because he knew that 'one studies foreign systems in order to find one's own system' (N II, 511 #220).[49] In a letter to August Wilhelm Schlegel, Novalis made the same point, though in a more facetious tone and with regard to natural science, which he studied with equal fervour. The study of the empirical sciences is here called a preferred means of speculation since it allows us to devise a world of our own choosing:

> Ich bin ziemlich fleißig und habe freylich jetzt mit so viel empirischen Wust zu thun, daß mir oft angst und bange wird — wo ich Verdauungskraft hernehmen soll. Wie wohl wird mir nicht, wenn ich zuweilen meine liebe Speculation hervorsuchen kann [...] da mache ich mir eine empirische Welt, wo alles hübsch nach speculativen Schlendrian geht.[50]

[I am fairly industrious, and now, of course, I have to deal with so much empirical rubbish that I often worry and ask myself — where to find the power to digest all that. How well I feel, by contrast, whenever I can revisit my dear speculations for a while [...] then I devise an empirical world in which all things go by the neat laws of speculative whimsy.]

The triadic diagram Novalis drew in one of his encyclopaedic notebooks (N II, 657 #767) suggests he had a clear idea about the course of study that would eventually take him to his own system. The study of 'logic', the traditional domain of philosophy, together with the 'doctrine of rationality' [Rationalistik], the core of the mathematical sciences, was meant to reveal the 'doctrine of fantasy' [Fantastick].[51] This trajectory corresponds exactly to the chronology of Novalis's major projects. He began with the *Fichte-Studien*, a philosophical study, then moved on to *Das allgemeine Brouillon*, a Romantic encyclopaedia concerning above all contemporary science, and finally attempted to unite these two domains under the signs of fantasy and poetry through *Heinrich von Ofterdingen*.

Another reason for categorically distinguishing Novalis's fragments from the philosophies that may have inspired them is, of course, their distinctly aesthetic character and purpose — the perplexing insights through which they first arrest the reader's mind, releasing him into strange repose thereafter. Rahel Villinger has recently drawn attention to the graphic and phonic features in Novalis enabling these partly physical, partly intellectual effects. Drawing on a few paradigmatic examples from the *Bouillon*, she illustrates how the use of dashes and graphic markers as well as phonic devices like repetition, alliteration, assonance, and rhyme shapes the apprehension and, indeed, perception of Novalis's fragments.[52]

Aesthetically, therefore, the fragmentary and transitory (or, following Beiser, 'sketchy' and 'inchoate') character of his fragments is not at all a failure. These characteristics are, on the contrary, just another means of involving the reader, whom Novalis famously calls, as mentioned in the Introduction, the 'extended author' (N II, 282 #125). Novalis addresses this point as he responds to a reader of his *Blüthenstaub* and *Glauben und Liebe* fragments. In his response, he describes the fragments not as parts of a philosophical system but, rather, as 'texts for thinking', many of which possess only 'transitory value', like 'tokens in a game':

> Es freut mich, wenn meine abgerissenen Gedanken Ihnen einige beschäftigte Stunden gemacht haben — wenn sie Ihnen gewesen sind, was sie mir waren, und noch sind, Anfänge interessanter Gedankenfolgen — Texte zum Denken. Viele sind Spielmarken und haben nur transitorischen Werth. (N I, 680)[53]

> [I am pleased if my fragmentary thoughts have brought you some busy hours — if they have been to you what they were to me and still are: beginnings of interesting trains of thought — texts for thinking. Many of them are tokens in a game and have only a transitory value.]

Novalis's fragments are 'texts for thinking' or, as he calls them elsewhere, *Denkaufgaben* (N II, 353). They seek to engage the reader in their development, soliciting a mode of reception that is more active and subjective — and also more corporeal — than the sober distance and attention needed to penetrate a philosophical system. In short, Novalis wishes for the reader to interact with his fragmentary texts. They, too, are placed in a relationship of reciprocity.[54]

'Wechselbestimmung'

Wechselbestimmung ('reciprocal determination') is the synthetic principle Fichte develops to account for the unity of the *Tathandlung* as a dual act of *Setzen* and *Entgegensetzen*. *Wechsel-Thun*, *Wechselwirkung*, and *Wechselerweis* are synonyms Fichte also uses as he fleshes out this principle, which takes up more or less the entire second half of the *Wissenschaftslehre*.[55] Ego and non-ego stand in a relation of reciprocal determination, says Fichte, thus neutralizing their opposition. Novalis immediately understood the centrality of this principle, employing it and its derivatives not only to account for the interrelation of *Setzen* and *Entgegensetzen* — in other words, the structural overlap between identification and differentiation — but also, as we shall see, to conceptualize sense perception.[56] Likewise, Friedrich Schlegel embraced this Fichtean principle, which is essential to his notion of irony.[57] Following Joseph Vogl, one might contextualize this Romantic affinity for reciprocity by relating it to the contemporaneous economic idea of self-regulatory equilibrium.[58]

Naturally, Fichte grounds reciprocal determination in the ego, a conceptual choice that is indicative of the foundationalism constituting his system. All acts of *Setzen* and *Entgegensetzen* are rooted in some 'absolute and unrestrictable' ego, so that the *empirical* cognizance of subjects or objects represents merely 'accidents' of this unifying ground: 'Ego and non-ego [...] are both aspects (accidents) of the ego as a divisible substance; they are both posited by the ego as an absolute and unrestrictable subject that has no equal, nor opposite [dem nichts gleich ist, und nichts entgegengesetzt ist]' (F I, 119). This monist resolution of the dual *Tathandlung* is repeated and confirmed at the beginning of the section introducing the idea of reciprocal determination, where he posits, with emphasis, that '*all reality has been placed in the ego*'.[59] Still, the nature of Fichte's monism is rather 'peculiar', Robert Pippin notes, since the single absolute foundation — the ego — designates a potentially infinite process of self-determination: 'To understand "the I as the ultimate foundation" simply means that there is no "end" to the self-critical, self-adjusting activity that makes up the "whole" of the self's positings.'[60]

For Novalis, too, cognition requires poetic making: 'We *know only* insofar as *we are active [machen]*', he notes in a fragment (N II, 218 #10). In a related reference to Kant, he likewise notes that 'we *perceive [erkennen]* it[61] only *insofar as we realize it*' (N II, 220 #13). It is in this Kantian, and also Fichtean, spirit that Novalis concludes that the ego is the quintessential form or 'principle' of cognition. But for Novalis, the implication of this assumption is altogether different, namely: 'the ego is fundamentally nothing — everything must be given to it — But something can only be *given* to it and the given only becomes something through the ego. The ego is not an encyclopaedia, but rather a universal principle' (N II, 185 #568).[62] The ego is not the single origin of cognition, nor its self-sufficient cause, but sits always on the receiving end, for 'everything must be given to it'.

Novalis thus renounces the possibility of an absolute (viz. simple and unconditioned) foundation, including the notion that the reciprocal determination of *Setzen* and *Entgegensetzen* can be grounded in, and hence reduced to, a single origin and self-positing agent, the 'absolute' ego. Every act of *Setzen*, Novalis writes in the *Fichte-Studien*, is always already affected by a reciprocal act of *Entgegensetzen*, and vice versa: 'Positing is *effectively* an opposing [Setzen ist ein *wirkliches* Entgegensetzen] — Positing is thus also a not-positing [Nichtsetzen] [...] An opposing is a not-positing [...] and thus also a positing' (N II, 56 #97).[63] As an isolated occurrence, each of these acts remains unreal and without effect. Only insofar as each is determined by its opposite do *Setzen* and *Entgegensetzen* produce a tangible cognition. These two actions thus take place under a condition of a reciprocity that cannot be grounded in a single unified cause, least of all in Fichte's 'absolute and unrestrictable' ego.

The supposed transcendental unity of the *Tathandlung* falls prey to the spiralling effects of reciprocity early on in the *Fichte-Studien*. Novalis's vertiginous reasoning pulls the reader ever further from any identifiable single foundation:

> Nachzuholen möchte noch seyn — daß die Urhandlung mit sich selbst in Wechselwirkung steht. Ihre relative erste Handlung [viz. *Setzen*] [...] ist ursprünglich die zweyte, ihre relative 2te Handlung [viz. *Entgegensetzen*] [...] ursprünglich die erste Handlung. Leztere ist ursprünglich absolut, Erstere relativ absolut — aber für sie allein muß es umgekehrt sein. Der relative Gesichtspunct dreht immer die Sache um — (N II, 27 #25)
>
> [It should perhaps be added — that the original act stands in reciprocal interaction with itself. Its relative first act [viz. *Setzen*] [...] is originally the second act, its relative second act [viz. *Entgegensetzen*] [...] is originally the first act. The latter is originally absolute, the former is relatively absolute — but for it alone it must be reversed. The relative point of view always turns the thing around —][64]

Novalis criticizes the ostensible priority of the ego from the very outset of the *Fichte-Studien*: 'Has not Fichte too arbitrarily [willkührlich] packed everything into the ego? with what warrant? [...] There has to be a non-ego for the ego to be able to posit itself [damit Ich sich, als Ich setzen kann]' (N II, 12 #5, #7).[65] Further on in the *Fichte-Studien*, Fichte's 'absolute' ego is simply called 'nonsense', a merely 'regulative idea' to avoid an infinite regress, because 'each *Tathandlung* presupposes another'.[66]

Such expressions are levelled not only against Fichte but the philosophical quest for absolutes in general. 'All searching for *a single principle*', Novalis notes in a key entry of the *Fichte-Studien*, 'would be like the attempt to square the circle', a pointless quest for 'perpetual motion' or the 'philosophers' stone'. True philosophy, Novalis continues, is based on the exact opposite, 'the deliberate renunciation [Entsagen] of the absolute' and 'the *interruption* of the drive toward knowledge of the ground' (N II, 180–81 #566). This 'absolute postulate' of thought, as Novalis paradoxically calls it, is reiterated in the *Brouillon*, though this time more polemically: 'Why bother with a *beginning* at all? This unphil[osophical] — or semiphil[osophical] — goal [Zweck] is the source of all errors' (N II, 622 #634).[67] Instead of attempting to solve Fichte's foundationalist antinomy of which comes first, the self-positing ego or some prior opposition, Novalis simply discards the question as unphilosophical. And unlike Hegel, Novalis does not wish to reveal, in the phrase of the *Phenomenology*, the synthetic ground of 'opposition in itself'[68] to be reflection or self-consciousness, because he does not believe in such absolute foundations. 'Everywhere we seek the absolute [das Unbedingte]', Novalis writes in *Blüthenstaub* (N II, 227 #1), 'and all we ever find are things'. It is the very first fragment of this collection. Wouldn't it be smarter, therefore, to stick to these, instead of reaching for the illusory no-thing called the Absolute? And so, insisting on things and the reciprocities among them, Novalis squarely defies the monist tendency, especially, of post-Kantian idealism.

Novalis does, however, reflect on Fichte's rhetorical strategies for hiding the conflicts of his system from his readers. In the *Brouillon*, Novalis calls Fichte's ego 'a Robinson — a scientific [wissenschaftliche] *fiction* — to facilitate the representation [Darstellung] and development of the *Wissenschaftslehre* [...] Description of the philosophical state of nature — of an isolated principle' (N II, 645 #717).[69] At first glance, this comparison between the 'scientific fiction' of the Fichtean ego and Defoe's *Robinson Crusoe* (which Novalis once dubbed the 'handbook of all clever men')[70] might appear far-fetched. But in combination with another note from the *Brouillon*, it becomes a striking observation:

> *Der Anfang des Ich* ist blos *idealisch*. [...] Der Anfang entsteht später, als das Ich, darum kann das Ich nicht angefangen habe. Wir sehn daraus, daß wir hier im Gebiet der *Kunst* sind — aber diese künstliche Supposition ist die Grundlage einer ächten Wissenschaft die allemahl aus *künstlichen Factis* entspringt. Das Ich soll construirt werden. Der Philosoph bereitet, schafft künstliche Elemente und geht so an die Construction. Die *Naturgeschichte* des Ich ist dieses nicht — Ich ist kein Naturproduct [...] sondern ein artistisches — eine *Kunst* — ein Kunstwerck. (N II, 485 #76)

> [*The beginning of the ego* is merely an *idea*. [...] The beginning originates later than the ego, thus the ego cannot have begun. Consequently, we see that here we are in the realm of *art* — yet this artificial supposition is the foundation of a genuine science that always arises from *artificial facts*. The ego should be constructed. The philosopher prepares, creates artificial elements and so tackles the construction. This is not the *natural history* of the ego — the ego is not a natural product [...] but rather something artistic — it is *art* — a work of art.][71]

Indeed, Fichte's *Wissenschaftslehre* is anything but 'the natural history' of the self. Fichte tells a highly artificial story. He invents a fiction justifying the degree of self-sufficiency and self-creation he ascribes to the ego. The earlier fragment identifies this fiction precisely as a Robinsonade. In reality, 'no man is an island', as the saying goes, but in the world of Fichtean fiction different rules apply. Fichte's ego, the isolated hero of the *Wissenschaftslehre*, acts like Robinson Crusoe on his island, colonizing a mental space — the 'philosophical state of nature' — through perfectly autonomous deeds, regardless of external forces or relations. Like Robinson, the ego has created a world in which it rules supreme and — ostensibly — all by itself.

Novalis does not take issue with the fictional character of foundations. On the contrary, he takes it as yet another indication of the close proximity between philosophy and poetry. Just as the literary writer is required to choose a beginning for his story, so is the philosopher required to devise, indeed invent, the foundation of his system. It is in that sense, Novalis writes in the aforementioned fragment comparing Fichte's ego and Defoe's Robinson, that poetry is philosophy of 'the highest degree':

> Jeder Anfang ist ein Actus d[er] Freyheit — eine *Wahl* — Construction eines abs[oluten] Anfangs. [...] Mit der Bildung und Fertigkeit [...] des Denkers, *wächst* die *Freyheit*. (Grade der Freyheit.) Die Mannichfaltigkeit der Methoden nimmt zu — am Ende weiß der Denker aus *Jedem* Alles zu machen — der Phil[osoph] wird zum Dichter. *Dichter* ist nur der höchste Grad des Denkers, oder Empfinders etc. (N II, 645 #717)
>
> [Every beginning is an act of freedom — a *choice* — a construction of an absolute beginning. [...] *Freedom increases* [...] with the education and skill of the thinker. (Degrees of freedom.) The diversity of the methods increases — the thinker eventually knows how to make everything, out of *each thing* — the philosopher becomes a poet. The *poet* is but the highest degree of the thinker, or senser etc.][72]

Considering all that, it seems mistaken to see 'the absolute' at the centre of Novalis's theories, as so many commentators do. On the contrary, Novalis articulates a dual logic of reciprocity undermining all claims to primordial unity and absolute beginnings.[73] Along with the notion of *Wechselbestimmung*, or 'reciprocal determination', Novalis uses several synonyms to describe that dual logic, such as *Wechselverhältnis*, *Wechselverbindung*, *Wechselprozess*, and *Wechselrepräsentation*. A line from the *Brouillon* can serve as a general definition of these procedures. In fact, this line expresses Novalis's Romantic metaphysics, since it reads: 'METAPHYSICS. Every thing is a general *formula* of something else — a function of another thing [...] a reciprocal connection [Wechselverbindung]' (N II, 623 #637).

None of these reciprocal connections produce dialectic unity and closure, as Hegelian commentators would have it.[74] Novalis's 'absolute postulate' against monist solutions (whether rationalistic, egological, or speculative in kind) remains intact, so that these connections involve in all cases duality and opposition, which is to say, reciprocal determination: 'Each thing is recognizable through opposition [im Entgegengesetzten] [...] There is no absolute form, and no absolute matter [Stoff]. They all condition [bedingen] each other reciprocally in a circle [wechselweise im Kreise]' (N II, 78 #226). Ego and non-ego, subject and object, reflection and perception, concept and intuition, understanding and memory, form and matter, time and space, even fact and fiction, or science and poetry: all these terms are intelligible only if understood *against* each other. 'Understanding and memory', for example, are 'opposite operations', though 'the one consists of, and is completed by, the other' (N II, 533 #331), an interrelations of opposites Novalis explains here, as he often does, in mathematical terms.[75]

In brief, and unmistakably, 'We can understand only that which is incomplete', wherefore 'every *definition* is *relative*'.[76] There is no such thing as absolute unity or original totality, but only relative reciprocity, a groundless ground relating separate and as such incomplete elements. Reciprocity is the absolute for Novalis, reciprocity as seen and expressed through the power of poetry; whence it follows that the Absolute does not exist. There is no such thing as simple unconditioned unity, complete in and of itself, some higher synthesis in which separate parts are made whole again, but only a myriad of reciprocal combinations. The Whole is not One but at least Two, which poetry freely and — just as important — interestingly *connects*, instead of uniting them.

Novalis applies this — *his* — principle of reciprocal determination to the workings of perception. A first example is found in the *Fichte-Studien*, at the end of the key fragment contradicting Fichte's foundationalism. Novalis concludes that 'I can never find intuition as such [die Anschauung] because I must look for it in reflection, and vice versa' (N II, 182 #566). The apprentices' exercises in poetic perception no doubt follow the same principle. As it is always already compounded with its seeming opposite, reflection, sensation cannot be considered in isolation. To illustrate this point, and also to counter possible objections, Novalis recalls an optical principle and turns it into a metaphor for perception: 'All our perceptual faculties [Wahrnehmungsvermögen] resemble the eye. The objects must pass through opposite media [entgegengesetzte Media] to appear on the pupil correctly' (N II, 229 #9). Just as external objects must pass through different media, namely cornea and lens, to produce a visible image on the retina, so must physical sensations pass through the medium of reflection to become intelligible perceptions — representations, as Novalis puts it in a related fragment, that 'appear correctly on the inner pupil'.[77] This logic of reciprocity applies to all senses. The visible, Novalis writes elsewhere, is always already compounded with its opposite, 'the invisible, the audible with the inaudible, the tangible with the intangible', and so forth.[78]

Reciprocal determination thus makes it impossible to explain perception in purely mechanical terms, as the immediate product of sensory stimuli. Perceptible contents — the visible, the audible, the tangible, and so forth — gain shape only in contrast to their imperceptible opposite, hence their negation. Novalis develops this notion in the same fragment wherein he concedes the difficulty of explaining the senses (N II, 183–85 #568). 'The ground of the senses, sense, must be a negative matter [Materie] and negative spirit [Geist]', he writes here, and is as such 'probably the element of the imagination — of the ego'. But, Novalis continues,

> wir [müssen] uns aber diesen Fund nicht materiell oder geistig denken — Es ist keins von beyden, weil es beydes auf gewisse Weise ist. Es ist ein Product der Einbildungskraft, woran wir *glauben*, ohne es seiner und unsrer Natur nach, je zu erkennen vermögen. Es ist auch nichts an und für sich vorhandnes, sondern dasjenige, was [...] den einzelnen Sinnen zum Grunde liegt und sie erklärt [...].
> (N II, 184 #568)

> [we must not think of this finding as material or mental [geistig] — It is neither one, because in a certain way it is both. It is a product of the imagination, which we *believe* in, without being able ever to know it according to its nature or ours. Nor is it something that exists in and of itself, but rather that which [...] constitutes the basis of the individual senses and explains them [...].][79]

If sense perception necessarily combines both the positive-material and the negative-immaterial, or the perceptible and the imperceptible, then it is an exemplary, if not the foremost, case of reciprocal determination. The senses function in this process as the 'medium of reciprocity':

> Es ist allgemein bekannt, daß man Seele und Körper unterscheidet. Jeder der diese Unterscheidung kennt wird dabey eine Gemeinschaft zwischen beiden statuiren, vermöge deren sie auf einander wechselseitig wirken. In dieser Wechselwirkung kommt beyden eine doppelte Rolle zur — entweder sie wirken selbst für sich auf einander oder ein drittes Etwas wirkt durch eins aufs Andere. Der Körper nemlich dient zugleich auch vermittelst der Sinne zu einer Communication der äußern Gegenstände mit der Seele, und insofern er selbst ein äußrer Gegenstand ist, wirkt er selbst, als solcher, mittelst der Sinne auf die Seele. Natürlich wirkt die Seele auf demselben Weg zurück und hieraus ergibt sich, daß dieser Weg, oder die Sinne, ein gemeinschaftliches, ungetheiltes Eigenthum des Körpers und der Seele sind. So gut es äußre Gegenstände giebt, zu denen der Körper mit gehört, eben so gut giebt es innre Gegenstände, zu denen die Seele mit gehört. Diese wirken auf den Körper und die äußern Gegenstände überhaupt, mittelst der Sinne, wie schon gesagt und erhalten die Gegenwirkung auf [auch?] auf diesem Wege zurück. Die Schwierigkeit ist nun die *Sinne* zu erklären.
> /Gattungsbegriff d[er] Sinne/
> Zu Sinnen gehört immer ein Körper und eine Seele. Ihre Vereinigung findet mittelst der Sinne statt. Die Sinne sind schlechthin nicht selbstthätig — Sie empfangen und geben, was sie erhalten — Sie sind das Medium der Wechselwirkung. (N II, 183 #568)
>
> [It is generally known that soul and body are distinct. Everyone who recognizes this distinction will at the same time assert a community between the two through which they interact. Both have a double role in this reciprocal interaction — either they affect each other in themselves directly or a third something acts through one of them upon the other. Indeed, the body serves to communicate outer objects to the soul via the senses, but insofar as it is itself an outer object, it at the same time acts by itself, through its senses, upon the soul. Naturally the soul responds in the same way, and so it is clear that this path, the senses, are a common, undivided property of the body and the soul. Just as there are outer objects to which the body belongs, so as well there are inner objects to which the soul belongs. These operate on the body and outer objects in general via the senses, as already mentioned, and are affected by this process in return. Now the difficulty is to explain the *senses*.
> /generic concept of the senses/
> The senses always belong to a body and a soul. Their union occurs by means of the senses. As such, the senses are not spontaneous — they receive and give what they get — they are the medium of reciprocity.][80]

The active use of the senses, perception, represents an intermediary system that relates the organic functions of the senses, their receptivity for certain matters, to the inner sense, reflection. Aesthesis is therefore the process investing physical or outer sense with an immaterial and intellectual or inner sense, so that its result, the sense of perception, is always both physical and mental, sensible and comprehensible in kind. Or as Novalis puts it, the word 'sense' indicates 'mediated knowledge', the *'contact'* and *'mixture'* — as opposed to union and identity — of these two different, if correlated, kinds of sense (N II, 482 #61).[81] Determining bodily sensations through reflection, and conversely the sense of reflection through sensation, perception generates 'modifications' as well as 'individual species of sense' [Individuen der Gattung Sinn], for instance, visible (and hence comprehensible) images, as well as audible (and hence understandable) sounds (N II, 185 #568). And so it is that 'every perception of sense [Sinnenwahrnehmung] comes at second hand', as Novalis writes, that sense is always 'both the means and the end', the physical vessel as well as the *'representative'* or *'symbolic'* content of perception (N II, 339 #118).[82]

Hegel once remarked on this double sense of sense. In his lectures on *Aesthetics* (TWA XIII, 173), he explains that '"sense" is this wonderful word' because it signifies both 'the organs of immediate apprehension' and the 'meaning' [Bedeutung] of such apprehension, 'its inner essence'. For that reason, a sensuous consideration deserving of the term *sinnvoll* (literally, 'filled with sense') 'does not cut the two sides apart' but combines them, thus recognizing 'in immediate sensation [im sinnlichen unmittelbaren Anschauen] at the same time essence and concepts'. Novalis's considerations of perception as reciprocal 'contact' are *sinnvoll* in that precise sense, as opposed to Hegel's philosophy. As a conceptual thinker, Hegel must disapprove of this way of considering things, since 'it does not bring to mind the concept as such but stops at intuiting it' (TWA XIII, 173).

Novalis's discussions of 'externalization' and 'self-alienation' expand on the reciprocity of sensation and reflection, or inner and outer sense, in perception. Novalis maintains that the perception of myself and external objects are interdependent operations. The ego, he writes in the *Fichte-Studien*, cannot be the immediate product of self-reflection or self-positing because it 'finds *itself outside* itself', through 'externalization' [Entäußerung] (N II, 56 #98). It exists and perceives itself only in opposition to 'a foreign entity' [ein Fremdartiges] (N II, 56, #97), a non-ego. This interdependency is, of course, the very reason why 'the ego is nothing by itself', least of all a self-sufficient 'encyclopaedia' (N II, 185 #568). Conversely, external perception (or in Fichtean terms, the perception of a non-ego) involves an 'alienation of myself', which in turn 'animates' the perceived object:

> Ich kann etwas nur erfahren, in so fern ich es in mir aufnehme; es ist also eine Alienation meiner selbst und eine Zueignung oder Verwandlung einer andern Substanz in die meinige zugleich: das neue Product ist von den beyden Factoren verschieden, es ist aus beyden gemischt. Ich vernehme nun jede Veränderung der zugeeigneten Substanz als die meinige und eine fremde zugleich; als die meinige, in so fern ich sie überhaupt vernehme; als eine fremde, in wie fern ich sie so oder so bestimmt vernehme. [...] Wir würden ohne diese Beseelung keine solchen Unterscheidungen in uns machen. (N II, 339 #118)
>
> [Something can be experienced only insofar as it is taken in by me; it is therefore both an alienation of myself and an assimilation or transformation of another substance into my own. The new product is different from both factors; it is a mixture of both. Each change in the assumed substance I perceive as a sensation of my own and as a foreign sensation — of my own insofar as I perceive the

change at all; as a foreign sensation insofar as I perceive a specific change. [...] Each of its attributes corresponds to features of cognition in me. [...] We would not make such distinctions within ourselves without this animation.]

A fragment from the *Brouillon* describes the same oscillation between alienation and assimilation as a correlation between 'self-*estrangement*' [Selbstfremdmachung] and '*self-alteration*' [Selbstveränderung] (N II, 670 #820). The feeling enabling these 'distinctions within ourselves', the passage suggests, is that of 'animation'. Being the 'original tendency and faculty' by which humans encounter the world, as Novalis notes in another fragment (N II, 343 #125), animation is the tangible point of intersection between reflection and sensation. It connects the inner to the outer sense, and by the same token enables their distinction, the differentiation between inanimate external properties and my own sensate body.

If it is true, as Novalis says, that perception involves animation and externalization, crucial boundaries of cognition are blurred. The stability of external objects is called into question, while subjects are in danger of losing themselves and their sense of reality in an unfathomable maze of reciprocal relations, a danger Uwe C. Steiner aptly describes as 'Romantic crises of objectivity'.[83] Despite the epistemological challenges of such crises (which, we shall later see, are addressed in Rilke's scenographies of looking as well), they are essential to phenomenologies of perception. For example, Husserl claims, like Novalis, that the apperception of external or 'transcendent' properties depends on the animation of sensory stimuli through consciousness.[84] Merleau-Ponty takes this thought further still in defining consciousness as 'being-towards-the-thing through the intermediary of the body', which is tantamount to saying that every cognition is body perception and, consequently, alive. This is especially true when perceiving inanimate objects, Merleau-Ponty explains, since here 'it is the investing of the object by my gaze which penetrates and animates it'.

> That is why we say that in perception the thing is given to us 'in person', or 'in the flesh' [...] the thing is correlative to my body [...] and if we try to describe the real as it appears to us in perceptual experience, we find it overlaid with anthropological predicates.[85]

The principle of reciprocal determination structures not only Novalis's critique of Fichte's foundationalism and his thoughts on sense perception. It also provides the basis of Novalis's famous definition of *Romantisierung* (N II, 334 #105). At issue in this fragment is the seeming opposition between the ordinary and the extraordinary, or the prosaic and the poetic world. To 'romanticize' either one means to determine the one sphere through the other, either by means of *Wechselerhöhung* or *Wechselerniedrigung*. These reciprocal operations of 'raising' and 'lowering' are then equated with the mathematical operations of exponentiation (*Potenzierung*) and logarithmization (*Logarithmisierung*), which invert each other. Romanticizing the prosaic world therefore means to raise it to a higher power, or to exponentiate it:

> Die Welt muß romantisirt werden. So findet man den urspr[ünglichen] Sinn wieder. Romantisiren ist nichts, als eine qualit[ative] Potenzirung. [...] Diese Operation ist noch ganz unbekannt. Indem ich dem Gemeinen einen hohen

> Sinn, dem Gewöhnlichen ein geheimnisvolles Ansehen, dem Bekannten die Würde des Unbekannten, dem Endlichen einen unendlichen Schein gebe so romantisire ich es — Umgekehrt ist die Operation für das Höhere, Unbekannte, Mystische, Unendliche — dies wird durch diese Verknüpfung logarythmisirt — Es bekommt einen geläufigen Ausdruck. [...] Wechselerhöhung und Erniedrigung. (N II, 334 #105)
>
> [The world must be romanticized. In that way we regain the original sense. Romanticization is nothing but a qualitative exponentiation. [...] This operation is as yet quite unknown. By giving the ordinary a mysterious appearance, the known the dignity of the unknown, the finite the appearance of the infinite, I romanticize it. The operation for the higher, unknown, mystical, infinite is the inverse — it is logarithmized in these connections — It takes on an ordinary form of expression. [...] Reciprocity of raising and lowering.][86]

The world of quotidian affairs must be regarded from infinite, mysterious heights (exponentiation), while the highest mysteries must be translated into familiar scenes and incidents (logarithmization). Instead of keeping the domains of life separate and distinct, as the sober mind would have it, the Romantic relates and combines them. He romanticizes them, transforming their random contiguity into 'magic affinity', thereby restoring, perhaps, the 'original sense' of the world.[87]

The idea of reciprocal determination also provides Novalis with the blueprint for his encyclopaedia project, the *Brouillon*. The following fragment makes this perfectly clear:

> PSYCH[OLOGIE] UND ENCYKLOP[AEDISTIK]. *Deutlich* wird etwas nu[r] [du]rch Repraesentation. Man versteht eine Sache am leicht[este]n, wenn man sie repraesentirt sieht. So versteht man das Ich nur insofern es vom N[icht]I[ch] repraesentirt wird. Das N[icht]I[ch] ist das Symbol des Ich, und dient nur zum Selbstverständniß des Ich. So versteht man das N[icht]I[ch] umgekehrt nur insofern es vom Ich repraesentirt wird, und dieses sein Symbol wird. In Hinsicht auf die Mathem[atik] läßt sich diese Bemerckung so anwenden, daß die Mathem[atik], um verständlich zu seyn repraesentirt werden muß. Eine Wissenschaft läßt sich nur durch eine andere wahrhaft repraesentiren. Die paedagogischen Anfangsgründe der Mathematik müssen daher *symbolisch* und *analogisch* sein. Eine bekannte W[isschenschaft] muß zum *Gleichniß* für die Mathem[atik] dienen und diese Grundgleichung muß das Princp der Darstellung der Mathematick werden. (N II, 478 #49)
>
> [PSYCHOLOGY AND ENCYCLOPEDISTICS. Something only becomes *clear* through representation. One understands a thing most easily if one sees it represented. Thus one understands the ego only insofar as it is represented by the non-ego. The non-ego is the symbol of the ego, and merely serves in the self-understanding of the ego. And conversely, one only understands the non-ego insofar as it is represented by the ego and becomes its symbol. In relation to mathematics one can say that in order to become understandable, mathematics must be represented. One science can only be truly represented by another science. Therefore the pedagogical foundations of mathematics must be *symbolic* and *analogical*. A known science must serve as an *allegory* for mathematics, and this fundamental equation must be the principle in the explication of mathematics.][88]

Notice how Novalis here transitions from egological or, as he puts it, 'psychological' issues to broader epistemic or 'encyclopaedic' concerns. The connection between Fichtean and 'encyclopaedic' problems is clearly visible in this fragment. In any case, the key concept of encyclopaedistics is clear: all comprehension occurs by way of analogy, and more precisely through reciprocal representation. Like sense perception, knowledge 'comes at second hand' (N II, 339 #118), for which reason the *Brouillon* points out analogies and reciprocities, instead of summarizing concepts.

One of Novalis's best readers, Ludwig Tieck, noticed this 'doctrine of *reciprocal representation*' [*Wechselrepraesentations*lehre] (N II, 499 #137) early on. In the preface to the first collection of Novalis's works, Tieck remarks that Novalis 'had planned to write an encyclopaedic work of his own in which experiences and ideas from various sciences would mutually explain, support and energize each other.'[89] The faculty to recognize *and* produce such analogies or 'degrees and types etc. of similarity' Novalis calls *Witz* (N II, 599 #555).[90]

The perception of poetry, or, 'the blue flower'

In the previous sections, I sought mainly to demonstrate three points. First, there is a tendency in Novalis's writings to connect perception and poetry conceptually. The transformation of merely receptive senses into creative instruments of poetry in the *Lehrlinge* is perhaps the most striking example thereof. This tendency is at once suggested and complicated by certain historical developments, to which Novalis alludes. Second, the study of Fichte further complicates Novalis's understanding of perception. Siding with Fichte's activist concept of self-consciousness, Novalis rejects a mechanical concept of perception, yet his rejection of Fichte's foundationalism makes it equally impossible to explain sense perception in purely egological terms. Perception thus turns — and here is the third point — into a dynamic wherein inner and outer sense determine each other reciprocally. Following this logic of reciprocity he developed in critical dialogue with Fichte, Novalis thinks of sensations as being determined and rendered intelligible through intentional acts of reflection such as attention, selection, and combination, as well as externalization and self-alienation. These inherently poetic acts of the mind would mean nothing, however, if they were not imbued with the tangible sense of the senses.

Taken together, these points may well represent a summary of Novalis's concept of sense perception. But Novalis is not solely a 'weaving loom of ideas' [Ideenwebstuhl] (N I, 624). He actualizes his ideas in and through poetry, as Hans Jürgen Balmes (N III, 149) pointed out. They are, and ought to be read as, inherent aspects of his poetic works. For that reason, his conception of the senses must be related to scenographies of perception in his poetic works. These scenographies delineate the territory wherein perception and poetry intermingle, wherein their reciprocity is not only posited but also represented and observed. The foremost example in this regard is, as I will demonstrate, the emergence of the blue flower at the beginning of *Heinrich von Ofterdingen*. The significance of this flower, its poetic sense, cannot be abstracted from its perceptual nature, from its sensuous sense, a reciprocity that in turn prompts the reader — 'the extended author' (N II, 282 #125) — to perceive the blue flower with his senses and mind together. As a result, perceptual process and poetic meaning are inseparable.[91]

This aesthesiological approach to the proverbial 'blue flower' has little in common with allegorical interpretations of *Heinrich von Ofterdingen*, which tend to read Heinrich's perceptions and experiences as figurations of deeper esoteric truths. For example, Detlef Kremer argued, in line with older scholarship, that Heinrich's story represents a 'journey into the realm of the imagination' revealing, at last, a 'vision of redemption', a golden age of love and poetry devised against the economic 'farce' that in Novalis's view concludes Goethe's *Wilhelm Meisters Lehrjahre*.[92] Similarly, Klingsohr's *Märchen* or tale is frequently singled out to illustrate the allegorical nature of *Heinrich von Ofterdingen* as a whole. This tale is then interpreted either as a 'myth of redemption' or as an allegory of contemporary science.[93]

These allegorical interpretations no doubt follow authorial leads. Klingsohr's tale, for instance, does allegorize contemporary discourses on galvanism, magnetism, and mineralogy, and Novalis planned to 'poeticize' still more sciences in the second part of *Heinrich von Ofterdingen*.[94] Novalis had also characterized Heinrich's development as 'years of transition' culminating in an 'apotheosis of poetry', hence as a 'transition from the real to the secret world', which seems to suggest that Heinrich's experiences are but prefigurations of higher truths to come.[95] The novel was supposed to 'gradually transform' into a 'fable' [Märchen], he wrote to Ludwig Tieck in April 1800 (N I, 740). But even so, visions of redemption and transfiguration — or still worse, mere allegory — are on Novalis's account not nearly enough to accomplish a work of poetry. Around the same time as he is working on *Heinrich von Ofterdingen*, Novalis comes to think of art as a technical, 'mechanical' [mechanisch] (N II, 713 #1113) achievement on the basis of artistic calculation and skill, rather than wild imagination and fancy.

In a note from the summer of 1799, Novalis underscores his pledge to sobriety most emphatically: 'I am convinced that a cold, technical mind [Verstand] and a calm moral sense are more likely to show us *true revelations* than our fantasy does, which only seems to lure us into the realm of ghosts, the antipode of the true heavens' (N I, 482). Novalis 'begins to love sobriety', he writes in a letter to Caroline Schlegel, because it is 'the way of real progress and improvement'.[96] In *Heinrich von Ofterdingen*, it is the arch-poet Klingsohr himself who promotes the idea of poetic sobriety. He warns Heinrich that poetry is a sober and very technical business wherein senseless enthusiasm and wild imaginations engender only 'confused talk' [verworrnes Geschwätz] and 'trembling vacuity' [zitternde Gedankenlosigkeit] (N I, 329).[97] Thus, the poetry envisioned by Novalis does not at all belong to some fairy-tale world of higher mystery but always points back to the concrete world of sensory experience.[98]

Accordingly, the 'apotheosis of poetry' Novalis hoped to achieve with *Heinrich von Ofterdingen* would have to be plotted out with careful craft and sobriety. And indeed, in a working note to *Heinrich von Ofterdingen* Novalis reminds himself of 'calmness and economy of style' as the technical means to accomplish this apotheosis, together with 'poetic cohesion and composition' [poëtischer Zusammenhang und

Anordnung] (N I, 389). These, however, are not sudden inspirations or spontaneous strokes of genius but involve above all the 'active association of ideas' (N II, 692 # 953). More precisely, poetic cohesion and composition involve the careful creation of what Novalis variously terms 'structured series' [gesezmäßige Reihe] (N II, 369 #242), 'reciprocal linkage' [Wechselglieder] (N II, 370 #242), 'catenation' (N II, 692 #953), 'exciting [reitzende] periods or chains' (N II, 807 #807), or 'secret concatenations' [geheime Verkettungen] (N I, 305) amongst words, sentences, characters, incidents, scenes, episodes. These and similar terms show up when Novalis discusses Goethe's *Wilhelm Meister* and, more generally, literary genres such as the tale (*Märchen*) and the novel.[99] The most sustained discussion of poetic cohesion, however, occurs in the fifth chapter of *Heinrich von Ofterdingen* (N I, 304–07), where the age-old Count of Hohenzollern explains the art of forming 'series' [Reihen] and concatenating signs in both fictional and historical narratives. In the *Lehrlinge* (cf. N I, 203, 207–09), series or 'figures' are topics of discussion as well, though here the apprentices wonder not about narrative but rather the arrangement of natural artefacts, the order in which the signs of nature ought to be concatenated. At any rate, what Novalis means by all these terms are, quite simply, *calculated* series, syntagms connected through semantic and/or sensory similarities, including phonic features such as assonance and rhythm, thereby anticipating quite precisely what Roman Jakobson will much later term the 'poetic function of language'.[100]

Although such technical considerations are very much at play in *Heinrich von Ofterdingen*, Novalis firmly believed that '[p]oetry must never be the main subject but at all times only the miracle' in his book, adding as a general rule that 'one should never *represent* things not seen in full and perceived clearly, things one has not fully mastered yet — e.g. when *representing the supersensible*'.[101] The consequence of this maxim is drawn in another working note from roughly the same period. The aspiring novelist, Novalis demands here, must practice above all the '*narration of tangible* [*wircklicher*] *scenes*' and, moreover, pay close 'attention to the strange effects that people have upon one another — in different situations [Zuständen]' (N II, 780 #207); a demand, I would add, that resonates perfectly with William Wordsworth's contemporaneous dictum that the poet ought to consider 'man and the objects that surround him as acting and re-acting upon each other' within a 'complex scene of ideas and sensations'.[102] Thus, the narration of both tangible and effective scenes — made so by means of 'exciting periods' or calculated series — represents for Novalis the technical basis of literary composition. In a word, scenographies are the essential means of accomplishing an 'apotheosis of poetry' beyond allegorical mystifications.

The so-called 'Berliner Papiere', which record ideas mainly for the second part of *Heinrich von Ofterdingen*, contain another version of the same rule: 'The epic period', Novalis notes here, 'should become a historical spectacle [Schauspiel], although the scenes are connected by means of narration' (N I, 396). Thus, *Heinrich von Ofterdingen* is fundamentally conceived as a series of scenes — scenes *showing*, rather than merely declaring or mystifying, the power of love and poetry such that these forces become a perceptible reality impacting the reader. Klingsohr expands on this imperative of literary composition in his final lesson:

> Wenn es schon für einen einzelnen Dichter nur ein eigenthümliches Gebiet giebt, innerhalb dessen er bleiben muß, um nicht alle Haltung und den Athem zu verlieren: so giebt es auch für die ganze Summe menschlicher Kräfte eine bestimmte Grenze der Darstellbarkeit, über welche hinaus die Darstellung die nöthige Dichtigkeit und Gestaltung nicht behalten kann, und in ein leeres täuschendes Unding sich verliert. Besonders als Lehrling kann man nicht genug sich vor diesen Ausschweifungen hüten, da eine lebhafte Fantasie nur gar zu gern nach den Grenzen sich begiebt, und übermüthig das Unsinnliche, Übermäßige zu ergreifen und auszusprechen sucht. Reifere Erfahrung lehrt erst, jene Unverhältnißmäßigkeit der Gegenstände zu vermeiden, und die Aufspürung des Einfachsten und Höchsten der Weltweisheit zu überlassen. Der ältere Dichter steigt nicht höher, als er es gerade nöthig hat, um seinen mannichfaltigen Vorrath in eine leichtfaßliche Ordnung zu stellen, und hütet sich wohl, die Mannichfaltigkeit zu verlassen, die ihm Stoff genug und auch die nöthigen Vergleichspunkte darbietet. [...] Die beste Poesie liegt uns ganz nahe, und ein gewöhnlicher Gegenstand ist nicht selten ihr liebster Stoff. (N I, 333–34)
>
> [If indeed there is for every single poet a proper district within which he must remain, in order not to lose all breath and vantage, then there is also for the whole sum of human powers a determinate limit of representation, beyond which representation cannot retain the necessary integrity and structure, but loses itself in an empty, delusive nonentity. Particularly as an apprentice, one cannot guard enough against these extravagances, since a lively fancy loves too well to fly to the outer limits, and arrogantly endeavors to seize upon and express the imperceptible and exuberant. Riper experience first teaches us to shun this disproportion of objects, and to leave the discovery of what is simplest and loftiest to worldly wisdom. The older poet rises no higher than is necessary for him to arrange his varied stock in a comprehensible order, and he is careful to forego the manifoldness, which provides him with enough material, and also with the necessary points of comparison. [...] The best poetry lies very near us, and an ordinary matter is not seldom its most beloved subject.][103]

Klingsohr instructs his student Heinrich to restrict his literary representations to ordinary matters and meanings that can be conveyed through — or rather shown within — real, tangible scenes. Simultaneously, he counsels Heinrich to leave the discovery of the 'simplest and loftiest' truths — the essence of cognition, the nature of self-consciousness, absolute knowledge, and so forth — to philosophers.

Taken together, all these remarks prohibit allegorical readings, suggesting instead that inner and outer, tangible and intangible, literal and figural, apparent and poetic sense belong together in *Heinrich von Ofterdingen*. The blue flower embodies this essential connection between perception and poetry, as that between text and scene. The blue flower is first mentioned in the opening sequence, a tense soliloquy. Tossing and turning restlessly on his bed, Heinrich recalls 'the stranger's tales', and still more acutely some 'blue flower', whose origin and provenance is not, and never will be, disclosed to the reader:

> Die Eltern lagen schon und schliefen, die Wanduhr schlug ihren einförmigen Takt, vor den klappernden Fenstern sauste der Wind; abwechselnd wurde die Stube hell von dem Schimmer des Mondes. Der Jüngling lag unruhig

auf seinem Lager, und gedachte des Fremden und seiner Erzählungen. Nicht die Schätze sind es, die ein so unaussprechliches Verlangen in mir geweckt haben, sagte er zu sich selbst; fern ab liegt mir alle Habsucht: aber die blaue Blume sehn' ich mich zu erblicken. Sie liegt mir unaufhörlich im Sinn, und ich kann nichts anders dichten und denken. So ist mir noch nie zu Muthe gewesen: es ist, als hätt' ich vorhin geträumt, oder ich wäre in eine andere Welt hinübergeschlummert; denn in der Welt, in der ich sonst lebte, wer hätte da sich um Blumen bekümmert, und gar von einer so seltsamen Leidenschaft für eine Blume hab' ich damals nie gehört. Wo eigentlich der Fremde herkam? Keiner von uns hat je einen ähnlichen Menschen gesehen; doch weiß ich nicht, warum nur ich von seinen Reden so ergriffen worden bin; die Andern haben ja das Nämliche gehört, und Keinem ist so etwas begegnet. Daß ich auch nicht einmal von meinem wunderlichen Zustande reden kann! Es ist mir oft so entzückend wohl, und nur dann, wenn ich die Blume nicht recht gegenwärtig habe, befällt mich so ein tiefes, inniges Treiben: das kann und wird Keiner verstehn. Ich glaubte, ich wäre wahnsinnig, wenn ich nicht so klar und hell sähe und dächte, mir ist seitdem alles viel bekannter. Ich hörte einst von alten Zeiten reden; wie da die Thiere und Bäume und Felsen mit den Menschen gesprochen hätten. Mir ist grade so, als wollten sie allaugenblicklich anfangen, und als könnte ich es ihnen ansehen, was sie mir sagen wollten. Es muß noch viel Worte geben, die ich nicht weiß: wüßte ich mehr, so könnte ich viel besser alles begreifen. Sonst tanzte ich gern; jezt denke ich lieber nach der Musik. (N 1, 240–41)

[The parents had already retired to rest; the clock ticked monotonously from the wall, the windows rattled with the whistling wind, and the chamber was lit by the flickering glimmer of the moon. The young man lay restless on his bed, thinking of the stranger and his tales. It is not the treasures, he said to himself, that have awakened in me such unutterable longings. Far from me is all avarice; but I long to behold the blue flower. It is constantly in my mind, and I can compose and think of nothing else. I have never been in such a mood. It seems as if I had been dreaming a moment ago, or slumbering into another world; for in the world, in which hitherto I have lived, who would trouble himself about a flower? — I never have heard of such a strange passion for a flower. Where did the stranger come from? None of us have ever seen his like; still I know not why I should be so fascinated by his conversation. The others have also listened to it, but none are struck by it as I am. I cannot even explain my strange condition in words! I am often full of rapture, and it is only when the blue flower is not fully present to my mind that this deep, heart-felt urge overwhelms me. But no one can and will comprehend all that. I would think myself mad if my vision and thought were not so lucid and clear. Since then everything is more familiar to me. I once heard that in ancient times beasts and trees and rocks had been conversing with men. Now it seems to me that they are about to speak at any moment, and that I could tell by their looks what they are about to say. There must yet be many words unknown to me. If I knew more, I could comprehend better. Formerly I loved to dance. Now I think rather to the music.][104]

Heinrich's soliloquy concerns an object that has not yet appeared, neither for him nor for the reader. It figures herein only in name, precisely as some 'blue flower'. Heinrich has yet to witness the blue flower in actuality, which is all he longs for. This flower, in other words, has yet to emerge as an object of perception, so that Heinrich and, by extension, the readers may see its magnificent appearance.

But Heinrich's soliloquy nonetheless describes the flower's irresistible spell. It has captivated his mind and his senses entirely, enchanting all of Heinrich's *Denken* and *Dichten* — cognitive activities, we have seen before, that both very much involve the senses.

The soliloquy thus indicates the strange double nature of the 'blue flower' as both a thing and a name, appearance and meaning. Indeed, the flower 'is special amongst all other words and things in that it functions both as name and image [Anschauung], signifier and signified' in the novel.[105] As an appearance to be witnessed, the flower captivates the senses, while it preoccupies the mind as an enigmatic meaning to be pondered. Uttering her name induces sheer physical delight, but at the same time a sense of significance. In Heinrich's soliloquy, however, the blue flower remains an abstraction, a mere name inspiring the deep longing to behold that flower. Her image is yet to be seen or, indeed, discovered.

The ensuing dreams bring Heinrich's initial soliloquy to completion in that they culminate in the appearance of a 'tall brilliant blue flower'. His dreams thus fulfil Heinrich's *Sehnsucht* to behold that thing known by the name of a 'blue flower', imbuing this name with sense and meaning:

> Endlich gegen Morgen, wie draußen die Dämmerung anbrach, wurde es stiller in seiner Seele, klarer und bleibender wurden die Bilder. Es kam ihm vor, als ginge er in einem dunkeln Walde allein. Nur selten schimmerte der Tag durch das grüne Netz. Bald kam er vor eine Felsenschlucht, die bergan stieg. Er mußte über bemooste Steine klettern, die ein ehemaliger Strom herunter gerissen hatte. Je höher er kam, desto lichter wurde der Wald. Endlich gelangte er zu einer kleinen Wiese, die am Hange des Berges lag. Hinter der Wiese erhob sich eine hohe Klippe, an deren Fuß er eine Oefnung erblickte, die der Anfang eines in den Felsen gehauenen Ganges zu seyn schien. Der Gang führte ihn gemächlich eine Zeitlang eben fort, bis zu einer großen Weitung, aus der ihm schon von fern ein helles Licht entgegen glänzte. Wie er hineintrat, ward er einen mächtigen Strahl gewahr, der wie aus einem Springquell bis an die Decke des Gewölbes stieg, und oben in unzählige Funken zerstäubte, die sich unten in einem großen Becken sammelten; der Strahl glänzte wie entzündetes Gold; nicht das mindeste Geräusch war zu hören, eine heilige Stille umgab das herrliche Schauspiel. Er näherte sich dem Becken, das mit unendlichen Farben wogte und zitterte. Die Wände der Höhle waren mit dieser Flüssigkeit überzogen, die nicht heiß, sondern kühl war, und an den Wänden nur ein mattes, bläuliches Licht von sich warf. Er tauchte seine Hand in das Becken und benetzte seine Lippen. Es war, als durchdränge ihn ein geistiger Hauch, und er fühlte sich innigst gestärkt und erfrischt. Ein unwiderstehliches Verlangen ergriff ihn sich zu baden, er entkleidete sich und stieg in das Becken. Es dünkte ihn, als umflösse ihn eine Wolke des Abendroths; eine himmlische Empfindung überströmte sein Inneres; mit inniger Wollust strebten unzählbare Gedanken in ihm sich zu vermischen; neue, niegesehene Bilder entstanden, die auch in einander flossen und zu sichtbaren Wesen um ihn wurden, und jede Welle des lieblichen Elements schmiegte sich wie ein zarter Busen an ihn. Die Flut schien eine Auflösung reizender Mädchen, die an dem Jünglinge sich augenblicklich verkörperten.
>
> Berauscht von Entzücken und doch jedes Eindrucks bewußt, schwamm er gemach dem leuchtenden Strome nach, der aus dem Becken in den

Felsen hineinfloß. Eine Art von süßem Schlummer befiel ihn, in welchem er unbeschreibliche Begebenheiten träumte, und woraus ihn eine andere Erleuchtung weckte. Er fand sich auf einem weichen Rasen am Rande einer Quelle, die in die Luft hinausquoll und sich darin zu verzehren schien. Dunkelblaue Felsen mit bunten Adern erhoben sich in einiger Entfernung; das Tageslicht [,] das ihn umgab, war heller und milder als das gewöhnliche, der Himmel war schwarzblau und völlig rein. Was ihn aber mit voller Macht anzog, war eine hohe lichtblaue Blume, die zunächst an der Quelle stand, und ihn mit ihren breiten, glänzenden Blättern berührte. Rund um sie her standen unzählige Blumen von allen Farben, und der köstlichste Geruch erfüllte die Luft. Er sah nichts als die blaue Blume, und betrachtete sie lange mit unnennbarer Zärtlichkeit. Endlich wollte er sich ihr nähern, als sie auf einmal sich zu bewegen und zu verändern anfing; die Blätter wurden glänzender und schmiegten sich an den wachsenden Stengel, die Blume neigte sich nach ihm zu, und die Blüthenblätter zeigten einen blauen ausgebreiteten Kragen, in welchem ein zartes Gesicht schwebte. Sein süßes Staunen wuchs mit der sonderbaren Verwandlung, als ihn plötzlich die Stimme seiner Mutter weckte, und er sich in der elterlichen Stube fand, die schon die Morgensonne vergoldete. Er war zu entzückt, um unwillig über diese Störung zu seyn; vielmehr bot er seiner Mutter freundlich guten Morgen und erwiederte ihre herzliche Umarmung.] (N 1, 241–42)

[In the morning, when day broke outside, his soul finally became calmer, and the images grew clearer and more lasting. He found himself walking alone in a dark forest, where the light shone only at intervals through the green net. He soon came to a passage through some rocks that led uphill. He had to climb over the mossy stones, which some stream in former times had torn down. The higher he went, the the forest became sparser, until at last he came to a small meadow situated on the declivity of the mountain. Behind the meadow rose a lofty cliff, at whose foot an opening was visible, which seemed to be the beginning of a path hewn in the rock. The path guided him gently along, ending in a wide expanse from which at a distance a bright light shone towards him. On entering this expanse, he beheld a mighty beam of light, which, like the stream from a fountain, rose to the ceiling of the cave, and then spread out into innumerable flashes, which came together below in a great basin. The beam shone like glowing gold; not the least noise was audible; a holy silence was around the splendid spectacle. He approached the basin, which trembled and undulated with ever-varying colors. The walls of the cave were coated with the golden liquid, which was not hot but cool to the touch, and which cast from the walls a dim blueish light. He dipped his hand in the basin and bedewed his lips. He felt as if a spiritual breath had pierced through him, and he was strengthened and refreshed from the inside. He was seized by an irresistible desire to bathe himself, and so he undressed and stepped into the basin. He thought himself surrounded by a cloud tinged with the glow of evening, and feelings as from heaven flowed into his soul; thoughts innumerable and full of rapture strove to mingle together within him; images never seen before arose before him and then flew into each other, becoming visible beings about him. Each wave of the lovely element pressed to him like a soft bosom. The flood seemed like a solution of alluring girls, who immediately embodied themselves upon contact.

Intoxicated with rapture, yet conscious of every impression, he swam gently down the glittering stream, which was flowing from the basin into the rock. A sweeter slumber now overcame him, and he dreamt of many indescribable occurrences — until a new vision woke him. He found himself sitting on the soft turf by the margin of a fountain, whose waters flowed into the air and seemed to vanish in it. Dark blue rocks with colored veins rose in the distance. The daylight around him was brighter and milder than usual; the sky was of a somber blue and perfectly clear. But what most attracted his notice, was a tall, brilliant blue flower, which stood close by the fountain, and touched it with its broad, glossy leaves. Around it grew numberless flowers of all colors, filling the air with the richest perfume. He saw nothing but the blue flower, and gazed long upon it with inexpressible tenderness. When he was about to approach it, it suddenly began to move and change its form. The leaves became still more radiant, nestling up against the growing stem. The flower bended towards him, and revealed among its leaves a blue, outspread collar, within which hovered a tender face. His sweet astonishment was increasing with this singular change, when suddenly his mother's voice awoke him, and he found himself in his parents' living room, already gilded by the morning sun. He was too enraptured to be angry at the sudden disturbance, bidding his mother instead a good morning and returning her hearty embrace.][106]

What does this sequence of two dreams accomplish? It actualizes the blue flower through acts of perception and situates it within a scene. It materializes the world to which the flower belongs as much as it sensualizes the flower's significance, and it does so by temporalizing and narrativizing what until then was nothing but an abstract empty name, some 'blue flower'. Heinrich's deep longing is thus filled with sense, with looks, smells, sounds, touch, and many more bodily sensations, for the reader as much as for Heinrich himself.

To this end, the scenography is carefully crafted. One important source of cohesion is obviously teleology: fulfilling Heinrich's express desire, the dream sequence drives towards the 'brilliant blue flower' as the enrapturing climax. Heinrich is utterly captivated by its appearance. Once again he cannot think or see anything but the flower, though this time it is fully present to his senses and his mind. Beholding the flower, Heinrich connects his 'strange condition' of *Sehnsucht* to a concrete object, whose tantalizing pleasures the name of the flower could only intimate. Displaying, in the end, also a 'tender face', the flower at the same time impresses a latent image of desire on Heinrich's soul. This is the flower's meaning, which is completely revealed only in retrospect, when Heinrich identifies the flower's 'tender face' with the countenance of his beloved Mathilde.[107]

It is upon this climactic convergence of splendid appearance and promising meaning that Heinrich, still 'enraptured' by the flower, is awakened by his mother, whose affectionate embrace he then reciprocates with conspicuous eagerness. Indeed, Heinrich's affectionate response to the motherly interruption of his dream seems to be an instance of transference. Instead of embracing the girl-flower, which in his dream had turned towards him as though she wanted to kiss him, Heinrich can only return his mother's 'hearty embrace', as he does not at all 'unwillingly' (N I, 242).[108] The scene consequently reverts to the parental living-room, where an 'industrious' [emsig] father dismisses the dream of his son with the disenchanting remark, 'Dreams are noise [Schäume]' (N 1, 243) — and this only moments before he narrates the remarkably similar dream he had as a young man (N 1, 245–48).

This apparent teleology is not the sole source of cohesion. At least as important is the intricate system of interdependent perceptions — the 'exciting periods or chains', to recall Novalis's formulation, running through his dreams, which altogether issue from, and circle back to, the 'blue flower'. Heinrich's perceptions either resemble the flower's *lichtblau* — literally 'light blue' — color, or they refer to the flower on the basis of a larger network of correspondences. These *aesthesiological series* inform the course of his dream. Since these series belong to a sceno*graphy*, however, they involve not only sensory but also phonic and semantic correspondences.

One such aesthesiological series or period is particularly obvious. Heinrich enters a tunnel wherein he perceives a 'bright *light*' and, thereafter, a liquid that gives off 'a dim *blueish light*' upon contact with the wall of the cave. Shortly before he discovers the site of the flower, Heinrich then notices 'dark *blue* rocks' and a 'somber *blue*' [schwarzblau] sky, as well as a type of 'day*light*' that seems 'brighter and milder' than ordinary daylight. All these perceptions are immediately associated with the flower in that they resemble its most distinctive feature, its radiant blue or *lichtblau* colour. In fact, this particular aesthesiological series extends throughout the entire novel in that many of the following episodes appear in shades of blue — and deliberately so: 'All is blue in my book', Novalis remarked as to its 'colour scheme' [Farbencharacter] (N 1, 396).

But what about those other perceptions that neither resemble the flower's radiant blueness, nor issue directly from its physical appearance? Those perceptions relate to the flower as well, but indirectly, on the basis of what Novalis called 'secret concatenations' (N 1, 305). The following example can illuminate the nature and the significance of those less obvious aesthesiological series. Bathing in the liquid that gives off 'a dim *bluish light*', Heinrich is imbued with *Wollust* — a 'lustful urge' that at the same time bears an intense self-enjoyment. Heinrich's *Wollust* eventually leads to very exciting erotic sensations, because he senses the liquid on his skin as though he had been touched by 'alluring girls' and thus feels 'intoxicated with rapture'. All these perceptions are connected to the flower by the following aesthesiological series:

> blueness of flower = blueness of liquid ↔ contact with liquid on hand and lips ↔ 'irresistible desire' to bathe ↔ *Wollust* while bathing ↔ erotic sensations: liquid feels like 'alluring girls' on the skin ↔ utter rapture.

The liquid relates to the flower on the basis of an immediate sensory correspondence (=), namely their blueness; Heinrich's 'irresistible desire' as well as his *Wollust* and the resulting ecstasy are contiguous with (↔), and indeed caused by, this liquid; so that these erotic sensations seem to betray a defining trait of the flower, namely feminine allure, her female touch. This anticipatory attribution of arousing femininity to the flower, suggested by the aesthesiological series on the basis of contiguity, is eventually confirmed and fulfilled when the flower exhibits a 'tender face' — the countenance, as it turns out later, of Heinrich's future lover, Mathilde. The fact that both the bath in the liquid and the later observation of the flower result in utter rapture only underscores the essential correspondence between the exciting liquid and the flower. Just as the blue flower animates Heinrich's thinking and sensing, so does the liquid excite his *Denken* and *Dichten*, giving rise to 'thoughts innumerable' in Heinrich and 'images never seen before'. One might think that these two things are composed of the same substance, pure poetry.

Further aesthesiological series are inscribed into Heinrich's very sensuous dreams. For example, the two landscapes (and more precisely dreamscapes) developing from Heinrich's perceptual movements show astonishing similarities. In fact, the second landscape in which the flower is situated appears to be a variation, if not a duplicate, of the first. The following juxtaposition might indicate the striking aesthesiological symmetry between them:

> ... he came to a small meadow ↔ mountain and lofty cliff ↔ path hewn in the rock leading to wide expanse ↔ fountain of light feeding a basin trembling in ever-varying colours.
>
> ... he found himself sitting on the soft turf by the margin of a water fountain ↔ dark blue rocks with coloured veins ↔ clear sombre blue sky ↔ brilliant blue flower close by the fountain, surrounded by flowers of all colours.

There are tangible, and for the analyst also legible, correspondences between these two dreamscapes. Indeed, they unfold on the basis of a nearly identical aesthesiological script. The topographical features Heinrich notices resemble each other closely, as well as the sequence by which he perceives them. Heinrich remarks in each case a meadow (*Wiese*, *Rasen*), then rocks, a fountain, and finally the flower, which the first landscape substitutes, however, with the basin of exciting liquid. The fact that Heinrich's second dream picks up near a fountain of light, the source of endless pleasures in his earlier dream, perfects the symmetry and reciprocity. One could almost say that Heinrich transitions seamlessly from the first into the second dreamscape by swimming 'gently down the glittering stream, which was flowing from the basin into the rock' — if this transition was not interrupted, strangely enough, by a dream within his current dream: 'A sweeter slumber now overcame him, and he dreamt of many indescribable occurrences — until a new vision [Erleuchtung] woke him' (N 1, 242).

This strange occurrence is indicative of the many tangled *mise en abyme* structures in *Heinrich von Ofterdingen*, which often make it hard to distinguish between reality and fantasy, or diegetic and metadiegetic spaces. Moreover, it beautifully illustrates the ambiguity of Novalis's *Athenäum* fragment that 'we are near waking when we dream that we dream'.[109] On the one hand, the dream within Heinrich's dream signals his imminent awakening; his mother's voice will wake him in a short while. This is the profane meaning of Heinrich's 'sweeter slumber'. On the other hand, the 'sweeter slumber' separating the first from the second dream sequence introduces his poetic *Erleuchtung* — his awakening in the land of poetry, where he will behold the blue flower for the first time. This is the metaphoric or, perhaps more accurately, the Romantic meaning of the dream within Heinrich's dream.

Aesthesiological series such as these determine not simply the course of Heinrich's perceptions; they regulate, properly speaking, *readerly* perception. The bath in the liquid prepares the emergence of the flower also in the reader's eyes, while the sense of this bath comes to completion by noticing, in retrospect, the similarly arousing effects of both liquid and flower. Similarly, the perceptual sequence by which the first dreamscape evolves anticipates also for the reader the second dreamscape, wherein the dream sequence finds its enrapturing completion. Taken together, these aesthesiological series constitute a network pointing to the flower as the retentional origin and the protentional telos of perception. They gradually instil, augment, and perfect the cohesion of the first scenography in *Heinrich von Ofterdingen* and, moreover, imbue it with sensory force, for its protagonist no less than for its reader.

What, then, is the blue flower? It is certainly a harbinger of that *Mährchenwelt* (N 1, 394) Heinrich was supposed to discover in the end, a wonderland in which he was supposed to intuit 'the meaning [Sinn] of the world' (N 1, 395) and have 'strange [wunderliche] *conversations* with the dead' (N 1, 397). Here, 'those who sing or kiss' would know more than 'learned men': *die so singen, oder küssen | Mehr als die Tiefgelehrten wissen*, Novalis rhymes, while 'fables' and 'poems' would represent the 'true histories of the world': *Und man in Märchen und Gedichten | Erkennt die alten wahren Weltgeschichten* (N 1, 395). Here, where 'the hourglass runs eternally' and the sky is forever 'blue and cloudless' (N 1, 400), all hurting, all mourning, all sorrow was supposed to come to an end. All these lines from poems intended for the novel's second part seem to describe key aspects of that 'secret' and 'supernatural' (N 1, 392) *Mährchenwelt* (N 1, 394) Heinrich was supposed to discover after his final 'transfiguration' (N 1, 394).

This is an enticing prospect, no doubt, but Heinrich never reaches the land of eternal bliss envisioned by these lines. It remains uncertain whether, and if so how, Novalis would have used these poems if he had been given the time to finish his novel. That notorious heaven of Universal and Perpetual Poesy, wherein the difference between life and death is eradicated and the 'alienation of man from nature' forever healed — this 'vision', or rather caricature, of redemption that some critics recognize in *Heinrich von Ofterdingen* does not appear in the novel.[110] Klingsohr's doctrine as to the 'limits of representation' [Grenze der Darstellbarkeit] (N 1, 333–34) explains why this could never happen: because heaven cannot be shown, nor described through tangible scenes. 'Poetry', to cite Novalis's golden rule again, 'must never be the main subject but at all times only the miracle' (N 1, 389). The blue flower therefore only *heralds* the promised *Mährchenwelt* — a world that might not even be as wonderful a place as it seems from a distance, since the kind of bliss it has to offer is, in truth, the bliss of death, as Novalis knew himself. The lines envisioning this 'blue and cloudless' wonderland are prefaced by the words: 'Blessed [Selig] are the dead *alone*' (N 1, 399; emphasis added).

What else is the blue flower, besides an unfulfilled and unfulfillable promise of redemption? The blue flower is something more fundamental and, perhaps, also more potent. It is, in the first place, a *prompt* to make active, magical use of the senses. It is an abstract name prompting Heinrich to develop its sense and meaning through perceptions. With his dream, Heinrich does just that: he *makes sense* of the enchanting words 'the blue flower'. The name of the flower is a spell turning his senses, to recall an earlier formulation, into an 'instrument of speech' [Sprachwerkzeug] (N II, 377 #264). They begin to translate a senseless name into a concatenated series of perceptions, thus creating the scene in which the flower can be both sensed and thought, beheld and understood, as he so much desires. His sense produces a dream wherein, to quote again from *Die Lehrlinge zu Saïs*, 'the perceptions of his senses crowded together in massive, colorful images: he heard, saw, touched, and thought simultaneously', finding 'familiarity everywhere, but oddly commingled and combined' (N I, 202). In doing so, Heinrich takes the critical first step on his journey to become a poet, for he started doing what the poets do: manipulate 'the sensory world at will' (N II, 335 #109) and use 'things and words like keys [wie Tasten]' (N II, 692 #935) by creating powerful combinations of sense and meaning — scenes.

The logical next step in becoming a poet would be learning to write such scenes down, and narrating them in a clear, effective, and captivating style. This is the kind of poetry and 'magical idealism'[111] practised by Novalis. For him, poetry is not an all-encompassing encyclopaedia but, like the ego, a universal form to which everything must be given. Nor is it spontaneous inspiration or wild enthusiasm but, like the senses, a 'medium of reciprocity', a language translating one sense into another in a controlled and deliberate way. This power of translation is the true 'magic' of both poetry and perception. The one transforms a complex mixture of sensations into species of organized sense, while the other skilfully concatenates the knowledge of history, fantasy, irony, science, experience, and anything else in literary texts such as novels, poems, tales, or, for that matter, scenographies. The intense perception of sense — in the double sense — is what it means to be under the spell of either language.

The blue flower is the emblem and common sense of this connection. It physically embodies, and by its name announces, the *Wechselbestimmung* between perception and poetry, and it does so by summoning aesthesiological series. These series remain invisible as such, and their logic cannot be sensed but needs to be read. However, their fundamentally abstract power to engender and concatenate perceptions precisely constitutes the flower's sensuousness. Such sensuousness captivates not only Heinrich's mind. The blue flower wants to arrest also our *Dichten* and *Trachten*. We readers are summoned, like Heinrich, to sense and ponder its name. Its powerful spell urges us, too, to conjure up complex conjunctions of thought and sensation — new scenes of oddly commingled perceptions in which a blue flower might blossom.

Notes to Part II — Novalis

1. N II, 533 #331.
2. 'Die Poësie ist das ächt absolut Reelle. Dies ist der Kern meiner Phil[osophie]. Je poëtischer, je wahrer' (N II, 420 #471).
3. The context of the quoted passage suggests the synonymity between *Dichten* and *Poesie*:

    Es ist recht übel, sagte Klingsohr, daß die Poesie einen besondern Namen hat, und die Dichter eine besondere Zunft ausmachen. Es ist gar nichts besonderes. Es ist die eigenthümliche Handlungsweise des menschlichen Geistes. Dichtet und trachtet nicht jeder Mensch in jeder Minute? (N I, 335)

    [It is quite unfortunate, said Klingsohr, that poetry has a particular name, and that poets constitute a particular class. It is nothing particular at all. It is the mind's inherent way of acting. Does not every man strive and act at every moment?]

    A contemporary reviewer in fact criticized this passage for its ambiguity, calling it, in 1803, a ridiculous wordplay 'zwischen Dichten als Poesie genommen, und dem Dichten und Trachten' (N III: 156). The ambiguity is of course intended. Klingsohr refers here to *die Poesie* with the at first puzzling pronoun *es* — puzzling because of the pronoun's ostensibly wrong gender. The third sentence, '*Dichtet* und *trachtet* nicht jeder Mensch in jeder Minute?', suggests, however, that the neuter of the preceding pronoun derives in fact from *das Dichten*. I therefore read *es* as referring here to both *die Poesie* and *das Dichten* and thus translate them with the same word, as 'poetry' (which of course also signifies the resulting product or composition, *Dichtung*). Alternatively, one might consider translating both *Dichten* and *Poesie* as 'poesy', which designates, according to the *New Oxford American Dictionary*, the 'art or composition of poetry'. But this old-fashioned word belongs to 'fairy lands forlorn', John Keats reminds us in his 'Ode to a Nightingale', 'Forlorn!' — which is why I am not using it.

4. In *Das Auge liest mit: Zur Visualität der Literatur* (Munich: Hanser, 2010), pp. 9–31, Friedmar Apel discusses the parallels between neuroscience and Romantic conceptions of vision. Apel claims that they overlap insofar as each of them represents vision as a poetic activity, specifically as 'ein ästhetischer, sowohl erzählförmiger wie metaphorischer Prozeß' involving 'Selektion und Kombination unter bestimmtem Orientierungsinteresse' (p. 44). This is, in a nutshell, what Apel later (pp. 65–74) presents as Novalis's conception of vision.
5. To Fr. Schlegel on 7 November 1798: 'Eins von den auffallenden Beyspielen unserer innern Symorganisation und Symevolution' (N I, 672) — the example of coevolution being, in this letter, that both friends came to think of 'die Idee *der Bibel* [...] als des *Ideals jedweden* Buchs' (N I, 673).
6. *Kritische Friedrich-Schlegel-Ausgabe*, XVIII [1963], 146 #279: 'Alle Bilder d[er] Dichter sind buchstäblich wahr; alles unser Empfinden, Fühlen, Wahrnehmen ist ein Dichten.' Schlegel thus suggests a literal interpretation of *wahrnehmen*, in the sense that poetic images are 'literally true' and should also be 'taken for a truth' by perceiving them. As discussed in the previous chapter, Hegel debunks the literal meaning of *Wahrnehmung* in the *Phenomenology*. Although perception itself wants to 'take in' the 'truth' (*wahr-nehmen*) of external objects, directly and immediately, we eventually see that the act of perceiving is 'entwined' with 'the movement of consciousness' (PhG 108/79*) — with attention, intention, and language.
7. In her *Hirnhöhlenpoetiken*, p. 205, as well as 'Die Grenzen des Menschen: Anthropologie und Ästhetik um 1800. Zum Verhältnis zwischen Physiologie und Autonomieästhetik bei Tieck und Novalis', in *Die Grenzen des Menschen: Anthropologie und Ästhetik um 1800*, ed. by Maximilian Bergengruen and others (Würzburg: Königshausen & Neumann, 2001), pp. 113–34 (pp. 126–27), Caroline Welsh connects Novalis's mention of *Chiffernschrift* and *Figuren* to S. T. Soemmerring's model of the human brain, specifically to his notion of a cerebral *Seelenorgan*, i.e. the liquid medium between skull and brain wherein all sensorial stimuli come together and turn into 'vibrations' and 'moving figures' — the 'letters', as it were, of sense perception. At the same time, Novalis alludes by *Chiffernschrift* and *Figuren* to ancient seers and their practice of discerning omens in natural appearances. The Roman augurs, for example, considered certain cloud formations and the behaviour of birds as prefigurations of things to come. Similarly, the

apprentices attempt to discern figures 'in clouds' (N I, 200), and they are instructed at a 'temple' (N I, 231), the traditional institution of these mantic practices. However, the immediate source of the term *Chiffernschrift* seems to be Kant's *Kritik der Urteilskraft*, where Kant precisely speaks of the 'Chiffreschrift [...] wodurch die Natur in ihren schönen Formen figürlich zu uns spricht' (A 167–68). The fact that August Wilhelm Schlegel cites this passage in his Berlin Lectures on Literature and Art held between 1801 and 1804 suggests that it had circulated amongst Jena Romantics; see A. W. Schlegel, *Kritische Ausgabe der Vorlesungen*, ed. by Ernst Behler, 4 vols (Paderborn: Schöningh, 1989–), I, 249. As for the essential connection between prophetic and poetic, or mantic and semantic, practices, see Philipp Theisohn, *Die kommende Dichtung: Geschichte des literarischen Orakels 1450–2050* (Munich: Fink, 2012).

8. Utz, p. 224.
9. Chad Wellmon, 'Lyrical Feeling: Novalis' Anthropology of the Senses', *Studies in Romanticism*, 47 (2008), 453–77, observes that in Novalis 'sensations are figured as letters and perception as such is figured as an act of reading' (p. 466). Wellmon's observation concerns specifically *Hymnen an die Nacht* and Novalis's reception of the Molyneux problem via Herder (cf. N II, 423 #480), although it most certainly applies to the *Lehrlinge* as well.
10. N II, 123 #302: 'Wahr — Derivation von währen — Wahrnehmen — beharrlich ergreifen. / Nehmen — ist active Rezeptivität./'
11. Apel, *Das Auge liest mit*, p. 69. In contrast to Apel, who foregrounds the visual elements, Utz conceives of the *Lehrlinge* primarily as an 'acoustic world' (p. 224).
12. Enhancing the sensory faculties of children was a notable goal of late eighteenth-century pedagogues, as Utz (p. 186) points out. For example, J. H. Campe proposed in 1785 various exercises to improve the seeing, hearing, and touching of infants.
13. Novalis, *The Novices of Sais*, trans. by Ralph Manheim (Brooklyn: Archipelago Books, 2005), p. 9.
14. 'Sehn — hören, schmecken — tasten, riechen sind nur *Zersplitterungen* der allg[emeinen] Wahrnehmung' (N II, 792 #251). Utz, pp. 195–212, understands the frequent representations of synaesthesia in Romantic texts as an attempt at restoring a lost totality through literary language. But these imaginations of synesthetic unity, Utz continues (pp. 213–24), conflict with the often fragmentary form of Romantic thinking and writing. Like perception itself, these fragments achieve unity and completion only through the work of the imagination. Wellmon identifies 'feeling' as 'the metonymic figure for individual senses' in Novalis and, therefore, as the basic sense of synaesthesia ('Lyrical Feeling: Novalis' Anthropology of the Senses', p. 468).
15. Cf. N II, 335–39 passim, 374–75 #253, 535–36 #338, 708 #1075; all these fragments describe the perception of the artist in a similarly 'magical' fashion.
16. Novalis, *Philosophical Writings*, pp. 71–72.
17. Silvio Vietta, *Ästhetik der Moderne: Literatur und Bild* (Munich: Fink, 2001), pp. 121–25.
18. Novalis, *Philosophical Writings*, p. 72.
19. The aspiration to 'speak' the senses like a language is echoed in *Heinrich von Ofterdingen*: 'Language, said Heinrich, is indeed a little world in signs and sounds. As man rules over it, so would he rule the great world and freely express himself therein' [Die Sprache, sagte Heinrich, ist wirklich eine kleine Welt in Zeichen und Tönen. Wie der Mensch sie beherrscht, so möchte er gern die große Welt beherrschen, und sich frey darinn ausdrücken können] (N I, 335). The arch-poet Klingsohr details, in the seventh and eighth chapter of *Heinrich von Ofterdingen*, the ways and means to become a poet; cf. N I, 327–32, 333–35. Amongst those, the training of and the reflection on language usage is a foremost task (N I, 334), as is, on Klingsohr's account, the sharpening of the senses and the cultivation of a sober mind (N I, 328–31).
20. Friedmar Apel, 'Die Poetik der Aufmerksamkeit bei Novalis', in *Novalis: Poesie und Poetik*, ed. by Herbert Uerlings (Tübingen: Niemeyer, 2004), pp. 141–50 (pp. 143).
21. Cf. N II, 366–67 #235, wherein *Aufmerksamkeit* is similarly characterized as the mental faculty to modify perception at will.
22. Kittler, *Aufschreibesysteme 1800/1900*, pp. 87–91, 139–43.
23. Novalis comments the 116th Athenäum fragment (see *Kritische Friedrich-Schlegel-Ausgabe*, II (1967), 182–83) with the following words: 'Zu herausgerissen eigenthümlich — nicht genetisch

— oder generirend — der letzte Satz hebt d[as] Ganze Vorhergehende auf' (Novalis, *Schriften: Die Werke Friedrich von Hardenbergs*, ed. by Paul Kluckhohn and Richard H. Samuel (Stuttgart: Kohlhammer, 1960–), II (1965), 623 #28.4). Still, Novalis too conceives of poetry as an act of translation, as in his 1797 letter to A. W. Schlegel: 'In the end, all poetry is translation' (N I, 648), as well as the notation: 'The imagination', and hence the faculty or organ of poetry, 'is the marvelous sense that can *replace* all senses for us' (N II, 423 #479; Novalis, *Philosophical Writings*, p. 118. Recall, finally, Novalis's sustained attempts at 'poeticizing the sciences' (N I, 662), which practically means the translation of scientific principles and terminologies into a poetic context, Klingsohr's tale (N I, 338–64) being perhaps the foremost example.

24. In the Grimms' *Deutsches Wörterbuch*, *Druckerstock* is defined as 'holzschnitt [...] vignette und dergleichen für bücher'.
25. In fact, speaker B desires still more books — but books that he authored himself: 'I wish to see before me a collection of books pertaining to all the arts and sciences — *as my mind's work*' [Ich möchte eine ganze Büchersammlung aus allen Kunst, und Wissenschaftsarten, *als Werck meines Geistes*, vor mir sehn] (N II, 429; emphasis added). Novalis expands on the challenge posed by the ever-growing stock of books in several notes; cf. N II, 598 #550, 602 #571, 603 #573–75. As for the seeming conflict between reading and the senses, a recurrent topic of literary texts and popular journals at the turn of the eighteenth century, see Erich Schön, *Der Verlust der Sinnlichkeit, oder, Die Verwandlungen des Lesers: Mentalitätswandel um 1800* (Stuttgart: Klett-Cotta, 1987). For a different view, cf. Sigmund von Lempicki, 'Bücherwelt und wirkliche Welt: Ein Beitrag zur Wesenserfassung der Romantik', *Deutsche Vierteljahrsschrift für Literaturwissenschaft und Geistesgeschichte*, 3 (1925), 339–86 (p. 361), who relates Romantic authorship to the 'poeta-philologus' of the Renaissance.
26. See Ulrich Stadler, 'Zur Anthropologie Friedrich von Hardenbergs (Novalis)', in *Novalis und die Wissenschaften*, ed. by Herbert Uerlings (Tübingen: Max Niemeyer, 1997), pp. 87–103; Nicholas Saul, '"Poetisierung d[es] Körpers": Der Poesiebegriff Friedrich von Hardenbergs (Novalis) und die anthropologiche Tradition', in *Novalis: Poesie und Poetik*, ed. by Herbert Uerlings (Tübingen: Niemeyer, 2004), pp. 151–69; Wellmon, 'Lyrical Feeling'; and Welsh, *Hirnhöhlenpoetiken*, pp. 9–111. Note also Noel Jackson, 'Archaeologies of Perception: Reading Wordsworth after Foucault', *European Romantic Review*, 18 (2007), 175–85, who traces the same epistemic shift but in the context of British romanticism.
27. Michel Foucault, *The Order of Things: An Archaeology of the Human Sciences*. (New York: Pantheon Books, 1970), pp. 386–87.
28. To Friedrich Schlegel on 10 January 1797 (N I, 607–08).
29. See, among others, Hans-Joachim Mähl's 'Einleitung' in Novalis, *Schriften*, II, 29–102; Géza von Molnár, *Novalis' 'Fichte Studies': The Foundations of his Aesthetics* (The Hague: Mouton, 1970); Manfred Frank, *Einführung in die frühromantische Ästhetik: Vorlesungen* (Frankfurt am Main: Suhrkamp, 1989), pp. 231–86, as well as his 'Philosophische Grundlagen der Frühromantik', *Athenäum: Jahrbuch für Romantik*, 4 (1994), 37–130 (pp. 70–106); Olivier Schefer, 'Les *Fichte-Studien* de Novalis et la "Tathandlung": à l'épreuve de la transcendance', *Les Études Philosophiques*, 1 (2000), 55–74; and Dieter Henrich, *Between Kant and Hegel: Lectures on German Idealism*, ed. by David S. Pacini (Cambridge, MA: Harvard University Press, 2003), pp. 216–30.
30. Fichte also concedes the circularity of his argumentation but thinks it 'inevitable' (F I, 92).
31. Dieter Henrich, 'Fichtes ursprüngliche Einsicht', in *Subjektivität und Metaphysik: Festschrift für Wolfgang Cramer*, ed. by Hans Wagner and Dieter Henrich (Frankfurt am Main: Klostermann, 1966), pp. 188–232, elaborates on this discrepancy at great length, including Fichte's various attempts to eliminate it in later drafts of the *Wissenschaftslehre*.
32. F I, 96: 'The ego *posits itself*, and by virtue of this mere self-assertion it *exists*. Conversely, the ego *exists* and *posits* its own existence by virtue of merely existing. It is at once the agent and the product of this action' [Das Ich *setzt sich selbst*, und es *ist*, vermöge dieses bloßen Setzens durch sich selbst; und umgekehrt: Das Ich *ist*, und es *setzt* sein Seyn, vermöge seines bloßen Seyns. — Es ist zugleich das Handelnde, und das Product der Handlung].
33. F I, 104: '*a non-ego is opposed absolutely to the ego*. All we have just said concerning opposition in general is derived from this opposition, which therefore represents an originary act: It is

absolutely unconditioned in form, but conditioned as to its material content' [*dem Ich* [wird] *schlechthin entgegengesetzt ein Nicht-Ich*. Von diesem ursprünglichen Entgegensetzen nun ist alles das, was wir soeben vom Entgegengesetzen überhaupt gesagt haben, abgeleitet; und es gilt daher ursprünglich: es ist also der Form nach schlechthin unbedingt, der Materie nach aber bedingt]. Thus, as a *formal* act, the *opposition* of a non-ego — which is invoked here in the passive voice (*wird entgegengesetzt*), hence without ascribing this act explicitly to the ego — is just as 'originary' and 'unconditioned' as the ego's self-assertion. Only the cognizance resulting from the act of *opposition* (e.g. the perception of *this* non-ego over there as *a green tree*) is conditioned by external properties.

34. The somewhat desperate title of this text reads in full: *Sonnenklarer Bericht an das grössere Publicum, über das eigentliche Wesen der neuesten Philosophie: Ein Versuch, die Leser zum Verstehen zu zwingen* [Crystal Clear Report to the General Public Concerning the Actual Essence of the Newest Philosophy: An Attempt to Force the Reader to Understand].
35. Henrich, *Hegel im Kontext*, p. 20.
36. The exclusively diachronic nature of experience is laid out in *Die Bestimmung des Menschen* (F II, 211). Fichte here also negates, just like Hume, the reality of spatial permanence and unity, considering them instead creations (or rather 'deeds') of the mind. But Fichte goes even further. Sensations are not passive impressions of external things in the sense of Locke and Hume. Cognitive action is necessary to register them as such, so that sensation must be an active process in itself. Or as Fichte puts it: '*Leiden*' — in the sense of passivity and specifically sensory receptivity — already implies '*a measure of activity*' [*ein Quantum Tätigkeit*] (F I, 139).
37. N II, 133 #323: 'Nicht die Handlung, sondern das Produkt ist fixierbar.'
38. Henrich, 'Fichtes ursprüngliche Einsicht', p. 198. My recapitulation of the Fichtean *Tathandlung* was partly based on Henrich's work, but I have also drawn on Rolf-Peter Horstmann, 'The Early Philosophy of Fichte and Schelling', in *The Cambridge Companion to German Idealism*, ed. by Karl Ameriks (Cambridge: Cambridge University Press, 2000), pp. 117–40 (pp. 117–27); Pippin, *Hegel's Idealism*, pp. 42–59; and Beiser, *German Idealism*, pp. 217–345.
39. Frank, *Einführung in die frühromantische Ästhetik*, pp. 228–29. Frank deduces the claim that the Jena Romantics remained oriented towards 'the absolute' chiefly from quotes by Friedrich Schlegel and Novalis (pp. 224–30). He finally groups these quotes around Schlegel's assertion that 'all knowledge is symbolic', interpreting this assertion as gesturing towards 'the absolute' (p. 229). This assertion, however, has much less to do with the absolute as it refers to a very different concept, namely, Schlegel's key principle of *Wechselerweis* (and synonymously *Wechselgrundsatz* as well as *Wechselbegriff*), which he derived, like Novalis, from Fichte. As for Frriedrich Schlegel's complex appropriation of Fichte, see Bärbel Frischmann, *Vom transzendentalen zum frühromantischen Idealismus: J. G. Fichte und Fr. Schlegel* (Paderborn: Schöningh, 2005), pp. 140–61 (regarding the notion of *Wechselerweis*), as well as Elizabeth Millan-Zaibert, *Friedrich Schlegel and the Emergence of Romantic Philosophy* (Albany: SUNY Press, 2007), pp. 133–74. For a critique of Frank's concept of Early Romanticism, see Ernst Behler, 'Über Manfred Frank: *Einführung in die frühromantische Ästhetik*', *Athenäum*, 1 (1991), 243–53.
40. Theodor Haering, *Novalis als Philosoph* (Stuttgart: Kohlhammer, 1954), pp. 126–42.
41. Berbeli Wanning, *Novalis zur Einführung* (Hamburg: Junius, 1996), pp. 149–97.
42. Alison Stone, 'The Romantic Absolute', *British Journal for the History of Philosophy*, 19 (2011), 497–517; Dalia Nassar, *The Romantic Absolute: Being and Knowing in Early German Romantic Philosophy, 1795–1804* (Chicago: University of Chicago Press, 2013); and Ralf Simon, *Die Idee der Prosa: Zur Ästhetikgeschichte von Baumgarten bis Hegel mit einem Schwerpunkt bei Jean Paul* (Munich: Fink, 2013), pp. 194–202.
43. Beiser, *German Idealism*, p. 408. As for the supposed impact of Jena Romanticism on the development of German Idealism, see Charles Larmore, 'Hölderlin and Novalis', in *Cambridge Companion to German Idealism*, pp. 141–60; Bärbel Frischmann, 'Der philosophische Beitrag der deutschen Frühromantik und Hölderlins', in *Handbuch Deutscher Idealismus*, pp. 326–54; Andrew Bowie, 'Romantic Philosophy and Religion', in *The Cambridge Companion to German Romanticism*, ed. by Nicholas Saul (Cambridge: Cambridge University Press, 2009), pp. 175–90; and *The Relevance of Romanticism: Essays on German Romantic Philosophy*, ed. by Dalia Nassar (Oxford: Oxford University Press, 2014).

44. Beiser, *German Idealism*, p. 434.
45. Friedrich Strack, 'Novalis und Fichte: Zur bewußtseinstheoretischen und zur moralphilosophischen Rezeption Friedrich von Hardenbergs', in *Novalis und die Wissenschaften*, pp. 193–206 (p. 201).
46. Jean Paul to his son Max on 10 May 1821; Nicolin, *Hegel in Berichten seiner Zeitgenossen*, p. 226 #345.
47. Novalis, *Philosophical Writings*, p. 79.
48. F I, 227: 'Es wird demnach hier gelehrt, dass alle Realität [...] bloss durch die Einbildungskraft hervorgebracht werde.'
49. Cf. N II, 618 #627, which makes the same point.
50. To A. W. Schlegel on 12 January 1798 (N I, 658). 'Empirischer Wust' refers to Novalis's studies in mining and related subjects such as physics, chemistry, and mineralogy he had taken up in 1797 at the Bergakademie of Freiberg.
51. In print, this diagram is rendered as follows:

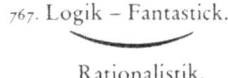

Looking at this diagram, it is clear that for Novalis, rationalism (viz. logic and mathematics) is not at all the antithesis to but rather an integral part of Early Romanticism. Following Remigius Bunia, *Romantischer Rationalismus: Zu Wissenschaft, Politik und Religion bei Novalis* (Paderborn: Schöningh, 2013), one might even say that Novalis radicalizes the rationalist tradition (p. 9).
52. Rahel Villinger, 'Gedankenstriche: Theorie und Poesie bei Novalis', *Deutsche Vierteljahrsschrift für Literaturwissenschaft und Geistesgeschichte*, 86 (2012), 547–77. Although the 'sense of rhythm' (p. 572) plays a key role in her argument, Villinger does not consider the letter to A. W. Schlegel (N I, 654–57) in which Novalis discusses the question of rhythm at length. But Villinger does acknowledge 'the constitutive role of the reader in "accomplishing" the theory of the fragment' (p. 569 n. 30).
53. To Coelestin August Just, the superior of Friedrich von Hardenberg in his professional capacity as mining inspector, on 26 December 1798. In a self-critical note (N II, 384 # 318) from the same year Novalis goes even further, calling his fragments 'rough' and 'hardly ready for publication', adding, however, that fragments are still 'the most tolerable' forms of communicating 'individual curiosities' [einzelne Merckwürdige Ansichten].
54. See Friedrich Strack, '"Fermenta Cognitionis": Zur romantischen Fragmentkonzeption von Friedrich Schlegel und Novalis', in *Subversive Romantik*, ed. by Volker Kapp and others (Berlin: Duncker und Humblot, 2004), pp. 343–64.
55. F I, 131–227. For a brief summary, see Frischmann, *Vom transzendentalen zum frühromantischen Idealismus*, pp. 86–90.
56. As for Novalis's immediate reception of the principle of *Wechselbestimmung*, see N II, 42 #48 and N II, 111–24 passim. Novalis also discusses the term in other places; cf. the index by Doris Strack (N III, 767).
57. See Frischmann, *Vom Transzendentalen zum frühromantischen Idealismus*, pp. 25, 198–200, 335–38; Manfred Frank, '"Wechselgrundsatz": Friedrich Schlegels philosophischer Ausgangspunkt', *Zeitschrift für philosophische Forschung*, 50 (1996), 26–50; as well as Guido Naschert, 'Friedrich Schlegel über Wechselerweis und Ironie', in *Athenäum: Jahrbuch für Romantik*, 6–7 (1996–97), 47–90 and 11–36.
58. Joseph Vogl, *Kalkül und Leidenschaft: Poetik des ökonomischen Menschen* (Zurich: diaphanes, 2004), pp. 246–70 (p. 264).
59. F I, 132. Fichte's foundationalism becomes increasingly dominant in subsequent attempts to explain the *Wissenschaftslehre*, for example, in the 1797 'Versuch einer neuen Darstellung der Wissenschaftslehre' (F I, 519–34 (pp. 526–28)).
60. Pippin, 'Fichte's Alleged Subjective, Psychological, One-Sided Idealism', in *The Reception of Kant's Critical Philosophy: Fichte, Schelling, and Hegel*, ed. by Sally Sadgwick (Cambridge: Cambridge University Press, 2000), pp. 147–70 (p. 157). See also Suzanne Dürr, 'Reflexion und Produktion: Zur Bestimmung des absoluten Ich in Fichtes Grundlage der gesammten

Wissenschaftslehre von 1794/95', in *Die Aktualität der Romantik*, ed. by Michael Forster and Klaus Vieweg (Berlin: Lit, 2012), pp. 163–81.
61. It is not entirely clear to which noun *es* refers in this last fragment from the *Kant-Studien* (N II, 220 #13). *Es* could refer to *das Unbedingte* mentioned in the preceding sentence paraphrasing Kant (cf. KrV B XX–XXI), or it could mean, more simply, *etwas* or an object in general, which is the reading that I propose.
62. Novalis, *Fichte Studies*, trans. by Jane Kneller (Cambridge: Cambridge University Press, 2003), p. 171.
63. Ibid., p. 48.
64. Ibid., pp. 20–21. Fichte also struggles with the transcendental unity of the *Tathandlung*, for in conceiving the ego not as a static point but as a dynamic temporal activity, Fichte constantly undermines the seeming stability and positivity of the ego as a 'self-positing' origin. This intrinsic paradox of Fichte's system — an origin that can never be grasped but only inferred, posited after the fact — is not far from the kind of *Nachträglichkeit* and 'originary non-originality' Derrida termed *différance*; see Harald Münster, *Fichte trifft Darwin, Luhmann und Derrida: 'Die Bestimmung des Menschen' in differenztheoretischer Rekonstruktion und im Kontext der 'Wissenschaftslehre novo methodo'* (Amsterdam: Rodopi, 2011).
65. Novalis, *Fichte Studies*, p. 7.
66. 'Jeder Zustand, jede Thathandlung sezt eine andere voraus [...] alles Suchen nach der Ersten ist Unsinn — es ist *regulative Idee*' (N II, 164 #472).
67. Novalis was perhaps not the first and certainly not the last to make this point. Nietzsche (II, 540), for example, uses the same argument to attack nineteenth-century historicism in *Der Wanderer und sein Schatten*, § 3.
68. In the *Phenomenology*, the transition from the understanding to self-consciousness is initiated by the sentence: 'We have to *think* pure change, or *opposition in itself* [*die Entgegensetzung in sich selbst*] — *contradiction as such*' (PhG 130/99*). According to Hegel, the unity and identity of self-consciousness is precisely based on such internal difference or 'opposition in itself'.
69. Novalis, *Notes for a Romantic Encyclopaedia: Das allgemeine Brouillon*, trans. by David W. Wood (Albany: SUNY Press, 2007), p. 132.
70. '*Robinson Crusoe* ist ein höchst lehrreiches Buch [...] das Handbuch des klugen Mannes sein' (To his brother Erasmus in June 1793; N I, 536).
71. Novalis, *Notes for a Romantic Encyclopaedia*, p. 12.
72. Ibid., p. 132.
73. N II, 182–83 #567, 609–10 #601, 614 #615 further evidence Novalis's firm anti-foundationalism.
74. Haering (pp. 143–94) characterizes, with direct reference to Hegel, the basic principle of Novalis's thinking as 'universale Repräsentationslehre', specifically as 'Wechselbeziehung, also dialektische[] Wechseleinheit' (p. 169). According to Haering, however, such reciprocity is just the negative reflection of some higher, dialectic unity.
75. Consider, for example, the note I have just quoted: 'METAPHYSICS. Every thing is a general *formula* of something else — a function of another thing. In applying this formula, a product emerges — which we can ascribe to the one or the other, just as 12 is [...] a 3 treated (*multiplied*) by 4', and hence 'a reciprocal connection [Wechselverbindung] of both numbers' (N II, 623 #637). In light of this and similar notes, one might say that reciprocal determination is the concept in which Novalis's study of Fichte and his mathematical studies intersect. There is, nonetheless, one critical difference: A mathematical formula — e.g. $y = 4x$, to generalize Novalis's example — represents a *universal* relation between elements, whereas Novalis's poetic and encyclopaedic applications of reciprocal determination do not reveal universal rules but only *specific* analogies between otherwise incommensurable elements or, indeed, 'opposite operations' (N II, 533 #331). As for the importance of mathematical concepts in Novalis, see Käte Hamburger, *Philosophie der Dichter: Novalis, Schiller, Rilke* (Stuttgart: Kohlhammer, 1966), pp. 11–82 (pp. 22–28, regarding functional calculus), and more recently Philippe Séguin, 'Von der Philosophie zur "ars combinatoria": Novalis' Erwartungen an die Mathematik und die Folgen', in *Zahlen, Zeichen und Figuren: Mathematische Inspirationen in Kunst und Literatur*, ed. by Andrea Albrecht and others (Berlin: De Gruyter, 2011), pp. 248–67.

76. N II, 348 #151: 'Nur das Unvollständige kann begriffen werden — kann uns weiter führen. [...] /Alle *Bestimmung* ist *relativ.*/'.
77. A note from the *Kant-Studien* reads almost alike: 'Isn't our faculty of apperception [Apperceptionsvermögen] like the membranes in the eye — representations must pass through opposite media to finally appear correctly on the inner pupil' (N II, 348 #151).
78. 'Alles Sichtbare haftet am Unsichtbaren — Das Hörbare am Unhörbaren — Das Fühlbare am Unfühlbaren. Vielleicht das Denkbare am Undenckbaren' (N II, 423 #479).
79. Novalis, *Fichte Studies*, p. 171
80. Ibid., p. 170.
81. 'Das Wort Sinn, das auf mittelbares Erkenntnis, *Berührung, Mischung* hindeutet' (N II, 482 #61). In light of his vehement insistence on *Wechselbestimmung*, I doubt that Novalis envisions here and in other places a 'non-distinction' of inner and outer sense, as Wellmon ('Lyrical Feeling', p. 468) claims. In fact, Wellmon's earlier observation that perceived sense possesses for Novalis always 'both a formal (or ideational) and material (or physiological) character' (p. 461) undermines this claim.
82. Novalis, *Philosophical Writings*, p. 61. Similarly, Samuel T. Coleridge conceives of perception as a reciprocal process of determination. In his notebooks, he writes that 'our consciousness originates in the modification' of 'the sensitive faculty'. Yet this modification cannot be ascribed to a single cause, he goes on, because it is impossible to determine 'what part proceeds from the sensitive faculty, and what from the outward Causes or the Things acting on the faculty [...] we become conscious both of the one and of the other in one & the same way; namely, as modifications of our own Being' (*Notebooks* iii #3605; quoted by McSweeney, p. 13).
83. Uwe C. Steiner, 'Die Tücken des Subjekts und der Einspruch der Dinge: Romantische Krisen der Objektivität bei Novalis, Eichendorff und Hoffmann', in *Schläft ein Lied in allen Dingen? Romantische Dingpoetik*, ed. by Christiane Holm and Günter Oesterle (Würzburg: Königshausen & Neumann, 2011), pp. 29–42 (p. 35).
84. *Husserliana*, XI (1966), 17: 'All noematic moments [...] are constituted through immanent sense data and *the ability of consciousness to animate them* [*vermöge des sie gleichsam beseelenden Bewußtseins*]' (emphasis added).
85. Maurice Merleau-Ponty, *Phenomenology of Perception*, trans. by Colin Smith (New York: Routledge, 2002), pp. 159–60, 308, 372.
86. Novalis, *Philosophical Writings*, p. 60. Novalis came up with this definition in 1798. Just a few years earlier, in 1795, Tieck had expressed a similar, if not the same, idea. In *Peter Lebrecht*, ironically subtitled 'a story without adventurous events [Abenteuerlichkeiten]', Tieck writes:

> Das Alltägliche und Langweilige bestimmen und messen wir immer nach dem, was dicht um uns herum ist, das, was uns ergötzen soll, suchen wir immer in der Ferne. [...] wir sollten es nur einmal versuchen, uns das Gewöhnliche fremd zu machen, und wir würden darüber erstaunen, wie nahe uns so manche Belehrung, so manche Ergötzung liegt, die wir in einer weiten, mühsamen Ferne suchen. Das wunderbare Utopien liegt oft dicht vor unsern Füßen, aber wir sehn mit unsern Teleskopen darüber hinweg. (I (1963), 124–25)

> [We define and measure ordinary and boring things always against our closest surroundings, looking for delightful experiences always in far-away places. [...] we should for once try to make the ordinary seem strange. We'd be surprised at how many an insight and how many a delight are near us that we otherwise seek in far-away and inconvenient places. A marvellous Utopia often lies right at our feet, but we fail to see it with our telescopes.]

Novalis likely knew Tieck's story.
87. Cf. N II, 499 # 137: 'MAGIE. (mystische Sprachl[ehre]) *Sympathie* des *Zeichens* mit dem Bezeichneten (Eine der Grundideen der Kabbalistik.)'.
88. Novalis, *Notes for a Romantic Encyclopaedia*, pp. 6–7.
89. Novalis, *Schriften*, ed. by Friedrich von Schlegel and Ludwig Tieck, 2 vols (Berlin: Buchhandlung der Realschule, 1802), I, i–xii (p. vii). Friedrich Kittler's summary of Novalis's encyclopaedic principle is virtually identical: 'The *Brouillon*'s method is to translate individual data from one science into another [...] via systematic analogies' (*Aufschreibesysteme 1800/1900*, p. 89). For a more detailed account of Novalis's syncretistic and non-hierarchical concept of encyclopedia, see

Andreas B. Kilcher, *Mathesis und Poiesis: Die Enzyklopädik der Literatur 1600 bis 2000* (Munich: Fink, 2003), pp. 402–16.

90. Novalis defines *Witz* as the 'principle of affinities' (N II, 250 #57), a creative faculty that indeed 'produces similarities' (N II, 649 # 732). Note also N II, 556 #431 (Novalis, *Notes for a Romantic Encyclopaedia*, p. 67): 'ENCYCLOPEDISTICS. *Analogistics*. Analogy — described as an instrument, and its myriad uses outlined'.

91. Klingsohr's tale and the *Hymnen an die Nacht*, as well as the late poems 'Es färbte sich die Wiese grün...' and 'Der Himmel war umgezogen...' (N I, 139–42), contain scenographies that demonstrate the reciprocity of perception and poetry in a similarly striking way as the emergence of the blue flower does, but discussing these examples would require an additional chapter.

92. Detlef Kremer, *Romantik* (Stuttgart: Metzler, 2001), pp. 126–27, which takes up Herbert Uerlings, *Friedrich von Hardenberg, genannt Novalis: Werk und Forschung* (Stuttgart: Metzler, 1991), p. 451, among others. Novalis's most severe stricture of Goethe reads:

> *Gegen* Wilhelm Meisters Lehrjahre. Es ist im Grunde ein fatales und albernes Buch — so pretentiös und pretiös — undichterisch im höchsten Grade, was den Geist betrifft — so poëtisch auch die Darstellung ist. Es ist eine Satyre auf die Poësie, Religion etc. Aus Stroh und Hobelspänen ein wohlschmeckendes Gericht, ein Götterbild zusammengesetzt. Hinten wird alles Farçe. Die Oeconomische Natur ist die Wahre — *Übrig bleibende*. [...] Die Poësie ist der Arlequin der ganzen Farce. [...] Avanturiers, Comoedianten, Maitressen, Krämer und Philister sind die Bestandtheile des Romans. Wer ihn recht zu Herzen nimmt, ließt keinen Roman mehr. (N II, 806–07 #320)

> [*Against* Wilhelm Meisters Lehrjahre. It is at bottom a fatal and foolish book — so pretentious and precious — unpoetic to the highest degree, as far as the spirit is concerned, however poetic the description. It is a satire on poetry, religion etc. A palatable dish, a divine image put together from straw and shavings. Behind it everything becomes farce. Economic nature is true — and *what remains*. [...] Poetry is the harlequin of the entire farce [...] Adventurers, comedians, mistresses, hucksters, and philistines constitute the novel. Whoever takes it to heart won't be reading novels any longer.] (Novalis, *Philosophical Writings*, p. 158)

Cf. the similar criticism in a letter to Ludwig Tieck (N I, 733).

93. Gerhard Schulz's editorial commentary (Novalis, *Werke*, ed. by Gerhard Schulz (Munich: Beck, 2001), pp. 711–22 (p. 714)) exemplifies the former, Frederick Burwick's *The Damnation of Newton: Goethe's Color Theory and Romantic Perception* (Berlin: De Gruyter, 1986), pp. 102–38, the latter tendency.

94. In the 'Berliner Papiere', Novalis notes with regard to the second part: 'All sorts of science poeticized, mathematics as well, competing with each other' [Allerhand Wissenschaft poëtisirt, auch Mathematik, im Wettstreit] (N I, 393).

95. My characterization combines three different sources: first, a letter to Caroline Schlegel: 'The word years of apprenticeship [Lehrjahre] is wrong — it expresses a specific goal. In my novel it will simply designate *years of transition* [*Übergangs Jahre*] from the infinite to the finite world. I thus hope to satisfy both my historical and my philosophical yearnings' (27 February 1799; N I, 691); a letter to Ludwig Tieck: 'My novel [...] shall be an apotheosis of poetry. In the 1st part, Heinrich von Afterdingen will mature as a poet — and in the second he will be transfigured [verklärt]' (23 February 1800; N I, 732); third, a working note in the so-called 'Berliner Papiere': 'The ending marks the transition from the real to the secret world — death — final dream and awakening' (N I, 392).

96. 'Ich fange an das Nüchterne, aber ächt fortschreitende, Weiterbringende zu lieben' (20 January 1799; N I, 685).

97. Cf. Klingsohr's entire speech in the seventh chapter (N I, 328–30), which is continued in the following chapter (N I, 333–35), as well as N II, 803 #305, where Novalis summarizes the gist of Klingsohr's doctrine regarding the education of young poets.

98. This is how I interpret the gnomic line: 'Man kann die Poësie nicht gering genug schätzen' (N II, 803 #304).

99. Cf. N II, 369–71 #242, 546–47 #390, 692 #953, 693 #959, 696–97 #986, 769 #113, 807 #321.
100. Roman Jakobson, 'Closing Statement: Linguistics and Poetics', in *Style in Language*, ed. by Thomas Albert Sebeok (Cambridge, MA: Technology Press of the Massachusetts Institute of Technology, 1960), pp. 350–77. The iconic phrase runs: '*The poetic function projects the principle of equivalence from the axis of selection into the axis of combination*. Equivalence is promoted to the constitutive device of the sequence' (p. 358). This idea of linking syntagms through paradigmatic correspondences is essential to all structuralist concepts of literariness. For example, Jurij M. Lotman, *The Structure of the Artistic Text*, trans. by Gail Lenhoff and Ronald Vroon (Ann Arbor: University of Michigan, 1977) identifies 'the process of "linkage"' with the essential 'structure' of poetic expression (p. 11).
101. N I, 389: 'Die Poësie muß nie der Hauptstoff, immer nur das Wunderbare seyn. Man sollte nichts *darstellen*, was man nicht völlig übersähe, deutlich vernähme, und ganz Meister desselben wäre — z. B. bey *Darstellungen des Übersinnlichen*.'
102. Wordsworth in the 1802 preface to the *Lyrical Ballads*, p. 248. Novalis's note reads in full: 'Resources regarding novels. *Practice in telling real scenes*. Idiom dictionaries and old books. Attention to the strange effects people have on each other — in different situations' [Hülfsmittel zu Romanen. *Übung in Erzählung wircklicher Szenen*. Idiotika und alte Bücher. Aufmercksamkeit auf die sonderbaren Wirckungen von Menschen aufeinander — in verschiedenen Zuständen] (N II, 780 # 207).
103. Novalis, *Henry of Ofterdingen: A Romance*, trans. by Frederick S. Stallknecht (Cambridge, MA: John Owen, 1842), pp. 146–47.
104. Ibid., pp. 23–24.
105. Friedrich A. Kittler, '*Heinrich von Ofterdingen* als Nachrichtenfluß', in *Die Wahrheit der technischen Welt: Essays zur Genealogie der Gegenwart* (Berlin: Suhrkamp, 2013), pp. 132–59 (p. 137).
106. Novalis, *Henry of Ofterdingen*, pp. 24–26.
107. See N I, 325: 'That face, which bowed towards me from the petals [aus dem Kelche], was Mathilde's heavenly face' (Novalis, *Henry of Ofterdingen*, p. 133).
108. Regarding the significance of mothers in *Heinrich von Ofterdingen*, see Friedrich A. Kittler, 'Die Irrwege des Eros und die "Absolute Familie": Psychoanalytischer und diskursanalytischer Kommentar zu Klingsohrs Märchen in Novalis' *Heinrich von Ofterdingen*', in *Psychoanalytische und psychopathologische Literaturinterpretation*, ed. by Bernd Urban and Winfried Kudszus (Darmstadt: Wissenschaftliche Buchgesellschaft, 1981), pp. 421–70.
109. *Fragments from German Prose Writers*, trans. by Sarah Austin (New York: Appleton, 1841), p. 21; the original runs: 'Wir sind dem Aufwachen nah, wenn wir träumen, daß wir träumen' (N II, 232 #16).
110. I was quoting, representatively, Wanning, pp. 191, 197.
111. Cf. N II, 395 #375, 535 #338, 623 #638, 671 #826.

§2. *Looking with Rilke*

> Wird nicht der Fels ein eigenthümliches Du, eben wenn ich ihn anrede?
> Und was bin ich anders, als der Strom, wenn ich wehmüthig in seine Wellen
> hinabschaue, und die Gedanken in seinem Gleiten verliere?[1]
>
> [Does the rock not turn into a peculiar You when I address him? And what am
> I if not the stream as I look down on his waves with wistful eyes, losing my
> thoughts in its drift?]

Seeing things

The prominence of vision and a preoccupation with things are characteristic features of Rilke's works. The references to looking, gazing, and seeing throughout Rilke's oeuvre are too many to count, yet one might be inclined to sum up their general tendency with a famous (though hardly unprecedented) line from *Die Aufzeichnungen des Malte Laurids Brigge*, which runs: 'I am learning to see' [Ich lerne sehen].[2] Malte Laurids Brigge, the protagonist of the *Aufzeichnungen*, reiterates this line three times at the beginning of his notations (R VI, 710, 711, 723). Learning to see is the goal he pursues in Paris. No surprise, then, that seeing, looking (*schauen*), and regarding (*anschauen*) are 'the most frequent main verbs' in the *Aufzeichnungen*, as August Stahl remarked, a quantitative fact that no doubt supports the view of Helmut Naumann that 'the long and arduous process of learning to see *is* the "plot" of the *Aufzeichnungen*'.[3] But the prominence of looking and seeing is not particular to Rilke's middle period, since these topoi recur throughout his entire work, including the late poetry. The ninth of the *Duineser Elegien*, for example, recalls the phrase of 'learning to see' almost verbatim, though by way of negation: 'Ach, in den andern Bezug, | wehe, was nimmt man hinüber? Nicht das Anschaun, das hier | langsam erlernte' [What, alas, to take across into that other realm? Not the way of looking learned so slowly here]. Additionally, learning to see was a personal goal of Rilke, as evidenced by texts such as *Worpswede* and the various writings on Rodin and Cézanne, wherein he attempted to translate minute observations into vivid descriptions. In learning to see, he at the same time sought to refine his ways of describing the newly seen details. For the poet, therefore, the training of his eye involved a training of his pen as well.[4]

Rilke's preoccupation with things, on the other hand, is evidenced by innumerable representations of concrete objects, often anthropomorphic in kind and sometimes addressed through incantatory gestures, in both his poetry and prose. Several personal confessions make this pervasive — some say obsessive and pathological — interest in things all the more evident. 'My world begins with things [bei den Dingen]', Rilke writes in a letter to Ilse Jahr on 2 December 1922.[5] Other letters convey similar sentiments, for example, when Rilke praises things as 'small batteries of life energy' in a letter to Ilse Erdmann on 20 March 1919, or when he draws, in a 1920 letter to Nanny Wunderly-Volkart, a detailed floor plan of his room in

Locarno, adding minute descriptions and further hand-drawn illustrations of the furniture.[6] In Rilke's middle period, the interest in things culminates in famous literary works, but also in two long confessional letters to Lou Andreas-Salomé. In these letters, Rilke reverently praises Rodin's *Kunst-Dinge* (viz. his sculptures), confessing on 8 August 1903 that 'only things speak to me' and then, two days later, that he wishes to make things as Rodin does, though 'not sculptural but written things — realities originating in craftsmanship' [nicht plastische, geschriebene Dinge, — Wirklichkeiten, die aus dem Handwerk hervorgehen]. Finally, Rilke's so-called *Schmargendorfer Tagebuch* contains an early, and due to its clumsy erotics somewhat embarrassing, praise of things as being 'so ready to entertain our many and often confused thoughts and desires, for a short while. — I want to rest with each thing for a night [...] sleep by its side one time and become tired from its warmth, dreaming [with my head] on its breathing body and feeling its soft and lovely nakedness closely on my limbs', etc.[7]

The significance of this particular fascination with things is routinely relativized in the study of Rilke, because it is potentially embarrassing and also serves as a precautionary measure against older accusations according to which Rilke's pathological 'cult' of things indicates commodification, fetishism, and psychological compensation, if not vulgar materialism itself. The other prominent feature of Rilke's works, the interest in visual processes, is frequently cleansed of all reference to the world of phenomena. Rilke's poetic observations are then perceived as purely linguistic fictions and rhetorical fabrications, whereas the observed objects count for little more than props in a self-referential 'play of signs'.[8] The picture changes drastically, however, if we regard these features as two sides of the same coin, namely, as aspects connected by a process of looking. For it is the process of looking — *Schauen* or *Anschauen* in German — that links vision and things, in Rilke's works no less than actual perception.

Seeing and things converge in Rilke's middle period in an exemplary way because *Die Aufzeichnungen des Malte Laurids Brigge*, thing-poems like 'Archaïscher Torso Apollos', as well as Rilke's texts on Rodin and Cézanne, contain striking scenes of looking and observing. How exactly things are regarded in these works is what I discuss in this chapter. It will not suffice, however, to discuss them solely in rhetorical terms, as fictions composed of tropes and figures of speech, since these scenographies ask for our participation. They call for readerly aesthesis. They address us phatically, often calling on the observed objects as well, and so claim our attention, and they tell stories of looking that place us in a spectatorial setting and direct our gaze at many a detail to be seen. One would do well, therefore, to combine the rhetorical analysis of how looking figures in Rilke's texts with a scrutiny of their inherent aesthetic potential. The rhetorical makeup and the scenic setup of looking should be examined together — and also weighed against one another whenever the rhetoric conflicts with the aesthetics of looking in Rilke's scenographies. Doing so certainly involves more than a reconstruction of the described 'sequence of events' — a narrative dimension, by the way, that scholars like Jonathan Culler want to separate from lyric poems altogether.[9] It requires a closer consideration of diegesis, but in the sense of both Plato and Genette, as the specific form or diction of poetic speech (*diēgēsis*) and the world evoked by such speech (*diégèse*). Paying close attention to both is what it means to look 'with' Rilke.

Admittedly, this approach is somewhat ahistorical. Doubts concerning the representational power of language peaked in literary and critical discourses around 1900, after which the so-called 'language crisis' unfolded. More than ever writers scrutinized the ostensibly natural but, in fact, purely convention-based bond between signs and meanings, signifiers and signified, to the point of rupture and radical divorce. According to some critics and writers, notably Hermann Bahr and Hugo von Hofmannsthal, words and phenomena were simply incommensurable, while the cognitive apparatus between them — consciousness — seemed elusive, unpredictable, opaque, if not 'unsalvageable'.

These historical crises of subjectivity and signification are quite literally spelled out in Rilke's *Aufzeichnungen*. Early on in the story, Brigge visits the most infamous psychiatric clinic of Paris, the Salpêtrière, where he hears 'a superior, self-satisfied voice' [eine überlegene, selbstgefällige Stimme] coming through the walls, demanding of a patient '*Dites-nous le mot: avant*' and reiterating this demand by spelling out the letters '*a-v-a-n-t*' (R VI, 764). According to Friedrich Kittler, who radically historicized Rilke's work, this psychiatric exercise used to be a cure for a form of aphasia first described by psychiatrist Hubert von Grashey (1839–1914). More importantly, it also reminds the acoustic witness Brigge of the critical difference between signifier and signified, between *a-v-a-n-t* and 'before', and in realizing this difference, Kittler concludes, Brigge decides to write accordingly, like a psychiatric patient. Instead of representing life in Paris or scenes from his childhood, Brigge merely 'archives' words in his notations, Kittler holds, because he no longer believes in the possibility of signification. Cured of this false belief, he produces only spontaneous notations and unmotivated records — precisely *Aufzeichnungen* — rather than meaningful memoirs, reflections, or poems representing phenomena through words.[10]

When this historical framework is applied to Rilke's texts in general, as Kittler did, they consequently lack the ability to show anything besides their own language. Instead of communicating experiences or meanings, and far from 'revealing phenomena or ascertaining facts', they would contain nothing but empty signifiers and self-referential fictions. They would constitute an 'archive' of words resembling the type of record psychiatrists and psychoanalysts kept of their patients' deranged speeches. In short, they would amount to 'a kind of madness that exists on paper only'.[11]

Kittler's radical view on Rilke and literary modernism in general may be historically accurate, but also radically sense-less, a lesson in literary history that, though brilliant in itself and unsurpassed in scope, has run its course. Meanwhile, the contrasting view that texts from Rilke's middle period can and do refer to processes of looking has gained critical currency. In the *Rilke-Handbuch*, Wolfgang G. Müller reports that the *Neue Gedichte* in particular are nowadays considered as 'representing processes of perception and cognition' in ways that resemble 'Husserl's phenomenological constitution of objects'.[12] This is a significant reorientation in comparison to the tendency, pervasive especially in older scholarship, to read Rilke's references to looking and seeing biographically, as expressions of a personal fascination with the visual arts, above all with Rodin's sculptures and Cézanne's paintings.[13]

It was Käte Hamburger who initiated this reorientation with her seminal essay 'Die phänomenologische Struktur der Dichtung Rilkes'. Hamburger here maintains that 'looking' [schauen] is a 'basic word' of Rilke's poetics carrying great phenomenological significance, drawing parallels between Rilke's poetic ways of looking and Husserl's key concepts of intentionality, phenomenological reduction, and transcendental subjectivity.[14] In remarking these parallels, she may have followed a lead Husserl himself gave when he associated poetry and phenomenology in an enthusiastic letter to Hugo von Hofmannsthal. In this remarkable letter of January 1907, Husserl praises precisely the close relationship between poems 'looking at' their subjects in a 'purely aesthetic' way and 'the phenomenological way of looking', two ways of looking that, according to Husserl, eschew sentimentality just as much as abstract judgements and opinions and thus share the descriptive attitude.[15]

How much of Husserl one can find in Rilke is of course subject to debate.[16] More important for my purposes is Hamburger's prudent reminder that Rilke writes 'lyric poetry instead of epistemology', because it indicates the essential limit of a phenomenological, and more specifically aesthesiological, approach to Rilke's work.[17] Even if it is true that Rilke thematizes issues of perception, his poetic texts are much more than a phenomenology of looking. They speak in a poetic voice rather than a conceptual terminology, and contain scenographies of looking instead of a philosophical theory of vision.

Still, Rilke's enduring poetic imperative 'to look' and 'to learn to see' [sehen lernen], of which the *Neue Gedichte* and the *Aufzeichnungen* are the foremost aesthetic expressions, should not be construed as a purely metaphoric phrase. Instead one had to say, with Hamburger, that in Rilke looking 'never means an "inner looking" [...] in a mystical sense but always the perception of the external world'.[18] This view in fact also holds true in a historical perspective. Far from being pure metaphors, 'looking' and 'learning to see' are specific expressions in a discourse flourishing around 1900 in which Enlightenment ideals in drawing instruction, the contemplative gaze of nineteenth-century aesthetics, psychophysical research on visual perception, phenomenology, and the *Kunsterziehung* movement of the early twentieth century are all implicated. Monika Fick, Ralph Köhnen, and Steffen Arndal have situated the works of Rilke's middle period in this particular historical nexus.[19]

Exchanging imprints

There is one pattern of looking that is characteristic of Rilke's middle period. This pattern consists of a paradoxical exchange of looks as two reciprocal but never strictly separable movements of looking. The one movement is marked by the inward impression or imprint (*Eindruck*) external objects leave on the observer or observers. Malte Laurids Brigge, the protagonist of the *Aufzeichnungen*, characterizes this procedure of being imprinted by the external world with the phrase: 'But this time I shall be written. I am the impression that will transform itself' [Aber diesmal werde ich geschrieben werden. Ich bin der Eindruck, der sich verwandeln wird] (R VI, 756).[20] Earlier in his notations, Brigge describes the procedure as follows: 'everything enters more deeply into me and no longer stops in the place where it used to cease. I have an inside of which I knew nothing. Now everything ends up there' [es geht alles tiefer in mich ein und bleibt nicht an der Stelle stehen, wo es sonst immer zu Ende war. Ich habe ein Inneres, von dem ich nicht wußte. Alles geht jetzt dorthin] (R VI, 710–11).[21]

The other, obverse movement of looking appears to be an imprint the viewer leaves on things by the very act of looking at them. This type of imprint seems to establish the things looked upon as stable objects and separate external entities available for usage and possession. A rather extreme example of such a lasting imprint — which I want to call 'cathexis'[22] — is the one Brigge's grandfather, Chamberlain Christoph Detlev Brigge, apparently left on the things of his household:

> Ja, es war für diese geistesabwesenden, verschlafenen Dinge eine schreckliche Zeit. Es passierte, dass aus Büchern, die irgend eine hastige Hand ungeschickt geöffnet hatte, Rosenblätter heraustaumelten, die zertreten wurden; kleine, schwächliche Gegenstände wurden ergriffen und, nachdem sie sofort zerbrochen waren, schnell wieder hingelegt, manches Verbogene auch unter Vorhänge gesteckt oder gar hinter das goldene Netz des Kamingitters geworfen. Und von Zeit zu Zeit fiel etwas, fiel unverhüllt auf Teppich, fiel hell auf das harte Parkett, aber es zerschlug da und dort, zersprang scharf oder brach fast lautlos auf, denn diese Dinge, verwöhnt wie sie waren, vertrugen keinerlei Fall.
>
> Und wäre es jemandem eingefallen zu fragen, was die Ursache von alledem sei, was über dieses ängstlich gehütete Zimmer alles Untergangs Fülle herabgerufen habe, — so hätte es nur *eine* Antwort gegeben: der Tod. Der Tod des Kammerherrn Christoph Detelv Brigge auf Ulsgaard. (R VI, 716–17)
>
> [Indeed, it was a terrible time for the absent-minded, sleepy things. When books were opened clumsily by hasty hands, rose petals would fall out and be trampled down; small and fragile objects were snatched up, instantly broken, and then quickly put back; a few things that had been bent were hidden behind the curtains or even tossed behind the golden mesh of the fire screen; and from time to time something would fall, fall with a thud on the carpet, fall with a sharp crack on the hard parquet, but breaking to pieces here and there, breaking with a crashing snap or almost without a sound, for these things, spoiled as they were, would not tolerate falling at all.
>
> And had anyone thought to ask what might be the cause of it all, what might have brought down the fullness of all destruction upon this anxiously guarded room, there could have been but one reply: death. The death of Chamberlain Christoph Detlev Brigge at Ulsgaard.]

The 'sleepy' objects in Chamberlain Brigge's room are disturbed in their peace. Formerly resting 'absent-mindedly' on shelves, they have now become disobedient, resisting the 'hasty' grasp of foreign hands. And 'the cause of it all' is the imminent death of their master. The cathectic imprint that Chamberlain Brigge left on his things is so powerful that his belongings are compelled to imitate his mortal agony.

Things are falling down to the ground where they 'instantly' break to pieces, thus experiencing, like their owner, 'the fullness of all destruction', death.[23]

Whereas Chamberlain Brigge had the cathectic power to take things into possession and subject them to his command, his grandson Malte Laurids Brigge feels haunted by things and their looks. He is, we shall see, unable to control them, let alone take possession of them and impress his will upon them. Indeed, in the *Aufzeichnungen* as well as other works the main difficulty seems to be that the observer's cathectic imprint is usually more precarious an endeavour than the inverse movement of looking, when things impress their faces on the observer.

But first a formulation by the psychoanalyst and psychiatrist Viktor Emil von Gebsattel will help me define the meaning of cathexis more closely. Incidentally, Gebsattel was also the analyst of Clara Rilke-Westhoff and would have become the analyst of Rilke himself if the latter had not shied away 'from this big tidying-up which is not the result of life — this correction of all those pages life has written thus far, pages I then image to look like an exercise book filled with revisions in red'.[24] At any rate, in his 1929 article 'Über Fetischismus' Gebsattel also mentions the 'discharge of foreign body-spirit into the world of things such that these appear to be animated and suffused with the fluid of such being', adding the curious claim that 'this ability to inscribe oneself into things is more pronounced in women than in men'.[25] This imaginary procedure, which for Gebsattel constitutes the necessary basis of fetishism, thus invests or impresses an object with mental energy, with a residue, as it were, of selfhood. It is this mental imprint left on an object — or rather the perception thereof — that I call cathexis, which is the standard translation of the Freudian term *Besetzung*. Whereas Freud used the term to describe libidinal investments in ideas, objects, and persons alike, I employ cathexis in the narrower sense of a personal signature of possession and ownership seemingly inhabiting an object. The cathectic signature in turn stabilizes the relation between object and owner and so facilitates future interactions, which is why cathexis could be considered an essential means of forming and maintaining object relations, an idea systematically developed by cultural theorist Hartmut Böhme.[26]

Rilke further illustrates the significance of cathexis in forming object relations in his 1914 essay 'Dolls' [Puppen] (R VI, 1063–74). This text contains perhaps the most explicit description of the joys, as well as the sufferings, cathectic procedures imply. The doll here appears in two ways. On the one hand, it is a medium that can potentially receive a child's, and presumably also an adult's, cathectic imprint, which is to say, mental and emotional investments like 'overflowing tenderness' [Überschwemmungen unserer Zärtlichkeit] (R VI, 1067). The doll thus functions as a container or vessel (*Gefäß*)[27] of selfhood, since 'we could impress ourselves in the doll and get lost in it' [wir konnten uns in sie hineindrücken und in ihr verlorengehen] (R VI, 1067). These are the moments of joy. But there are also moments, Rilke writes in the same passage, when the doll resists its appropriation. Then it appears to be 'the terrifying foreign body on which we have squandered our most sincere warmth' [der grausige Fremdkörper, an den wir unsere lauterste Wärme verschwendet haben] (R VI, 1067). These moments of objective resistance and rejection are the moments of suffering.

Considering the examples given, one might say they all investigate, in one way or another, the interaction between observer and observed thing. During that period of observation, the perceived thing does not immediately appear as a distinct external entity, or as an object, while the observer does not immediately recognize himself as the subject causing and controlling the gaze. Their perceptual interaction thus marks a moment before the positions of a seeing subject and the seen object are firmly established, constantly shifting and confusing them instead.

If this is true, we are faced with a terminological difficulty. The word 'object' derives from the Latin *obiectum*, combining *ob* ('towards', 'against') and *iacere* ('to throw'), so that it could be rendered as that which is 'thrown towards' the eye. The German *Gegen-stand* — an eighteenth-century loan translation of *Objekt* — repeats this spatial notion. Therefore, either concept presupposes a subject-position as antithesis, as well as the separation between subject and object, interiority and exteriority.

To avoid these tacit presuppositions, I suggest differentiating three moments of perception. First of these is the actual thing, the material referent as such, whose physical existence and visual features have to be bracketed when dealing with scenic descriptions — sceno*graphies* — rather than scenes of looking. The second element is the thing of perception, its sensory appearance in the observer's mind, which may be referred to with the Greek term *aisthēton*. This literally means 'thing perceived', or more plainly 'perception', including feelings and affections of the body. Practically, however, the *aisthēton* always involves a complex of *aisthēta* or 'things perceived', since the thing of perception consists even in the most elementary cases of a bundle of at first indistinct and unseparated sensations. This understanding no doubt contrasts with the common idea, dominant in seventeenth- and eighteenth-century thought, that discrete 'sense impressions' constitute the basic matter and immediate units of perception. However, philosophers and psychologists began to challenge this idea in the nineteenth century. For example, Ernst Mach claimed, in his widely read treatise *Die Analyse der Empfindungen und das Verhältnis des Physischen zum Psychischen* (1886), that perception means to impose 'functional relationships' on a bundle of a priori indeterminate stimuli.[28] More recent theories of sense perception continue to emphasize the necessity of both cognitive and corporeal or 'embodied' action in perception so as to produce and then discern 'impressions'. This 'enactive' approach, which philosophers like Alva Noë adopt, draws inspiration above all from psychologist James J. Gibson, who claimed that:

> Perceiving is an achievement of the individual, not an appearance in the theater of his consciousness. [...] The act of picking up information, moreover, is a continuous act, an activity that is ceaseless and unbroken. The sea of energy in which we live flows and changes without sharp breaks. Even the tiny fraction of this energy that affects the receptors in the eyes, ears, nose, mouth, and skin is a flux, not a sequence. [...] Discrete percepts, like discrete ideas, are 'as mythical as the Jack of Spades'.[29]

The third moment and epistemic result of perception is the object as a whole. To identify something as a coherent external entity with distinctive properties, and hence as an object, means to comprehend what the perceived 'things' signify altogether. It means, in other words, to objectify the 'things' seen through a self-conscious act of apperception, thus producing objective unity. Extending this line of thought, one might describe the procedure connecting all three moments of perception as a 'realization' of objective meaning: The momentary sensory appearance of some thing, the *aisthēton*, consisting of not just one but many perceptions is eventually comprehended and realized in objective form, which in the domain of discursive cognition corresponds to a name or caption designating, as it were, 'the meaning of it all'.

By calling this perceptual procedure 'realization' (which need not occur in succession but might, in complex cases, also vacillate or even break down, as it so often happens in Rilke) I refer to Paul Cézanne. He used the term of *réalisation* in letters and conversations, remarking in one of them that 'painting from nature is not copying the object, it is realizing one's sensations'.[30] For Cézanne, the objective form in which one ought to realize sensations was of course painting. But he also cautioned that in doing so one must never abandon the labour of looking, the colour sensation physically felt in the eye. Instead, one should attempt to preserve — and render visible — the laborious process of looking through the painted image.

Owing to this bold aesthetic demand, the realization even of trivial subject matters like apples on a table became virtually impossible for Cézanne. 'The realization of my sensations', he wrote in a letter to his son Paul six weeks before his death in 1906, 'is always painful' because 'I cannot attain the intensity that unfolds itself before my senses' with pigment on a canvas.[31] Still, Rilke fervently admired such tenacity in the face of inevitable failure, praising Cézanne as a champion of looking who was never nervous or distracted but at all times focused and objective in his attention to things, just like a humble 'dog'.[32] Rilke was also aware of Cézanne's notion of *réalisation*, explaining it in a letter to his wife Clara Rilke-Westhoff and translating it as *Dingwerdung* into German (literally 'becoming-a-thing'), a notion some scholars in fact regard as the key to Rilke's poetics.[33]

With all this in mind, I now turn to a passage from a letter Rilke wrote to Clara Rilke-Westhoff on 8 March 1907. This passage is an instructive scenography in that it vividly illustrates the complexities involved in realizing all those 'things' to see while looking:

> Das Anschauen ist eine so wunderbare Sache, von der wir noch so wenig wissen; wir sind mit ihm ganz nach außen gekehrt; aber gerade wenn wirs am meisten sind, scheinen in uns Dinge vor sich zu gehen, die auf das Unbeobachtetsein sehnsüchtig gewartet haben, und während sie sich, intakt und seltsam anonym, in uns vollziehen, ohne uns, — wächst in dem Gegenstand draußen ihre Bedeutung heran, ein überzeugender, starker, — ihr einzig möglicher Name, in dem wir das Geschehnis in unserem Innern selig und ehrerbietig erkennen, ohne selbst daran heranzureichen, es nur ganz leise, ganz von fern, unter dem Zeichen eines eben noch fremden und schon im nächsten Augenblick aufs neue entfremdeten Dinges begreifend —.

> [Looking is such a wonderful thing of which we still know so little. It turns us completely to the outside; but just when we are turned to the outside most of

all, certain things seem to take place within us that have waited longingly until they are unobserved. And while these proceed within us, intact and strangely anonymous, without us, their meaning is growing up in the object outside, a convincing, a strong name — their only possible name, in which we blissfully and reverently recognize the procedure inside us, but without reaching it, comprehending it only very quietly and from afar under the sign of a thing that was strange initially and in the next moment will be estranged from us again —.]

Looking at things and grasping their meaning seems to be a complex process for Rilke. Nonetheless, this dense passage contains a theory of looking in miniature, but in a scenographic form. What happens in the scene he describes? As looking turns the observer's attention fully to the outside, 'things seem to take place within us', yet these inner 'things' are perceived only by means of 'the object outside'. The external object is intertwined with the impenetrable 'procedure [Geschehnis] inside us' looking has started. Similarly, the meaning of those 'things' inside us gradually develops outside us, 'growing up' in the external object.

Looking, one might therefore say, involves in this scene a con-fusing reversal between inside and outside, a strange vacillation amongst noticed 'things' whose combined 'meaning', however, cannot be 'reached'. Looking cannot come to a close because it lacks both definite meaning and permanent location. Instead of converging in the place where the external object permanently stands, the noticed 'things' constituting the thing of perception or *aisthēton* keep wavering, while their proper 'name' constantly escapes, despite the 'convincing name' occasionally presenting itself during brief moments of faint recognition. Consequently, the relation between observer and object is continually 'estranged'. The observing subject can neither distinguish his looking from and against the external object, nor stop the endless reversals of positions by pinning down this 'one and only name' [einzig möglicher Name] of it all. The perpetual con-fusion of boundaries prevails, as it does, strangely enough, 'without us'. Looking is not only name- and placeless. It is also a 'strangely anonymous' occurrence that belongs to no one.

What, then, could restore clear boundaries? How to sort out the con-fusing reversals of looking? How once more to separate inside and outside, looking subject and seen object? In the 1907 lectures on sense perception known as *Ding und Raum*, given the same year as Rilke wrote his letter, Edmund Husserl ascribes objectivity squarely to consciousness. For him, all object perception originates in the ability of consciousness to *intend* a series of perceptions *as* a unified object. Husserl calls this process the 'constitution' of the perceptual object, which happens through active as well as passive acts of synthesis, including interplay between 'intention' and 'fulfilment' or, equally possible 'disappointment' of expectations. What results from such syntheses is a 'consciousness of identity'. This type of identity, however, does not simply duplicate physical realities. Husserl insists that 'properties do not constitute the object [of perception] as pieces constitute a whole', claiming, on the contrary, that consciousness produces objective unity through intentional acts such as identification and discrimination, thereby connecting sensations, just like predicates within judgements, 'grammatically'.[34]

Consciousness in Husserl's model serves to determine origin and cause of perception. His model, much like Fichte's, stipulates the author and grammar of looking in advance. In Rilke's scenography, however, the author and grammar of looking are quite unclear, because it involves constant reversals and displacements that happen 'without us'. The external thing appears to be always already inside, while this inside is always already projected towards the outside, so that both moments escape permanently. The movement of looking staged by Rilke is continually 'estranged'. Instead of discovering the object's proper name, there are only anonymous 'things' to see. The process of looking thus blurs the boundaries between subject and object while simultaneously dynamizing their hierarchy.

Anxiety and objectification

Although at odds with Husserlian phenomenology, Rilke's scenographic representation of looking does prefigure newer phenomenological theories. Philosopher Bernhard Waldenfels, for example, similarly contests concepts of visual perception that a priori ascribe the gaze to a subject:

> If something is naïve, it is the rash humanization and personalization of the gaze, which immediately turns it into an act of looking [Blickakt] and ascribes it to an author. [...] Like the voice of a stranger, the foreign gaze surprises us. It presents itself as an event of looking [Blickereignis] that seems at first anonymous and nameless, not as someone's gaze. One should say 'it sees'. [...] A kind of seeing that is not a priori certain of itself and its objects will not eschew the confrontation with the look [Blick] of things, and it will take seriously the feeling that things look at us, look at themselves in us. [...] This transfer of the gaze to the outside can be dismissed as an animistic relic or a metaphoric excuse only insofar as we suppose that the seeing subject is in perfect control of his gaze and projects it to the outside, thus endowing the things, as it were, with eyes. The thought, however, that things see themselves in us assumes an entirely different meaning if we understand seeing as a process [Geschehen] *that remains to a certain degree anonymous and begins elsewhere.*[35]

The 'event of looking', Waldenfels writes, cannot be said to belong immediately and unambiguously to a subject, but is instead a process that 'begins elsewhere' and 'remains to a certain degree anonymous'. This conclusion (which is rooted in similar remarks by Maurice Merleau-Ponty and has been further developed by Lambert Wiesing)[36] renders explicit some of the 'things' Rilke's letter has us see. Indeed, the scene of looking set up by Rilke invites anything but a 'hasty humanization and personalization of the gaze'. It is, on the contrary, the de-personalized interplay of glances and the anonymous exchange of imprints that prevails therein.

These reflections on the original anonymity of looking cast a different light on the prevalence of anthropomorphisms in Rilke. Anthropomorphisms thus no longer appear as indicative of an ideologically compromised 'cult of things' [Dingkult] Adorno and his disciples discovered in Rilke.[37] Nor would they necessarily constitute signs of mental illness, a pathological 'displacement of traumatic symptoms from subjects to objects' noted by scholars like Andreas Huyssen and Erich Simenauer.[38]

Instead of concealing more fundamental truths about capitalist economy, modern society, or traumatized subjectivity, Rilke's anthropomorphism would simply tell us something about the process of looking itself. His scenographies would indeed 'present a range of encounters between subject and object, interior and exterior, man and animal, beholder and work of art, during which the boundaries of either party are being called into question', but not, as Andreas Kramer thinks, because they reflect the essential 'malaise' of modernity, the 'condition of alienation'.[39] On the contrary, the anthropomorphic suspension of clear boundaries between animate subjectivity and inanimate objectivity could be understood as an inherent moment of looking, which Rilke captures in scenographic form.

Rilke's anthropomorphisms frequently take the form of prosopopoeia: things return the observer's gaze as if they too had a looking 'face' (*prosōpon* in Greek). This is the reversal of looking that so often transpires in Rilke's scenographies of looking. The *Aufzeichnungen* are replete with such reversals, when things suddenly impress their insistent looks on the observer in return. Brigge describes such a reversal one lonesome evening in his Paris chamber. He feels haunted by a certain 'lid of a can' [Büchsendeckel] and is generally horrified by the spiteful grimaces he discovers in the look of things. The surrounding items seem to exchange conspiring glances while resisting human dominion: 'They join forces to trouble, to frighten, and to lead him astray, knowing that they can do so. Winking at one another they begin their seduction, which then grows beyond measure' [Da verbinden sie sich, um ihn zu stören, zu schrecken, zu beirren, und wissen, daß sie es können. Da fangen sie, einander zuzwinkernd, die Verführung an, die dann ins Unermessene weiter wächst] (R vi, 878).

As Brigge sees it, such spiteful winks betray the general resistance and, literally, ob-jective being of things — the fact that they have finally liberated themselves from human control to indulge in 'debauchery':

> Hier [beim Umgang mit dem Büchsendeckel] zeigt es sich so recht, wie verwirrend der Umgang mit den Menschen auf die Dinge gewirkt hat. Die Menschen nämlich, wenn es angeht, sie ganz vorübergehend mit solchen Deckeln zu vergleichen, sitzen höchst ungern und schlecht auf ihren Beschäftigungen. [...] Die Dinge sehen das nun schon seit Jahrhunderten an. Es ist kein Wunder, wenn sie verdorben sind, wenn sie den Geschmack verlieren an ihrem natürlichen, stillen Zweck und das Dasein so ausnutzen möchten, wie sie es rings um sich ausgenutzt sehen. Sie machen Versuche, sich ihren Anwendungen zu entziehen, sie werden unlustig und nachlässig, und die Leute sind gar nicht erstaunt, wenn sie sie auf einer Ausschweifung ertappen. [...] Wo aber einer ist, der sich zusammennimmt, ein Einsamer etwa, der so recht rund auf sich beruhen wollte Tag und Nacht, da fordert er geradezu den Widerspruch, den Hohn, den Haß der entarteten Geräte heraus, die, in ihrem argen Gewissen, nicht mehr vertragen können, daß etwas sich zusammenhält und nach seinem Sinne strebt. (R vi, 877–78)

> [This [viz. Brigge's interaction with the lid] perfectly illustrates how confusing it has been for things to interact with humans. Humans (if it is appropriate to compare them to can lids for a moment) sit on their occupations very badly and reluctantly. [...] Things have now been observing this for centuries. No wonder

they are corrupted and lose the taste for their natural, silent functions and want to take advantage of their existence just as they see it happen all around them. They attempt to evade their usage; they grow listless and neglectful, and people are not at all surprised to catch them in a moment of debauchery. [...] But wherever there is one who pulls himself together, some loner who wants to rest roundly upon himself day and night, he provokes opposition, the scorn and the hatred of the depraved devices, whose wicked consciences cannot tolerate the thought that anything might control itself and follow its own purpose.]

For Brigge, the disconcerting lid of the can is representative of all the other items of daily use that were confused by the interaction with humans. It is one among many 'depraved devices' seeking to assault him with 'scorn' and 'hatred'. The objective meaning that these devices have in the eyes of Brigge is thus identified and asserted: they precisely mean scorn and hatred. For him, objects therefore become *ecstatic*, or literally depart (ex-) from a simple, 'static' standing. They now 'stand out', impressing their spiteful grimaces on the observer.

These spiteful looks in return need not be interpreted psychologically, as a projection of traumatic symptoms and hence a form of compensation, nor in a Marxist vein, as indicating the violent rule of merchandise over man in capitalist society. Read in an aesthesiological way, the look of things effects instead a critical demarcation of difference, namely: subject versus object(s), or in Brigge's words, 'some loner' versus those 'depraved devices'. Brigge receives the overpowering imprint of the object world, but with the consequence that the confusing anonymity of looking is resolved and clear boundaries are restored.

This demarcation of difference usually takes a rather unpleasant turn in Brigge's *Aufzeichnungen*, since it is often accompanied by the sensation of *Angst* ('anxiety', 'fear'). And indeed, in countless entries he describes feelings of anxiety and fear. It frequently happens to him that 'a bit of anxiety evolves inside me' [ein wenig Angst in mir anfing] (R VI, 769), which then quickly grows into more severe forms of horror and dread. The long paragraph listing Brigge's manifold anxieties attests to the dominance of this feeling. Lying in bed, Brigge realizes that all those fears of his childhood have returned, namely:

> Die Angst, daß ein kleiner Wollfaden, der aus dem Saum der Decke heraussteht, hart sei, hart und scharf wie eine stählerne Nadel; die Angst, daß dieser kleine Knopf meines Nachthemdes größer sei als mein Kopf, groß und schwer; die Angst, daß dieses Krümchen Brot, das jetzt von meinem Bette fällt, gläsern und zerschlagen unten ankommen würde, und die drückende Sorge, daß damit eigentlich alles zerbrochen sei, alles für immer; die Angst, daß der Streifen Rand eines aufgerissenen Briefes etwas Verbotenes sei, das niemand sehen dürfe, etwas unbeschreiblich Kostbares, für das keine Stelle in der Stube sicher genug sei; die Angst, daß ich, wenn ich einschliefe, das Stück Kohle verschlucken würde, das vor dem Ofen liegt; die Angst, daß irgendeine Zahl in meinem Gehirn zu wachsen beginnt, bis sie nicht mehr Raum hat in mir; die Angst, daß das Granit sei, worauf ich liege, grauer Granit; die Angst, daß ich schreien könnte und daß man vor meiner Türe zusammenliefe und sie schließlich aufbräche, die Angst, daß ich mich verraten könnte und alles das sagen, wovor ich mich fürchte, und die Angst, daß ich nichts sagen könnte, weil alles unsagbar ist, — und die anderen Ängste... die Ängste. (R VI, 766–67)

[The fear [or anxiety] that a small thread of wool sticking out of the hem of the blanket might be hard, hard and sharp as a needle; the fear that this little button on my nightshirt might be larger than my head, large and heavy; the fear that this crumb of bread, falling right now from the bed, might be glass when it hits the floor, and smash, and the oppressive worry that, when it does, everything will be shattered, everything, forever; the fear that the edge of a torn-open letter might be something forbidden which no one should see, something indescribably precious for which no place in the room is safe enough; the fear that if I fell asleep, I might swallow that piece of coal in front of the stove; the fear that some number might start growing inside my brain until it has no more room; the fear that I might be lying on granite, grey granite; the fear that I might scream, and people would come running and gather at my door and eventually break it open; the fear that I might betray myself and speak of everything I am afraid of; and the fear that I might not be able to say anything, because it is all unspeakable — and the other fears... the fears.]

Contextualizing Brigge's experience of the 'depraved' lid with this passage, one might say that *Angst* represents the main force of objectification in the *Aufzeichnungen*. Anxiety and fear are Brigge's primary means of separating his subjectivity from the world of objects. Though detrimental to his emotional well-being, his fear at the same time stabilizes the object world in a fundamental way. For being afraid of something automatically introduces the mark of otherness — of objectivity. Fear, that is, implies the difference between me and that foreign something which makes itself felt as anxiety, dread, horror, etc.

The image suggested by the etymology of *Angst*, going back to Greek *agchein* ('to squeeze, to strangle, to throttle') via Latin *angor* (the 'choking', and already 'anxiety, fear'), supports this observation. Fear manifests itself in and through my body. It is my feeling; but at the same time a foreign sensation, a grip from the outside tightening my chest and squeezing my throat — the proverbial 'grip of fear'. Being immersed in fear, the self stands always already in opposition to something else, which just emphasizes the fundamental difference between me ('the loner') and the feared objects (e.g. 'depraved devices'). And although the sensation of fear physically indicates these foreign elements, it is not identical to them. The external, anxiety-inducing cause and the inner sensation constitute two distinct poles, and it is precisely this implicit distinction of fear that enables Brigge to reassert the boundary between his self and those 'depraved' objects surrounding him.

Therefore, fear (*Angst*) has both an egocentric and an intentional structure, in Brigge's *Aufzeichnungen* as well as in common experience. It inevitably points back at a subject position, 'me', the sentient locus of experience, while simultaneously directing the awareness towards something else, something ob-jective, to that foreign element which neither belongs to me nor feels like me. This basic structure also applies to fears and anxieties whose causes are not readily known or simply unclear. Although these fears lack a specific object and direct cause, as the intransitive statement 'I am afraid' indeed suggests, they nonetheless imply an objective counterpart, namely that foreign sensation of fear in my body, which as such directs my attention towards something ob-jective. This implicit directionality or intentionality is of course the very reason why the sensation of fear immediately begs the question whence it came.

One famous thinker of *Angst* confirms the observation that this feeling combines self-centeredness or egocentricity with intentionality, the being-towards something else. In *Sein und Zeit*, Martin Heidegger maintains that anxiety represents the 'basic feeling' [Grundbefindlichkeit] of 'being in the world' [In-der-Welt-sein]. This means, on the one hand, that the feeling of anxiety necessarily 'individuates' [vereinzelt] one's 'existence' [Dasein]. Being anxious, we are 'thrown back' onto ourselves. The quotidian affairs of life lose their significance, so that our attention is redirected towards the 'genuine potential' [Eigentlichkeit] of existence — what we 'could be' [Sein-können] as individuals. On the other hand, the feeling of anxiety directs our attention to the external world as the sum of all possible concerns and fears, thus shifting the centre of 'existence' from inside to outside, from self to world. For that reason, anxiety represents for Heidegger the 'mode of feeling' [Modus der Befindlichkeit] that 'discloses, primordially and directly, the world as world'.[40]

One incident in the *Aufzeichnungen* makes it particularly obvious that Brigge can objectify his perceptions and thus restore the boundary between self and object world only by way of fear. This incident is Brigge's encounter with 'the wall' [die Mauer] — a passage that Heidegger quotes in his 1927 lecture *Die Grundprobleme der Phänomenologie* to illustrate the basic feeling of being in the world, anxiety.[41] Attending to this 'wall', the remains of one or multiple demolished buildings, Brigge makes mostly visual and olfactory perceptions. He notices a wide range of sensory properties:

> Ich weiß nicht, ob ich schon gesagt habe, daß ich diese Mauer meine. Aber es war sozusagen nicht die erste Mauer der vorhandenen Häuser (was man doch hätte annehmen müssen), sondern die letzte der früheren. Man sah in den verschiedenen Stockwerken Zimmerwände, an denen noch die Tapeten klebten, da und dort den Ansatz des Fußbodens oder der Decke. Neben den Zimmerwänden blieb die ganze Mauer entlang noch ein schmutzigweißer Raum, und durch diesen kroch in unsäglich widerlichen, wurmweichen, gleichsam verdauenden Bewegungen die offene, rostfleckige Rinne der Abortröhre. Von den Wegen, die das Leuchtgas gegangen war, waren graue, staubige Spuren am Rande der Decken geblieben, und sie bogen da und dort, ganz unerwartet, rund um und kamen in die farbige Wand hineingelaufen und in ein Loch hinein, das schwarz und rücksichtslos ausgerissen war. Am unvergeßlichsten aber waren die Wände selbst. Das zähe Leben dieser Zimmer hatte sich nicht zertreten lassen. Es war noch da, es hielt sich an den Nägeln, die geblieben waren, es stand auf dem handbreiten Rest der Fußböden, es war unter den Ansätzen der Ecken, wo es noch ein klein wenig Innenraum gab, zusammengekrochen. Man konnte sehen, daß es in der Farbe war, die es langsam, Jahr um Jahr, verwandelt hatte: Blau in schimmliches Grün, Grün in Grau und Gelb in ein altes, abgestandenes Weiß, das fault. Aber es war auch in den frischeren Stellen, die sich hinter Spiegeln, Bildern und Schränken erhalten hatten; denn es hatte ihre Umrisse gezogen und nachgezogen und war mit Spinnen und Staub auch auf diesen versteckten Plätzen gewesen,

die jetzt bloßlagen. Es war in jedem Streifen, der abgeschunden war, es war in den feuchten Blasen am unteren Rande der Tapeten, es schwankte in den abgerissenen Fetzen, und aus den garstigen Flecken, die vor langer Zeit entstanden waren, schwitzte es aus. Und aus diesen blau, grün und gelb gewesenen Wänden, die eingerahmt waren von den Bruchbahnen der zerstörten Zwischenmauern, stand die Luft dieser Leben heraus, die zähe, träge, stockige Luft, die kein Wind noch zerstreut hatte. Da standen die Mittage und die Krankheiten und das Ausgeatmete und der jahrealte Rauch und der Schweiß, der unter den Schultern ausbricht und die Kleider schwer macht, und das Fade aus den Munden und der Fuselgeruch gärender Füße. Da stand das Scharfe vom Urin und das Brennen vom Ruß und grauer Kartoffeldunst und der schwere, glatte Gestank von alterndem Schmalze. Der süße, lange Geruch von vernachlässigten Säuglingen war da und der Angstgeruch der Kinder, die in die Schule gehen, und das Schwüle aus den Betten mannbarer Knaben. Und vieles hatte sich dazugesellt, was von unten gekommen war, aus dem Abgrund der Gasse, die verdunstete, und anderes war von oben herabgesickert mit dem Regen, der über den Städten nicht rein ist. Und manches hatten die schwachen, zahm gewordenen Hauswinde, die immer in derselben Straße bleiben, zugetragen, und es war noch vieles da, wovon man den Ursprung nicht wußte. Ich habe doch gesagt, daß man alle Mauern abgebrochen hatte bis auf die letzte —? Nun von dieser Mauer spreche ich fortwährend. (R VI, 749–51)

[I'm not sure I have already said that I mean this wall. It was not, as it were, the first wall of the existing houses (as one would have supposed) but the last of the earlier ones. You could see their inner side. On the various floors you could see walls of rooms with wallpaper still adhering, and here and there the beginnings of the floor or ceiling. Next to these rooms, a dirty white space ran down the entire wall, and through it crept the open, rust-speckled groove of the toilet pipe in the inexpressibly disgusting, wormlike manner of a digestive tract. The paths which the gas of the lamps had formerly taken were still visible as grey, dusty traces along the edge of the ceiling, and sometimes they unexpectedly turned around and ran into the coloured wall and finally into some black hole that had been torn open ruthlessly. Most unforgettable of all, though, were the walls themselves. The stubborn life of those rooms had refused to be stamped out. It was still there, it clung to the nails that were left, it stood on the hand's breadth of the floor that had remained, it huddled up in the little bit of space left underneath the corners. You could see it was in the paint, which it had slowly changed, from year to year: blue into mouldy green, green into grey, and yellow into an old, stale, putrefying white. But it was also in the fresher spots that had survived behind mirrors, pictures, and wardrobes; for it had traced and retraced the outlines of these things and had been, with spiders and dust, even in these hidden places, which were now exposed. It was in every flayed strip, it was in the damp blisters at the bottom edges of the wallpaper, it flapped in the torn-off shreds, and it sweated out of nasty stains made long ago. And from these walls that had once been blue, green, or yellow and were now framed by the remains of demolished partition walls, there issued the air of those lives, a persistent, motionless, fuggy air that no wind had yet dispersed. There it was, the air of midday meals and the illnesses and the exhaled breaths and the smoke of years and the sweat from armpits that makes clothing heavy, and the stale breath from mouths and the boozy odour of fermenting feet. There it was, the acrid tang of urine and the smell of burning soot and grey fumes of potatoes, and the heavy, slick stink of old lard. The sweet, lingering smell of neglected infants was there, and the smell of anxious children setting off to school, and the stuffiness of pubescent boys' beds. And a good deal more was admixed: vapours that had come up from down below in the street, while other things had seeped in with the rain, which is not clean over cities. And still more had been wafted in by the weak, tame breezes that always stay in the same street. And there was a lot more besides of unknown origin. I did say, did I not, that all the walls had been demolished except for the last — ? It is this wall I have been talking about the entire time.]

This passage represents the most detailed scenography of perception in the *Aufzeichnungen*. The wall emerges for Brigge, and by extension also for the reader, in great and vivid detail through a continuous process of perception. It is described as an evolving phenomenon, an *aisthēton* composed of an ever-growing range of sensations: 'And there was a lot more besides of unknown origin.' But sensory inexhaustibility is precisely the problem Brigge confronts when facing the wall. His perception does not produce a coherent object but only a bundle of disconnected aspects and glimpses. Brigge is simply unable to consolidate the myriad 'things' the wall impresses on him into a connected whole, so that objective meaning constantly escapes. What the wall truly *is* cannot be said; it can only be pointed out through deictic gestures (wherefore the entire episode represents, philosophically speaking, an instance of sense-certainty). First introduced precisely as 'this' wall, the thing of perception remains a sheer 'this' still at the end of Brigge's account: 'It is *this* wall I have been talking about the entire time.'

The remark preceding his descriptions similarly betrays the difficulties of conveying the nature of 'this' wall — difficulties that must be troubling for someone who wishes to 'learn to see' (R VI, 710, 711, 723) and then write down his new discoveries. Brigge adds a reassuring preface to his description:

> Wird man es glauben, daß es solche Häuser giebt? Nein, man wird sagen, ich fälsche. Diesmal ist es Wahrheit, nichts weggelassen, natürlich auch nichts hinzugetan. [...] Häuser? Aber, um genau zu sein, es waren Häuser, die nicht mehr da waren. Häuser, die man abgebrochen hatte von oben bis unten [...] Ich weiß nicht, ob ich schon gesagt habe, daß ich diese Mauer meine. (R VI, 749)

> [Will anyone believe that there are houses such as these? No; they will say I am giving a false account. This time it is the truth, with nothing omitted and of course nothing added. [...] Houses? Rather, to be exact, they were houses that were no longer there. Houses that had been torn down, top to bottom. [...] I'm not sure I have already said that I mean this wall.]

This preface of course means to subdue doubts as to the accuracy of all those 'things' Brigge will subsequently claim to have perceived in the face of the wall, but its strained rhetoric only raises more suspicion. The reader is brought to wonder whether 'this' unspeakable wall does exist at all.

At the very end of the encounter, however, a retroactive act of objectification does occur. Brigge then recognizes everything about that wall:

> Man wird sagen, ich hätte lange davorgestanden; aber ich will einen Eid geben dafür, daß ich zu laufen begann, sobald ich die Mauer erkannt hatte. Denn

das ist das Schreckliche, daß ich sie erkannt habe. Ich erkenne das alles hier, und darum geht es so ohne weiteres in mich ein: es ist zu Hause in mir. (R VI, 751)

[You might say I stood looking at it for a long time. But I swear I started to run the moment I recognized the wall; for the terrible thing is that I recognized it. I recognize all about it, and that is why it enters into me so readily: it is at home inside me.]

This recognition does not result from external impressions — impressions of buildings, paradoxically, 'that were no longer there'. Instead, it involves the intervention of something that belongs only to Brigge, something inside him. But what is it, exactly, that is entirely 'at home inside me'? Brigge's endless fear, his inexhaustible anxiety. The apperception of the wall — as *this* wall, precisely, in contrast to 'me', subject — bears Brigge's cathectic imprint, the stamp of *his* anxiety, which produces the division between 'me' and 'not-me', observer and wall, in the first place. This is no doubt a 'terrible thing' to realize, that you can see neither 'this' nor any other object without *Angst*. And so a flight from the wall becomes simply impossible, for its very essence, anxiety, is 'at home inside me'.[42]

Nachträglichkeit

Certain thing-poems from the *Neue Gedichte* represent looking in such a way that a reciprocal exchange of looks produces a strange reversal and, consequently, objective meaning. The outstanding example for such a reversal resulting in object recognition is the sonnet 'Archaïscher Torso Apollos' (reproduced below). Paul de Man was one of the first to describe these reversals as typical of Rilke's poetry, drawing attention in particular to the 'chiastic' tendency of his thing-poems. 'Chiasmus' in this context means that these poems tend to invert the properties of the depicted objects by presenting, for example, the inside of a violin as its outside, but only, de Man adds, to revoke these seeming oppositions eventually through a final gesture of 'totalization'. Rilke therefore chose, says de Man, only those objects as poetic motifs whose 'attributes allow for such a reversal and for such an (apparent) totalization'.[43] In 'Archaïscher Torso', de Man recognizes also a totalizing chiasmus, namely the transformation of 'the eyeless sculpture [in]to an Argus eye capable of engendering, by itself, all the dimensions of space'.[44]

In contrast to de Man, whose interpretations were driven by the express desire to reveal the 'original violence' and 'pseudo-dialectic' of Rilke's chiastic 'totalizations', I will focus on the temporality of looking in 'Archaïscher Torso'.[45] Moreover, a closer look at this poem will help me to clarify an inherent tension of all scenographies, namely the discrepancy between diegetic scene and diegetic form, which is both constitutive of scenographies and a prerequisite for readerly perception, since words can and need be translated into perceptions only if these are different media indeed. In poems, the discrepancy between text and scene, or form and meaning, is particularly conspicuous, and 'Archaïscher Torso' is perhaps the most extreme example from the *Neue Gedichte* of textual form dislocating diegetic scene. This poem is by no means a straightforward representation in plain German. On the contrary, the constraints of the sonnet form — fourteen lines of iambic pentameter, a predefined stanza scheme, as well as end rhymes — constantly undermine the cohesion within and between sentences, causing abrupt breaks (as between the first and the second stanza) as well as confusing collisions (as in the second line), so that it takes time and effort to perceive the scene. We shall see, however, that the eminent tension between diegetic scene and textual form directly reflects the paradoxical temporality of looking that unites the poem as a whole, which is also true for 'Die Fensterrose' and 'Schwarze Katze', two poems I analyse in the next section.

Archaïscher Torso Apollos

Wir kannten nicht sein unerhörtes Haupt,
darin die Augenäpfel reiften. Aber
sein Torso glüht noch wie ein Kandelaber,
in dem sein Schauen, nur zurückgeschraubt,

sich hält und glänzt. Sonst könnte nicht der Bug
der Brust dich blenden, und im leisen Drehen
der Lenden könnte nicht ein Lächeln gehen
zu jener Mitte, die die Zeugung trug.

Sonst stünde dieser Stein entstellt und kurz
unter der Schultern durchsichtigem Sturz
und flimmerte nicht so wie Raubtierfelle;

und bräche nicht aus allen seinen Rändern
aus wie ein Stern: denn da ist keine Stelle,
die dich nicht sieht. Du mußt dein Leben ändern.

Archaic Torso of Apollo

We did not know his unheard-of head
in which the eyeballs were ripening. But
his torso is still glowing like a candelabrum
in which his looking, although turned down,

just holds and shines. Otherwise the front
of his breast could not blind you, and the silent turn
of the loins could not send a smile
towards that center where begetting once was.

Otherwise this stone would stand defaced and short
below the shoulder's transparent arch[46]
and would not glimmer like a predator's coat

and would not, from within all its edges,
burst like a star: for there is no place
that does not see you. You must change your life.

By the end of the poem, the observer (or several observers, since the poem begins with a 'we') has comprehended the torso's meaningful look.[47] The torso exhorts the observer to change his or her life. There are good reasons to consider this exhortation a quasi-religious command, not least because it is issued by a work of art representing the god of art and poetry, Apollo.[48] Before the divine command is heard, however, the awareness of a foreign 'looking' [Schauen] is growing in the observer. In fact, this foreign looking is present from the beginning. Its origin appears to be the sculpture's absent head. The head seems to have impregnated the stony torso with its gaze. Thanks to the head, or so it seems, the torso 'is still glowing' [glüht noch] — present tense in the German indicating an actual perception — from the inside 'like a candelabrum', but with diminished radiance, as though the torso was a branched gas lamp having been *zurückgeschraubt* — turned down using a screw knob. The absent head must have caused the glowing, the two following subjunctive clauses hypothesize, because 'otherwise' the torso 'could not' blind the observing eye, nor 'would' it glimmer like fur and burst like a shining star.

The penultimate line, 'for there is no place | that does not see you', finally identifies the reason and essence of it all: there are countless looking places on the stony torso. The surface of the torso is shining all over *because* every place of the torso has been looking at you the whole time. The presence of an ob-jective gaze, intuited at first as a glowing and glinting, is thus confirmed with conclusive certainty ('*for* there is...'), and as it is stated in the present tense also currently experienced. Rilke describes the same powerful perception in his *Rodin* monograph, noting that Rodin's sculptures bear 'places without end, none of which was not active. There were no empty places [...] only lively patches beyond counting.'[49] 'Archaïscher Torso' echoes these lines, which is not surprising given that this poem also depicts a sculpture and, moreover, belongs to a cycle dedicated to 'mon grand Ami Auguste Rodin'.

The accusative pronoun 'you' [dich] in the final line evidences the shift in direction from perception to realization happening at the end of the poem, a reversal that could be called 'noematic'. Since the publication of his *Ideen zu einer reinen Phänomenologie* in 1913, Husserl uses 'noema' basically to refer to those aspects signified by, but not manifest in, current perceptions, which he calls 'noesis'. Noema therefore designates the 'unreal' or 'inactual' (*nicht-reell*) background of an ongoing perceptual (viz. noetic) process, specifically in terms of modality and identity, *how* something is perceived and what such perception *means*. The noema of a perceptual process represents, in Husserl's words, 'the How of objective determinations' [der Gegenstand im Wie seiner Bestimmtheiten], but 'in abstraction from all predicates', hence the logical structure or meaning uniting the constitutive noetic manifold.[50]

In 'Archaïscher Torso', the noematic reversal consists precisely in the turn from perception to comprehension, from seeing individual sensory signs (noesis) to finally understanding their overall meaning (noema) in the two last lines. In the beginning, the torso has been the object of observation, but now the torso itself returns the gaze in the form of countless looking places. The observer realizes that his or her gaze is reflected and thrown back by the torso — objectified in the literal sense. Now he is the direct and, grammatically speaking, accusative object of a gaze issuing from within the torso. The perception of individual 'places' or parts has thus revealed the essential meaning or noema of the entire scene, 'You must change your life' — a meaning, however, that is not seen within but rather inferred from the scene.

Endowed with such significance, the torso seems no longer fragmentary, an unending series of glinting bits and glowing pieces, but emerges as a meaningful *object* — as the work of art that it once was and still is. The sculpture thus impresses the observer with an image of unity and completeness concerning not only the past, when it was supposedly still intact, but also the present moment, during which there is *no* place not looking back. The torso embodies a wholeness in which every place partakes. At the same time, the observer's subjectivity is restored, for in exhorting the observer to 'change your life', the sculpture in fact addresses him in the subject position, as 'you' [Du]. And so it might seem that 'Archaïscher Torso' stages a mutual recognition process between subject and object, eventually giving rise to self-consciousness through a 'movement of *recognition*' in the Hegelian sense (cf. PhG 145–46/111*). Carsten Strathausen hints at such a Hegelian reading of 'Archaïscher Torso' when he concludes that for Rilke, 'to see is to be seen in return. [...] Things look back at us once we have learned to look at them, enabling a mutual recognition process that gives way to self-awareness'.[51]

But the poem's strange first sentence, which announces as much a lack of knowledge as it points out a vacant place, complicates the explanation of the poem's final reversal, the turn from actual perception to noematic comprehension. Perhaps, the first sentence subverts it altogether, since the thing mediating between observer and torso is missing: 'We did not know his unheard-of[52] head | in which the eyeballs were ripening.' The supposed cause of all those looking places *was* unheard of, and the 'eyeballs ripening therein' *were* not known to us. The head simply is not there, and so it cannot be recognized and affirmed. As far as is known, this head was never seen and heard of, so that its existence can only be posited and any assertion as to its efficacy must remain speculative. Indeed, it is only by dint of grammatical inference (*sein Schauen* ⟶ *das Haupt*) that the reader, not the observer, could connect the foreign looking to the head and its eyes. But within the scene the origin of looking is missing, although each and every place on the stony torso is looking back.

The poem's first sentence thus represents a paradox only language can produce. It *asserts* an origin, but at the same time *evokes* a lack, a thing yet unseen and unheard of, a vacancy. It summons an origin whose originality remains purely hypothetical and unheard-of, while textually restoring an origin of looking by grammatically suggesting that the head's gaze had infiltrated the torso and so brought about all those looking places on the torso's surface. The figure of an *unerhörtes Haupt* repeats this paradox in a nutshell, since it names an origin of looking no one has ever heard of, thereby disputing, or at least casting doubt on, its very existence.

Although an origin of looking does not appear within the scene, its attribution to the head is nonetheless suggested by that scene, but in retrospect. The restoration of the head by way of grammatical inference represents the logical consequence of what transpired between observer and torso. Hence, looking finds its 'origin' in this poem by way of *Nachträglichkeit*. Jean Laplanche has provided a succinct definition of this ambiguous term, defining it chiefly as a temporal structure with three connected layers:

> In the first place, [*nachträglich*] has the simple meaning of 'additional' or 'secondary'; and hence, in a temporal sense, of 'later'. A second use implies movement from past time in the direction of the future, while a third implies the opposite, a movement from the future towards the past.[53]

How does this vexed temporality match up with the process of looking represented in Rilke's sonnet? *Nachträglich* in the simple sense of additional and retrospective is the closing exhortation, 'you must change your life', since it encapsulates the cognitive result and meaning of the scene. The process of looking itself is driven by a movement in two opposite temporal directions, thus forming a temporal loop. Moving at once forward and backward in time, this double movement departs from, and simultaneously returns to, the unheard-of head as the apparent 'origin' of looking. The textual sequence and the diegetic scene differ precisely with regard to their temporal direction. According to the textual sequence, looking originates in the past (earlier in the text) and is then noticed in the future (later in the text). Looking thus departs from the head or is caused by it. The described scene reverses this temporal order of causation. It first confronts us with an anonymous and literally headless looking, so that the 'origin' of looking is caused by the scene rather than some pre-existent head. As a result of the scene, looking is transferred back to an unknown past, an 'origin' the first line hypothetically restores.

The *Nachträglichkeit* of looking in 'Archaïscher Torso' is in fact analogous to the two-way logic of imprinting that characterizes most of Rilke's scenographies. According to the diegetic scene, the observer casts his gaze first on the torso and then backward in time, on an imaginary head, thereby impressing the absent head with a look; the object has been marked by the observer. The textual sequence suggests, in reverse, that the head has transmitted its looking forward in time, to the future, thereby impressing first the torso and then, through countless looking places, the observer with its look; the observer has been marked by the object. The last line concludes this mutual exchange of imprints with an additional meaning. Taken together, those three movements of looking establish the kind of circularity a truly reciprocal exchange demands. Neither takes precedence over the other, because each depends on the other. In a word, they are inseparable due to their *Nachträglichkeit*.

Finally, it should be noted that the *Nachträglichkeit* of looking in 'Archaïscher Torso' is also the reason why the poem can be read both forward and backward to the same effect. Whether you start with the first line (the void, the head that is not there), the middle part (the stony torso), or the final line (the inscription on its pedestal, if you will), the object stands unchanged. Rilke's poem thus resembles the object it represents, a sculpture, but without *being* one.[54]

Anonymity and inexhaustibility

The preceding sections may have shown that in a typical Rilkean scenography, the anonymous interplay of looks, with all its reversals and retrospective repositionings, remains the paradoxical but necessary procedure for objects to take shape. There are more examples to support this point. Brigge's description of the wall, for instance, bears further witness to the anonymity of looking. Before he finally recognizes its objective meaning, Brigge notices 'something' that apparently occupies the wall from the inside. At first he wants to call it 'the stubborn life of those rooms' — rooms, however, that no longer exist. But as he traces the manifestations of this 'stubborn life' in and on the wall, the choice of a more precise name becomes increasingly impossible, and so he starts referring to what he sees simply as 'it':

> *Es* war noch da, *es* hielt sich an den Nägeln, die geblieben waren, *es* stand auf dem handbreiten Rest der Fußböden, *es* war unter den Ansätzen der Ecken, wo *es* noch ein klein wenig Innenraum gab, zusammengekrochen. Man konnte sehen, daß *es* in der Farbe war, die *es* langsam, Jahr um Jahr, verwandelt hatte [...] Aber *es* war auch in den frischeren Stellen [...] *es* [...] *es* [...] (R VI, 750; emphases added)
>
> [*It* was still there, *it* clung to the nails that were left, *it* stood on the hand's breadth of floor that had remained, *it* huddled up in a little bit of space underneath the corners. You could see *it* was in the paint, which *it* had slowly changed, from year to year [...] But *it* was also in the fresher spots [...] *it* [...] *it* [...]]

The cumulative employment of the pronoun 'it' seems to express once again the nameless anonymity that belongs to the actuality of looking. 'I' does not see discrete objects, but 'it' shows many 'things', whose proper name continually eludes the observer. This elusiveness resonates with the 1905 lecture manuscript on Rodin, in which Rilke draws attention precisely to the difficulty of naming the 'things' to see while looking at Rodin's works. His sculptures appear as 'immortal, untouchable, yet higher beings' [ein Nicht-Sterbendes, ein Un-Antastbares, ein Nächst-Höheres] (R V, 261) for which Rilke has neither words nor names: 'And here my words become powerless. What should I say to you: things — things — things — without name — vessels' (R V, 269).

The poems 'Die Fensterrose' and 'Schwarze Katze' are my final examples to demonstrate the characteristic double movement of looking in Rilke's scenographies. Together with 'Archaïscher Torso', these poems represent the most striking scenes of exchanged glances in *Neue Gedichte*. In both cases looking loses its seemingly self-evident origin the moment it starts to see, thereby discovering its essential anonymity — that 'it' looks, not me — as well as its *Nachträglichkeit* — that seeing starts only after looking has begun.

Die Fensterrose

Da drin: das träge Treten ihrer Tatzen
macht eine Stille, die dich fast verwirrt;
und wie dann plötzlich eine von den Katzen
den Blick an ihr, der hin und wieder irrt,

gewaltsam in ihr großes Auge nimmt, —
den Blick, der, wie von eines Wirbels Kreis
ergriffen, eine kleine Weile schwimmt
und dann versinkt und nichts mehr von sich weiß

wenn dieses Auge, welches scheinbar ruht,
sich auftut und zusammenschlägt mit Tosen
und ihn hineinreißt bis ins rote Blut —:

So griffen einstmals aus dem Dunkelsein
der Kathedralen große Fensterrosen
ein Herz und rissen es in Gott hinein.

The Rose Window

In there: the sluggish steps of their paws
creates a silence that almost confuses you;
but as one of the cats suddenly
fixates the look on her, which strays now and then,

with her big eye violently —
that look which, as if caught in a whirl,
swims a short while
and then drowns and forgets itself

when this eye, which seems to rest,
opens up and crashes together with a swoosh
pulling it deep into the red blood — :

so it was when in the darkness
of cathedrals big rose windows
seized a heart and pulled it into God.

Schwarze Katze

Ein Gespenst ist noch wie eine Stelle,
dran dein Blick mit einem Klange stößt;
aber da, an diesem schwarzen Felle
wird dein stärkstes Schauen aufgelöst:

wie ein Tobender, wenn er in vollster
Raserei ins Schwarze stampft,
jählings am benehmenden Gepolster
einer Zelle aufhört und verdampft.

Alle Blicke, die sie jemals trafen,
scheint sie also an sich zu verhehlen,
um darüber drohend und verdrossen
zuzuschauern und damit zu schlafen.
Doch auf einmal kehrt sie, wie geweckt,
ihr Gesicht und mitten in das deine:
und da triffst du deinen Blick im geelen
Amber ihrer runden Augensteine
unerwartet wieder: eingeschlossen
wie ein ausgestorbenes Insekt.

> *Black Cat*
>
> A ghost is still like a spot
> into which your gaze bumps with a ring;
> but here, on this black fur,
> your strongest looking is absorbed:
>
> like a madman's frenzied raving
> and stamping around in the dark
> is abruptly stopped by the padded wall
> of a cell and turned into air.
>
> All the glances that ever struck her
> thus seem to be rejected,
> while she, with a menacing grumpy purr,
> goes to sleep with them.
> But all the sudden, as if awakened, she turns
> her face straight at yours:
> and here you meet your gaze again, within
> the yellow[55] amber of her round eye-stones,
> against your expectation: locked in
> like an extinct insect.

In 'Die Fensterrose', the anonymity of looking is evidenced by the unclear setup of the scene. Who is looking at whom here, and who is seeing what? Is it the cat that looks at the rose window? or the rose window looking at the cat? Whose 'big eye' absorbs that unsteady 'look' on whom? — or on what? After all, the shape of a rose window resembles a big eye, too, especially those mighty rose windows in old cathedrals. These diegetic uncertainties directly correlate with grammatical ambiguities, and necessarily so, since we are dealing with a sceno*graphy* of looking. The identical grammatical gender of *Katze* and *Fensterrose*, which are both feminine in German, makes it difficult to determine whose gaze and eye it is, exactly, the pronoun 'her' stands for in the first and the second stanzas of 'Die Fensterrose'. Moreover, what is the role of the observer in the scene, what happens to her looking as she watches the confusing spectacle 'in there'? Is her gaze affected as well, perhaps even implicated in it?

Even if we were to attribute the initial gaze to the cat, who would thus cast 'her' big eye at 'her', the rose window, what happens then, after looking has begun? That, however, the poem makes explicit: looking loses its origin. The gaze 'swims', 'drowns', and finally 'forgets itself', disappearing in a stream of 'red blood' — whose location and affiliation seems no more certain than that of 'the look on her' or 'her' big eye. Looking belongs to no one in this scene — and to everyone, everything, multiplying everywhere, in all kinds of places. The last stanza further complicates the matter, because this retroactive moment of realization suggests, by way of a complex simile, that just as 'the look on her' was captured by 'her' eye, so the big rose windows of cathedrals used to seize a human heart and pull it into God.

A similar displacement occurs in 'Schwarze Katze'. At first, 'your' — the observer's — looking is 'absorbed' and literally 'dissolved' [aufgelöst] by the cat's sleek black fur. The rhyme between the third and first line, *Felle* | *Stelle*, naturally recalls 'Archaïscher Torso', in which the torso's *Stellen* glimmer like *Raubtierfelle*. Much like this stony surface, the cat's fur does not allow its observer to focus on one single spot but instead refracts and blurs 'all the glances that ever struck' it. This surface, too, is impervious to sight — and, paradoxically, still less seeable than a 'ghost', a shape upon which the gaze would still hit 'with a ring' [mit einem Klange]. There is no place on the cat's sleek black fur where the gaze could rest, no matter how determined you look at it. Her thick black fur absorbs every single glance, just as the padded wall of a prison cell absorbs a prisoner's frenzied ravings. The cat hardly acknowledges receipt of these glances. She seems to tacitly 'reject' and 'do away with' all of them (as I read the unique formulation *an sich zu verhehlen*), responding with no more than a grumpy purr, or some sort of a shivering motion (*zuzuschauern*), while she continues her sleep. The third stanza thus brings the dissolution — and dispossession — of 'your strongest looking' to completion.

Paradoxically, this process of dissolution at the same time enables the observer to regain his vision. He finally recognizes *his* possession, 'your gaze', in and through the eyes of someone else: 'and here you meet your gaze again, within | the yellow amber of her round eye-stones, | against your expectation: locked in | like an extinct insect.' The moment the observer, 'you', finds his gaze again and in consequence starts to see, he must also realize that, unexpectedly, his 'strongest looking' has *already* been retracted, and his possession displaced. The cat's sleek fur has absorbed it completely — and consequently killed it: the observer discovers an 'extinct' gaze in the cat's eyes, not just a mirror image thereof on her eyes. Now 'your' looking, formerly strong and alive, is put to rest in her eyes, like a dead insect preserved in amber. The gaze, ostensibly 'your' possession, has disappeared in there. 'You' was buried in there, and the only reminder of such loss is the lifeless image enshrined in the cat's eye-stones. These eye-stones become the gravestones of 'your' looking, a final image that in fact recalls the 'ghost' from the first line — another extinct gaze — which by the end of the poem returns in the form of a *déjà vu*, as Ralf Simon observes.[56]

Much like the examples discussed in the preceding sections, these two scenographies make manifest a singularly unsettling experience: the effective disappearance of the subject as it faces the 'things' of looking. These undermine the seeming egocentricity of the gaze, indicating instead that the prior attribution of looking to a subject is nothing but an interpretation, a *fictum* after the fact. Looking pertains to a pre-personal order in Rilke's scenographies, because at first there are only '*things to see* and *nobody who sees*', as Maurice Merleau-Ponty describes the topology of vision.[57] At the same time, the noticed 'things' seem to slip away at the same pace as they gain in sensory detail. It is precisely not the closer look or the collection of ever more precise impressions whereby the *aisthēton* could be consolidated and the objective meaning revealed. The assiduous apprentice of looking, Brigge, knows of this paradox. He attempts to study closely and then describe in full and accurate detail the moment when they pierced the breast of his dead father so as to ensure his death. But the attempt is doomed to fail:

> Nein, nein, vorstellen kann man sich nichts auf der Welt, nicht das Geringste. Es ist alles aus so viel einzigen Einzelheiten zusammengesetzt, die sich nicht absehen lassen. Im Einbilden geht man über sie weg und merkt nicht, dass sie fehlen, schnell wie man ist. Die Wirklichkeiten aber sind langsam und unbeschreiblich ausführlich. (R VI, 854)[58]
>
> [No, no, there is nothing in the world that we can imagine, not the least thing. Everything is composed of so many unique details that the eye cannot absorb. In forming an image, we pass over them, not noticing in our haste that they are lacking. But realities are slow and indescribably detailed.]

In showing 'realities' that consist of 'so many unique details', actual perception becomes an inexhaustible process. It is impossible to apprehend the real in a purely empirical way — by 'absorbing' all details with the eye. At the same time, no act of imagination can integrate and identically represent such inexhaustible or 'indescribably detailed' complexity, nor can writerly description. Rilke expands on this double paradox in a famous letter on Cézanne:

> Heute schließt der Salon. Und schon, da ich zum letzten Mal von dort nach Hause gehe, möchte ich ein Violett, ein Grün oder gewisse blaue Töne wieder aufsuchen, von denen mir scheint, daß ich sie hätte besser, unvergeßlicher sehen müssen. Schon, obwohl ich so oft aufmerksam und unnachgiebig davorgestanden habe, wird in meiner Erinnerung der große Farbenzusammenhang der Frau im roten Fauteuil so wenig wiederholbar wie eine sehr vielstellige Zahl. Und doch hab ich sie mir eingeprägt, Ziffer für Ziffer. In meinem Gefühl ist das Bewußtsein ihres Vorhandenseins zu einer Erhöhung geworden, die ich noch im Schlafe fühle; mein Blut beschreibt sie in mir, aber das Sagen geht irgendwo draußen vorbei und wird nicht hereingerufen.
>
> [Today the Salon closes. And already as I am on my way home for the last time I would like to revisit a violet, a green or certain blue tones that I feel I ought to have seen better, more unforgettably. Although I have stood in front of the painting so often, attentively and stubbornly, the comprehensive colour scheme of the woman in the red armchair has already become as impossible for me to reproduce in my memory as a number with a great many digits. Still, I memorized her, digit by digit. As an inner feeling, my awareness of her existence has become an exaltation that I sense even in my sleep. My blood describes her inside me, yet my speech misses that feeling and, instead of being called in, ends up somewhere outside.] (To Clara Rilke on 22 October 1907)

No act of recollection can repeat the 'colour scheme' of Cézanne's painting, in spite of 'relentless' attempts to absorb each visual 'digit' and every shade of colour with the eye. Simultaneously, no act of speaking (or writing) can ever express the received impression, the unique traces that looking produced in blood and feeling. Our sensory 'headlights' [Scheinwerfern], Rilke writes in his essay 'Ur-Geräusch' (R VI, 1091), illuminate only tiny segments of the world, leaving so much more in the dark. The composition and 'cohesion of color' [Farbenzusammenhang] of Cézanne's painting is therefore both inexhaustible and irreproducible.

If learning to see means to *totally* apprehend 'the real' [das Wirkliche] and then describe what has been overlooked 'for millennia', as a famously immodest passage in the *Aufzeichnungen* demands (R VI, 726–28), one could never achieve, in the sense of bringing to completion, such learning. One can only approximate this goal, which is why Brigge commits himself, like all true phenomenologists, to ceaseless description: 'he will have to write, yes, that will be the end' [ja er wird schreiben müssen, das wird das Ende sein] (R VI, 728).

The impossibility of exhaustive perception, let alone of comprehensive description, did not only occur to Rilke. It was also a fundamental premise of nineteenth-century psychophysics, which for that reason replaced qualitative descriptions of phenomena with quantitative methods. But even Husserl, who always rejected the reduction of phenomena to measurable units because he was committed to a descriptive approach, declares the inexhaustibility of perception. In *Ding und Raum*, he points out that, unless the *aisthēton* is apprehended under the *concept* of objecthood, the process of perception 'can go on *in indefinitum*':

> Ist eine Erscheinung vorausgesetzt, so sind damit unendlich viele Möglichkeiten für Erscheinungsreihen offen, die Erscheinungsreihen eines und desselben Dinges wären. [...] Immer ist die Möglichkeit offen, daß es, dasselbe Ding, neue Bestimmtheiten habe, die in den jetzt erscheinenden nicht dargestellt [sind] [...] Im Wesen der Erscheinungen gründet keine Möglichkeit absoluter Sättigung. Jede Sättigung läßt, ideal gesprochen, die Möglichkeit weiterer Sättigung offen.
>
> [If an appearance is presupposed, then infinitely many possible series of appearance are thereby open, which would be series of appearances of one and the same thing. [...] The possibility is always open that it, the same thing, might have new determinations, ones which are not presented in the current appearance [...] The possibility of absolute saturation does not obtain in the essence of appearances. Every saturation leaves open, ideally speaking, the possibility of further saturation.][59]

Despite the increasing detail closer looking yields, there will always be aspects that cannot be simultaneously perceived. What we actually see are never entire objects, steady 'substantial unit[s]' with permanent properties, but only a continual 'change of appearances'.[60] Sensory perception is unable to exhaust its object and apprehend it in full, although perception naturally 'pretends' it could do so, as Husserl remarks elsewhere:

> Die äußere Wahrnehmung ist eine beständige Prätention, etwas zu leisten, was sie ihrem eigenen Wesen nach zu leisten außerstande ist. [...] Was damit gemeint ist, wird Ihnen alsbald klarwerden, wenn Sie schauend zusehen, wie sich der objektive Sinn als Einheit [in] den unendlichen Mannigfaltigkeiten möglicher Erscheinungen darstellt [...] und wie gegenüber den faktischen, begrenzten Erscheinungsabläufen doch beständig ein Bewußtsein von darüber hinausreichenden, von immer neuen Erscheinungsmöglichkeiten besteht. [...] Eine äußere Wahrnehmung ist undenkbar, die ihr Wahrgenommenes in ihrem sinndinglichen Gehalt erschöpfte, ein Wahrnehmungsgegenstand ist undenkbar, der in einer abgeschlossenen Wahrnehmung im strengsten Sinn allseitig, nach der Allheit seiner sinnlich anschaulichen Merkmale gegeben sein könnte.
>
> [External perception is a constant pretension to accomplish something that, by its very nature, it cannot accomplish. [...] My meaning will soon become clear to you once you observe with me how the objective sense presents itself as unity

> [in] the unending manifolds of possible appearances [...] and how a consciousness of ever new possibilities of appearance constantly persists against the factual, limited courses of appearance and so transcends these. [...] It is unthinkable that an external perception could ever be exhausted by its purely sensible content [sinndinglichen Gehalt], and it is equally unthinkable that a perceptual object could ever be given through a strictly self-contained perception, showing the totality of sensory features all at once.][61]

Certain facets cannot be seen and remain to us, as it were, 'in the shadow' (*abgeschattet*), for example, the rear of a house apprehended from the front. We can never see the entire object at once, presently perceive all its attributes, so in turn we come to know that there is always more to see — but again only aspects, parts, pieces. This fact feeds right into Husserl's concept of phenomenological reduction, meaning the 'reduction of being to consciousness'.[62] For if the reality of an object cannot be exhausted through perception, then it is only logical — Husserl would say necessary — to bracket it off, focusing instead on the question of how the object appears to, and is generated by, consciousness. At any rate, Cézanne's works speak, not only on Rilke's account, precisely to the great difficulties of exhausting and then integrating the heterogeneity of a visual field, difficulties that seemed at times insurmountable even to Cézanne himself, despite his dogged objectivity.[63]

Given that perception can neither exhaust nor define the targeted object through physical sensation alone, abstraction becomes a necessary means of comprehension. Without applying an integrative rule to the sensory manifold — an objective meaning *referring* to the *aisthēton* without ever truly re-presenting it — the apperception of an object cannot take its course. This integrative rule, which Rilke in his 1907 letter seems to call 'convincing name', while Husserl names it the noema of perception, is ultimately not to be found *within* perception. Mere receptivity supplies neither the name nor the meaning of the object. The 'convincing name' escapes as soon as it comes into sight, Rilke wrote, while the noema is, according to Husserl himself, an unreal element of perception, 'the pure X abstracted from all predicates' — nothing.[64] In a manner of speaking, the rule unifying, and hence objectifying, the *aisthēton* is in both cases an absent head, too — or, literally, an unseen *Mitte, die die Zeugung trug*: an unseen centre that somehow creates synthesis.

What, then, *do* Rilke's scenographies *know* about looking? What can they tell about perception if they capture this process with neither names nor concepts? They communicate the essential anonymity, *Nachträglichkeit*, and strange reciprocity of looking, among other things, but they tend to do so in a metaphoric way, through figures of speech like personifications, anthropomorphisms, oxymorons, and chiasmata. Their aesthesiology is therefore rooted in metaphors of looking. Indeed, understood as a mode of expression that is not detached from but fundamentally related to the phenomenal world, metaphors would possess the power to represent perceptual occurrences that in experience might at first seem name- and placeless. The reciprocal exchange of imprints staged in so many Rilkean scenographies would amount to much more than a fanciful fiction, or a 'pseudo-dialectical' chiasmus 'that exists only on paper'. Similarly, the associated imagery — revolting devices, undead walls that appear soulful, a torso suffused with the looking of an unknown head, a sleek black fur that absorbs every single gaze, 'knowing' things,[65] and similar anthropomorphisms — would hardly betray symptoms of a mental disorder or, still worse, false consciousness. Instead, all those figures would constitute 'absolute metaphors', to use Hans Blumenberg's term, metaphors characterizing phenomena and occurrences that elude the grasp of conceptual language.[66] Their target and referent, the process of looking, in a sense necessitates metaphoric description, since it marks, not only for Rilke, 'a vacancy of terminology that can only be filled by the imagination'.[67]

Accordingly, the epistemological and more precisely aesthesiological significance of Rilke's scenographies consists largely in their metaphorology. Such 'knowledge' is neither certain nor universally valid, and least of all purely immanent to the text. The reason for this is that we are involved in the emergence of that knowledge. If not seen from within a scene, and hence in abstraction from perception, the presence of an absent head means just a plain contradiction, a pointless oxymoron, while an undead wall inside me represents at best a self-referential metaphor, and at worst a misapplication of language. Rilke's metaphors of looking, like any other poetic figure, do not signify outside the scene of their application. Knowing their meaning requires readerly perception. We must make sense of these metaphors, in the literal sense.[68]

Despite their 'knowledge', Rilke's scenographies are mindful of the blind spot of visual cognition: the lack of certainty and clarity in the con-fusing process of looking. And perhaps, precisely in renouncing conceptual language and its pretence to apprehend the real in favour of scenographies and metaphors, Rilke comes closer to showing the 'things' we see — before the still object comes into sight.

Notes to Part II — Rilke

1. Novalis in *Die Lehrlinge zu Saïs* (N I, 224).
2. Inevitably, Brigge's maxim of 'learning to see' was anticipated by the other great *Augenmensch* of German literature. In the diary he kept for Charlotte von Stein while travelling through Italy, Goethe described his main occupation similarly: 'Ich gehe nur immer herum und herum und sehe und übe mein Aug und meinen innern Sinn' (Goethe, *Italienische Reise*, ed. by Christoph Michel and Hans-Georg Dewitz, 2 vols (Berlin: Deutscher Klassiker Verlag, 2011), I, 660; 21 September 1786).
3. August Stahl, 'Kommentar', in Rilke, *Werke: Kommentierte Ausgabe in vier Bänden*, ed. by Manfred Engel and others, 4 vols (Frankfurt am Main: Insel, 1996), III, 913; Helmut Naumann, *Malte-Studien: Untersuchungen zu Aufbau und Aussagegehalt der 'Aufzeichnungen des Malte Laurids Brigge' von Rainer Maria Rilke* (Rheinfelden: Schäuble, 1983), p. 56.
4. The importance of looking and seeing in Rilke is widely recognized; see, among others, Käte Hamburger, 'Die phänomenologische Struktur der Dichtung Rilkes', in *Rilke in neuer Sicht*, ed. by Käte Hamburger (Stuttgart: Kohlhammer, 1971), pp. 83–158 (first published 1966 in her *Philosophie der Dichter*); Carsten Strathausen, *The Look of Things: Poetry and Vision around 1900* (Chapel Hill: The University of North Carolina Press, 2003), pp. 190–236; Karine Winkelvoss, *Rilke, la pensée des yeux* (Asnières: PIA, 2004); and Anette Horn and Peter Horn, 'Ich lerne sehen': *Zu Rilkes Lyrik* (Oberhausen: Athena, 2010). Though I am concerned specifically with Rilke's middle period, one might ask if and how his notion of seeing changes over time. In *Die fünffingrige Hand: Die Bedeutung der sinnlichen Wahrnehmung beim späten Rilke* (Berlin: De Gruyter, 2002), pp. 34–102, Silke Pasewalck concludes that it changes significantly in Rilke's late works.

However, the notion of seeing Pasewalck ascribes primarily to the late Rilke — i.e. the blurring and finally suspension of the boundary between inside and outside — is equally essential to his middle period, as I will show.

5. I quote Rilke's letters throughout from the edition *Gesammelte Briefe in sechs Bänden*, ed. Ruth Sieber-Rilke, 6 vols (Leipzig: Insel, 1936–40), identifying them by date and recipient.
6. Rilke's curious and very detailed drawing is reproduced in Wolfgang Leppmann, *Rilke: Sein Leben, seine Welt, sein Werk* (Berne: Scherz, 1981), p. 401.
7. In full, the entry reads:

    Alle Dinge sind so bereit, unsere vielen und oft verirrten Gedanken und Wünsche zu bewirten, für kleine Zeit. — In jedem Ding will ich eine Nacht ruhen, wenn ich am Tage mit meinem Tun durch die anderen Dinge ging. — Bei jedem Ding will ich einmal schlafen, von seiner Wärme müd werden, auf seinen Atemzügen auf und nieder träumen, seine liebe gelöste nackte Nachbarschaft an allen meinen Gliedern spüren und stark werden durch den Duft seines Schlafes und dann am Morgen früh, eh es erwacht, vor allem Abschied weitergehen, weitergehen. (Rilke, *Tagebücher aus der Frühzeit*, ed. Ruth Sieber-Rilke und Carl Sieber (Leipzig: Insel, 1942), p. 130; 10 March 1899)

    For further professions of love towards things, see Bernhard Marx's biographical study '*Meine Welt beginnt bei den Dingen': Rainer Maria Rilke und die Erfahrung der Dinge* (Würzburg: Königshausen & Neumann, 2015).

8. This line of scholarship essentially dates back to Paul de Man. The term 'play of signs' [Zeichenspiel], recurrent in deconstructionist interpretations of Rilke, I take from Sabine Schneider, *Verheißung der Bilder: Das andere Medium in der Literatur um 1900* (Tübingen: Niemeyer, 2006), pp. 236–39. Schneider here defends the rhetorical approach to Rilke's thing-poems, including de Man's.
9. David Wellbery, 'Zur Poetik der Figuration beim mittleren Rilke: "Die Gazelle"', in *Zu Rainer Maria Rilke*, ed. by Egon Schwarz (Stuttgart: Klett, 1983), pp. 125–32, discusses the scene of Rilke's thing-poems merely, and only briefly, in terms of 'sequence of events' [Handlungsablauf], while Jonathan Culler, 'Why Lyric?', *PMLA*, 123 (2008), 201–06, generally opposes lyric poetry to narrative representations by contradicting the 'conception of poetry as a dramatization of the encounter between a consciousness and the world', a point he develops in his *Theory of the Lyric*, pp. 91–109. For a contrasting view, see Brian McHale, 'Beginning to Think about Narrative in Poetry', *Narrative*, 17 (2009), 11–27, as well as the contributions gathered in *Narrative* 22 (2014), where the discussion on their relationship is continued.
10. Kittler, *Aufschreibesysteme 1800/1900*, pp. 267–68, 383–85. Kittler's powerful conclusion reads: 'Brigge entkoppelt sein Schreiben von Mündlichkeit und Kommunikation [...] Das Medium Schrift kehrt seine Kälte hervor; es ist Archivieren und sonst nichts. Deshalb kann es das Leben nicht ersetzen, darstellen, sein, sondern nur erinnern, wiederholen, durcharbeiten' (p. 385).
11. Kittler, *Aufschreibesysteme 1800/1900*, pp. 368, 372. For a less polemical account of literary modernism in the context of contemporary psychology, see Judith Ryan, *The Vanishing Subject: Early Psychology and Literary Modernism* (Chicago: University of Chicago Press, 1991).
12. *Rilke-Handbuch: Leben, Werk, Wirkung*, ed. by Manfred Engel (Stuttgart: Metzler, 2004), pp. 303, 299. Note also Luke Fischer, *The Poet as Phenomenologist: Rilke and the New Poems* (New York: Bloomsbury, 2015).
13. This biographic interpretation remains influential to this day; e.g. Rick Barot, 'Rilke's Blue Flower', *The Virginia Quarterly Review*, 82 (2006), 225–39, describes the *Neue Gedichte* as a 'secret homage to what Rilke had seen upon first visiting the studio at sculptor Auguste Rodin's villa' (p. 226). Marx, '*Meine Welt beginnt bei den Dingen'* falls into the same category.
14. Hamburger, 'Die phänomenologische Struktur der Dichtung Rilkes', p. 85.
15. Edmund Husserl, *Arbeit an den Phänomenen: Ausgewählte Schriften*, ed. by Bernhard Waldenfels (Munich: Fink, 2003), pp. 118–21.
16. Wolfgang G. Müller, 'Rilke, Husserl und die Dinglyrik der Moderne', in *Rilke und die Weltliteratur*, ed. by Manfred Engel and Dieter Lamping (Zurich: Artemis & Winkler, 1999), pp. 214–35, largely supports Hamburger's thesis that Rilke's poetic ways of looking resemble Husserlian phenomenology, although he does not consider the phenomenological reduction an inherent

aspect of Rilke's poetry (pp. 224–27). Jennifer A. Gosetti, 'Phenomenological Literature: From the Natural Attitude to "Recognition"', *Philosophy Today*, 45 (2001), 18–27, similarly recognizes a proximity between Husserl and Rilke, though she is unaware of Hamburger's essay. David Wellbery, by contrast, criticizes Hamburger, maintaining that Rilke's thing-poems cannot be read as an 'evocation' [Vergegenwärtigung] (p. 131) of objects and recommends focusing on their self-referential rhetoric and intertextual allusions instead.
17. Hamburger, 'Die phänomenologische Struktur der Dichtung Rilkes', p. 84.
18. Ibid., p. 87.
19. Monika Fick, *Sinnenwelt und Weltseele: Der psychologische Monismus in der Literatur der Jahrhundertwende* (Tübingen: Niemeyer, 1993), pp. 184–223, 300–18; Fick, 'Präsenz: Sinnesphysiologische Konstruktion und ästhetische Transformation der Wahrnehmung: am Beispiel von Przybyszewski, Benn und Rilke', *Scientia Poetica*, 9 (2005), 114–35; Steffen Arndal, '"Ohne alle Kenntnis von Perspektive"? Zur Raumperzeption in Rainer Maria Rilkes *Aufzeichnungen des Malte Laurids Brigge*', *Deutsche Vierteljahrsschrift für Literaturwissenschaft und Geistesgeschichte*, 76 (2002), 105–37; Arndal, 'Sehenlernen und Pseudoskopie: Zur visuellen Verarbeitung des Pariserlebnisses in R. M. Rilkes *Die Aufzeichnungen des Malte Laurids Brigge*', *Orbis Litterarum*, 62 (2007), 210–29; and Ralph Köhnen, 'Das physiologische Wissen Rilkes und seine Cézanne-Rezeption', in *Poetik der Evidenz: Die Herausforderung der Bilder in der Literatur um 1900*, ed. by Helmut Pfotenhauer and others (Würzburg: Königshausen & Neumann, 2005), pp. 141–62. Kittler, *Aufschreibesysteme 1800/1900*, pp. 383–94, 398–405, was the first to detail the influence of both psychophysics and the *Kunsterziehung* movement on Rilke.
20. My translations from Rilke's *Aufzeichnungen* are partly based on those of Michael Hulse (*The Notebooks of Malte Laurids Brigge* (London: Penguin, 2009)) and William Needham (*The Notebooks of Malte Laurids Brigge*, <https://archive.org/details/TheNotebooksOfMalteLauridsBrigge> [accessed 1 April 2019]).
21. Possibly, these two dictions allude to photography. Rilke's letters of 21 October 1913 to Lou Andreas-Salomé would support this assumption: 'Paris war diesmal genau wie ich mir's versprach; schwer. Und ich komme mir vor wie eine photographische Platte, die zu lange belichtet wird, indem ich immer noch dem hier, diesem heftigen Einfluß, ausgesetzt bleibe.' Interestingly, Fernando Pessoa uses the exact same image in his *Livro do desassossego*, a lifelong book project that resembles Rilke's *Aufzeichnungen* not only stylistically due to its fragmentary nature but also thematically, since its protagonist, Bernardo Soares, is likewise concerned with the complex details of perception: 'I'm an ultrasensitive [prolixamente impressionável] photographic plate. All details are engraved in me out of all proportion to any possible whole. The plate fills up with nothing but me. The outer world that I see is pure sensation. I never forget that I feel [sinto]' (Fernando Pessoa, *The Book of Disquiet*, trans. by Richard Zenith (London: Penguin, 2002), p. 543). Regarding Rilke and photography, see Kenneth Scott Calhoon, 'Personal Effects: Rilke, Barthes, and the Matter of Photography', *MLN*, 113 (1998), 612–34, and Stefanie Harris, 'Exposures: Rilke, Photography, and the City', *New German Critique*, 33 (2006), 121–49. In contrast to these scholars, Kittler, *Aufschreibesysteme 1800/1990*, pp. 238–42, 380–83, connects the figure of being 'imprinted' and 'inscribed', recurrent in German literature around 1900, to the typewriter.
22. For a preliminary definition, see 'cathexis' (*Besetzung*) in Jean Laplanche and J. B. Pontalis, *The Language of Psychoanalysis* (London: The Hogarth Press, 1973), pp. 62–65.
23. It is not insignificant that 'dieses ängstlich gehütete Zimmer', in which Chamberlain Brigge chose to die, was also the room in which his mother died (R VI, 715). Her imaginary presence even seems to amplify the Chamberlain's cathectic powers. In light of this and other passages, one could maintain that the spirit of the Mother, that is, the invocation of her name, is a major means of cathexis as it stabilizes Brigge's perception of objects; see my '"Das Anschauen ist eine so wunderbare Sache, von der wir noch so wenig wissen": Szenographien des Schauens beim mittleren Rilke', *Zeitschrift für Ästhetik und Allgemeine Kunstwissenschaft* 59, no. 1 (2014), 141–60 (pp. 150–51 n. 31).
24. In the original, Rilke writes that he is afraid of 'diesem großen Aufgeräumtwerden, das nicht das Leben tut, — von dieser Korrektur der ganzen bisher beschriebenen Seite Leben, die ich mir

dann so rot durchverbessert denke wie in einem Schulheft' (to Gebsattel on 14 January 1912). As for the connection between Rilke and Gebsattel, see Erich Simenauer, *Rainer Maria Rilke: Legende und Mythos* (Berne: Haupt, 1953), pp. 134–35, 192.

25. Viktor Emil von Gebsattel, *Prolegomena einer medizinischen Anthropologie: Ausgewählte Aufsätze* (Berlin: Springer, 1954), p. 151 n. 1: 'Es gibt allerdings ein Einstrahlen der fremden leib-seelischen Wesenheit in den Bereich der Sachwelt, derart, dass diese wie beseelt und durchdrungen erscheint vom Fluidum solcher Wesenheit. Diese Fähigkeit, sich selbst auf Dinge zu übertragen, eignet dem Weibe mehr als dem Mann'.

26. Hartmut Böhme, *Fetishism and Culture: A Different Theory of Modernity*, trans. by Anna Galt (Berlin: De Gruyter, 2014), pp. 91–96, 104, 246, 287–88, 355.

27. In his 1905 lecture manuscript on Rodin, Rilke defines a thing essentially as a 'vessel': 'Ein Ding, im Grunde wieder nur ein Gefäß' (R v, 269).

28. See Ryan, *Vanishing Subject*, pp. 6–22, who charts the development of empirical psychology in the 1880s, including Ernst Mach's *Die Analyse der Empfindungen und das Verhältnis des Physischen zum Psychischen* (1886), as well as Crary, *Techniques of the Observer*, who traces the emergence 'of an emanative, autonomous vision' (p. 142) in physiological optics in the first half of the nineteenth century. Naturally, both these developments are at odds with the idea of static sense impressions.

29. James J. Gibson, *The Ecological Approach to Visual Perception* (Boston: Houghton Mifflin, 1979), pp. 239–40. Noë, p. 17, acknowledges his debt to Gibson, specifically his concept of affordances mentioned in the Introduction (pp. 12–13).

30. *Conversations with Cézanne*, ed. by Michael Doran, trans. by Julie Lawrence Cochran (Berkeley: University of California Press, 2001), p. 198.

31. Ibid., p. 198. Vladimir Vukićević, *Cézannes Realisation: Die Malerei und die Aufgabe des Denkens* (Munich: Fink, 1992) further specifies the concept and practice of *réalisation*, including Cézanne's usage of the term (pp. 15–27, 152–55).

32. Rilke's admiration for Cézanne culminates in the motif of the looking dog, symbolizing the unwavering attention of looking that Rilke recognized in Cézanne's works: '[Cézanne] sat there in front of it like a dog, just looking, without any nervousness, without any ulterior motive [Nebenabsicht]' (to Clara Rilke on 12 October 1907). Similarly, Rilke praises the 'incorruptible sobriety' and 'humble objectivity' of his gaze, which Rilke likens to 'the detached interest of a dog [der sachlich interessierten Teilnahme eines Hundes] that looks at itself in the mirror and thinks: there is another dog' (to Clara Rilke on 23 October 1907).

33. To Clara Rilke on 9 October 1907; cf. Martina Kurz, *Bild-Verdichtungen: Cézannes Realisation als poetisches Prinzip bei Rilke und Handke* (Göttingen: Vandenhoeck & Ruprecht, 2003).

34. *Husserliana*, xvi (1973), 25–41 (pp. 34–35). Ernst Wolfgang Orth, 'Zu Husserls Wahrnehmungs-begriff', *Husserl Studies* 11 (1994), 153–68, provides a competent introduction to Husserl's complex concept of objectivity.

35. Bernhard Waldenfels, *Sinnesschwellen: Studien zur Phänomenologie des Fremden 3* (Frankfurt am Main: Suhrkamp, 1999), pp. 145–46; emphasis in the original.

36. Merleau-Ponty, *Phenomenology of Perception*, p. 250:

> Every perception takes place in an atmosphere of generality and is presented to us anonymously [...] I ought to say that one perceives in me, and not that I perceive. Every sensation carries within it the germ of a dream or depersonalization.

In his phenomenological 'autopsy', *Das Mich der Wahrnehmung: Eine Autopsie* (Frankfurt am Main: Suhrkamp, 2009), Wiesing (pp. 7–9) holds that it is the very process of perceiving by which self-awareness — Me — emerges, thereby reversing the common view that perceptions are produced and owned by Me.

37. Adorno, *Noten zur Literatur*, p. 52, considered Rilke's poetry ideologically compromised and also aesthetically flawed because Rilke attempted to hide, precisely through *Dingkult*, the foreignness of objects, behind the 'lyrical aura' of 'subjective expression', thereby covering up the 'real violence' of commodification.

38. Simenauer, *Rainer Maria Rilke*, p. 158, and Andreas Huyssen, *Twilight Memories: Marking Time in a Culture of Amnesia* (New York: Routledge, 1995), pp. 105–26, both interpret the occurrence of

anthropomorphisms as psychopathological symptoms, though Simenauer links them directly to Rilke's psyche. The direct quotation is Huyssen, p. 115.

39. Andreas Kramer, 'Rilke and Modernism', in *The Cambridge Companion to Rilke*, ed. by Karen Leeder and Robert Vilain (Cambridge: Cambridge University Press, 2010), pp. 113–30 (pp. 120–21). Kramer understands alienation in this context 'not in a Marxian but in a vitalist sense', citing the very passage from Rilke's letter of 8 March 1907 I quoted before to support his argument.

40. Heidegger, *Sein und Zeit* (Tübingen: Niemeyer, 1967), pp. 187–88.

41. Heidegger, *Gesamtausgabe*, XXIV (1975), pp. 244–45. According to Hans-Georg Gadamer, 'Erinnerungen an Heideggers Anfänge', *Dilthey-Jahrbuch*, 4 (1986), 13–26 (p. 14), Heidegger was 'hardly acquainted' with the literature of his day and did not read Rilke's *Aufzeichnungen* until 1924, doing so upon Gadamer's recommendation. Twenty years later, the enthusiastic endorsement of the *Aufzeichnungen* is tacitly withdrawn. In 'Wozu Dichter?', Heidegger first restricts the 'valid' part of Rilke's oeuvre to the *Duineser Elegien* and the *Sonette an Orpheus* (*Gesamtausgabe*, V (1977), 274), and then goes on to criticize these works for remaining within the scope of Western metaphysics (pp. 284–85, 305–07). The rest of Rilke's oeuvre interests Heidegger only insofar as it illuminates the 'essence of technology' (pp. 290–94).

42. I would therefore challenge the interpretation that Rilke's *Aufzeichnungen* represent 'one of the most radical deconstructions of the notion of self we find in modernist writing' (Kramer, p. 123), indeed a 'devolution of the self' (Walter H. Sokel, 'The Devolution of the Self in *The Notebooks of Malte Laurids Brigge*', in *Rilke: The Alchemy of Alienation*, ed. by Frank Baron and others (Lawrence: The Regents Press of Kansas, 1980), pp. 171–90). Surely, selfhood appears fragile in Brigge's *Aufzeichnungen* — after all, Brigge thinks of himself as the 'the impression that will be transformed' [der Eindruck, der sich verwandeln wird] (R VI, 756), but the notion itself is by no means undone. Selfhood remains an indispensable concept in the *Aufzeichnungen* insofar as anxiety — Brigge's innermost feeling and therefore core of his self — is the chief means of objectification.

43. Paul de Man, *Allegories of Reading: Figural Language in Rousseau, Nietzsche, Rilke, and Proust* (New Haven: Yale University Press, 1979), pp. 20–56 (pp. 38, 40).

44. Ibid., pp. 44–45. In *Natur und Subjekt* (Frankfurt am Main: Suhrkamp, 1988), pp. 251–53, Hartmut Böhme made a similar observation, but came to a different conclusion. Rilke's 'Archaïscher Torso', Böhme writes here, stages the 'ocular character of works of art' and specifically the fact that each of these becomes, quoting Hegel's *Ästhetik*, a 'thousand-eyed Argus' (TWA XIII, 203) when looked at. However, Böhme regards the transformation of the torso into an Argus eye at the end of the poem not as a spurious 'totalization', as de Man does, but as a 'reconciliation' between the observer and the aesthetic object.

45. De Man, *Allegories of Reading*, pp. 30, 34. For an incisive critique of de Man's method of reading, not only in the case of Rilke, see Stanley Corngold, 'Error in Paul de Man', *Critical Inquiry*, 8 (1982), 489–507. Corngold's key observation (pp. 500–03) is that the method of composition de Man attributed to Rilke — setting up an apparent opposition, arranging for its chiastic inversion, and finally showing the spuriousness of that opposition through a totalizing gesture — is virtually identical to his own method of interpretation.

46. *Sturz* has the common meaning of a 'fall' or a 'tumble', but it is also an architectural term designating the horizontal support on top of two vertical structures. A *Türsturz* or 'lintel', the horizontal beam supporting the top of a door, would be an example, as opposed to the threshold at its bottom, *Türschwelle*. I think the poem invokes primarily this architectural meaning, which my rendition of *Sturz* as 'arch' seeks to imitate.

47. Neither one nor multiple observers are mentioned verbatim in 'Archaïscher Torso'. In representing a process of looking, however, the poem at least implies the place of an observer, thus prompting readerly aesthesis.

48. Regarding the 'religious' authority of this 'command from within the stone', see Peter Sloterdijk, *Du musst dein Leben ändern: Über Anthropotechnik* (Frankfurt am Main: Suhrkamp, 2009), pp. 37–51.

49. R V, 149–50: 'und es gab Stellen ohne Ende und keine, auf der nicht etwas geschah. Es gab keine Leere [...] nur unzählbar viele lebendige Flächen'; one of many passages in which Rilke

calls attention to the vivid surface structure of Rodin's sculptures. As for Rilke's suggestive appropriation of Rodin's sculptures in the domain of language, see Brigid Doherty, 'Rilke's Magic Lantern: Figural Language and the Projection of "Interior Action" in the Rodin Lecture', in *Interiors and Interiority*, ed. by Ewa Lajer-Burcharth and Beate Söntgen (Berlin: De Gruyter, 2016), pp. 313–45.
50. *Husserliana*, III.I (1977), 200–313 (pp. 301–03, 231).
51. Strathausen, *The Look of Things*, p. 27.
52. The German term *unerhört* bears several interpretations, so that different translations are possible. The head could be *unerhört* in the sense of having 'never been heard of' and of being 'unprecedented', either in a positive or a negative way. But the head could also be *unerhört* in terms of appearance, again in either a positive or a negative way. It may have looked 'exceptional' and 'extraordinary', or even 'shocking' and 'bizarre'.
53. Laplanche on 'deferred action' in *International Dictionary of Psychoanalysis*, ed. by Alain de Mijolla, 3 vols (Detroit: Thomson Gale, 2005), I, 378. Laplanche here also suggests that it was neither Freud nor Lacan who fully developed the concept of *Nachträglichkeit* but in fact 'Jean-Bertrand Pontalis and Jean Laplanche' (ibid.). This assertion might seem self-aggrandizing, but has a sound basis in fact, as shown by Jonathan House and Julie Slotnick, 'Après-Coup in French Psychoanalysis: The Long Afterlife of Nachträglichkeit: The First Hundred Years, 1893 to 1993', *The Psychoanalytic Review*, 102 (2015), 683–708.
54. Norbert Fuerst, *Phases of Rilke* (Bloomington: Indiana University Press, 1958) similarly observes that the *Neue Gedichte* 'stand, in crowded galleries, like immovable statues' (p. 67), and also that it is 'characteristic of many of these chiseled and sculptured poems that one can read them backwards, or that one can read back and forth in them. They are more spatial than temporal' (p. 75). However, the enabling factor is not their spatiality — Rilke's poems *are not* sculpture — but the *Nachträglichkeit* of looking.
55. The strange adjective *geel* also calls to mind the German noun *Gel*, 'gel, jelly'. Therefore, 'within the jellylike amber' is the other possible translation of *im geelen Amber*.
56. Simon, *Der poetische Text als Bildkritik*, p. 99. Simon thinks of this and all the other thing-poems by Rilke as 'images', by which he means, somewhat vaguely, the 'force field connecting the scene' as a whole (p. 96). But the poem's content is not exclusively visual. It is not an 'image', but describes an entire process — precisely a scene — of perception, potentially activating other senses too. For example, the tangible description of the fur's surface qualities, its sleek, glossy, upholstered appearance, instils a strong sense of touch as well. For that reason, Rilke's poem seems best described as a scenography — unless, that is, the word 'image' is itself turned into a rather vague metaphor.
57. Merleau-Ponty, *Phenomenology of Perception*, p. 275.
58. Cf. the radical concept of literary modernism Kittler derives from this passage in his *Aufschreibesysteme 1800/1900*, p. 396.
59. *Husserliana*, XVI (1973), 130–31; Husserl, *Thing and Space: Lectures of 1907*, trans. by Richard Rojcewicz (Dordrecht: Kluwer, 1997), pp. 108–09. Cf. Husserl's summary, XVI, 135–39.
60. Husserl makes this contrast in 'Philosophie als strenge Wissenschaft' (*Husserliana*, XXV (1986), 26–31), juxtaposing his dynamic temporal concept of perception with substantialist notions of thinghood.
61. *Husserliana*, XI (1966), 3; Husserl, *Analyses Concerning Passive and Active Synthesis: Lectures on Transcendental Logic*, trans. by Anthony J. Steinbock (Dordrecht: Kluwer, 2001), pp. 39–40.
62. *Husserliana*, II (1973), viii: 'die Auflösung des Seins in Bewusstsein'. This is in fact Walter Biemel's brilliant paraphrase of the following pp. 4–7, where Husserl explains the phenomenological reduction.
63. These difficulties are documented by Merleau-Ponty, 'Cézanne's Doubt', in *Sense and Non-Sense*, trans. by Hubert L. Dreyfus and Patricia Allen Dreyfus (Evanston: Northwestern University Press, 1964), pp. 9–25. 'Dogged objectivity' is my paraphrase of Rilke; see n. 32.
64. *Husserliana*, III.I (1977), 302.
65. 'Knowing' things: a puzzling cipher Rilke used repeatedly. A foremost example is the letter to his Polish translator, Witold Hulewicz, dating 13 November 1925. Rilke here voices the

concern that 'the things that know us [die uns mitwissenden Dinge] are vanishing, and there is no way of replacing them anymore. *We are perhaps the last ones who will have known such things.*' Rilke here also professes that the loss of 'knowing' things is caused by the intrusion of 'empty, indifferent things from America', fake objects he condemns as 'Schein-Dinge, *Lebens-Attrappen*'. For a contextualization of this letter, see Christoph Jamme, 'Der Verlust der Dinge: Cézanne — Rilke — Heidegger', *Deutsche Zeitschrift für Philosophie*, 40 (1992), 385–97.

66. According to Blumenberg, *Theorie der Unbegrifflichkeit*, ed. by Anselm Haverkamp (Frankfurt am Main: Suhrkamp, 2007), an 'absolute metaphor' cannot be replaced with a non-figurative expression or concept, because its very imagery is, or has become, the only way to state its meaning. Metaphors must be regarded as absolute, Blumenberg writes, '[falls] sie sich gegenüber dem terminologischen Anspruch als resistent erweisen, nicht in Begrifflichkeit aufgelöst werden können' (p. 11). An example for an absolute metaphor would be the phrase 'God is the eternal light', with the metaphoric predicate, 'light', expressing the meaning of the highly abstract subject, 'God', in irreducible concreteness.

67. Ibid., p. 74.

68. Even Franz Kafka, whom many interpreters consider the epitome of literary self-reference and 'intransitive' writing, concedes (with much regret, of course) the impossibility of detaching literary language from the world of phenomena. In the case of metaphorical expressions, the dependency strikes him as particularly strong. Considering the trivial metaphor 'I warm myself at [your words] in this sad winter' in his so-called 'diaries' (Kafka, *Tagebücher*, ed. Hans-Gerd Koch and others (Frankfurt am Main: Fischer, 1990), p. 875 (6 December 1921)), Kafka concludes that this expression, too, only makes sense in the context of a scene, which he then spells out (ibid.): 'I warm myself at ...' quite naturally calls to mind 'a stove', around which we might see gathered 'a maid who tends the fire', as well as 'a cat' enjoying its warmth, even some 'poor old person' sitting nearby.

§3. *Listening to Proust's* Recherche

Vertrau den Büchern nicht zu sehr; sie sind | Gewesenes und Kommendes.¹

[Do not trust the books too much; they | Have been and will come.]

Music and memory, or, the leitmotif

Music plays a major role in Marcel Proust's *À la recherche du temps perdu*. One of the first commentators who sought to unravel the import of music in Proust's magnum opus was the French art critic and musicologist André Cœuroy. In 1923, shortly after Proust's death, but predating the publication of *La Prisonnière* and *Le Temps retrouvé*, writings particularly rich in discussions and performances of music, Cœuroy published a chapter on 'Music in the Work of Marcel Proust'. At the end of the chapter, Cœuroy concludes that:

> music is so marvelously exciting to Marcel Proust [...] because it is ceaselessly arousing the memory of which it is so bounteously the purveyor, because it suddenly springs forth from the unconscious at the summons of an attentive power. For anyone who attempts, as does Proust, the resurrection of a life by means of memory, music is the most precious auxiliary. Without a musical memory, would Swann be Swann at all? The *petite phrase de Vinteuil*, sign of a complex love [...] is the very key to his soul, just as, in another sense, it is the key to Proust's whole theory of art.²

Cœuroy supports his conclusion by citing René Laloue, according to whom Proust 'has informed us that "in the last volume he bases the whole of his theory of art upon unconscious recollections", and these to him are realities after the style of the *petite phrase de Vinteuil* which the musician by no means invented but simply released into freedom'.³

Evidently, Cœuroy draws a connection between music and memory. He calls music the 'purveyor' and 'most precious auxiliary' of memory and, therefore, the key to 'the resurrection of a life by means of memory'. Cœuroy thus likens the evocative power of music to the culmination of the protagonist's lifelong quest for 'lost time' in moments of involuntary memory at the end of the *Recherche* (which in 1923, when Cœuroy published his piece, was yet to be told: *Le Temps retrouvé* did not appear for another four years). The experience of music and particularly the music of Vinteuil, 'the key to Proust's whole theory of art', would prepare and inspire the resurrection of the past through involuntary memory. Music and involuntary memory would be two sides of the same coin.

Since Cœuroy's early observations, the demonstration of the *Recherche*'s 'musical structure' has become a classic goal of Proust scholarship. And although the doyen of modern Proust scholarship, Jean-Yes Tadié, issued the warning to not fall for the 'metaphor' of 'musical structure',⁴ it is hard to disagree with Françoise Leriche's general verdict that Proust was 'at heart a musician who writes in a musical rather than logical fashion'.[5] Or as Timothy Mathews recently put it, 'Proust's music, like any novelist's, is music in words and not sound'.[6]

Proust's musical style is audible in the prosody of individual phrases, but it also pervades key episodes of the *Recherche*, so that one might say his book has a fundamentally musical architecture. Defending this point and specifying the supposed musicality of the *Recherche* in a concrete, technical sense is my immediate goal in this chapter. To achieve this goal, I will employ two modes of listening. On the one hand, I listen closely to the music *of* the *Recherche*, to the sound of its verbal texture, which shapes the perceptions of the reader. On the other hand, I listen closely to the music *in* the *Recherche*, to the ways in which music shapes the life of the protagonist — whom I call, following the author's own suggestion, 'Marcel'[7] — and finally summons him to become a writer. The division of the chapter into two sections, 'Longtemps' and 'The music of Vinteuil', reflects this difference.

That Proust *intended* to connect involuntary memory to music is already evident in the earliest drafts of *Le temps retrouvé*, composed in 1910/11 but not published until 1982. These draft notebooks describe, among other things, a reception at the palace of the Princess de Guermantes. A heavily revised version of this reception — it is a matinee concert — still constitutes the end of *Le temps retrouvé*. In the early drafts, however, the concert includes a performance of Richard Wagner's so-called *Karfreitagszauber* ('Good Friday Spell'), an orchestral arrangement of motifs from the third act of *Parsifal*. At one point during the concert, a certain 'motif of the "Good Friday Spell"' triggers speculations about the essence of reality, of which involuntary memory affords an epiphanic perception. Shortly thereafter, the narrator of the draft version compares the 'spiritual essence' of reality to 'truly musical moments'. In yet another, later draft, Proust explicitly reminds himself to 'present the discovery of Time regained in the sensations induced by the spoon, the tea, etc.' — the famous instances of involuntary memory which in *Le temps retrouvé* herald the end of Marcel's quest and simultaneously the birth of his book — 'as an illumination à la Parsifal'.[8] From these passages from Proust's early drafts, musicologist and semiotician Jean-Jacques Nattiez concludes that 'as early as 1910–11 [...] music, and most particularly the "Good Friday Spell", was seen as [...] a perfect model for the workings of involuntary memory' and hence 'for the literary enterprise' as a whole.[9]

Why is it that Wagner figures so prominently in these early drafts? Why should it be a Wagner opera that reveals the essential link between music and memory? Personal taste certainly played a role. Proust was an ardent Wagnerian, and this to such a degree, as anecdote has it, that 'in spite of asthma, he mounted on to the platform of the great tower of the château de Coucy, while Bertrand de Fenelon, to encourage him, sang softly the "Good Friday Music" from *Parsifal*'.[10] *Parsifal* was an all-time favourite of his that greatly influenced the composition of the *Recherche*, notably its conception as a quest for redemption. Nattiez detailed Proust's debt to *Parsifal*, demonstrating in particular the parallels between Charles Swann and Amfortas on the one hand and Marcel and Parsifal on the other. Margret Mein similarly related the 'progression towards perfect redemption' in the *Recherche* to

Wagner's *Parsifal*.[11] Additionally, *Tannhäuser, Lohengrin, Tristan und Isolde*, and *Der Ring des Nibelungen* have left their marks on the *Recherche* — works, Proust once said, he knew 'almost by heart'.[12] There are, for example, resemblances between the ingestion of the madeleine and the ingestion of the love potion in *Tristan und Isolde*, as well as striking parallels between Tristan's sickening love for Isolde and Swann's fatal love for Odette.[13] At moments, hearing itself becomes Wagnerian in the *Recherche* — for example, when the sirens' warning of an imminent German Zeppelin raid are described as sounding like riding Valkyries (*Retrouvé* 65–66/vi, 84).[14]

Proust later consciously diminished Wagner's significance by replacing his works partly with compositions of Vinteuil. For example, the aforementioned matinee concert concluding the novel now features Vinteuil's Septet. Nonetheless, the fictional works of Vinteuil cannot eclipse the great technical significance of Wagner for Proust, for the composition of the *Recherche* crucially depends on the compositional method for which Wagner is most famous — his leitmotif technique.

A musical leitmotif, to be clear, is usually based on a short acoustic figure or phrase that recurs throughout a musical piece in more or less the same form. In Wagner's operas, however, a leitmotif is not an independent acoustic figure, nor are its recurrences determined by purely musical rules and conventions. Wagner's leitmotifs are interwoven with the dramatic action on the stage. They essentially combine music and scene, recurring acoustic motifs and dramatic actions (which is why Wagner's operas, against his express desire, are frequently described as 'music-dramas').[15] Wagner makes this point about leitmotifs succinctly in his late essay 'Über die Anwendung der Musik auf das Drama' (1879) — although he uses that term neither here nor elsewhere in his writings, referring to recurring motifs instead as *Grundthemen, Grundmotive*, or *melodische Momente*.[16] The unity of 'the new form of dramatic music', Wagner explains in the essay, results from

> einem das ganze Kunstwerk durchziehenden Gewebe von Grundthemen, welche sich, ähnlich wie im Symphoniesatze, gegenüberstehen, ergänzen, neu gestalten, trennen und verbinden: nur daß hier die ausgeführte und aufgeführte dramatische Handlung die Gesetze der Scheidungen und Verbindungen gibt [...]
>
> [a web of basic themes that pervade the entire work and that are juxtaposed, complemented, reshaped, separated, and combined in a way resembling symphonic movements, the only difference being that the laws of separation and combination are given by the performed and staged dramatic plot [...]][17]

The 'only' of the qualifying clause is undoubtedly a drastic understatement. If the recurrences and interactions of the 'basic themes' or leitmotifs are indeed 'given' by the 'performed and staged dramatic plot', they are no longer independent figures in an immanent musical process resembling 'a symphonic movement'. Instead, leitmotifs are *musicodramatic* units evolving on stage and through dramatic action. They are audio-visual gestures emphasizing and commenting on the scene, which is why their recurrences are based on dramaturgic rather than purely musical considerations. In a word, leitmotifs are scenographic devices and as such achieve their full reality only during the operatic performance — in the context of scenes to be heard, seen, and felt by the audience.

The architecture of the Bayreuth Festspielhaus directly reflects this priority of the stage in relation to the musical substance of leitmotifs. In an essay concerning its architectural design, Wagner explains that the orchestra is intentionally hidden from sight so as to minimize 'ugly interruptions' and distraction from the dramatic scene. At Bayreuth, the 'always irritating visibility [die stets sich aufdrängende Sichtbarkeit] of the technical apparatus for the production of tone' had to disappear in the 'mythical abyss' between auditorium and stage.[18] It was precisely for this prioritization of the stage — or 'the drama', as Wagner likes to call it — that Nietzsche charged Wagner, 'our *scenic artist* par excellence', with having degraded music to a 'theatrical rhetoric', to a 'semiotics of tone' based on 'the hallucination [...] of gestures' on stage.[19] That leitmotifs appeal as musicodramatic units to two senses simultaneously, eyes and ears, only amplifies their rhetorical power of persuasion.

Wagner discusses the scenographic implementation of leitmotifs and their dramaturgic function on stage in his lengthy book *Oper und Drama* (1852). Here, he conceives of leitmotifs essentially as signals and gestural cues. They are means of conveying 'the deepest secret of the poet's intention', Wagner writes, and more specifically means for the poet-composer to provide the audience with 'emotional signposts [Gefühlswegweisern] through the complex architecture of the drama', as they do by producing 'anticipation' [Ahnung] and 'remembrance' [Erinnerung] upon recurrence.[20] The return of a leitmotif reminds the audience of things previously seen and words previously heard, thereby adding an invisible layer of retrospective, and possibly also prospective, meaning to the current scene.

The 'musical prose' of the *Ring* cycle represents perhaps the most stringent application of this method to convey reminiscences or the air of prophecy through musical cues, as well as psychological undercurrents and overarching dramatic intentions. At the same time, the *Ring* betrays, more than any other work, Wagner's often tedious urge to explain himself. Driven by the constant fear of being misinterpreted — undoubtedly an indication of vanity — Wagner was, as Carl Dahlhaus wrote, obsessed with the 'perfect justification and drastic illustration' of his dramatic ideas.[21] The notion to employ leitmotifs primarily as scenographic means and to dramaturgic ends is the natural consequence of such a disposition. Wagner was simply unable to think of leitmotifs in abstraction from their scenic context. For him, the 'scenic-musical implementation' of the overall idea was therefore the sole measure of aesthetic success, Dalhaus points out, whereas musical ingenuity became just a means to dramatic ends.[22] Regarding Wagner primarily as a scenic artist, rather than a musical genius, as Nietzsche did, is therefore no denigration, really, but entirely in line with Wagner's self-understanding.

The power of leitmotifs to add commentary and explanation obviously depends on acts of recollection, the third essential component of a leitmotif technique. Indeed, it is both the musical and scenic memory of the audience that brings a leitmotif into full effect. In order to interpret its dramatic meaning, the opera viewers have first to recognize the motif acoustically, then recall, however dimly, its scenic origins and past uses, and then apply this memory to the context in which the motif resounds anew. At the same time, the recurrence of a leitmotif may generate fresh memories. Heard in a new dramatic context, a certain musical figure might take on an additional, if not entirely different, meaning and thus involuntarily trigger yet unknown associations upon its next return. For that reason, musicologists regularly stress the pivotal role of memory in perceiving and interpreting leitmotifs.[23]

The mnemonic power of leitmotifs — which Baudelaire had characterized by that exact term[24] — must have been intriguing to an author who was preoccupied with questions of memory, memory formation, and more generally the passage (if not the essence) of time. And indeed, a letter to Lucien Daudet Proust suggests this precise connection, because in it Proust compares the first volume of the *Recherche* to an 'overture' filled with 'leitmotifs' — or rather 'pieces you don't recognize as leitmotifs when heard in isolation', not yet knowing 'how they will be set afterwards'.[25] An overture is pure music, whereas leitmotifs signify only in a dramatic context, as part of a scene.

Realizing the ambition to fill a novel with leitmotifs is quite another matter, of course, for it is self-evident that Wagner's *musical* leitmotif technique cannot be directly transferred onto a *verbal* composition, a work of literature. As always, mere intentions have little bearing on what is actually possible and can be accomplished in a work. Terms such as 'leitmotif', 'leitmotif technique', and also 'musicality' must therefore achieve an intrinsic meaning. They must be shown to designate actual literary features, namely, recurring patterns in the verbal texture of the *Recherche*. Such patterns of verbal recurrences, one of which I will single out in the next section, would correspond to the iterations of musical motifs. Yet equally important, as in the case of Wagner, would be the literary scene of recurrence, the scenography in which these verbal motifs recur, because their significance derives precisely from the scene in which they occur, not from their literal meaning.

If both go hand in hand, one could justly call that system of verbal recurrences the literary equivalent of a musicodramatic (i.e. Wagnerian) leitmotif technique. Understood in this way, a literary leitmotif technique would be a concrete scenographic arrangement with an implicit logic of perception or aesthesiology. Its actualization, however, depends on the memory of the listening reader. He or she actualizes each leitmotif and brings it into bodily effect by associating a recurrent verbal motif with diegetic situations and actions. The text provides only the raw material, the score to be staged by the reader. And this is almost inevitable if Gérard Genette was right in saying that 'the whole of Proust's narrative text can be defined as scene', a series of scenes glued together through essayistic reflection and ellipses, rather than narratorial summaries, as was customary before Proust.[26]

The impression that the *Recherche* is pervaded by leitmotifs — not in the trivial sense of recurrent topics or themes, but precisely in the Wagnerian manner — was articulated early on. Of these early articulations, Edmund Wilson's 1928 review is, as we shall soon see, particularly striking as to its precision. Wilson notices that:

> Proust's novel is [...] a symphonic structure rather than, in the ordinary sense, a narrative. Like so many other important modern writers, Proust had been

> reared in the school of symbolism and had all the symbolist's preoccupation with musical effects. Like many of his generation, he was probably as deeply influenced by Wagner as by any writer of books, and it is characteristic of his conception of his art that he was in the habit of speaking of the 'themes' of 'A La Recherche du Temps Perdu.' The book begins with what is really an overture, of which it is important [...] to note the first chord: '*Longtemps, je me suis couché de bonne heure*', followed by a second sentence in which the word '*temps*' twice recurs.[27]

Wilson does not follow up on this important intuition regarding the opening phrase or 'chord' of *Du côté de chez Swann*. Other commentators who intuited leitmotifs in Proust similarly neglected to specify their meaning. Of course, considering Proust's stated intentions and personal tastes it seems only natural to suppose that his literary composition should contain leitmotifs, yet this supposition is hardly ever supported through technical analysis and concrete examples.[28]

The notable exceptions to this common neglect are studies by Uwe Daube and Inge Backhaus. But regrettably, these two studies have little bearing on the issue to which I am attending, the music of and in the *Recherche*. Daube negates any meaningful connection between Wagner's musical and Proust's literary leitmotif technique, focusing instead on the semantics of recurrent themes or topoi such as Balbec and Venice. According to Daube, leitmotifs are little more than hermeneutic riddles, allegories of moral questions the reader gradually deciphers, just as Marcel ostensibly does.[29] Backhaus, on the other hand, draws conceptual parallels between Wagner and Proust, but she understands leitmotifs in Proust neither as verbal and hence acoustic figures, nor as affecting readers, and so knowingly disregards two defining traits of leitmotifs according to Wagner: their materiality, sound, and their effective target, the audience. Instead, she explains leitmotifs in purely fictional terms, as something that has existence and effect only within the imaginary world of Proust's narrative. The 'difference between stage (as the site of musical and dramatic action) and audience (as the site of perception)', constitutive of Wagner's — and frankly any — leitmotif technique, consequently breaks down, as she notes herself. Leitmotifs become fictional impressions triggering fictional sensations the reader can only imagine.[30]

'Longtemps'

'Longtemps, je me suis couché de bonne heure' (*Swann* 3).[31] This placid opening phrase will turn out, upon further reading and reflection, to have set the stage for Marcel's long-lasting search for 'lost time', initiated as he hovers between memories of the past and the present situation, as between sleep and waking.

What does the phrase specifically introduce? Two things: a recurring sound, and the nucleus of a diegetic theme. It exposes the recurring sound *longtemps*, which is privileged in a remarkable way: it is the very first resonance of the first chapter, 'Combray', and hence the opening chord of the entire *Recherche*. Accordingly, *longtemps* rings out as a distinct acoustic motif. As it rings out in the context of a scene, however, this acoustic motif is immediately associated with the situation on the literary stage: Lying on his bed, not quite awake or asleep, Marcel finds himself in an intermediate state of self-awareness, in a transitory sphere between no and full consciousness of the temporal and spatial situation — a state that continues to fascinate phenomenologists.[32] Immersed in this state outside linear time and physical space, the sound *longtemps* makes its entrance. Then Marcel starts to drift. He feels in a position to 'apply himself' to events, places, stories that, while palpably present to his mind, lack spatiotemporal reality in themselves:

> [J]e n'avais pas cessé en dormant de faire des réflexions sur ce que je venais de lire, mais ces réflexions avaient pris un tour un peu particulier; il me semblait que j'étais moi-même ce dont parlait l'ouvrage: une église, un quatuor, la rivalité de François Ier et de Charles Quint. Cette croyance survivait pendant quelques secondes à mon réveil; elle ne choquait pas ma raison, mais pesait comme des écailles sur mes yeux et les empêchait de se rendre compte que le bougeoir n'était plus allumé. Puis elle commençait à me devenir inintelligible, comme après la métempsycose les pensées d'une existence antérieure; le sujet du livre se détachait de moi, j'étais libre de m'y appliquer ou non [...] [*Swann* 3]

> [I had gone on thinking, while I was asleep, about what I had just been reading, but these thoughts had taken a rather peculiar turn; it seemed to me that I myself was the immediate subject of my book: a church, a quartet, the rivalry between François I and Charles V. This impression would persist for some moments after I awoke; it did not offend my reason, but lay like scales upon my eyes and prevented them from registering the fact that the candle was no longer burning. Then it would begin to seem unintelligible, as the thoughts of a previous existence must be after reincarnation; the subject of my book would separate itself from me, leaving me free to apply myself to it or not [...]] [1, 1]

With this diegetic specification of the motif *longtemps* the exposition of the narrator's leitmotif is complete. Associated with the place of some timeless in-between as its corresponding diegetic theme, the sound of *longtemps* now embodies a feeling in which the usual experience of temporality as a steady progression of discrete moments is suspended. The symbol of such hovering between different times and places, present in the scene, is the bed. Henceforth, the motif *longtemps* may recall and so render present precisely that peculiar feeling, or rather the memory of how it feels. Its evocative force, heard and felt many times throughout the novel, thus exceeds its plain lexical meaning, 'for a long time'.

A leitmotif is recurrent by definition, and the motif *longtemps* returns at several key moments of the *Recherche*. Whenever it rings out, it summons both the presence and the extra-temporal position of the narrator Marcel, that hovering in-between whence he looks back and reflects upon the story of his life, his lifelong search. I will provide five paradigmatic examples to demonstrate the systematicity of its recurrences, as well as its scenographic implementations.[33]

The narratorial leitmotif rings out after the opening episode of *Du côté de chez Swann* — known as 'Awakenings' [Reveils] — has come to a close:

> À Combray, tous les jours dès la fin de l'après-midi, *longtemps* avant le moment où il faudrait me mettre au lit et rester, sans dormir, loin de ma mère et de ma grand'mère, ma chambre à coucher redevenait le point fixe et douloureux de mes préoccupations. (*Swann* 9; emphasis added)

At Combray, as every afternoon ended, long before the time when I should have to go to bed and lie there, unsleeping, far from my mother and grandmother, my bedroom became the fixed point on which my melancholy and anxious thoughts were centred. (I, 8)

Longtemps here rings out in the same diegetic context as it initially does, in the bedroom, where young Marcel lies 'unsleeping', thus recalling the timeless and strangely displaced feeling of in-betweenness of old Marcel at the beginning. The bedroom sets also the main stage for the childhood reminiscences to follow, first the unsettling projections of Marcel's magic lantern, and shortly thereafter the painful deprivation of the motherly good-night kiss due to the evening visits of Monsieur Swann.

The leitmotif returns a second time at the beginning of the brief interlude connecting the shorter first with the longer second part of the Combray chapter: 'C'est ainsi que, pendant *longtemps*, quand, réveillé la nuit, je me ressouvenais de Combray, je n'en revis jamais que cette sorte de pan lumineux' [And so it was that, for a long time afterwards, when I lay awake at night and revived old memories of Combray, I saw no more of it than this sort of luminous panel] (Swann 43/I, 49; emphasis added). This recurrence musically prepares the first experience of involuntary memory, the madeleine episode described shortly thereafter. Just as a leitmotif triggers a memory through a sensory and more precisely acoustic cue, so does the taste of the madeleine remind an aged Marcel of his childhood in Combray. The motif *longtemps* impels the drifting back in time precisely by summoning that feeling of timelessness which by now has been firmly, if involuntarily, associated with its sound. This temporal drift, which for the narrator is caused by a taste, but for the reader triggered by a sound, finally culminates in a full resurrection of Combray.

The leitmotif returns a third time at the end of the Combray chapter, opening the final cadence and last paragraph: 'Certes quand approchait le matin, il y avait bien *longtemps* qu'était dissipée la brève incertitude de mon réveil' [It is true that, when morning drew near, I would long have settled the brief uncertainty of my waking dream (I, 223)] (Swann 184/I, 223; emphasis added). This leitmotific recurrence is consistent with the symphonic convention that after a period of development main themes are finally recapitulated in their original form. This recapitulation concluding the piece confirms the continuity of the themes, specifically their ability to withstand those variations and alterations, even re-combinations and omissions that have taken place since their first introduction, thereby producing symmetry and closure.

However, this third recurrence of *longtemps* happens not at all without dramatic motivation. Once more ringing out in the bedroom of the narrator, the leitmotif returns to its diegetic origin. The recurrence is thus strictly in line with Wagner's aforementioned doctrine that the musical process must be driven by dramatic necessities rather than purely formal musical conventions. In comparison to the opening scene, however, the situation is subtly altered. The leitmotif now occurs in the context of a scene of awakening and for that reason shimmers in fresh and as yet unknown hues: The 'state of darkness' (*Swann* 3/I, 1) of Marcel's waking dream on the first page of 'Combray' is now brightened by feeble traces of daylight, by a 'first white, correcting ray' coming through 'the darkness' like an 'uplifted forefinger of dawn' [le doigt levé du jour] (*Swann* 184/I, 224).

Just these three recurrences of *longtemps*, and especially the second one, raise the question of how this leitmotif relates to 'the miracle of an analogy' (*Retrouvé* 178/VI, 223) effected by involuntary memory. The 'miracle of an analogy', to be clear, refers to the famous flashbacks that were prompted by, for example, the taste of the madeleine and the feel of the uneven paving stones in the courtyard of the Guermantes' palace. In these moments, a present perception brings back a remembrance of things past. Involuntarily, that sensory cue revives the essence of past experience, which as a singular occurrence would appear to be lost forever, suffusing present perceptions with past sensations and memories, and vice versa. The result is the virtual coexistence or simultaneity of chronologically distinct incidents.

Marcel describes this experience as being 'at the present moment and at the same time in the context of a distant moment, so that the past was made to encroach upon the present and I was made to doubt whether I was in the one or the other', placing him above or 'outside time' (*Retrouvé* 177–78/VI, 222–23). This involuntary coincidence of moments consequently reveals to him a hitherto unknown analogy, if not identity, between the past and the present and so transcends the singularity of each. Marcel celebrates this kind of miracle as sheer 'extra-temporal joy' (*Retrouvé* 184/VI, 231), because it has 'the power [...] to make me rediscover days that were long past [les jours anciens], the Time that was Lost [le temps perdu]' (*Retrouvé* 178/VI, 223). 'By writing his novel, by translating the transcendent, extra-temporal quality of these experiences to the level of esthetic form', the narrator of course 'hoped to reveal their nature to the world'.[34]

Evidently, involuntary memory — that 'miracle of an analogy' described by the narrator — follows the same aesthesiology as a musical leitmotif does: in both cases a sensory cue triggers an associated memory. The verbal leitmotif *longtemps* appropriates the same mechanism, translating its crucial effect, the spontaneous coincidence of presently heard sound and felt memory, into a literary discourse. The sound *longtemps* is a concrete sensory — and more precisely scenographic — means to trigger involuntary memories in the reader, thereby '*realizing thought*', as Wagner would put it, 'in sensory form'.[35] As musicologist Arne Stollberg points out, this means the motif

> not only inscribes itself into the listener's memory through repetition; it becomes a physical experience that is reactualized each time the corresponding acoustic figure returns. It literally achieves a 'presentation' of the past — meaning the motif's occurrences earlier in the composition — instead of merely 'recalling' it, thus restoring this past, similar to a *déjà entendu*, to the Here and Now and reviving it for aesthetic perception.[36]

Marcel comes very close to stating the aesthesiological similarity between musical leitmotifs and instances of involuntary memory. He writes that:

nothing resembled more closely than a beautiful[37] phrase of Vinteuil the peculiar pleasure which I had felt at certain moments in my life, when gazing, for instance, at the steeples of Martinville [...] or, more simply, at the beginning of this book [ouvrage], when I tasted a certain cup of tea. (*Prisonnière* 360–61/v, 428)

The fact that Marcel previously identified Wagner as the 'grandfather' of Vinteuil (*Prisonnière* 148/v, 174) makes it even more plausible to think of the mentioned 'phrase of Vinteuil' precisely as a musical leitmotif.

Following Gilles Deleuze, involuntary memory and, by extension, leitmotifs could be described as self-contained acts of signification — as 'sensuous signs' that have 'imprisoned and enveloped' their meaning.[38] The narratorial leitmotif thoroughly exploits that kind of embodied significance. In contrast to purely conventional signs, which do not carry their meaning *within* themselves, *longtemps* summons a complex feeling without abstracting from the corporeal acuity of that feeling. Based on corporeal acuity and embodied memory, it skirts the divide between signifier and signified, as well as that between presence and absence. By dint of its sheer acoustic materiality, its being a *sensible* trace, it reminds the reader of a diegetic theme, the feeling of the 'timeless' drift that Marcel experienced in his bed. It summons and renders present such a feeling, but nonetheless preserves its singularity — the fact that this occurrence does, in fact, belong to a specific moment of the past, to an earlier scene. At the same time, the leitmotif preserves and indeed enforces the perception of its acoustic materiality, since the associated scenic context cannot be remembered or 'seen' without attending to the sound of *longtemps*, an inextricable two-sidedness that precisely defines a leitmotif as a musicodramatic unit.

Yet the possibility of such embodied significance issues from the very lack of specific meaning. The meaning of the *adverb* 'longtemps' in the novel's first sentence, 'Longtemps, je me suis couché de bonne heure', remains unclear, as does its immediate reference. Semantically, this first word represents nothing but an indeterminate, even obfuscating deictic marker, which in the context of the first sentence becomes what Gérard Genette called a 'pseudo-iterative' suggesting habitual action (namely the habit of going to bed early), although the 'richness and precision of detail' of the ensuing sentences 'ensure that no reader can seriously believe' this habit would 'occur and reoccur in that manner, several times, without any variation'.[39] Understood as a temporal adverb without clear reference, the frequent mention of *longtemps* contributes to the chronic temporal indeterminacy of the chapter 'Combray'. Being such an empty deictic marker, an abstract sign for an unspecific duration before and outside the novel's time, *longtemps* indeed *refers to* that 'timeless' place that the leitmotif means to summon musically and that Marcel will search for for a very long time.

My fourth and penultimate example is a perplexing hint at the end of 'Un amour de Swann', the second chapter of *Du côté de chez Swann*. Here, the narrator's leitmotif is associated with seemingly unrelated sounds and diegetic themes, thus generating a fresh motific-thematic complex.

Wagner uses this subtle technique of motific association to realize, on the one hand, his idea of 'endless melody' — a seamless stream of music without noticeable breaks. On the other hand, and dramaturgically more important, these musical associations are often made to disclose secret affinities. One such association occurs, for example, in the Prelude to *Tristan und Isolde*, even before the drama commences on the stage. The so-called *Leidensmotiv* expressing the mutual suffering of Tristan and Isolde in the scenes to follow is here immediately associated with the *Sehnsuchtsmotiv*, the melody of their passionate yearning for one another. The *Leidensmotiv*, to be clear, is the descending movement in the lower register opening the Prelude, while the *Sehnsuchtsmotiv* is the pressing, irresistible chromatic ascension starting in the second bar. Both together produce a pregnant dissonance, the world-famous 'Tristan chord'.[40]

This subtle musical hint already contains the essence of the piece. On the surface, suffering and passionate yearning are opposite feelings — dissonances indeed. But it is precisely the ensuing drama on stage demonstrating their complementarity, the fact that they are inextricable, perhaps even indistinguishable, aspects of love, that in turn justifies their musical combination in the first place. That the one leitmotif is musically simply the 'inversion' of the other, as Carl Dahlhaus points out, makes their complementarity audible.[41] Due to the inevitable limitations in verbalizing and visualizing emotions, it is primarily the music of *Tristan and Isolde* that demonstrates the dissonance of love — if it is a genuine dissonance indeed. Since the audible coincidence of suffering and yearning — the 'Tristan chord' — has resounded so many times throughout the opera, this chord no longer requires resolution in consonance, persisting instead, like love itself, as a harmony charged with discord. Still more motivic associations and derivations as well as contrastive juxtapositions occur in Wagner's tetralogy *Der Ring des Nibelungen*. More than any other Wagner opera, the *Ring* is precisely famous for its evocative 'musical prose', for a rich network of interrelated motifs explaining the scene. Carl Dalhaus and Thomas S. Grey, among others, provide striking examples thereof.[42]

It cannot be, nor need it be, clear to what extent Proust consciously imitates what Wagner called his subtle 'art of transition' [Kunst des Übergangs].[43] Nonetheless, we can recognize Marcel's leitmotif in the following passage from 'Swann In Love':

> il n'était pas loin de voir quelque chose de providentiel dans ce fait qu'il se fût décidé à aller à la soirée de Mme de Saint-Euverte, parce que son esprit désireux d'admirer la richesse d'invention de la vie et incapable de se poser *longtemps* une question difficile [...] considérait dans les souffrances qu'il avait éprouvées ce soir-là et les plaisirs encore insoupçonnés [...] une sorte d'enchaînement nécessaire.
>
> Mais tandis que, une heure après son réveil, il donnait des indications au coiffeur... (*Swann* 375; emphasis added)

> [he was not far short of seeing something providential in the fact that he had at last decided to go to Mme. de Saint-Euverte's that evening, because his mind, anxious to admire the richness of invention that life shews, and incapable of facing a difficult problem for a long time [...] came to the conclusion that the sufferings through which he had passed that evening, and the pleasures, at that time unsuspected [...] were linked by a sort of concatenation of necessity.

But while, an hour after his awakening, he was giving instructions to the barber...] (I, 459)

This passage relates the end of a dream in which Swann had developed a series of strained reflections about his unhappy love for Odette de Crecy. *Longtemps* rings out here seemingly unmotivated and without great significance, almost as if it were redundant. If we hear it as a recurrence of the narratorial leitmotif, however, the passage discloses a more sophisticated meaning. In that case *longtemps* recalls the established thematic connotation of a transitional drift, thus signalling the imminent awakening of Swann mentioned in the following paragraph.

At the same, *longtemps* inserts a strange sound — one associated with Marcel — into the misty, absent-minded aftermath of Swann's dream. This association intimates, on the one hand, the subcutaneous connection between Swann and Marcel, one Marcel will later acknowledge in stating that, ultimately, it was Swann who provided him with the 'raw material' of his life (*Retrouvé* 221/VI, 278). Without Swann, it would have been impossible for Marcel to become a writer. His leitmotif would have never emerged.

On the other hand, the return of the narratorial leitmotif in the context of Swann's dream produces a sharp dissonance. *Longtemps* rings out as a foreign sound in this scene: It does not belong to Swann and especially not to a dream reviving his *amour fou* for Odette, for unlike the narrator and his musical reader, Swann is indeed 'incapable' of hearing the evocative echo of *longtemps*. Associating Swann's dream with the narratorial leitmotif, the quoted scenography makes palpable the fundamental difference of character between the two. The 'extra-temporal' place between waking and dreaming summoned by *longtemps* contrasts sharply with the profane message of Swann's dream: that things proceeded according to 'a sort of concatenation of necessity'. 'Incapable of facing a difficult problem for a long time [*longtemps*]', least of all his relationship with Odette, Swann responds with fatalistic resignation. Marcel, by contrast, will eventually respond to his big challenge, the transformation of fleeting moments of life into a work of art, with uncompromising determination. The fact that *longtemps* could be omitted from the phrase without significantly altering its meaning — 'incapable of facing a difficult problem' means virtually the same as 'incapable of facing a difficult problem *for a long time*' — emphasizes all the more its function as a musical cue.

Within Swann's story, *longtemps* sounds dissonant. The leitmotif that clearly belongs to Swann is *la petite phrase*, in the double sense of the term as combining an acoustic motif (the sound of these words) with a diegetic theme, which in his case is the passion this little phrase from Vinteuil's *sonate en fa dièse* arouses inside him. Subsequently, the motif *la petite phrase* is also associated with a secondary theme, namely Swann's love for Odette. In truth, however, that love was enkindled by the irresistible sound of the little phrase itself rather than the allure of Odette's appearance and personality. Or as the narrator puts it, 'Odette had been merely by his side [à côté de lui], not (as the phrase had been) within him [non en lui comme le motif de Vinteuil]' (*Filles* 104/II, 123). For that reason, the word 'Odette' does not constitute a genuine leitmotif — an issue I will consider in more detail in the next section.

My fifth and final example is the very last phrase of *Le Temps retrouvé*, which could be understood as the ultimate transfiguration of Marcel's leitmotif:

> Aussi, si elle [la force de maintenir longtemps attaché à moi] m'était laissée assez *longtemps* pour accomplir mon œuvre, ne manquerais-je pas d'abord d'y décrire les hommes, cela dût-il les faire ressembler à des êtres monstrueux, comme occupant une place si considérable, à côté de celle si restreinte qui leur est réservée dans l'espace, une place au contraire prolongée sans mesure puisqu'ils touchent simultanément, comme des géants plongés dans les années à des époques, vécues par eux si distantes, entre lesquelles tant de jours sont venus se placer — dans le Temps. (*Retrouvé* 353; emphasis added)

> [So, if I were given long enough to accomplish my work, I should not fail, even if the effect were to make them resemble monsters, to describe men as occupying so considerable a place, compared with the restricted place which is reserved for them in space, a place on the contrary prolonged past measure, for simultaneously, like giants plunged into the years, they touch the distant epochs which they have lived, between which so many days have come to range themselves — in Time.] (VI, 451)

'Longtemps [...] simultanément [...] le Temps': Time itself resonates from within the leitmotif, and the final phrase just announces their fundamental correspondence. One last time, the vague sound opening the *Recherche* is transfigured and, by associating it with essential Time, finally determined and completed. The leitmotif has found its innermost meaning and ultimate referent.[44]

That thing, however, is highly elusive — a 'pure and disembodied' perception or, alternatively, an 'undifferentiated memory' (*Retrouvé* 175–76/VI, 220). Marcel can describe Time, the glorified solution of his lifelong quest, only as that which it is not, namely, as such 'necessarily imperfect' things like external perception, linear time, and voluntary memories. What he truly regains *dans le Temps* defies verbalization. His final discovery remains a promise and as such a sound, as it was in the beginning, another resonance, precisely, another echo of the narrator's leitmotif *longtemps*. Consequently, it might be more appropriate to reverse the order of the equation, pronouncing instead 'le Temps [...] simultanément [...] longtemps'. Essential Time, which at first reveals itself to the protagonist Marcel only in the form of epiphany, or through involuntary memory, has been set free by the narrator Marcel, for in writing his book he transformed that 'miracle' of experience into a deliberate way of writing — into a literary leitmotif technique. After a very long time of searching for the substance of Time, Time became a narrative procedure.

The preceding examples of scenographies in which the narratorial leitmotif serves increasingly different dramaturgic purposes might warrant a few general conclusions. It would be a misunderstanding to conceive of a literary leitmotif as a fixed motific-thematic unit to which one could assign a definitive name or concept, a misunderstanding that in the case of Wagner dates back to Hans von Wolzogen's various *Leitfäden*. In assigning names and concepts to recurring musical figures, these explanatory guides seemed to provide the listeners precisely with their proper meanings, the themes they *really* stand for. But a leitmotif, whether literary or operatic in kind, does not proceed according to a logic of identity, as though it were an unchanging sign, nor does it have one specific denotation, as if it were a sounding caption. Pinning down the meaning of a leitmotif is simply impossible, since its sole function is to proliferate and change in meaning over the course of time. A growing number of thematic connotations (or scenic associations) is what forms and sustains leitmotifs, for Wagner as well as for Proust.[45]

The brief mentioning of Swann's leitmotif, *la petite phrase*, may have indicated this necessary discrepancy between a leitmotif's constant acoustic shape and its changing connotations. In contrast to Swann's simple identification of *la petite phrase* with Odette — a major theme connected with that motif, but not the only and not the first one — the sound of a leitmotif can and indeed must absorb multiple connotations. Otherwise, it would appear to be nothing but the inane repetition of the always-same figure. It can be enriched with fresh and unknown hues, and modified up to the point that a new motific-thematic ensemble emerges. The reiteration of verbal motifs in the context of different scenographies facilitates both.

The examples may have also shown that the musicality of the *Recherche* reaches well beyond momentary euphony — the beautiful ring of certain words, the consonance amongst phrases, the lovely melody of sentences, etc. Indeed, these two categories should be kept apart, rather than treated interchangeably, as they too often are. The euphony of phrases derives from alliteration and rhyme, the accumulation of open vowels, recurring rhythmic patterns, and the like, whereas musicality is fundamentally inaudible because it is a syntactic schema, for example, a leitmotif technique. Understood as syntax, musicality may go unheard at first; perhaps it cannot be recognized without analysis, without being 'read', as Roland Barthes said.[46] But whether it is heard as such or not, musical syntax nonetheless exerts sensuous force upon the listening reader. It is this syntactic form of musicality, I believe, that Proust recognized in Flaubert as someone who 'treated [the change of tempo] in terms of music' and then appropriated for his own composition.[47] In any case, the composition of an 'œuvre cathédrale', as Proust characterized his novel, involves an acoustic architecture as well.[48]

If the vagueness of meaning is indeed a constitutive feature of a verbal leitmotif, then it is only logical to base it on a word or a short pattern of words carrying little semantic weight. Their relative indeterminacy and initial lack of connotation then allow in turn for even more flexibility in absorbing diegetic contexts. This metamorphic potential of leitmotifs (which Armand Pierhal had identified in Proust as early as 1929)[49] ensures and indeed demands an ongoing explication through the dramatic scene. Enriching its more or less identical acoustic substance with different thematic connotations is a necessary means to sustain interest in a leitmotif, and also a way of keeping up the expectation of its 'redemption'. Indeed, the ongoing explication seems to promise a final revelation of the motif's innermost meaning, often supporting this expectation with a final gesture of transfiguration, as so often happens at the end of Wagner's operas and perhaps also in the final phrase of the *Recherche*, wherein *longtemps* and *Le Temps* are conflated. Whether such gestures of 'redemption' amount, in either case, to more than empty rhetoric and an absurd 'circus finale', as Adorno critically remarked, stands to question.[50]

The initial indeterminacy of leitmotifs can be a pleasurable affair, at least for some listeners. Marcel, for one, admits to 'the joy that my mind derived [...] from this task of modelling a still shapeless nebula [modelage d'une nébuleuse encore informe]' (*Prisonnière* 358/v, 425). This is an indulgence he shares with Wagner, who in the Prelude to *Das Rheingold* carves no less than 136 bars out of the shapeless nebula of one and the same E flat major chord.

The return to Wagner is perhaps the logical outcome of this first section, and it provides a suitable transition to all those matters connected to the music of Vinteuil. At a certain moment in *La Prisonnière* (149/v, 173), when Marcel can 'detach' his thoughts 'for a moment from Albertine' because she is physically absent, he describes the texture of Wagner's music in a beguiling phrase:

> Je me rendais compte de tout ce qu'a de réel l'œuvre de Wagner, en revoyant ces thèmes insistants et fugaces qui visitent un acte, ne s'éloignent que pour revenir, et, parfois lointains, assoupis, presque détachés, sont à d'autres moments, tout en restant vagues, si pressants et si proches, si internes, si organiques, si viscéraux qu'on dirait la reprise moins d'un motif que d'une névralgie. (*Prisonnière* 149)

> [I was struck by how much reality there is in the work as I contemplated once more those insistent, fleeting themes which visit an act, recede only to return again and again, and, sometimes distant, dormant, almost detached, are at other moments, while remaining vague, so pressing and so close, so internal, so organic, so visceral, that they seem like the reprise not so much of a musical motif as of an attack of neuralgia.] (v, 174–75)

These words very precisely describe the irresistible sensuality, the musicality of Proust's own literary composition: so pressing, so visceral — 'la reprise moins d'un motif que d'une névralgie'.

The music of Vinteuil

The previous section was concerned with the scenographic functions of one particularly versatile sound, *longtemps*. However, the main story told in the *Recherche* — the life of Marcel up to the realization of his literary 'vocation' — follows a similar system of recurrences, namely the systematic recurrences of music by Vinteuil. Vinteuil's music drives the story of his life forward, gradually leading Marcel, implicitly as well as explicitly, towards a comprehension of his true vocation to become a writer. Consequently, Vinteuil's music could be considered a recurrent *theme* (as opposed to motif) generating and concatenating key episodes of the novel's plot.[51] This gradually shifts attention from words to representations, from what the reader actually sees and hears (words such as *la petite phrase*) to what Marcel is said to see and hear (for example, an actual phrase of music).

Speaking of Vinteuil, however, one must again speak of Wagner. Wagner represents the conceptual link between the verbal texture and the storyline of the *Recherche*. He is the most influential proponent of leitmotif technique — a technique, we have seen, inscribed into key scenographies — and he is also the most extensively discussed artist in the *Recherche* after Vinteuil, hence a major theme in the novel. This does not mean, however, that one should regard the plot of Wagner's operas as blueprints for Proust's novel, as critics have often done, even if certain parallels are striking, as I mentioned before. Instead, it is once again Wagner's compositional method Proust appropriates as he plots out Marcel's story, with Vinteuil's music functioning as leitmotif.

The consanguinity between Vinteuil and Wagner is explicitly stated in *La Prisonnière*. Marcel here ponders Wagner's subtle art of leitmotif, finally identifying him as Vinteuil's 'grandfather':

> [U]ne mesure de la sonate [de Vinteuil] me frappa, mesure que je connaissais bien pourtant, mais parfois l'attention éclaire différemment des choses connues pourtant depuis longtemps et où nous remarquons ce que nous n'y avions jamais vu. En jouant cette mesure, et bien que Vinteuil fût là en train d'exprimer un rêve qui fût resté tout à fait étranger à Wagner, je ne pus m'empêcher de murmurer: '*Tristan!*', avec le sourire qu'a l'ami d'une famille retrouvant quelque chose de l'aïeul dans une intonation, un geste du petit-fils qui ne l'a pas connu. (*Prisonnière* 148)

> [I was struck by a passage in the [Vinteuil] sonata. It was a passage with which I was quite familiar, but sometimes our attention throws a different light upon things which we have long known, and we remark in them what we have never seen before. As I played the passage, and although Vinteuil had been trying to express in it a fancy which would have been wholly foreign to Wagner, I could not help murmuring 'Tristan', with the smile of an old family friend discovering a trace of the grandfather in an intonation, a gesture of the grandson who has never set eyes on him.] (v, 174)

In fact, their kinship is already noticeable when Vinteuil's music is played during the soireé at the Verdurins' (*Swann* 205–09/I, 250–54). On that occasion, Vinteuil's sonata in F sharp and in particular the sound of its first, andante movement, are portrayed in a parlance recalling works by Wagner. Take, as an example, the characterization of the Andante movement as 'a sort of liquid rippling [un clapotement liquide] of sound, multiform but indivisible, smooth yet restless [plane et entrechoquée], like the deep blue tumult of the sea [comme la mauve agitation des flots]', which makes it impossible for Swann to distinguish between 'phrase' and 'harmony' (*Swann* 205/I, 250). This description strikes me as an unmistakable allusion to the oceanic scenery and timbre of *Tristan und Isolde*. Proust himself also named *Lohengrin* and *Parsifal* as sources of inspiration for the Vinteuil sonata, along with compositions by César Franck, Saint-Saëns, Fauré, and Schubert.[52]

During the soirée at the Verdurins', it also becomes clear that Vinteuil treats motifs in a Wagnerian style. The narrator of 'Swann in Love' describes the sonata's 'motifs which from time to time [par instants] emerge, barely discernible, to plunge again and disappear' (*Swann* 206/I, 251) in a wording similar to Marcel's understanding of Wagner's 'insistent, fleeting themes which visit an act, recede only to return again and again [ne s'éloignent que pour revenir]' (*Prisonnière* 149/V, 174). The stream of music is structured by an erratic coming and going of 'fugitive' and 'vague' motifs, while these motifs issue, in turn, from a 'long-drawn sonority, stretched like a curtain of sound [rideau sonore]', from a seamless musical texture that veils 'the mystery' of their 'incubation' (*Swann* 208/I, 254). The foremost example of such a 'fleeting' motif is, of course, the endearing *petite phrase*, which constitutes the nucleus of Swann's leitmotif.

This *petite phrase* is also of paramount importance for Marcel, since this 'little phrase' initiates and in some ways even compels Marcel's quest for 'lost time'; which is just another way of claiming, as I have done before, that Vinteuil's music, including the 'little phrase' from his sonata, generates and concatenates pivotal episodes of his story, just as a leitmotif does. However, thematic connections of episodes are not simply given by the text; they are actively produced. They result from my reading and 'plotting', as Peter Brooks[53] calls it, from my selective recasting of Marcel's story such that his journey assumes coherence and closure.

Where, then, and when does Marcel's story chronologically begin? It all starts with Monsieur Swann, of course, with Swann hearing a piece of music. 'Tinged already with disenchantment' [déjà un peu désabusé] (*Swann* 193/I, 235), Swann encounters the 'little phrase', which arouses a 'passionate longing' to hear it again (*Swann* 207/I, 251). This longing is initially attached to the music itself; it is a 'passion [amour] for a phrase of music' (*Swann* 207/I, 252). On the occasion of the Verdurin Soirée, Swann rediscovers Vinteuil's sonata, where it is performed in a piano reduction. During this performance, he remembers having heard the sonata once before, when he failed to appreciate its perfect beauty. The sonata consequently causes 'a sort of rejuvenation' (*Swann* 207/I, 252), replacing the 'rather ephemeral satisfactions' in which Swann had been inclined to indulge with the 'exquisite and inexpressible pleasure' [le plaisir spécial et intraduisible] offered by the 'little phrase' (*Swann* 208/I, 253).[54] And so Swann 'had been filled [éprouvé] with love for the "little phrase", as with a new and strange desire [comme un amour inconnu]' (*Swann* 206/I, 251). Vinteuil's music has imbued Swann with the pure form of passionate desire, yet without providing an object to which he can attach his newfound passion. The ensuing attachment to Odette fills this vacancy. 'L'amour est ici une résultante', as Ortega y Gasset aptly remarked.[55]

Swann attaches the musically induced passion to a woman whose 'type' of beauty had initially left him 'indifferent' (*Swann* 193/I, 234). Marcel discloses this transference later in the book, retrospectively concluding that Swann 'mistakenly assimilated [that happiness which the little phrase of the sonata promised] to the pleasures of love' (*Retrouvé* 184/VI, 231). Vinteuil's *petite phrase* thus eroticizes a scenario that previously existed merely in Swann's head, namely, the idea of possession 'without any foundation in desire' (*Swann* 193; I, 235). Once the musically induced passion and the pleasing notion of possession are conflated, the 'little phrase' becomes 'the national anthem' of the love between Swann and Odette (*Swann* 215/I, 262). By means of supplementary aesthetic media, foremost among these Botticelli's *Zipporah*, Swann seeks to increase, enrich, and sustain his passion for Odette. Swann thus turns the liaison with Odette into that self-referential obsession Niklas Luhmann calls 'romantic love', of which 'a peculiar combination of circular closure and openness for anything that can enrich this love' is characteristic.[56]

Following that exact logic of 'romantic love', Swann feels compelled to silence Odette upon their first and highly comical act of intimacy in a carriage. For unlike the many aesthetic enrichments Swann has attached to her effigy, Odette's actual looks and utterances do not arouse his passion. On the contrary, Swann finds her rather off-putting as a real person, a perception that threatens to disenchant the passion Vinteuil's 'little phrase' ignited in him. When Swann repeatedly exclaims in the carriage: 'Whatever you do, don't utter a word, just make a sign' [Surtout, ne me parlez pas, ne me répondez que par signes] (*Swann* 229/I, 279), it is because he could not otherwise preserve the more beautiful things and experiences he associates with his leitmotif.[57]

As a result of the musically induced romance, which is followed by the agonies of jealousy and finally indifference, Swann fathers a child with Odette, marries her, and settles down with his family in Combray. Here, Swann finds himself in a position to exert a formative influence on Marcel. He becomes the 'unwitting author' [l'auteur inconscient] of Marcel's sufferings in depriving him of the maternal kiss (*Swann* 43/I, 50). At the same time, however, he is the 'author' of his first encounters with works of art: Swann shows Marcel photographs of paintings and encourages his passion for Bergotte, the writer. Moreover, the offspring of Swann's musical passion, his daughter Gilberte, becomes the archetype of Marcel's sexual desires, after her commanding visage was inextinguishably imprinted on his mind one sunny day (*Swann* 139–40/I, 168–70). It is also Gilberte who brings 'the famous "Albertine"' to Marcel's attention, the future object of his own obsessive love, whom Swann praises in the same context as 'charming, pretty, intelligent [...] even quite witty [spirituelle]' (*Filles* 83/II, 98).

All this happens because of Vinteuil's 'little phrase'. Vinteuil is, as it were, the begetter of Swann's adult life, while Swann, in turn, provides Marcel in his own assessment with no less than

> la matière de mon expérience, laquelle serait la matière de mon livre [...] non pas seulement par tout ce qui le concernait lui-même et Gilberte. Mais c'était lui qui m'avait dès Combray donné le désir d'aller à Balbec, où sans cela mes parents n'eussent jamais eu l'idée de m'envoyer, et sans quoi je n'aurais pas connu Albertine, mais même les Guermantes [...] ma présence même en ce moment chez le prince de Guermentes, où venait de me venir brusquement l'idée de mon œuvre (ce qui faisait que je devais à Swann non seulement la matière mais la décision), me venait aussi de Swann. (*Retrouvé* 221–22)

> [the raw material of my experience, which would also be the raw material of my book [...] not merely because so much of it concerned Swann himself and Gilberte, but because it was Swann who from the days of Combray had inspired in me the wish to go to Balbec, where otherwise my parents would never have had the idea of sending me, and but for this I should never have known Albertine. [...] had I not gone to Balbec I should have never known the Guermantes either [...] so that even my presence at this very moment in the house of the Princess de Guermantes, where out of the blue the idea for my work had just come to me (and this meant that I owed to Swann not only the material but also the decision), came to me from Swann.] (VI, 278–79)[58]

After the death of Swann, the 'begetter' [auteur] (*Retrouvé* 222/VI, 279) of Marcel's life, things become increasingly complex and cannot be traced in detail here. But, reviewing Marcel's aesthetic *curriculum vitae*, it seems fair to regard music as the foremost art form in it. The early exposure to the sensuous world of Combray, an environment drenched with bodily sensation, and the later encounter with Elstir's paintings at Balbec are crowned, and in a way completed, by Vinteuil's music. Taking up the term Swann mentions during a conversation with Marcel, several critics have indeed argued for such a teleological 'hierarchy' (*Swann* 96/I, 115) of art forms, associating this idea with Schopenhauer.[59]

Whether or not music is set above the other arts in the *Recherche*, Marcel could not have found his true vocation without it. As he, in *La Prisonnière*, plays the Vinteuil sonata for himself, the music reanimates his forgotten aesthetic ambitions and at the same time indicates a place where the shortcomings of 'everyday existence' — the maddening strain of jealousy, for example — are overcome:

> prenant la sonate à un autre point de vue, la regardant en soi-même comme l'œuvre d'un grand artiste, j'étais ramené par le flot sonore vers les jours de Combray — je ne veux pas dire de Montjouvain et du côté de Méséglise, mais des promenades du côté de Guermantes — où j'avais moi-même désiré d'être un artiste. En abandonnant, en fait, cette ambition, avais-je renoncé à quelque chose de réel? La vie pouvait-elle me consoler de l'art, y avait-il dans l'art une réalité plus profonde où notre personnalité véritable trouve une expression que ne lui donnent pas les actions de la vie? Chaque grand artiste semble, en effet, si différent des autres, et nous donne tant cette sensation de l'individualité que nous cherchons en vain dans l'existence quotidienne! (*Prisonnière* 148)

> [Approaching the sonata from another point of view, regarding it in itself as the work of a great artist, I was carried back upon the tide of sound to the days at Combray — I do not mean Montjouvain and the Méséglise way, but to my walks along the Guermantes way — when I myself had longed to become an artist. In abandoning that ambition *de facto*, had I forfeited something real? Could life console me for the loss of art? Was there in art a more profound reality, in which our true personality finds an expression that is not afforded it by the activities of life? For every great artist seems so different from all the rest, and gives us so strongly that sensation of individuality for which we seek in vain in our everyday existence!] (v, 173–74)

A related passage from *Le Temps retrouvé* is even more assertive as concerns the role of music in Marcel's aesthetic becoming:

> Et, repensant à cette joie extra-temporelle causée, soit par le bruit de la cuiller, soit par le goût de la madeleine, je me disais: 'Était-ce cela, ce bonheur proposé par la petite phrase de la sonate à Swann [...] ce bonheur que m'avait fait pressentir comme plus supra-terrestre encore que n'avait fait la petite phrase de la sonate, l'appel rouge et mystérieux de ce septuor que Swann n'avait pu connaître, étant mort, comme tant d'autres avant que la vérité faite pour eux eût été révélée ? (*Retrouvé* 184)

> [And thinking again of the extra-temporal joy which I had been made to feel by the sound of the spoon or the taste of the madeleine, I said to myself: 'Was this perhaps the happiness that the little phrase of the sonata promised to Swann [...] was this the happiness of which long ago I was given a presentiment — as something more supraterrestrial even than the mood evoked by the little phrase

of the sonata — by the call, the mysterious, rubescent call of that septet which Swann was never privileged to hear, having died like so many others before the truth that was made for him had been revealed?'] (VI, 231)

The supraterrestrial 'call' [appel] that resounds in Vinteuil's music, especially in the septet, prefigures the triumphant, blissful, and also pregnant instant when Marcel finally understands the 'miracle of an analogy', involuntary memory, enabling him to 'escape from the present' (*Retrouvé* 178/VI, 223). No wonder, then, that 'the last works of Vinteuil had seemed [...] to combine the quintessential character' and concentrate 'the same happiness' of all his previous experiences of involuntary memory (*Retrouvé* 173/VI, 216–17).

It was also the septet, Marcel discovers in retrospect, that made him realize for the first time that only works of art can 'give permanence' [fixer] to those miracles of simultaneity that involuntary memories make manifest for just a moment; Vinteuil's septet 'had seemed to point to the [...] conclusion' [eût semblé me dire] that such a miraculous coincidence of past and present could be preserved in art (*Retrouvé* 183–84/VI, 230). Vinteuil's musical art thus indicates the precise way to 'link for ever' [enchaîner à jamais] those 'two sets of phenomena' [les deux termes différentes] that experience 'joins together', if involuntarily (*Retrouvé* 196/VI, 246); which can only mean, I think, that Vinteuil had mastered the musical art to link momentary perception and recollection — the art of leitmotif. Just as involuntary memory associates a 'material pattern' [figure matérielle] with 'the outline [trace] of the impression that it made upon us' (*Temps*, 186/VI, 234), so does his music associate an acoustic figure with a recollection of its earlier usage.

Considering the developmental schema I have just delineated, from Swann's love for a phrase to Marcel's crucial discovery in Vinteuil's septet, it seems justified to call Vinteuil's music the source '*sine materia*'[60] of Proust's composition. Polymorphously shimmering through the discursive texture, this theme secures the cohesion of the storyline — most notably as a 'little phrase' that would 'from time to time emerge, barely discernible, to plunge again and disappear [...], recognized [connus] only by the particular kind of pleasure' it gives (*Swann* 206/I, 251). The music of Vinteuil, in all its guises and 'iridescent' metamorphoses, for example, during the striking Saint-Euverte Soirée (*Swann* 339–47/I, 415–25), provides Proust's fiction with thematic consistency. His 'little phrase' is both the original and indispensable fiction inside the fiction, so that one might say it embodies for the reader what it eventually comes to embody for Swann: 'no longer pure music, but rather design, architecture, thought' (*Swann* 206/I, 251).

Marcel too ponders the aesthetic exemplarity of Vinteuil's music at several critical junctures. But what is the lesson he learns from Vinteuil's music? What is it, exactly, that Marcel understands when he hears a 'mysterious, rubescent call' [l'appel rouge et mystérieux] in the septet (*Retrouvé* 184/VI, 231)? In the case of Swann, Vinteuil's 'little phrase' inflames a hitherto unknown passion and, in consequence, the fatal desire for a woman endowed 'with a kind of beauty which left him indifferent, which aroused in him no desire, which gave him, indeed, a sort of physical repulsion' (*Swann* 193; I, 234). To Swann, Vinteuil's music is essentially

Gemütherregungskunst,⁶¹ a 'technique to agitate the soul' that stands, consciously or unconsciously, in the service of his *amour fou*. Swann thus fails to perceive musical utterances in their own right. To Marcel, the same piece sounds entirely different. Playing Vinteuil's sonata in a free moment (in the absence of *his* fatal object of desire, Albertine), he is reminded of a time when his life was not dominated by the 'spasmodic disease' of jealousy, which he obviously shares with Swann. More importantly, the sonata makes him understand that the 'sensation of individuality for which we seek in vain in our everyday existence' (*Prisonnière* 148/v, 174) is to be found in art alone, never in the love for another person:

> Comme le spectre extériorise pour nous la composition de la lumière, l'harmonie d'un Wagner, la couleur d'un Elstir nous permettent de connaître cette essence qualitative des sensations d'un autre où l'amour pour un autre être ne nous fait pas pénétrer. [...] Même ce qui est le plus indépendant du sentiment qu'elle nous fait éprouver garde sa réalité extérieure et entièrement définie, le chant d'un oiseau, la sonnerie de cor d'un chasseur [...] découpent à l'horizon leur silhouette sonore. (*Prisonnière* 149)

> [As the spectrum makes visible to us the composition of light, so the harmony of a Wagner, the colour of an Elstir, enable us to know that essential quality of another person's sensations into which love for another person does not allow us to penetrate. [...] Even that which, in this music, is most independent of the emotion that it arouses in us preserves its outward and absolutely precise reality; the song of a bird, the call of a hunter's horn [...] each carves its silhouette of sound against the horizon.] (v, 175)

Marcel develops in this scene an intrinsic aesthetic appreciation of Vinteuil's music: 'Was there in art a more profound reality, in which our true personality finds an expression that is not afforded it by the activities of life [que ne lui donnent pas les action de la vie]?' (*Prisonnière* 148/v, 174). For Marcel, this 'profound reality' exists solely in art; it has no reality outside its own aesthetic domain, no representation in 'everyday existence'. It is only logical that this decisive breakthrough is, in fact, hailed by a recurrence of the narratorial leitmotif:

> Même en celle-ci [la sonate], je ne m'attachai pas à remarquer combien la combinaison du motif voluptueux et du motif anxieux répondait davantage maintenant à mon amour pour Albertine, duquel la jalousie avait été si *longtemps* absente que j'avais pu confesser à Swann mon ignorance de ce sentiment. (*Prisonnière* 148; emphasis added)

> [I did not even go out of my way to notice how, in the latter [the sonata], the combination of the sensual and the anxious motifs corresponded more closely now to my love for Albertine, from which jealousy had been for so long absent that I had been able to confess to Swann my ignorance of that sentiment.] (v, 174)

Though it is created and appreciated under ordinary circumstances, the work of art situates its true origin, cause, and meaning — its reality — nowhere else than within itself. This means, however, that this 'reality' belongs to a 'fatherland' [patrie] that is always already 'lost' and 'unknown', even to its creator, the artist (*Prisonnière* 245/v, 290). Marcel eventually claims such radical autonomy and indeterminacy for his own work, his book to come:

> En réalité, chaque lecteur est quand il lit le propre lecteur de soi-même. L'ouvrage de l'écrivain n'est qu'une espèce d'instrument optique qu'il offre au lecteur afin de lui permettre de discerner ce que, sans ce livre, il n'eût peut-être pas vu en soi-même. La reconnaissance en soi-même, par le lecteur, de ce que dit le livre est la preuve de la vérité de celui-ci [...] (*Retrouvé* 217–18)
>
> [In reality every reader is, while he is reading, the reader of his own self. The writer's work is merely a kind of optical instrument which he offers to the reader to enable him to discern what, without this book, he would perhaps never have experienced in himself. And the recognition by the reader in his own self of what the book says is the proof of its veracity [...]] (VI, 273)[62]

André Gide once described the *Recherche* as a composition that requires the reader to individually 'orchestrate' and 'nuance' its 'endless phrases', a description reminiscent of Mallarmé's notion of 'the total arabesque'.[63] The quoted passage from *Le Temps retrouvé* says as much.

In contrast to Marcel, Swann never recognizes the radical autonomy and indeterminacy of art — its radically 'arabesque' meaning, because Swann fails to detach aesthetic experience from both his personal feelings and the supposed intentions of the artist. This conclusion applies even to the Saint-Euverte concert, during which Swann tries hard to detach the 'little phrase' from what it came to signify for him — his feelings for Odette. It might seem as though Swann then achieves a degree of aesthetic comprehension comparable to that of Marcel, for example, when music is described, during the Saint-Euverte concert, as 'an immeasurable keyboard [clavier incommensurable] [...] showing us what richness, what variety lies hidden, unknown to us, in that vast, unfathomed and forbidding night of our soul which we take to be an impenetrable void [cette grande nuit impénétrée et décourageante de notre âme que nous prenons pour du vide et pour du néant]' (*Swann* 344/I, 420–21). Moreover, Swann is said to note 'the audacity of a Vinteuil experimenting, discovering the secret laws that govern an unknown force' (*Swann* 345/I, 423). This formulation resembles the metaphor Marcel will later use to describe his artistic task, namely, the deciphering of the 'inner book of unknown symbols [signes inconnus]' so as to reveal its inherent 'law' of concatenation and 'necessary' syntax (*Retrouvé* 186–88/VI, 233–36).

Unlike the third-person narrator telling his story, however, Swann is unable to attend to the inherent and autonomous significance of Vinteuil's music. As soon as the musicians start to play, Odette, 'who was entirely absent' until then, is summoned 'as though she had entered, and this apparition was so agonizingly painful [une si déchirante souffrance] that his hand clutched at his heart' because of 'the forgotten strains [refrains] of happiness', and also the sufferings, that her apparition recalled (*Swann* 339/I, 415). Once again, Swann reduces a musical utterance to a conventional act of signification, so that the inherent meaning of Vinteuil's *petite phrase* — and hence his leitmotif — is obliterated. To Swann, the 'dilettante of intangible [immatérielles] sensations' (*Swann* 263/I, 321), Vinteuil's music never speaks about itself. It merely signifies his love for Odette — whose bitter-sweet happiness, Swann realizes that evening, is lost forever: 'From that evening onwards, Swann understood that the feeling which Odette had once had for him would never revive [ne renaîtrait jamais], that his hopes of happiness would not be realized now [ne se réaliseraient plus]' (*Swann* 347/I, 425).

Swann finally gives up his hopes of happiness. Does he, by the same token, detach the 'little phrase' from Odette and so come to appreciate Vinteuil's sonata as an autonomous work of art? The text provides no explicit answer to this question, but it seems unlikely, since Swann's realization that his love has come to an end can hardly eradicate the memory thereof. Vinteuil's 'little phrase' would still remind Swann of the passionate love he once felt for Odette. The Saint-Euverte soirée would thus effect one final metamorphosis of Swann's leitmotif, transforming Vinteuil's *petite phrase*, in happier days the 'national anthem' of his love for Odette (*Swann* 215/I, 262), into a funeral march.[64]

Marcel, by contrast, realizes the necessity for an inherent appreciation of music. Listening in that attitude, music speaks indeed — in sheer immediacy. As the first Andante movement of the septet, 'to which [Marcel] had entirely surrendered' (*Prisonnière* 246/V, 291), comes to an end and refreshments are handed around, Marcel laments the loss of the enrapturing immediacy he had just experienced:

> Des personnes plus agréables causèrent un moment avec moi. Mais qu'étaient leurs paroles, qui, comme toute parole humaine extérieure, me laissaient si indifférent, à côté de la céleste phrase musicale avec laquelle je venais de m'entretenir? J'étais vraiment comme un ange qui, déchu des ivresses du Paradis, tombe dans la plus insignifiante réalité. Et de même que certains êtres sont les derniers témoins d'une forme de vie que la nature a abandonnée, je me demandais si la musique n'était pas l'exemple unique de ce qu'aurait pu être — s'il n'y avait pas eu l'invention du langage, la formation des mots, l'analyse des idées — la communication des âmes. Elle est comme une possibilité qui n'a pas eu de suites [...] (*Prisonnière* 246–47)

> [Other more agreeable people chatted for a moment with me. But what were their words, which like every human and external word left me so indifferent, compared with the heavenly phrase of music with which I had just been communing? I was truly like an angel who, fallen from the inebriating bliss of paradise, subsides into the most humdrum reality. And, just as certain creatures are the last surviving testimony to a form of life which nature has discarded, I wondered whether music might not be the unique example of what might have been — if the invention of language, the formation of words, the analysis of ideas had not intervened — the means of communication between souls. It is like a possibility that has come to nothing [...]] (V, 292)

While listening, Marcel heard a resonance of those riches that lie 'hidden, unknown to us, in that vast, unfathomed and forbidding night of our soul' (*Swann* 344/I, 421), to quote again the narrator's anticipatory phrase from 'Swann in Love'. These riches of the soul cannot be verbalized but only heard in music, says Marcel.

However, the bewildering turn of Marcel's reflection should not go unheard: 'It is like a possibility that has come to nothing'. Not even composers remember the musical paradise of angelic communication, 'this lost fatherland', although each of them 'remains all his life unconsciously attuned to it' [accordé en un certain unisson avec elle] (*Prisonnière* 245; V, 290). Having drowned in the blissful waves of resonance, Marcel, now a reasoning earthling again, is unsettled by the conclusion that music is after all an impossible way of *communicating*. Indeed, 'communing' *in private* with a 'heavenly phrase of music' as a means of gaining access to one's 'angelic' self is the exact opposite of *sharing* experiences with others. Understanding this difference between private associations and the actual possibilities of aesthetic communication would be one critical lesson taught by the septet.

The other lesson is perhaps even more important for Marcel's artistic development, at least in practical terms. Some time after the performance, he discovers that the septet was not conceived among the stars, as it were. It was Mlle Vinteuil's girlfriend who 'deciphered' the dead master's 'indecipherable scribblings', assembling them 'by dint of patience, intelligence and respect' (*Prisonnière* 249/v, 295) so as to bring forth Vinteuil's unfinished masterwork. The divine septet, which sounded already during the performance at the Princess Guermantes' at moments 'laboriously earthbound' [traînait si péniblement à terre] (*Prisonnière* 239/v, 283), is nothing but a result of profane labour. In truth, it is a second-hand pastiche rather than a so-called 'original'.[65]

This revelation also represents the late denouement of the (in)famous scene of 'sadism', as Marcel terms it, at Montjouvain, Vinteuil's house, which was told many hundred pages earlier (*Swann* 157–61/I, 190–96). Learning that Mlle Vinteuil's girlfriend compiled, nay *created*, the septet, one must concede that it was not only 'ritual profanations' that old Vinteuil received in return for sacrificing his life to his daughter, as it initially appeared. Rather, the completion of the septet is the 'form' in which both the naughty daughter and her girlfriend honour Vinteuil's memory, the 'reward' [salaire] to make up for his self-sacrificing devotion.[66] It was, as the narrator puts it, the 'profound union between genius' and 'the sheath of vices' that brought about a masterwork (*Prisonnière* 252/v, 298).

The laborious and prosaic fabrication of the septet foreshadows the arduous task Marcel will take up himself in the end, namely, the deciphering and assemblage of hitherto indecipherable scribblings, of those 'unknown symbols' life had left in his soul or 'inner book' (*Retrouvé* 186–88/VI, 233–36). Marcel's reflections on the septet therefore pertain to the core of the *Recherche*'s aesthetics, as Malcolm Bowie points out:

> These pages are a gloriously impure, lumber-filled rhapsody. In them Proust's art reveals art, lays bare its inner workings, comes clean about its insecurities and low motives, and pins snapshots of the production-process on to the finished product. This combined description and reinvention has unparalleled summative force: it is an allegorical representation both of what the narrator's book will eventually be like and of what Proust's book has already been like from its first page.[67]

Marcel's final commitment, inspired by Vinteuil's septet, to the aesthetic labour of writing represents a very bourgeois turn indeed, whereby Vinteuil's 'grandfather' Richard Wagner is summoned one last time. For Wagner is the perfect example of bourgeois work ethic — the nagging duty always to fulfil the daily quota. In 1854,

Wagner reportedly writes to Julie Ritter, his benefactress, that 'a morning without work feels like a day in hell'.[68] Baudelaire expressed the sentiment in more sober words, maintaining that 'inspiration is definitely the sister of daily labor'.[69] Not bouts of genius but diligence and persistent labour are the necessary conditions for creating a work of art with which 'we do really fly from star to star', just as 'we can do with an Elstir, with a Vinteuil' (*Prisonnière* 246/v, 291). This the 'laboriously earthbound' septet makes abundantly clear, too.

There are also the sorrows of aesthetic labour, twinges of insufficiency and underachievement, for example, depressions even, and above all the fear of running out of time — mortal time of the kind written in lower-case letters — before the great work about Time is complete. Proust's narrator is haunted by this worst fear, pondering it repeatedly.[70] It is no small irony, of course, that the fate of Vinteuil became Proust's own. In the end, someone else had to decipher his indecipherable scribblings on so-called *paperoles* to complete the last volume of his great work. And so, thanks to the patient hands and respectful minds of philologists, the musicality of his work lives on, carving 'its silhouette of sound against the horizon' (*Prisonnière* 149/v, 175).

Notes to Part II — Proust

1. The first lines from a poem Rilke wrote in November 1907 (R vi, 1228), not long before Proust's started writing on his book. — In this chapter, I expand on arguments first developed in 'Music and Musical Semiology in Marcel Proust's *À la recherche du temps perdu*', *Narrative*, 23 (2015), 1–26.
2. André Cœuroy, 'Music in the Work of Marcel Proust', trans. by Fred Rothwell, *The Musical Quarterly*, 12 (1926), 132–51 (pp. 150–51; translation slightly modified). This article is the English translation of a chapter from Cœuroy's *Musique et littérature: Études de musique et de littérature comparées* (Paris: Bloud & Gay, 1923).
3. Cœuroy, 'Music in the Work of Marcel Proust', p. 151 n. 2.
4. Jean-Yes Tadié, *Lectures de Proust* (Paris: Colin, 1971), p. 196, which repeats, perhaps unwittingly, Costil, p. 469.
5. *Dictionnaire Marcel Proust*, ed. by Annick Bouillaguet and Brian G. Rogers (Paris: Champion, 2004), p. 666 ('Musique').
6. Timothy Mathews, 'Foreword', *Romance Studies*, 32 (2014), 69–70 (p. 69). Classic studies of Proust's musicality include Pierre Costil, 'La construction musicale de la *Recherche du Temps perdu*', *Bulletin de la société des amis de Marcel Proust*, 8–9 (1958–59), 469–89 and 83–110; Georges Piroué, *Proust et la musique du devenir* (Paris: Denoël, 1960); Georges Matoré and Irène Tamba-Mecz, *Musique et structure romanesque dans 'La recherche du temps perdu'* (Paris: Klincksieck, 1973); Claude-Henry Joubert, *Le fil d'or: étude sur la musique dans 'À la recherche du temps perdu'* (Paris: Corti, 1984); Jean-Jacques Nattiez, *Proust as Musician* (Cambridge: Cambridge University Press, 1989). Recent discussions include *Marcel Proust und die Musik*, ed. by Albert Gier (Berlin: Insel, 2012); *Marcel Proust: Une vie en musiques*, ed. by Pierre Ivanoff (Paris: Archimbaud, 2012); as well as the special issue 'Unsettling Scores: Proust and Music' of *Romance Studies*, 32.2 (2014).
7. 'Then [Albertine] would find her tongue and say: "My —" or "My darling —" followed by my Christian name, which, if we give the narrator the same name as the author of this book, would be "My Marcel", or "My darling Marcel"' (*Prisonnière* 67/v, 77). Cf. *La Prisonnière* 147/v, 172).
8. I quote from the early drafts of *Le temps retrouvé*, published as *Matinée chez la princesse de Guermantes: Cahiers du 'Temps retrouvé'*, ed. by Henri Bonnet and Bernard Brun (Paris: Gallimard, 1982), after Nattiez, pp. 28, 29, 31.
9. Nattiez, p. 29.

10. Cœuroy, 'Music in the Work of Marcel Proust', p. 134 n. 1.
11. Nattiez, pp. 12–33; Margaret Mein, 'Proust and Wagner', *Journal of European Studies*, 19 (1989), 205–22 (p. 212).
12. Early in 1911, Proust subscribed to the *théâtrophone*, a system for the transmission of concerts and operas over telephone cable, but he was dissatisfied with the sound quality. In the case of Wagner, however, this was not a problem, he told Georges de Lauris in February 1911: 'Mais enfin pour les opéras de Wagner que je connais presque par cœur, je supplée aux insuffisances de l'acoustique' (Proust, *Correspondance*, ed. by Philip Kolb, 21 vols (Paris: Plon, 1970–93), x (1983), 254). Thanks to the *théâtrophone*, Proust also fell in love with Debussy's *Pelléas et Mélisande*, as shown by William C. Carter, *Marcel Proust: A Life* (New Haven: Yale University Press, 2013), pp. 497–501, a passion that finds literary expression in *Sodome et Gomorrhe* (IV, 243–49), where 'with the gestures of a wild woman' Madame de Cambremer praises the beauties of *Pelléas et Mélisande*.
13. Mein, pp. 206–08. Note, in this context, the curious biographical parallel drawn by Marc A. Weiner, 'Zwieback and Madeleine: Creative Recall in Wagner and Proust', *MLN*, 95 (1980), 679–84.
14. As for the Wagnerian traces in the *Recherche*, see also Armand Pierhal, 'Sur la composition wagnérienne de l'œuvre de Proust', *Bibliothèque Universelle et Revue de Genève* (1929), 710–19; Emile Bedriomo, *Proust, Wagner et la coïncidence des arts* (Tübingen: Narr, 1984); Albrecht Betz, 'Suche und Initiation: Proust als Wagnerianer', *Merkur: Deutsche Zeitschrift für europäisches Denken*, 598 (1998), 74–80; as well as the two detailed entries on 'Proust' in the excellent *Dictionnaire encyclopédique Wagner*, ed. by Timothée Picard (Arles: Actes sud, 2010), 1673–85. James Connelly has compiled a 170-page list of all musical references in the *Recherche*, including the many allusions to Wagner: 'Music in Marcel Proust's *À la recherche du temps perdu*: A Playlist Resource', <http://www.proust-ink.com/s/proust_playlist.pdf> [accessed 1 April 2019].
15. The dictionary defines a 'music drama' very aptly as 'an opera whose structure is governed by considerations of dramatic effectiveness, rather than by the convention of having a series of formal arias', citing Wagner for good reason as the champion of the genre. The irony is, of course, that Wagner rejected the term *Musikdrama*, although his works *are* just that, describing his works instead as operas, although he hated the opera of his time. See Wagner's rebuttal 'Über die Benennung "Musikdrama"' (1872), in Wagner, *Sämtliche Schriften und Dichtungen* ('Volks-Ausgabe'), ed. by Richard Sternfeld and others, 16 vols, 6th edn (Leipzig: Breitkopf & Härtel, 1912), IX, 302–08.
16. The term *Leitmotiv* owes its currency chiefly to the explanatory guides by Hans von Wolzogen, such as his *Thematischer Leitfaden durch die Musik zu Rich. Wagner's Festspiel 'Der Ring des Nibelungen'* (Leipzig: Schloemp, 1876) and *Thematischer Leitfaden durch die Musik zu Richard Wagner's 'Tristan und Isolde'* (Leipzig: Feodor Reinboth, 1882). The conceptual history of leitmotifs is discussed by Jörg Riedlbauer, '"Erinnerungsmotive" in Wagner's *Der Ring des Nibelungen*', *The Musical Quarterly*, 74 (1990), 18–30, and Thomas S. Grey, '"... wie ein rother Faden": On the Origins of "Leitmotif" as Critical Construct and Musical Practice', in *Music and Theory in the Age of Romanticism*, ed. by Ian Bent (Cambridge: Cambridge University Press, 1996), pp. 187–210.
17. Wagner, , X, 185. For an introduction to Wagner's leitmotif technique, see the entry 'leitmotiv' in both the *Dictionnaire encyclopédique Wagner* and *The Cambridge Wagner Encyclopedia*, ed. by Nicholas Vazsonyi (Cambridge: Cambridge University Press, 2013).
18. Wagner, IX, 322–44 (pp. 336–38).
19. Nietzsche, *Der Fall Wagner*, §§ 7–9 (*Kritische Studienausgabe*, VI, 26–35). As for the semiotic (or rhetorical) dimension of Wagner's leitmotif technique, see Christian Thorau, *Semantisierte Sinnlichkeit: Studien zu Rezeption und Zeichenstruktur der Leitmotivtechnik Richard Wagners* (Stuttgart: Steiner, 2003), pp. 90–96, where Thorau sums up 'the complementary relationship of determining denotation (language/scene) and indeterminate exemplification (music)' (p. 92) in Wagner's operas.
20. Wagner, IV, 200. Cf. the similar but more meandering passage on pp. 201–03.
21. Carl Dahlhaus, *Richard Wagners Musikdramen* (Stuttgart: Reclam, 1996), pp. 164–65; Dahlhaus, *Richard Wagner's Music Dramas*, trans. by Mary Whittall (Cambridge: Cambridge University Press, 1979), p. 115.

22. Dahlhaus, *Wagners Musikdramen*, pp. 125–26; *Wagner's Music Dramas*, pp. 84–86. *Szenisch-musikalische Ausführung* is a formulation from Wagner's letter of 12 November 1851 to Theodor Uhlig.
23. See, for example, Thomas S. Grey, 'Leitmotif, Temporality, and Musical Design in the *Ring*', in *The Cambridge Companion to Wagner*, ed. by Thomas S. Grey (Cambridge: Cambridge University Press, 2008), pp. 85–114 (pp. 111–14).
24. In his 1861 'Richard Wagner et *Tannhäuser* à Paris', Baudelaire describes Wagner's leitmotif technique literally as a 'système mnemonique' (*Critique d'art suivi de Critique musicale*, ed. by Claude Pichois (Paris: Gallimard, 1992), p. 461), supporting his observation with a quote from Franz Liszt's 1851 book *Lohengrin et Tannhäuser*.
25. Lucien Daudet, *Autour de soixante lettres de Marcel Proust* (Paris: Gallimard, 1929), p. 76:

    l'ouvrage est impossible à prévoir par ce seul premier volume qui ne prend son sens que par les autres [...] ce sera comme les morceaux dont on ne sait pas qu'ils sont des leitmotive quand on les a entendus isolément au concert dans une Ouverture sans compter tout ce qui se situera après coup.

26. Genette, *Narrative Discourse*, p. 109.
27. Edmund Wilson, 'A Short View of Proust', *The New Republic*, 54 (21 March 1928), pp. 140–47 (p. 140).
28. Ernst Robert Curtius, *Französischer Geist im neuen Europa* (Stuttgart: Deutsche Verlags-Anstalt, 1925), pp. 15–16, remarks the import of 'recurring phrases', but without specifying his observation. Costil, pp. 83–84, 90, also remarks the importance of leitmotifs for the composition of the *Recherche*, but he does not provide a single example of one such leitmotif. Similarly unspecific are the discussions of leitmotif in Piroué, pp. 197–202, and Matoré und Mecz, pp. 246–54.
29. Uwe Daube, 'Dechiffrierung und strukturelle Funktion der Leitmotive in Marcel Prousts *À la recherche du temps perdu*' (PhD, Heidelberg, 1963), pp. 2–7, 235–47. The two complementary moral powers in which Daube sees all these riddles grounded are 'l'Esprit du Bien und l'Esprit du Mal' (p. 7), regarding these at the same time as the formative principles of Proust's novel. For a critique of Daube's allegorical approach, see Peter Bürger's review in *Romanistisches Jahrbuch* 18 (1967), 190–93.
30. Inge Backhaus, *Strukturen des Romans: Studien zur Leit- und Wiederholungsmotivik in Prousts 'À la recherche du temps perdu'* (Berlin: Schmidt, 1976), pp. 49–53, 114–17. Backhaus identifies several 'constitutive' leitmotifs such as the little phrase of Vinteuil and the taste of the madeleine, as well as 'prefiguring' leitmotifs like the steeples (*clochers*) of Martinville. These examples already betray her fundamental assumption that leitmotifs in Proust are not acoustic figures but intrafictional sensations of any kind (a taste, a smell, a sound, etc.) and as such trigger involuntary memories only in the protagonist. This conception of leitmotifs conflicts with Wagner's position, as Backhaus concedes herself: 'The separation between stage (the place of music/dramatic action) and auditorium (the place of perception) characterizing Wagner's operas is suspended [...] in the novel' (p. 22); similar assertions on pp. 18, 20, 21, 22, 28–29. Suspending this division, however, Backhaus creates two conceptual problems. On the one hand, she fails to describe a leitmotif technique as a method of composition inscribed into the acoustic fabric or *textual* score of the *Recherche*. On the other hand, the ways in which leitmotifs signify become strangely tautological, as indicated by the following passage: 'It is not actually the reader but the protagonist who hears leitmotifs in the Wagnerian sense. He draws the connection between sensory impression and specific contents the author has intended' (p. 28). A fictional character (Swann), to paraphrase this, associates a fictional sense impression (Vinteuil's little phrase) with fictional contents (memories of his love for Odette) because his author (Proust) has intended for him to produce this association. That, clearly, is mere tautology. Fictional leitmotifs are just ideas, whereas an actual leitmotif technique is an audible reality affecting listeners, or for that matter readers. For a more detailed critique of Backhaus, see Rainer Zaiser, *Die Epiphanie in der französischen Literatur: Zur Entmystifizierung eines religiösen Erlebnismusters* (Tübingen: Narr, 1995), pp. 28–29.
31. I quote only in French to stress the sonority of the original phrase, which Moncrieff translates as 'For a long time I would go to bed early' (I, 1).

32. Not least because Merleau-Ponty (*Phenomenology of Perception*, pp. 210–11) quotes the same passage (*Swann* 6/1, 4–5) to illustrate the constitutive role of corporeality in self-awareness.
33. It would be quite impossible to provide a complete index, since the motif *longtemps* is reiterated roughly 600 times throughout the entire *Recherche*, an obstinacy that recalls the endless repetition of certain motifs in Wagner's operas.
34. Joseph Frank, 'Spatial Form in Modern Literature: An Essay in Three Parts', *The Sewanee Review*, 53 (1945), 221–40, 433–56, 643–53 (p. 235). For a more detailed account of involuntary memory as 'extra-temporal' or simultaneous perception triggered by a sensory cue, see Joseph Frank, pp. 235–40, and Laïla El Hajji-Lahrimi, *Sémiotique de la perception dans 'À la recherche du temps perdu de Marcel Proust'* (Paris: L'Harmattan, 1999), pp. 69–71.
35. Wagner, IV, 183: 'Verwirklichung des Gedankens in der Sinnlichkeit'.
36. Arne Stollberg, 'Die Sinnlichkeit des Gedenkens: Aspekte der Leitmotivik bei Wagner und Proust', in *Marcel Proust und die Musik*, pp. 87–103 (p. 9). More recently, John Hamilton made the interesting suggestion that, 'if the Wagnerian leitmotif supplies the methodological basis for Proust's literary endeavor, it is arguably the gramophone that establishes the technological ground for the conversion from the musical to the literary' (John Hamilton, '"Cette douceur, pour ainsi dire wagnérienne": musical resonance in Proust's Recherche', in *Proust and the Arts*, ed. by Christie McDonald and François Proulx (Cambridge: Cambridge University Press, 2015), pp. 90–98 (p. 95)).
37. The revised Moncrieff translation still has 'some such phrase' here (v, 428), although the current Pléiade edition reads 'une [t]belle phrase de Vinteuil' (*Prisonnière* 360).
38. Deleuze, *Proust and Signs*, pp. 59–60.
39. Genette, *Narrative Discourse*, p. 121.
40. I rely here on the classic nomenclature of Hans von Wolzogen, *Leitfaden durch die Musik zu Richard Wagner's Tristan und Isolde*, p. 15:

41. Dahlhaus, *Wagners Musikdramen*, pp. 92–93; *Wagner's Music Dramas*, pp. 62–63.
42. Dahlhaus, *Wagners Musikdramen*, pp. 166–70; *Wagner's Music Dramas*, pp. 116–18, and Grey, 'Leitmotif', pp. 88–93.
43. See Wagner's famous letter of 29 October 1859 to Mathilde Wesendonck (*Richard Wagner über Tristan und Isolde: Aussprüche des Meisters über sein Werk*, ed. by Edwin Lindner (Leipzig: Breitkopf & Härtel, 1912), pp. 126–27).
44. The first edition of *Le Temps retrouvé* (Paris: Gallimard, 1927) renders the last sentence without 'longtemps': 'Si du moins il m'était laissé assez de temps pour accomplir mon œuvre' (II: 261). Despite their significant differences, both the first and the second, current Pléiade edition of *Le Temps retrouvé*, published in 1954 and 1989, respectively, establish 'assez longtemps' in this passage — an editorial decision that my observations would support. The text I quote is identical with the second Pléiade edition. Regarding the editorial difficulties with the posthumous parts of the *Recherche*, see Nathalie Mauriac Dyer, 'Mille feuilles de l'écriture: Les Cahiers manuscrits "au net" de Marcel Proust et la question éditoriale', *The Journal of Social Sciences and Humanities (University of Tokyo)*, 355 (2004), 7–30.
45. Similar points are made by Dahlhaus, *Wagners Musikdramen*, pp. 90–91; *Richard Wagner's Music Dramas*, p. 61, and Grey, 'Leitmotif', pp. 88, 95–97.
46. Roland Barthes, *Image, Music, Text*, trans. by Stephen Heath (New York: Fontana Press, 1977) cites Beethoven's *Diabelli Variations* as an example for a fundamentally 'inaudible' musical piece that can only be 'read', as opposed to the bodily practice of performing music (pp. 152–53).
47. Marcel Proust, *Contre Sainte-Beuve: Précédé de pastiches et mélanges et suivi de essais et articles*, ed. by Pierre Clarac (Paris: Gallimard, 1971), p. 595; quoted after Genette, *Narrative Discourse*, p. 155.
48. Proust to Comte Jean de Gaigneron, 1 August 1919 (*Correspondance*, XVIII (1990), 359). As for the wide-ranging metaphor of the cathedral in the *Recherche*, see Luc Fraisse, *L'Œuvre cathédrale: Proust et l'architecture médiévale* (Paris: Corti, 1990), pp. 77–119.

49. Pierhal, p. 711.
50. Theodor Adorno, *Die musikalischen Monographien* (Frankfurt am Main: Suhrkamp, 1971), p. 139; *In Search of Wagner*, trans. by Rodney Livingstone (London: Verso, 2005), p. 138. Similarly critical of the phantasm of a redemption in art is Leo Bersani, '"The Culture of Redemption": Marcel Proust and Melanie Klein', *Critical Inquiry* 12.2 (1986), 399–421.
51. The genetic importance of Vinteuil for Marcel's development is widely recognized, e.g. by Françoise Leriche, 'Vinteuil ou le révélateur des transformations esthétiques dans la genèse de *À la recherche du temps perdu*', *Bulletin d'Informations Proustiennes*, 16 (1985), 25–39.
52. See the editor's note *Swann* 496. In other contexts, Proust alluded to still more sources of inspiration (e.g. Reynaldo Hahn and Debussy), which suggests that he sought to undermine attempts at associating Vinteuil with any particular composer, period, or style. More recently, Marshall Brown, *The Tooth That Nibbles at the Soul: Essays on Music and Poetry* (Seattle: University of Washington Press, 2010), pp. 26–36, has connected Vinteuil's sonata to Fauré's song op. 21, 'Rencontre', which is also an andante movement. Brown's suggestion is particularly charming because of the song's lyrics. Its beginning captures Swann's initial mood perfectly: 'J'étais triste et pensif quand je t'ai rencontrée, | Je sens moins aujourd'hui mon obstiné tourment; | Ô dis-moi, serais-tu la femme inespérée, | Et le rêve idéal poursuivi vainement?' As for the connection between Proust and Fauré, see also Antoine Compagnon, 'Fauré, Proust et l'unité retrouvée', *Romanic Review*, 78 (1987), 114–21.
53. Brooks, *Reading for the Plot*, pp. xiii, 27 et passim.
54. Before he fell in love with Vinteuil's 'little phrase', when he was 'one of the most distinguished [élégants] members of the Jockey Club' (*Swann* 15/I, 16), Swann would take a fancy preferably to 'the good-looking daughter of a local squire or town clerk' [la fille du hobereau ou du greffier] (*Swann* 188/I, 229).
55. José Ortega y Gasset, 'Le temps, la distance, et la forme chez Proust', *Nouvelle Revue Française*, no. 112 (1923), 267–79 (p. 274). Claudia Brodsky, 'Remembering Swann: Memory and Representation in Proust', *MLN*, 102 (1987), 1014–42 (p. 1017 n. 11), brought Ortega y Gasset to my attention, similarly claiming that 'Swann, the self-effacing frequenter of a circle "where on proscribed *les phrases*", [is] in "love" with a "phrase" instead' (p. 1024).
56. Luhmann, *Liebe als Passion*, p. 177: 'eine eigentümliche Kombination von zirkulärer Geschlossenheit und Offenheit für alles, was die Liebe anreichern kann'. Wandering in Swann's footsteps, Marcel later also instrumentalizes artworks to arouse and maintain his 'love' for Albertine. First he uses Elstir's paintings to see her face in a more flattering light, and then Vinteuil's music to maintain tender feelings for her, despite his rampant jealousy. Backhaus, pp. 91–113, discusses the importance of music in their relation, but also how Marcel's behaviour differs from Swann's (ab)use of Vinteuil in matters of the heart.
57. John W. Kneller, 'The Musical Structure of Proust's "Un Amour de Swann"', *Yale French Studies*, 4 (1949), 55–62, traces the recurrences of the 'little phrase' throughout 'Swann in Love' in greater detail. Kneller's general argument is that Swann's love has a musical form, the 'sonata-allegro', though he regards Odette as the 'principal' and Vinteuil's little phrase only as the 'subordinate subject' (p. 57) of the chapter.
58. Evidently, the revised Moncrieff does not incorporate the deletions applied in the current Pléiade edition of *Le temps retrouvé*.
59. Taking up a term Swann mentions during a conversation with Marcel, several critics have argued for such a teleological 'hierarchy' (*Swann* 96/I, 115) of art forms, associating this idea with Schopenhauer; see Anne Henry, *Marcel Proust: Théories pour une esthétique* (Paris: Klincksieck, 1981), esp. p. 87 and Nattiez, pp. 53, 78–87.
60. The narrator of 'Un amour de Swann' suggests that 'purely musical impressions' are, 'so to speak, *sine materia*', without matter, thus 'vanishing in an instant' (*Swann* 206/I, 251).
61. 'Poésie = *Gemütherregungskunst*' (N II, 801 #292) is Novalis's shorthand for poetry.
62. The prominence of reading in this passage recalls the fact, stressed by Georges Poulet, *La conscience critique* (Paris: Corti, 1971), pp. 49–55, that Proust's novel originated from a practice of critical reading. Poulet thinks that in privileging the act of reading here and elsewhere in his novel, Proust also suggests a fundamental analogy between Marcel's quest for Time and

literary criticism, since both occupations rest on the discovery of similarities through reading and rereading (or remembering); in other words, both involve the selection and comparison of crucial passages in a text, or in the latter case, a life.

63. Gide made these observations six years before the publication of *Le Temps retrouvé*, in his 'Billet à Angèle', *La Nouvelle Revue Française*, 16 (1921), 586–91 (p. 588). Ironically, Gide had advised the *Nouvelle Revue Française* in 1912 not to publish *Du côté de chez Swann*, a refusal that soon thereafter he considered 'the greatest error of the N.R.F.' (*Swann* 460–61). Mallarmé, whose *Coup de dés* Gide compares to Proust's novel in 'Billet à Angèle', develops the notion of 'the total arabesque' in *Oxford, Cambridge: La Musique et les Lettres* (Paris: Perrin, 1895), pp. 46–47. Frédéric Sounac, *Modèle musical et composition romanesque: Genèse et visages d'une utopie esthétique* (Paris: Classiques Garnier, 2014), pp. 296–97, brought these two references to my attention.
64. Nattiez, pp. 34–57, discusses at length Swann's continued failure to detach the meaning of Vinteuil's 'little phrase' from his feelings for Odette, also during the Saint-Euverte soirée (pp. 50–55).
65. As for the genesis of Vinteuil's septet, see Kazuyoshi Yoshikawa, 'Vinteuil ou la genèse du septuor', *Études proustiennes*, 3 (1979), 289–347. Sounac, pp. 327–34, draws interesting parallels between Vinteuil's septet and Beethoven's late string quartets.
66. 'Poor M. Vinteuil', my mother would say, 'he lived for his daughter, and now he has died for her, without getting his reward [son salaire]. Will he get it now, I wonder, and in what form? It can only come to him from her'. (*Swann* 158/1, 192)
67. Malcolm Bowie, *Proust among the Stars* (London: HarperCollins, 1998), pp. 86–87.
68. '[E]in Vormittag ohne Arbeit ist mir ein Tag in der Hölle'; quoted after Thomas Mann, 'Leiden und Größe Richard Wagners', in *Essays*, ed. by Hermann Kurzke and Stephan Stachorski, 6 vols (Frankfurt am Main: Fischer, 1993–97), IV (1995), 11–72 (p. 58).
69. 'L'inspiration est décidément la sœur du travail journalier' — perhaps the most famous line from Baudelaire's 'Conseils aux jeunes littérateurs' (1846), *Baudelaire journaliste: Articles et chroniques*, ed. by Alain Vaillant (Paris: Flammarion, 2011), pp. 57–66 (p. 64).
70. Joshua Landy, 'Proust, his Narrator, and the Importance of the Distinction', *Poetics Today*, 25 (2004), 91–135 (pp. 119–20 n. 47), documents the narrator's concern that he could run out of time before his work is finished.

CONCLUSION

The whole truth, Hegel wrote, is 'essentially a *result*' (PhG 24/11★) — not a 'bare result', of course, but the result of a development (PhG 13/2★). In less pompous terms, you really know what you mean only after you have said it all. What, then, have I been saying, and what conclusions might be drawn from it?

This book examines the interplay of perception and narration, or aesthesis and diegesis, as it presents itself in scriptings of perception I call scenographies — scenes described in words. Readerly aesthesis is what brings these narrative scenes to life, or rather to the senses, for their inner spirit, one might say, are aesthesiologies — the (hi)stories connecting signs and sensations. These (hi)stories are the perceptual logic inscribed into, and by the same token the sensory force projected onto, scenographies, and thus language patterns that make sense only in relation to the senses. What a reader ultimately makes of scenographies, and how he or she perceives their aesthesiologies, is hard to generalize. The general effect, however, is evident: scenographies engage the senses and so invite each reader to produce the most fundamental and most individual kind of sense, sensate sense, a sense filling body and mind with sensation for a period of time. Herein lies the aesthetic power and momentary pleasure of scenographies, the sensuousness they both hold *and* produce.

The relationship of aesthesis and diegesis, as well as the aesthesiology connecting them, is conceived by writers differently in each case, as we have seen. Hegel highlights throughout the fundamental discrepancy between noticing and saying, perceiving and knowing, seeing and understanding. Only the signs of language — indexicals, adjectives, and nouns, as well as their syntactic combination in the process of explanation — can overcome these discrepancies, because they enable logical reflection. Indeed, language makes it possible to reunite *theoretically* what in diachronic experience must come apart, but preserving these differences of experience through explanatory descriptions and, hence, only in a manner of speaking. Thus, for Hegel, plain description or narration (*haplē diēgēsis*, in Plato's words) simply *is* the truth of perception — the form by means of which to reflect on, and thereby organize, the contents of perception without contradiction.

Scenographies are the passages in which this logical reflection takes place, in Hegel's *Phenomenology* no less than in any other phenomenology of consciousness. Here, the (hi)stories of conscious experience are told, including those of perception and sense-certainty. Yet the *whole* truth escapes sequential narration, Hegel maintains, because the truth is, in essence, a synchronic totality that is fully grasped only in the form of a conceptual system. Eventually, therefore, the scenographic mode of explanation characterizing crucial parts of the *Phenomenology* must give way to speculation and conceptualization proper. This is the 'turning point' (PhG 145/110*) of consciousness, as Hegel puts it, at which truth becomes fundamentally abstract: (Hi)storical explanations are then reduced to 'absolute' concepts, and the scenographies of experience are consummated by the system of philosophy. Consciousness thus grasps the universal concept of knowledge — self-conscious reflection — at the expense, however, of 'the colourful appearance of the sensory world' [dem farbigen Scheine des sinnlichen Diesseits] (PhG 145/110*).

For Hegel, scenographies are a means to conceptual ends. He confronts us with (hi)stories of consciousness only to reveal the concept of knowledge. Novalis, Rilke, and Proust, by contrast, do not elaborate theories of perception, let alone of knowledge. Although they all share Hegel's interest in the knowledge of perception and think about it in their works, they never sacrifice the sensory world for the grey in grey of systematic philosophy. They stay true to the language of the senses, to scenographies, using that language — in writing and as lovers of 'the mighty world | Of eye, and ear',[1] and all the other senses — to stage (hi)stories of perception.

The (hi)stories Novalis, Rilke, and Proust have inscribed into their scenographies to conjure up both vivid and complex perceptions clearly differ. Novalis insists throughout his works on the poetic productivity of the senses, indeed on the reciprocity of poetic composition and sensory perception. He thinks that poetic works do not merely seem magical but truly become magic if they are filled with sensuousness and composed with skill. Then poetry becomes a magical spell with the power to direct a listener's, or for that matter a reader's, senses at will. How the spells of poetry are composed, and the kind of aesthetic training they presuppose, is the point of *Die Lehrlinge zu Novalis*, while *Heinrich von Ofterdingen* shows that literature originates not simply in the intuition of poetry but rather in the aesthetic perception of signs — of a phrase such as 'the blue flower'. Enchanted by this puzzling and at first rather senseless phrase, Heinrich begins to dream, poeticizing 'the blue flower' by way of perception. He thus fills its name, just as the poet ought to, with the manifest sense of a scene, which in turn bears the sensuous traces of its name.

Unlike Novalis's Romantic interlacing of inner sense and outer senses, and squarely against Hegel's radical faith in conceptual terminology, Rilke portrays the relation between aesthesis and diegesis as problematic. In many of his poems and prose texts, the 'things' to see are not only inexhaustible but they also seem to resist the names we ordinarily attach to them when describing them objectively. The recurrent metaphor of such resistance is an anonymous exchange of looks or visual 'imprints' that establishes the subjects and objects of looking, but only in hindsight. This paradoxical metaphor of anonymity and *Nachträglichkeit* variously employed in Rilke's middle period is not, however, an anthropomorphic fiction of visual perception, a trope designed to deceive the reader's sense — and senses. Neither is Rilke's metaphor merely an attempt at compensating feelings of alienation and trauma. What the metaphor of anonymously exchanged looks represents instead is an aesthesiology of looking that Rilke takes from experience to experiment with it in scenographic form.[2]

Proust's characteristic style of narration fundamentally derives from Wagner's music dramas, though he still follows, if unwittingly, the important poetic principle Novalis so fervently advocated: for a literary work to charm the senses, its sensuousness must not be an authorial fantasy but must originate from the work's composition. The interplay of aesthesis and diegesis must be a textual reality, a logic structuring the text. Therefore, Proust has inscribed leitmotifs into the verbal texture of his *Recherche*, employing these as a means of associating themes and episodes throughout the novel and, most importantly, as a scenographic means of triggering involuntary perceptions in his readers. In terms of narrative development, Proust's leitmotifs drive the storyline forward, finally leading to Marcel's revelation that he will regain the Time of his life only by writing it down. Ironically, the literary resurrection of times past does not succeed, because Proust and his narrator ran out of time before the work about Time was complete. By incorporating leitmotifs into his prose, Proust may have chosen the aesthesiology best suited for telling the story of remembering Time, but the meaning of Time in the end still escapes him. The point of his long-time search for Time remains veiled in sound, the sound of phrases whose musical force ultimately escapes all semantics.

As different as these literary accounts of perception may be, what they all share is that they describe perceptions scenographically. A translation of text into scene through readerly aesthesis is therefore required to make sense of them. No matter what these scenographies show and regardless of how they were composed — for they are compositions indeed, scenes composed in writing that, nonetheless, ask to be perceived as truths — aesthesis is essential to both shaping and understanding their contents. Each chapter made this point in one way or another, though without determining the manifest contents of readerly aesthesis — what *you* will see, for instance, in the place of 'seeing places' or an 'unheard-of head', what *you* will feel while Heinrich bathes in the exciting waters and sees the face of some 'blue flower', or what kind of physical memory the sound of 'longtemps' will trigger in *you*. The whatness of readerly aesthesis and the physical sense so created has had to be left out precisely because I am concerned with scenographic texts in this book, rather than individual perceptual responses.

Consequently, my readings of Novalis, Rilke, and Proust concern readerly aesthesis only insofar as they examine its textual conditions — those patterns and descriptions that at once enable (or evoke) and constrain (or guide) readerly aesthesis. This aesthesiological approach to literature I see anticipated above all in Novalis's observation that books engender 'a thousand *sensations* and *functions* — *determinate* or *specific* and *free* ones' (N II, 356/#205). My readings largely explore this relationship between perceptual freedom and textual determinacy in scenographies, the result being, I hope, a better understanding of that strange scene within which readerly aesthesis develops, and *for a moment* form, feeling, and intellect *in a sense* coincide.

Vivid perceptions are but one type of response to literary texts. On the whole, however, the experience of literature is not solely perceptual in kind, nor always scenic in appearance. There are other varieties of literary experience. Consider the sense of wonder and curiosity triggered by an oracular verdict like 'Wo aber

Gefahr ist, wächst | Das Rettende auch'; or the sense of political urgency glowing in an exclamation like 'Seid umschlungen, Millionen!'; or the bewilderment at an event like one's having turned overnight into *ein ungeheueres Ungeziefer*; or the sense of uncertainty and hesitation in the face of an enigmatic proposition like 'Alles Vergängliche | Ist nur ein Gleichniß; | Das Unzulängliche | Hier wird's Ereigniß'; or the fun to be had with a silly two-liner like 'Oft ist das Denken schwer, indes, | das Schreiben geht auch ohne es'; or finally (though without exhausting the possibilities of literary experience) the strange mixture of fascination and revulsion when contemplating a man who killed two women to prove his, for want of a better word, 'philosophical genius'. Prophetic, political, surreal, cerebral, comical, and moral senses such as these no doubt belong to the experience of literature. But whenever they figure in scenographies, they can influence their corresponding aesthesiologies only indirectly, which is to say, in the context of a scene and through the medium of perception.

Similarly, not every narrative engages the senses. Many narrations have little to do with perception, and still less to say about logics of perception, since they lack scenographies almost entirely. Narrative prose like *Das Kalkwerk* by Thomas Bernhard is a good example in this regard. What this text 'depicts', or rather reports in print, are not vivid scenes but instead the rambling speeches of a Mr Konrad, who supposedly murdered his 'crippled' wife. In fact, the book consists of nothing but reported, and at times merely purported, speech. The scenes, however, in which Konrad must have uttered those words remain elusive throughout. The few scenographic elements the text contains are monotonous *inquit* formulae, like 'Konrad reportedly said', 'he said according to Wieser', 'he reportedly said to Fro', and so on — indications that are, nonetheless, unspecific and at least two degrees removed from the original scene of enunciation. Consequently, the voice identified as 'Konrad' becomes ever more abstract, disembodied, placeless as the narrative unfolds — a voice from nowhere, mere sound.

For a reader to make literary perceptions, however, sound bites are not enough. He or she needs to be informed about the scene of perception. Scenographies provide this kind of information: what there is to sense and see, what happens in it, and to whom, etc. Therefore, and in contrast to the classic but misleading distinction of 'summary narrative (telling) vs immediate scene (showing)', there is no scene without scenic description, no 'showing' without someone 'telling' what there is to observe. An immediate 'showing' of scene is simply impossible in the medium of language, and there is no way for a narrator to dramatize 'words and gestures [...] directly'.[3] All a narrator can ever do is present words and actions, and likewise thoughts and perceptions, *indirectly* — scenographically, for instance.

Dramatic texts are instructive as to the 'showing' of scenes. Although these texts surely *contain* theatrical scenes, namely in the form of dialogue, they hardly ever include scenographies. They usually lack detailed descriptions regarding the situation (What? Where?) and unfolding (How?) of the scene. Thus, instead of describing scenes through precise stage directions, as is possible and as occasionally happens (for example, in *Waiting for Godot*), dramatic texts consist, by and large, of speech. Consider, as an example, the text of *Much Ado About Nothing*, which is almost entirely made up of speech. Directions as to scenic location and setting are spare, while directions regarding the perceptions, reactions, feelings, gestures, and actions of characters are entirely absent from the text and must be inferred from their respective utterances. This, however, is what theatrical productions are all about: staging text, or deriving scenes from dialogue, as theatre companies do by first developing an effective scenography for each segment of text and then realizing this script through scenic design as well as actions and utterances on stage.

Even if a text clearly describes a scene of perception, it can be difficult to piece that scene together, as we have seen in Grünbein and above all in Rilke. Scenographies often bear resistance to readerly aisthesis, while some of them make full sense on paper only. Thinking of Kafka, whose works include many such paradoxical and ever so slightly surreal scenographies, one might say there are diegetic scenes that, although appealing to the senses, nonetheless follow the laws and logic of perception only *gewissermaßen*, or, 'in a manner of speaking'. The narrative logic (or grammar) of stories here clashes with the sensuous logic (or appearance) of incidents, so that our reading vacillates between the two without ever resolving their conflict. But in this conflict between aesthesis and diegesis lies a pleasure of its own, an in-between that, in bearing *complex* stories, belongs to the aesthetics of literature as well.

'What, then, does the poet do?' Wordsworth famously asked, answering that he 'considers man and the objects that surround him as acting and re-acting upon each other [...] he considers [man] as looking upon this complex scene of ideas and sensations. [...] The objects of the Poet's thoughts are every where; though the eyes and senses of man are, it is true, his favorite guides.'[4] This may oversimplify the laborious process of poetic composition as a verbal, writerly activity.[5] It is clear, however, that perception is essential to the scenes of literature. Literature is more than a mind game about problems of intelligibility that perpetually frustrate our desire for meaning with rhetorical undecidability and non-perceptual ('figural') non-sense. And it is more than a historical document concerning the social, political, aesthetic, epistemic, moral, etc. climate of a certain era.[6] Literature can be productively interpreted in these ways, no doubt, but what makes it truly worth reading is its lasting aesthetic power: the ability to concentrate *and* poeticize perceptions in language. Scenographies are the texts in which such poetic concentration or *Verdichtung* happens, and likewise the style of narration through which ideas and sensations come into contact, acting and re-acting upon each other in the process of reading.

Notes to the Conclusion

1. Lines from William Wordsworth's 'Tintern Abbey'.
2. A learned reader took issue with my choice 'to not engage with Rilke's personal metaphysics'. With regard to Novalis, he criticized my 'readiness to accept Novalis's claims at face value and insufficient willingness to challenge or apply pressure to them'. Surely, if these authors were up for election or applying for funding, it would be irresponsible not to scrutinize their strange idiosyncrasies. Similarly, their claims about perception would have to be challenged if the veracity and/or historical milieu of these claims were at issue. But, since the former is not

the case, and the latter not within the scope of my book, it seemed justified to forego lengthy historical contextualizations, as well as epistemological, scientific, political, or moral criticisms of authors and their ideas. In an aesthesiological, and hence a reader-oriented, perspective, all of that, including ideas *about* perception, is relevant only insofar as it illuminates the force *of* perception that emerges in the process of reading.

3. Norman Friedman, 'Point of View in Fiction: The Development of a Critical Concept', *PMLA*, 70 (1955), 1160–84 (pp. 1169, 1165). Friedman knows, however, that the showing/telling distinction does not hold: 'Not dialogue alone but concrete detail within a specific time-place frame is the *sine qua non* of scene. [...] even the most concrete of scenes will require the exposition of some summary matter' (p. 1170).

4. Wordsworth in the 1802 preface to the *Lyrical Ballads*, p. 248, 249.

5. However, Wordsworth (*Lyrical Ballads*, pp. 237–38, 248–49) considers poetic composition not so much a 'spontaneous overflow of powerful feelings' as he thinks of it as a 'mechanical' procedure involving 'habits of mind' the poet is to acquire through the constant training of both his 'organic sensibility' and his faculty of verbal expression. Novalis has similar ideas about poetic composition; cf. N II, 713 #1113, 803 #305, and N I, 482, 329.

6. A curiosity about the historical contexts of literature that too often strikes me as forced, if not feigned, and also as a bad excuse for what it lacks in the first place: a passion for literature.

BIBLIOGRAPHY

ADORNO, THEODOR W., *Beethoven: Philosophie der Musik: Fragmente und Texte*, ed. by Rolf Tiedemann (Frankfurt am Main: Suhrkamp, 2004)
—— *In Search of Wagner*, trans. by Rodney Livingstone (London: Verso, 2005)
—— *Die musikalischen Monographien* (Frankfurt am Main: Suhrkamp, 1971)
—— *Noten zur Literatur*, ed. by Tiedemann Rolf (Frankfurt am Main: Suhrkamp, 1981)
—— *Zur Metakritik der Erkenntnistheorie/Drei Studien zu Hegel*, ed. by Rolf Tiedemann (Frankfurt am Main: Suhrkamp, 1970)
AMERIKS, KARL, ed., *The Cambridge Companion to German Idealism* (Cambridge: Cambridge University Press, 2000)
ANDERSEN, NATHAN TODD, 'Example, Experiment and Experience in Hegel's *Phenomenology of Spirit*' (PhD, The Pennsylvania State University, 2000)
ANDRIOPOULOS, STEFAN, *Ghostly Apparitions: German Idealism, the Gothic Novel, and Optical Media* (New York: Zone Books, 2013)
APEL, FRIEDMAR, *Das Auge liest mit: Zur Visualität der Literatur* (Munich: Hanser, 2010)
—— 'Die Poetik der Aufmerksamkeit bei Novalis', in *Novalis: Poesie und Poetik*, ed. by Herbert Uerlings (Tübingen: Max Niemeyer, 2004), pp. 141–50
APEL, FRIEDMAR, and OTHERS, eds, *Wahrnehmen und Handeln: Perspektiven einer Literaturanthropologie* (Bielefeld: Aisthesis, 2004)
ARNDAL, STEFFEN, '"Ohne alle Kenntnis von Perspektive"? Zur Raumperzeption in Rainer Maria Rilkes *Aufzeichnungen Des Malte Laurids Brigge*', *Deutsche Vierteljahrsschrift für Literaturwissenschaft und Geistesgeschichte*, 76 (2002), 105–37
—— 'Sehenlernen und Pseudoskopie: Zur visuellen Verarbeitung des Pariserlebnisses in R. M. Rilkes *Die Aufzeichnungen des Malte Laurids Brigge*', *Orbis Litterarum*, 62 (2007), 210–29
ATELIER BRÜCKNER, *Scenography: Making Spaces Talk/Szenografie: Narrative Räume* (Ludwigsburg: Avedition, 2011)
AUGUSTINE, *Confessions*, trans. by William Watts, 2 vols (London: Heinemann, 1912)
AUSTIN, SARAH, TRANS., *Fragments from German Prose Writers* (New York: Appleton, 1841)
BACKHAUS, INGE, *Strukturen des Romans: Studien zur Leit- und Wiederholungsmotivik in Prousts 'A la recherche du temps perdu'* (Berlin: Schmidt, 1976)
BAL, MIEKE, *Narratology: Introduction to the Theory of Narrative* (Toronto; Buffalo: University of Toronto Press, 1997)
BARNETT, STUART, ed., *Hegel after Derrida* (London ; New York: Routledge, 1998)
BAROT, RICK, 'Rilke's Blue Flower', *The Virginia Quarterly Review*, 82 (2006), 225–39
BARTHES, ROLAND, 'L'activité structuraliste' (1963), in *Œuvres complètes*, ed. by Eric Marty, 3 vols (Paris: Le Seuil, 1993–95), I, 1328–33
—— *Image, Music, Text*, trans. by Stephen Heath (New York: Fontana Press, 1977)
BAUDELAIRE, CHARLES, *Critique d'art suivi de Critique musicale*, ed. by Claude Pichois (Paris: Gallimard, 1992)
—— 'Conseils aux jeunes littérateurs' (1846), in *Baudelaire journaliste: Articles et chroniques*, ed. by Alain Vaillant (Paris: Flammarion, 2011)

BEDRIOMO, EMILE, *Proust, Wagner et la coïncidence des arts* (Tübingen: Narr, 1984)
BEHLER, ERNST, 'Friedrich Schlegel und Hegel', *Hegel-Studien*, 2 (1963), 203–50
—— 'Über Manfred Frank: Einführung in die frühromantische Ästhetik', *Athenäum*, 1 (1991), 243–53
BEISER, FREDERICK C., *German Idealism: The Struggle against Subjectivism, 1781–1801* (Cambridge, MA: Harvard University Press, 2002)
—— *Schiller as Philosopher* (Oxford: Oxford University Press, 2005)
BENNETT, JONATHAN, *Kant's Analytic* (Cambridge: Cambridge University Press, 1966)
BERGSON, HENRI, *Essai sur les données immédiates de la conscience* (Paris: Presses Universitaires de France, 1991)
BERNHARD, THOMAS, *Alte Meister: Komödie* (Frankfurt am Main: Suhrkamp, 1985)
BERSANI, LEO, '"The Culture of Redemption": Marcel Proust and Melanie Klein', *Critical Inquiry*, 12 (1986), 399–421
BETZ, ALBRECHT, 'Suche und Initiation: Proust als Wagnerianer', *Merkur: Deutsche Zeitschrift für europäisches Denken*, 598 (1998), 74–80
BLUMENBERG, HANS, *Theorie der Unbegrifflichkeit*, ed. by Anselm Haverkamp (Frankfurt am Main: Suhrkamp, 2007)
—— *Zu den Sachen und zurück*, ed. by Manfred Sommer (Frankfurt: Suhrkamp, 2002)
BODAMMER, THEODOR, *Hegels Deutung der Sprache: Interpretationen zu Hegels Äußerungen über die Sprache* (Hamburg: Meiner, 1969)
BÖHME, GERNOT, *Aisthetik: Vorlesungen über Ästhetik als allgemeine Wahrnehmungslehre* (Munich: Fink, 2001)
BÖHME, HARTMUT, *Fetishism and Culture: A Different Theory of Modernity*, trans. by Anna Galt (Berlin: De Gruyter, 2014)
—— *Natur und Subjekt* (Frankfurt am Main: Suhrkamp, 1988)
BOHN, RALF, and HEINER WILHARM, eds, *Inszenierung und Ereignis: Beiträge zur Theorie und Praxis der Szenografie* (Bielefeld: transcript, 2009)
BOUILLAGUET, ANNICK, and BRIAN G. ROGERS, eds, *Dictionnaire Marcel Proust* (Paris: Champion, 2004)
BOWIE, ANDREW, 'Romantic Philosophy and Religion', in *The Cambridge Companion to German Romanticism*, ed. by Nicholas Saul (Cambridge: Cambridge University Press, 2009), pp. 175–90
BOWIE, MALCOLM, *Proust among the Stars* (London: HarperCollins, 1998)
BOWMAN, BRADY, *Sinnliche Gewissheit: Zur systematischen Vorgeschichte eines Problems des deutschen Idealismus* (Berlin: Akademie Verlag, 2003)
BRANDOM, ROBERT, 'Understanding the Object/Property Structure in Terms of Negation: An Introduction to Hegelian Logic and Metaphysics', 19 October 2014, <http://www.pitt.edu/~brandom/downloads/UOSTN%2014-10-19%20b.docx> [accessed 1 April 2019]
BREITHAUPT, FRITZ, *Jenseits der Bilder: Goethes Politik der Wahrnehmung* (Freiburg im Breisgau: Rombach, 2000)
BROCKETT, OSCAR GROSS, MARGARET MITCHELL, and LINDA HARDBERGER, *Making the Scene: A History of Stage Design and Technology in Europe and the United States* (Austin: University of Texas Press, 2010)
BRODSKY, CLAUDIA, *The Imposition of Form: Studies in Narrative Representation and Knowledge* (Princeton: Princeton University Press, 1987)
—— 'Remembering Swann: Memory and Representation in Proust', *MLN*, 102 (1987), 1014–42
—— 'Szondi and Hegel: "The Troubled Relationship of Literary Criticism to Philosophy"', *Telos*, 140 (2007), 45–63

BROOKS, PETER, *Reading for the Plot: Design and Intention in Narrative* (New York: Alfred A. Knopf, 1984)
BROWN, MARSHALL, *The Tooth That Nibbles at the Soul: Essays on Music and Poetry* (Seattle: University of Washington Press, 2010)
BUNIA, REMIGIUS, *Faltungen: Fiktion, Erzählen, Medien* (Berlin: Erich Schmidt, 2007)
—— *Romantischer Rationalismus: Zu Wissenschaft, Politik und Religion bei Novalis* (Paderborn: Schöningh, 2013)
BÜRGER, PETER, 'Uwe Daube: Dechiffrierung und strukturelle Funktion der Leitmotive in Marcel Prousts *À la recherche du temps perdu*', *Romanistisches Jahrbuch*, 18 (1967), 190–93
BURKE, KENNETH, *A Grammar of Motives* (Berkeley: University of California Press, 1969)
BURNHAM, SCOTT G., *Beethoven: Hero* (Princeton, NJ: Princeton University Press, 1995)
BURWICK, FREDERICK, *The Damnation of Newton: Goethe's Color Theory and Romantic Perception* (Berlin: De Gruyter, 1986)
CALHOON, KENNETH SCOTT, 'Personal Effects: Rilke, Barthes, and the Matter of Photography', *MLN*, 113 (1998), 612–34
CARTER, WILLIAM C., *Marcel Proust: A Life* (New Haven: Yale University Press, 2013)
CASSIN, BARBARA, ed., *Dictionary of Untranslatables : A Philosophical Lexicon*, trans. by Steven Rendall and others (Princeton: Princeton University Press, 2014)
CASSIRER, ERNST, *Das Erkenntnisproblem in der Philosophie und Wissenschaft der neueren Zeit*, 4 vols (Berlin: Cassirer, 1906–52)
CHATMAN, SEYMOUR BENJAMIN, *Coming to Terms: The Rhetoric of Narrative in Fiction and Film* (Ithaca: Cornell University Press, 1990)
—— *Story and Discourse: Narrative Structure in Fiction and Film* (Ithaca: Cornell University Press, 1978)
CHRISTIANS, HEIKO, 'Inszenieren', in *Historisches Wörterbuch des Mediengebrauchs*, ed. by Heiko Christians and others (Cologne: Böhlau, 2015), pp. 297–321
CLASSEN, CONSTANCE, and OTHERS, eds, *A Cultural History of the Senses*, 6 vols (London: Bloomsbury, 2014)
CŒUROY, ANDRÉ, 'Music in the Work of Marcel Proust', trans. by Fred Rothwell, *The Musical Quarterly*, 12 (1926), 132–51
—— *Musique et littérature: Études de musique et de littérature comparées* (Paris: Bloud & Gay, 1923)
COLERIDGE, SAMUEL TAYLOR, *Biographia Epistolaris: Being the Biographical Supplement of Coleridge's Biographia Literaria, with Additional Letters, Etc.*, ed. by Arthur Turnbull, 2 vols (London: G. Bell and Sons, 1911)
COMPAGNON, ANTOINE, 'Fauré, Proust et l'unité retrouvée', *Romanic Review*, 78 (1987), 114–21
CONNELLY, JAMES, 'Music in Marcel Proust's *À la recherche du temps perdu*: A Playlist Resource', <http://www.proust-ink.com/s/proust_playlist.pdf> [accessed 1 April 2019]
CORNGOLD, STANLEY, *Complex Pleasure: Forms of Feeling in German Literature* (Stanford, CA: Stanford University Press, 1998)
—— 'Error in Paul de Man', *Critical Inquiry*, 8 (1982), 489–507
COSTIL, PIERRE, 'La construction musicale de la *Recherche du Temps perdu*', *Bulletin de la société des amis de Marcel Proust*, 8–9 (1958–59), 469–89 and 83–110
CRARY, JONATHAN, *Techniques of the Observer : On Vision and Modernity in the Nineteenth Century* (Cambridge, MA: MIT Press, 1990)
CULLER, JONATHAN, *Theory of the Lyric* (Cambridge, MA: Harvard University Press, 2015)
—— 'Why Lyric?', *PMLA*, 123 (2008), 201–06
CURTIUS, ERNST ROBERT, *Französischer Geist im neuen Europa* (Stuttgart: Deutsche Verlags-Anstalt, 1925)

DAHLHAUS, CARL, *Richard Wagner's Music Dramas*, trans. by Mary Whittall (Cambridge: Cambridge University Press, 1979)
―― *Richard Wagners Musikdramen* (Stuttgart: Reclam, 1996)
DAUBE, UWE, 'Dechiffrierung und strukturelle Funktion der Leitmotive in Marcel Prousts *À la recherche du temps perdu*' (PhD, Heidelberg, 1963)
DAUDET, LUCIEN, *Autour de soixante lettres de Marcel Proust* (Paris: Gallimard, 1929)
DAVIDSON, DONALD, 'Seeing through Language', *Royal Institute of Philosophy Supplement*, 42 (1997), 15–28
DELEUZE, GILLES, *Bergsonism*, trans. by Barbara Habberjam and Hugh Tomlinson (New York: Zone Books, 1991)
―― *Proust and Signs: The Complete Text*, trans. by Richard Howard (Minneapolis: University of Minnesota Press, 2000)
DELEUZE, GILLES, and FÉLIX GUATTARI, *What Is Philosophy?* (New York: Columbia University Press, 1994)
DERRIDA, JACQUES, *Glas*, trans. by John P. Leavey and Richard Rand (Lincoln: University of Nebraska Press, 1986)
―― *Of Grammatology*, trans. by Gayatri Chakravorty Spivak (Baltimore: Johns Hopkins University Press, 1976)
―― *Margins of Philosophy*, trans. by Alan Bass (Chicago: University of Chicago Press, 1982)
―― *Speech and Phenomena, and Other Essays on Husserl's Theory of Signs* (Evanston: Northwestern University Press, 1973)
DESMOND, WILLIAM, 'Art, Philosophy and Concreteness in Hegel', *The Owl of Minerva*, 16 (1985), 131–46
DEWEY, JOHN, 'The Reflex Arc Concept in Psychology', *Psychological Review*, 3 (1896), 357–70
DOHERTY, BRIGID, 'Rilke's Magic Lantern: Figural Language and the Projection of "Interior Action" in the Rodin Lecture', in *Interiors and Interiority*, ed. by Ewa Lajer-Burcharth and Beate Söntgen (Berlin: De Gruyter, 2016), pp. 313–45
DONALD, MERLIN, 'Art and Cognitive Evolution', in *The Artful Mind: Cognitive Science and the Riddle of Human Creativity*, ed. by Mark Turner (New York: Oxford University Press, 2006), pp. 3–20
DORAN, MICHAEL, ed., *Conversations with Cézanne*, trans. by Julie Lawrence Cochran (Berkeley: University of California Press, 2001)
DÜRR, SUZANNE, 'Reflexion und Produktion: Zur Bestimmung des absoluten Ich in Fichtes *Grundlage der gesammten Wissenschaftslehre* von 1794/95', in *Die Aktualität der Romantik*, ed. by Michael Forster and Klaus Vieweg (Berlin: Lit, 2012), pp. 163–81
ECKERMANN, JOHANN PETER, *Gespräche mit Goethe in den letzten Jahren seines Lebens*, ed. by Christoph Michel and Hans Grüters (Berlin: Deutscher Klassiker Verlag, 2011)
EICHENDORFF, JOSEPH VON, *Werke in sechs Bänden*, ed. by Wolfgang Frühwald, Bibliothek deutscher Klassiker, 6 vols (Frankfurt am Main: Deutscher Klassiker-Verlag, 1985–93)
EL HAJJI-LAHRIMI, LAÏLA, *Sémiotique de la perception dans 'À la recherche du temps perdu' de Marcel Proust* (Paris: L'Harmattan, 1999)
ELLRICH, LUTZ, 'Entgeistertes Beobachten: Desinformierende Mitteilungen über Luhmanns allzu verständliche Kommunikation mit Hegel', in *Die Logik der Systeme: Zur Kritik der systemtheoretischen Soziologie Niklas Luhmanns*, ed. by Peter-Ulrich Luhmann and Gerhard Wagner (Konstanz: UVK, 2000), pp. 73–126
EMDEN, CHRISTIAN, 'Metapher, Wahrnehmung, Bewußtsein: Nietzsches Verschränkung von Rhetorik und Neurophysiologie', in *Text und Wissen: Technologische und anthropologische Aspekte*, ed. by Renate Lachmann and Stefan Rieger (Tübingen: Narr, 2003), pp. 127–51

EMPSON, WILLIAM, *Seven Types of Ambiguity* (New York: New Directions, 1966)
ENGEL, MANFRED, ed., *Rilke-Handbuch: Leben, Werk, Wirkung* (Stuttgart: Metzler, 2004)
ENZENSBERGER, HANS MAGNUS, *Die Furie des Verschwindens: Gedichte* (Frankfurt am Main: Suhrkamp, 1980)
FALKENBURG, BRIGITTE, *Die Form der Materie: Zur Metaphysik der Natur bei Kant und Hegel* (Frankfurt am Main: Athenäum, 1987)
FICHTE, JOHANN GOTTLIEB, *Sämmtliche Werke*, ed. by Immanuel Hermann Fichte, 8 vols (Berlin: Veit & Comp., 1845–46)
—— *The Vocation of Man*, trans. by William Smith (London: Chapman, 1848)
FICK, MONIKA, 'Präsenz: Sinnesphysiologische Konstruktion und ästhetische Transformation der Wahrnehmung: Am Beispiel von Przybyszewski, Benn und Rilke', *Scientia Poetica*, 9 (2005), 114–35
—— *Sinnenwelt und Weltseele: Der psychologische Monismus in der Literatur der Jahrhundertwende* (Tübingen: Niemeyer, 1993)
FISCHER, LUKE, *The Poet as Phenomenologist: Rilke and the New Poems* (New York: Bloomsbury, 2015)
FISH, STANLEY, 'Why No One's Afraid of Wolfgang Iser', *Diacritics*, 11 (1981), 2–13
FORSTER, MICHAEL, and KLAUS VIEWEG, eds, *Die Aktualität der Romantik* (Berlin: Lit, 2012)
FOUCAULT, MICHEL, *The Order of Things: An Archaeology of the Human Sciences* (New York: Pantheon Books, 1970)
FRAISSE, LUC, *L'Œuvre cathédrale: Proust et l'architecture médiévale* (Paris: Corti, 1990)
FRANK, JOSEPH, 'Spatial Form in Modern Literature: An Essay in Three Parts', *The Sewanee Review*, 53 (1945), 221–40, 433–56, 643–53
FRANK, MANFRED, *Ansichten der Subjektivität* (Berlin: Suhrkamp, 2012)
—— *Einführung in die frühromantische Ästhetik: Vorlesungen* (Frankfurt am Main: Suhrkamp, 1989)
—— 'Philosophische Grundlagen der Frühromantik', *Athenäum: Jahrbuch für Romantik*, 4 (1994), 37–130
—— *Präreflexives Selbstbewusstsein: Vier Vorlesungen* (Stuttgart: Reclam, 2015)
—— '"Wechselgrundsatz": Friedrich Schlegels philosophischer Ausgangspunkt', *Zeitschrift für philosophische Forschung*, 50 (1996), 26–50
FRICKE, HARALD, and OTHERS, eds, *Reallexikon der deutschen Literaturwissenschaft*, 3rd edn, 3 vols (Berlin: De Gruyter, 1997–2003)
FRIEDMAN, NORMAN, 'Point of View in Fiction: The Development of a Critical Concept', *PMLA*, 70 (1955), 1160–84
FRISCH, MAX, *Tagebuch 1946–1949* (Frankfurt am Main: Suhrkamp, 1985)
FRISCHMANN, BÄRBEL, 'Der philosophische Beitrag der deutschen Frühromantik und Hölderlins', in *Handbuch Deutscher Idealismus*, ed. by Hans-Jörg Sandkühler (Stuttgart: Metzler, 2005), pp. 326–54
—— *Vom transzendentalen zum frühromantischen Idealismus: J. G. Fichte und Fr. Schlegel* (Paderborn: Schöningh, 2005)
FRYE, NORTHROP, *Anatomy of Criticism: Four Essays* (Princeton: Princeton University Press, 1957)
FUERST, NORBERT, *Phases of Rilke* (Bloomington: Indiana University Press, 1958)
GADAMER, HANS-GEORG, 'Erinnerungen an Heideggers Anfänge', *Dilthey-Jahrbuch*, 4 (1986), 13–26
—— 'Phänomenologischer und semantischer Zugang zu Paul Celan?', in *Gesammelte Werke*, 10 vols (Tübingen: Mohr Siebeck, 1999), IX, 461–69
GANDER, HANS-HELMUTH, ed., *Husserl-Lexikon* (Darmstadt: Wissenschaftliche Buchgesellschaft, 2010)

GEBSATTEL, VIKTOR EMIL VON, *Prolegomena einer medizinischen Anthropologie: Ausgewählte Aufsätze* (Berlin: Springer, 1954)

GENETTE, GÉRARD, *Figures III* (Paris: Seuil, 1972)

—— *Narrative Discourse: An Essay in Method* (Ithaca, NY: Cornell University Press, 1980)

GERRIG, RICHARD J., *Experiencing Narrative Worlds: On the Psychological Activities of Reading* (New Haven: Yale University Press, 1993)

GIBSON, JAMES J., *The Ecological Approach to Visual Perception* (Boston: Houghton Mifflin, 1979)

GIDE, ANDRÉ, 'Billet à Angèle', *La Nouvelle Revue Française*, 16 (1921), 586–91

GIER, ALBERT, ed., *Marcel Proust und die Musik* (Berlin: Insel, 2012)

GOETHE, JOHANN WOLFGANG, *Italienische Reise*, ed. by Christoph Michel and Hans-Georg Dewitz, 2 vols (Berlin: Deutscher Klassiker Verlag, 2011)

GOETHE, JOHANN WOLFGANG VON, *Werke* (Hamburger Ausgabe), ed. by Erich Trunz, 14 vols (Munich: Beck, 1981), XIII

GOODMAN, NELSON, *Ways of Worldmaking* (Hassocks: Harvester, 1978)

GOSETTI, JENNIFER A., 'Phenomenological Literature: From the Natural Attitude to "Recognition"', *Philosophy Today*, 45 (2001), 18–27

GREGORY, RICHARD L., *Eye and Brain : The Psychology of Seeing*, Princeton Science Library, 5th edn (Princeton: Princeton University Press, 1997)

—— 'Perceptions as Hypotheses', *Philosophical Transactions of the Royal Society*, 290 (1980), 181–97

GREIMAS, A. J., *Structural Semantics : An Attempt at a Method* (Lincoln, NB: University of Nebraska Press, 1983)

GREY, THOMAS S., 'Leitmotif, Temporality, and Musical Design in the *Ring*', in *The Cambridge Companion to Wagner*, ed. by Thomas S. Grey (Cambridge: Cambridge University Press, 2008), pp. 85–114

—— '"... wie ein rother Faden": On the Origins of "Leitmotif" as Critical Construct and Musical Practice', in *Music and Theory in the Age of Romanticism*, ed. by Ian Bent (Cambridge: Cambridge University Press, 1996), pp. 187–210

GRÜNBEIN, DURS, *Koloß Im Nebel: Gedichte* (Berlin: Suhrkamp, 2012)

—— *Limbische Akte: Gedichte* (Stuttgart: Reclam, 2011)

HAERING, THEODOR, *Novalis als Philosoph* (Stuttgart: Kohlhammer, 1954)

HÄGGLUND, MARTIN, *Radical Atheism: Derrida and the Time of Life* (Stanford University Press, 2008)

HAMBURGER, KÄTE, 'Die phänomenologische Struktur der Dichtung Rilkes', in *Rilke in neuer Sicht*, ed. by Käte Hamburger (Stuttgart: Kohlhammer, 1971), pp. 83–158

—— *Philosophie der Dichter: Novalis, Schiller, Rilke* (Stuttgart: Kohlhammer, 1966)

HAMILTON, JOHN, '"Cette douceur, pour ainsi dire wagnérienne": musical resonance in Proust's Recherche', in *Proust and the Arts*, ed. by Christie McDonald and François Proulx (Cambridge: Cambridge University Press, 2015), pp. 90–98

HARRIS, H. S., 'Hegel's Intellectual Development to 1807', in *The Cambridge Companion to Hegel*, ed. by Frederick C. Beiser (Cambridge: Cambridge University Press, 1993), pp. 25–51

HARRIS, STEFANIE, 'Exposures: Rilke, Photography, and the City', *New German Critique*, 33 (2006), 121–49

HARTMANN, NICOLAI, 'Aristoteles und Hegel', *Beiträge zur Philosophie des deutschen Idealismus*, 3 (1923), 1–36

HEGEL, G. W. F., *Encyclopedia of the Philosophical Sciences in Basic Outline*, trans. by Klaus Brinkmann and Daniel O. Dahlstrom (Cambridge: Cambridge University Press, 2010)

—— *Encyklopädie der philosophischen Wissenschaften im Grundrisse* (Heidelberg: Oßwald, 1817)

―― *Gesammelte Werke*, ed. by Walter Jaeschke and others (Hamburg: Meiner, 1968–)
―― *Hegel and the Human Spirit: A Translation of the Jena Lectures on the Philosophy of Spirit (1805–06) with Commentary*, trans. and ed. by Leo Rauch (Detroit: Wayne State University Press, 1983)
―― *Hegel's Philosophy of Nature*, trans. and ed. by Michael John Petry, 3 vols (London: Allen and Unwin, 1970)
―― *Heidelberg Writings: Journal Publications*, trans. and ed. by Brady Bowman and Allen Speight (Cambridge: Cambridge University Press, 2009)
―― *The Science of Logic*, trans. and ed. by George di Giovanni (Cambridge: Cambridge University Press, 2010)
―― *Vorlesungen über die Philosophie der Natur, Berlin 1819/1820: Nachgeschrieben von Johann Rudolf Ringier*, ed. by Martin Bondeli and Hoo Nam Seelmann (Hamburg: Meiner, 2002)
―― *Werke* ('Theorie-Werkausgabe'), ed. by Eva Moldenhauer and Karl Markus Michel, 20 vols (Frankfurt am Main: Suhrkamp, 1986)
HEIDEGGER, MARTIN, *Gesamtausgabe*, ed. by Friedrich-Wilhelm von Hermann and others, 102 vols (Frankfurt am Main: Vittorio Klostermann, 1976–), V (1977), XXIV (1975)
―― *Sein und Zeit* (Tübingen: Niemeyer, 1967)
HELLER-ROAZEN, DANIEL, *The Inner Touch: Archaeology of a Sensation* (New York: Zone Books, 2007)
HENRICH, DIETER, *Between Kant and Hegel: Lectures on German Idealism*, ed. by David S. Pacini (Cambridge, MA: Harvard University Press, 2003)
―― 'Fichtes ursprüngliche Einsicht', in *Subjektivität und Metaphysik: Festschrift für Wolfgang Cramer*, ed. by Hans Wagner and Dieter Henrich (Frankfurt am Main: Klostermann, 1966), pp. 188–232
―― *Hegel im Kontext* (Berlin: Suhrkamp, 1971)
―― 'Selbstbewusstsein: Kritische Einleitung in eine Theorie', in *Hermeneutik und Dialektik*, ed. by Rüdiger Bubner and others (Tübingen: Mohr, 1970), pp. 257–84
HENRY, ANNE, *Marcel Proust: Théories pour une esthétique* (Paris: Klincksieck, 1981)
HERMAN, DAVID, and OTHERS, eds, *Routledge Encyclopedia of Narrative Theory* (London ; New York: Routledge, 2008)
HÖRISCH, JOCHEN, and MICHAEL WETZEL, eds, *Armaturen der Sinne: Literarische und technische Medien 1870 bis 1920* (Munich: Fink, 1990)
HORN, ANETTE, and PETER HORN, *'Ich lerne sehen': Zu Rilkes Lyrik* (Oberhausen: Athena, 2010)
HORSTMANN, ROLF-PETER, 'The Early Philosophy of Fichte and Schelling', in *The Cambridge Companion to German Idealism*, ed. by Karl Ameriks (Cambridge: Cambridge University Press, 2000), pp. 117–40
HOULGATE, STEPHEN, 'G. W. F. Hegel', in *The Blackwell Guide to the Modern Philosophers: From Descartes to Nietzsche*, ed. by Steven M. Emmanuel (Malden: Blackwell, 2000), pp. 278–305
―― *Hegel's Phenomenology of Spirit: A Reader's Guide* (New York: Bloomsbury, 2013)
HOUSE, JONATHAN, and JULIE SLOTNICK, 'Après-Coup in French Psychoanalysis: The Long Afterlife of Nachträglichkeit: The First Hundred Years, 1893 to 1993', *The Psychoanalytic Review*, 102 (2015), 683–708
HUME, DAVID, *A Treatise of Human Nature: A Critical Edition*, ed. by Mary J. Norton and David Fate Norton, 2 vols (Oxford: Oxford University Press, 2007)
HUSSERL, EDMUND, *Analyses Concerning Passive and Active Synthesis: Lectures on Transcendental Logic*, trans. by Anthony J. Steinbock (Dordrecht: Kluwer, 2001)
―― *Arbeit an den Phänomenen: Ausgewählte Schriften*, ed. by Bernhard Waldenfels (Munich: Fink, 2003)

—— *Husserliana: Gesammelte Werke*, ed. by H. L. van Breda and others, 42 vols (The Hague: Nijhoff, 1950–)
—— *Thing and Space: Lectures of 1907*, trans. by Richard Rojcewicz (Dordrecht: Kluwer, 1997)
HUYSSEN, ANDREAS, *Twilight Memories: Marking Time in a Culture of Amnesia* (New York: Routledge, 1995)
INGARDEN, ROMAN, *Das literarische Kunstwerk, mit einem Anhang von den Funktionen der Sprache im Theaterschauspiel* (Tübingen: Niemeyer, 1931)
—— *The Literary Work of Art: An Investigation on the Borderlines of Ontology, Logic, and Theory of Literature.*, trans. by George G. Grabowicz (Evanston: Northwestern University Press, 1973)
INWOOD, MICHAEL J., *A Hegel Dictionary* (Oxford: Blackwell, 1992)
ISER, WOLFGANG, *Der Akt des Lesens: Theorie ästhetischer Wirkung*, 2nd edn (Munich: Fink, 1984)
—— *Die Appellstruktur der Texte: Unbestimmtheit als Wirkungsbedingung literarischer Prosa* (Konstanz: UVK, 1970)
—— 'Indeterminacy and the Reader's Response in Prose Fiction', in *Aspects of Narrative: Selected Papers from the English Institute*, ed. by J. Hillis Miller (New York: Columbia University Press, 1971), pp. 1–45
—— 'Talk like Whales: A Reply to Stanley Fish', *Diacritics*, 11 (1981), 82–87
ITTNER, ROBERT T., 'Novalis' Attitude toward *Wilhelm Meister* with Reference to the Conception of his *Heinrich von Ofterdingen*', *The Journal of English and Germanic Philology*, 37 (1938), 542–54
IVANOFF, PIERRE, ed., *Marcel Proust: Une vie en musiques* (Paris: Archimbaud, 2012)
JACKSON, NOEL, 'Archaeologies of Perception: Reading Wordsworth after Foucault', *European Romantic Review*, 18 (2007), 175–85
—— *Science and Sensation in British Romantic Poetry* (Cambridge: Cambridge University Press, 2008)
JAESCHKE, WALTER, *Hegel-Handbuch: Leben — Werk — Schule*, 3rd edn (Stuttgart: Metzler, 2016)
JAKOBSON, ROMAN, 'Closing Statement: Linguistics and Poetics', in *Style in Language*, ed. by Thomas Albert Sebeok (Cambridge, MA: MIT Press, 1960), pp. 350–77
JAMME, CHRISTOPH, 'Der Verlust der Dinge: Cézanne — Rilke — Heidegger', *Deutsche Zeitschrift für Philosophie*, 40 (1992), 385–97
JAUSS, HANS ROBERT, *Ästhetische Erfahrung und literarische Hermeneutik* (Frankfurt am Main: Suhrkamp, 1982)
—— 'Der Leser als Instanz einer neuen Geschichte der Literatur', *Poetica*, 7 (1975), 325–44
—— *Literaturgeschichte als Provokation* (Frankfurt am Main: Suhrkamp, 1970)
—— *Toward an Aesthetic of Reception*, trans. by Timothy Bahti (Minneapolis: University of Minnesota Press, 1981)
JAY, MARTIN, *Downcast Eyes: The Denigration of Vision in Twentieth-Century French Thought* (Berkeley: University of California Press, 1993)
JOUBERT, CLAUDE-HENRY, *Le fil d'or: Étude sur la musique dans 'À la recherche du temps perdu'* (Paris: Corti, 1984)
KANT, IMMANUEL, *Critique of Pure Reason*, trans. and ed. by Paul Guyer and Allen W. Wood (Cambridge: Cambridge University Press, 1998)
Gesammelte Schriften (Akademieausgabe), 29 vols (Berlin: Reimer; De Gruyter, 1902–)
—— *Werke*, ed. by Wilhelm Weischedel, 12 vols (Frankfurt am Main: Suhrkamp, 1977)
KAUFMANN, WALTER A., *Hegel: A Reinterpretation* (Garden City: Anchor Books, 1966)
KETTNER, MATTHIAS, *Hegels 'sinnliche Gewissheit': Diskursanalytischer Kommentar* (Frankfurt am Main: Campus, 1990)

KHURANA, THOMAS, 'Kant, Heidegger und das Verhältnis von Repräsentation und Abstraktion', *Zeitschrift für Ästhetik und allgemeine Kunstwissenschaft*, 58 (2013), 203–24
KILCHER, ANDREAS B., *Mathesis und Poiesis: Die Enzyklopädik der Literatur 1600 bis 2000* (Munich: Fink, 2003)
KITTLER, FRIEDRICH A., *Aufschreibesysteme 1800/1900*, 4th edn (Munich: Fink, 2003)
—— 'Heinrich von Ofterdingen als Nachrichtenfluß', in *Die Wahrheit der technischen Welt: Essays zur Genealogie der Gegenwart* (Berlin: Suhrkamp, 2013), pp. 132–59
—— 'Die Irrwege des Eros und die "absolute Familie": Psychoanalytischer und diskursanalytischer Kommentar zu Klingsohrs Märchen in Novalis' *Heinrich von Ofterdingen*', in *Psychoanalytische und psychopathologische Literaturinterpretation*, ed. by Bernd Urban and Winfried Kudszus (Darmstadt: Wissenschaftliche Buchgesellschaft, 1981), pp. 421–70
—— 'Die Laterna magica der Literatur: Schillers und Hoffmanns Medienstrategien', *Athenäum: Jahrbuch für Romantik*, 4 (1994), 219–37
—— *Musik und Mathematik*, 2 vols (Munich: Fink, 2006–09)
—— *Optische Medien: Berliner Vorlesung 1999* (Berlin: Merve, 2002)
—— *Philosophien der Literatur: Berliner Vorlesung 2002* (Berlin: Merve, 2013)
KNELLER, JOHN W., 'The Musical Structure of Proust's "Un Amour de Swann"', *Yale French Studies*, 4 (1949), 55–62
KOCH, ANTON FRIEDRICH, 'Hegel's Science of Logic', Lectures at Emory University, 2009, <http://www.philosophie.uni-hd.de/imperia/md/content/fakultaeten/phil/philosophischesseminar2/koch/emory09.pdf> [accessed 1 April 2019]
—— 'Sinnliche Gewißheit und Wahrnehmung: Die beiden ersten Kapitel der *Phänomenologie des Geistes*', in *Hegels Phänomenologie des Geistes: Ein kooperativer Kommentar zu einem Schlüsselwerk der Moderne*, ed. by Klaus Vieweg and Wolfgang Welsch (Frankfurt am Main: Suhrkamp, 2008), pp. 135–52
KÖHNEN, RALPH, *Das optische Wissen: Mediologische Studien zu einer Geschichte des Sehens* (Paderborn: Fink, 2009)
—— 'Das physiologische Wissen Rilkes und seine Cézanne-Rezeption', in *Poetik der Evidenz: Die Herausforderung der Bilder in der Literatur um 1900*, ed. by Helmut Pfotenhauer and others (Würzburg: Königshausen & Neumann, 2005), pp. 141–62
KRACAUER, SIEGFRIED, *History: The Last Things before the Last*, ed. by Paul Oskar Kristeller (Oxford: Oxford University Press, 1969)
KRAMER, ANDREAS, 'Rilke and Modernism', in *The Cambridge Companion to Rilke*, ed. by Karen Leeder and Robert Vilain (Cambridge: Cambridge University Press, 2010), pp. 113–30
KREMER, DETLEF, *Romantik* (Stuttgart: Metzler, 2001)
KRUG, WILHELM TRAUGOTT, *Entwurf eines neuen Organon's der Philosophie, oder, Versuch über die Prinzipien der philosophischen Enkenntniss* (Meissen: Erbstein, 1801)
KURZ, MARTINA, *Bild-Verdichtungen: Cézannes Realisation als poetisches Prinzip bei Rilke und Handke* (Göttingen: Vandenhoeck & Ruprecht, 2003)
LACOUE-LABARTHE, PHILIPPE, *Heidegger, Art and Politics: The Fiction of the Political*, trans. by Chris Turner (Oxford: Blackwell, 1990)
LANDY, JOSHUA, 'Proust, his Narrator, and the Importance of the Distinction', *Poetics Today*, 25 (2004), 91–135
LAPLANCHE, JEAN, and J. B. PONTALIS, *The Language of Psychoanalysis* (London: The Hogarth Press, 1973)
LARMORE, CHARLES, 'Hölderlin and Novalis', in *The Cambridge Companion to German Idealism*, ed. by Karl Ameriks (Cambridge: Cambridge University Press, 2000), pp. 141–60
LEMPICKI, SIGMUND VON, 'Bücherwelt und wirkliche Welt: Ein Beitrag zur Wesenserfassung der Romantik', *Deutsche Vierteljahrsschrift für Literaturwissenschaft und Geistesgeschichte*, 3 (1925), 339–86

LEPPMANN, WOLFGANG, *Rilke: Sein Leben, seine Welt, sein Werk* (Bern: Scherz, 1981)
LERICHE, FRANÇOISE, 'Vinteuil ou le révélateur des transformations esthétiques dans la genèse de *À la recherche du temps perdu*', *Bulletin d'Informations Proustiennes*, 16 (1985), 25–39
LESSING, GOTTHOLD EPHRAIM, *Laokoon; Briefe, Antiquarischen Inhalts*, ed. by Wilfried Barner (Frankfurt am Main: Deutscher Klassiker Verlag, 2007)
LINDNER, EDWIN, ed., *Richard Wagner über Tristan und Isolde: Aussprüche des Meisters über sein Werk* (Leipzig: Breitkopf & Härtel, 1912)
LOCKE, JOHN, *An Essay Concerning Human Understanding*, ed. by Alexander Campbell Fraser, 2 vols (Oxford: Clarendon Press, 1894)
LONGUENESSE, BÉATRICE, *Kant and the Capacity to Judge: Sensibility and Discursivity in the Transcendental Analytic of the Critique of Pure Reason* (Princeton: Princeton University Press, 1998)
LOTMAN, JURIJ M., *The Structure of the Artistic Text*, trans. by Gail Lenhoff and Ronald Vroon (Ann Arbor: University of Michigan, 1977)
LOWE, E. J., 'Substance and Identity', in *Substanz: Neue Überlegungen zu einer klassischen Kategorie des Seienden*, ed. by Käthe Trettin (Frankfurt am Main: Klostermann, 2005), pp. 33–51
LÖWITH, KARL, *Von Hegel zu Nietzsche : Der revolutionäre Bruch im Denken des neunzehnten Jahrhunderts* (Hamburg: Meiner, 1995)
LUHMANN, NIKLAS, *Art as a Social System*, trans. by Eva M. Knodt (Stanford: Stanford University Press, 2000)
—— *Die Gesellschaft der Gesellschaft* (Frankfurt am Main: Suhrkamp, 1997)
—— *Die Kunst der Gesellschaft* (Frankfurt am Main: Suhrkamp, 1995)
—— *Liebe als Passion: Zur Codierung von Intimität* (Frankfurt am Main: Suhrkamp, 1982)
MACKSEY, RICHARD, and EUGENIO DONATO, eds, *The Languages of Criticism and the Sciences of Man* (Baltimore: Johns Hopkins University Press, 1970)
MAGEE, GLENN ALEXANDER, *The Hegel Dictionary* (London; New York: Continuum, 2010)
MALLARMÉ, STÉPHANE, *Oxford, Cambridge: La Musique et Les Lettres* (Paris: Perrin, 1895)
DE MAN, PAUL, *Blindness and Insight : Essays in the Rhetoric of Contemporary Criticism* (Minneapolis: University of Minnesota Press, 1983)
—— *The Resistance to Theory* (Minneapolis: University of Minnesota Press, 1986
MANN, THOMAS, 'Leiden und Größe Richard Wagners', in *Essays*, ed. by Hermann Kurzke and Stephan Stachorski, 6 vols (Frankfurt am Main: Fischer, 1993–97), IV (1995), 11–72
MARX, BERNHARD, *'Meine Welt beginnt bei den Dingen': Rainer Maria Rilke und die Erfahrung der Dinge* (Würzburg: Königshausen & Neumann, 2015)
MATALA DE MAZZA, ETHEL, and CLEMENS PORNSCHLEGEL, eds, *Inszenierte Welt: Theatralität als Argument literarischer Texte* (Freiburg im Breisgau: Rombach, 2003)
MATHEWS, TIMOTHY, 'Foreword', *Romance Studies*, 32 (2014), 69–70
MATORÉ, GEORGES, and IRÈNE TAMBA-MECZ, *Musique et structure romanesque dans 'La recherche du temps perdu'* (Paris: Klincksieck, 1973)
MATT, PETER VON, *Sieben Küsse: Glück und Unglück in der Literatur* (Munich: Hanser, 2017)
MAURIAC DYER, NATHALIE, 'Mille feuilles de l'écriture: Les cahiers manuscrits "au net" de Marcel Proust et la question éditoriale', *The Journal of Social Sciences and Humanities (University of Tokyo)*, 355 (2004), 7–30
MCCUMBER, JOHN, *The Company of Words: Hegel, Language, and Systematic Philosophy* (Evanston: Northwestern University Press, 1993)
MCHALE, BRIAN, 'Beginning to Think about Narrative in Poetry', *Narrative*, 17 (2009), 11–27
MCKINNEY, JOSLIN, and PHILIP BUTTERWORTH, *The Cambridge Introduction to Scenography* (Cambridge: Cambridge University Press, 2009)

McSweeney, Kerry, *The Language of the Senses: Sensory-Perceptual Dynamics in Wordsworth, Coleridge, Thoreau, Whitman, and Dickinson* (Montreal: McGill-Queen's University Press, 1998)
Mein, Margaret, 'Proust and Wagner', *Journal of European Studies*, 19 (1989), 205–22
Meiners, Christoph, *Briefe über die Schweiz: Zweiter Theil* (Berlin: Spener, 1785)
Melville, Herman, *Moby Dick*, ed. by Tony Tanner (Oxford: Oxford University Press, 2008)
Mendelsund, Peter, *What We See When We Read: A Phenomenology* (New York: Vintage Books, 2014)
Merleau-Ponty, Maurice, 'Cézanne's Doubt', in *Sense and Non-Sense*, trans. by Hubert L. Dreyfus and Patricia Allen Dreyfus (Evanston: Northwestern University Press, 1964), pp. 9–25
―― *Phenomenology of Perception*, trans. by Colin Smith (New York: Routledge, 2002)
Meyer, Theodor A., *Das Stilgesetz der Poesie* (Leipzig: Hirzel, 1901)
Mijolla, Alain de, ed., *International Dictionary of Psychoanalysis*, 3 vols (Detroit: Thomson Gale, 2005)
Millan-Zaibert, Elizabeth, *Friedrich Schlegel and the Emergence of Romantic Philosophy* (Albany: SUNY Press, 2007)
Molde, Klas, 'Enchantment and Embarrassment in the Lyric' (PhD, Cornell University, 2016)
Molnár, Géza von, *Novalis' 'Fichte Studies': The Foundations of his Aesthetics* (The Hague: Mouton, 1970)
Mukarovsky, Jan, *Kapitel aus der Poetik* (Frankfurt am Main: Suhrkamp, 1967)
Müller, Günther, *Morphologische Poetik: Gesammelte Aufsätze*, ed. by Elena Müller (Tübingen: Niemeyer, 1968)
Müller, Wolfgang G., 'Rilke, Husserl und die Dinglyrik der Moderne', in *Rilke und die Weltliteratur*, ed. by Manfred Engel and Dieter Lamping (Zurich: Artemis & Winkler, 1999), pp. 214–35
Münster, Harald, *Fichte trifft Darwin, Luhmann und Derrida: 'Die Bestimmung des Menschen' in differenztheoretischer Rekonstruktion und im Kontext der 'Wissenschaftslehre novo methodo'* (Amsterdam: Rodopi, 2011)
Naschert, Guido, 'Friedrich Schlegel über Wechselerweis und Ironie', *Athenäum: Jahrbuch für Romantik*, 6–7 (1996/97), 47–90 and 11–36
Nassar, Dalia, *The Romantic Absolute: Being and Knowing in Early German Romantic Philosophy, 1795–1804* (Chicago: University of Chicago Press, 2013)
―― ed., *The Relevance of Romanticism: Essays on German Romantic Philosophy* (Oxford: Oxford University Press, 2014)
Nattiez, Jean Jacques, *Proust as Musician* (Cambridge: Cambridge University Press, 1989)
Naumann, Helmut, *Malte-Studien: Untersuchungen zu Aufbau und Aussagegehalt der 'Aufzeichnungen des Malte Laurids Brigge' von Rainer Maria Rilke* (Rheinfelden: Schäuble, 1983)
Neumann, Gerhard, and others, eds, *Szenographien: Theatralität als Kategorie der Literaturwissenschaft* (Freiburg im Breisgau: Rombach, 2000)
Nicolin, Günther, ed., *Hegel in Berichten seiner Zeitgenossen* (Hamburg: Meiner, 1970)
Nietzsche, Friedrich, *Sämtliche Werke: Kritische Studienausgabe*, ed. by Giorgio Colli and Mazzino Montinari, 15 vols (Munich: Deutscher Taschenbuch Verlag, 1999)
Noë, Alva, *Action in Perception* (Cambridge, MA: MIT Press, 2004)
Novalis, *Fichte Studies*, trans. by Jane Kneller (Cambridge: Cambridge University Press, 2003)
―― *Henry of Ofterdingen: A Romance*, trans. by Frederick S. Stallknecht (Cambridge, MA:

John Owen, 1842) <http://nrs.harvard.edu/urn-3:FHCL:11729593> [accessed 1 April 2019]

―― *Notes for a Romantic Encyclopaedia: Das allgemeine Brouillon*, trans. by David W. Wood (Albany: SUNY Press, 2007)

―― *The Novices of Sais*, trans. by Ralph Manheim (Brooklyn: Archipelago Books, 2005)

―― *Philosophical Writings*, trans. by Margaret Mahony Stoljar (Albany: State University of New York Press, 1997)

―― *Schriften*, ed. by Friedrich Schlegel and Ludwig Tieck, 2 vols (Berlin: Buchhandlung der Realschule, 1802)

―― *Schriften: Die Werke Friedrich von Hardenbergs*, ed. by Paul Kluckhohn and Richard H. Samuel, 6 vols (Stuttgart: Kohlhammer, 1960–)

―― *Werke*, ed. by Gerhard Schulz (Munich: Beck, 2001)

―― *Werke, Tagebücher und Briefe Friedrich von Hardenbergs*, ed. by Hans-Joachim Mähl and Richard H. Samuel, 3 vols (Munich: Hanser, 1978)

NÜNNING, VERA, and OTHERS, eds, *Cultural Ways of Worldmaking: Media and Narratives* (Berlin: De Gruyter, 2010)

OHASHI, RYOSUKE, 'Die Tragweite des Sinnlichen', in *Hegels Phänomenologie des Geistes: Ein kooperativer Kommentar zu einem Schlüsselwerk der Moderne*, ed. by Klaus Vieweg and Wolfgang Welsch (Frankfurt am Main: Suhrkamp, 2008), pp. 115–34

OITTINEN, VESA, 'Mephisto und die List der Vernunft', *Deutsche Zeitschrift für Philosophie*, 39 (1991), 825–38

O'NEILL SURBER, JERE, ed., *Hegel and Language* (Albany: SUNY Press, 2006)

ORTEGA Y GASSET, JOSÉ, 'Le temps, la distance, et la forme chez Proust', *Nouvelle Revue Française*, 112 (1923), 267–79

ORTH, ERNST WOLFGANG, 'Zu Husserls Wahrnehmungsbegriff', *Husserl Studies*, 11 (1994), 153–68

OUELLET, PIERRE, 'The I's Eye: Perception and Mental Imagery in Literature', trans. by Larry Marks, *SubStance*, 22 (1993), 64–73

PASEWALCK, SILKE, *Die fünffingrige Hand: Die Bedeutung der sinnlichen Wahrnehmung beim späten Rilke* (Berlin: De Gruyter, 2002)

PATSCH, HERMANN, '"... ach! Philosophie": Fichte, Schelling und Hegel über Goethes *Faust*. Ein Fragment', *Jahrbuch des Freien Deutschen Hochstifts* (2015), 80–122

PESSOA, FERNANDO, *The Book of Disquiet*, trans. by Richard Zenith (London: Penguin, 2002)

PETERS, JOHN DURHAM, '"The Root of Humanity": Hegel on Language and Communication', in *Figuring the Self: Subject, Absolute, and Others in Classical German Philosophy*, ed. by David E. Klemm and Günter Zöller (Albany: SUNY Press, 1997), pp. 227–44

PICARD, TIMOTHÉE, ed., *Dictionnaire encyclopédique Wagner* (Arles: Actes sud, 2010)

PIERHAL, ARMAND, 'Sur la composition wagnérienne de l'œuvre de Proust', *Bibliothèque Universelle et Revue de Genève* (1929), 710–19

PINKARD, TERRY P., *Hegel's Phenomenology: The Sociality of Reason* (Cambridge: Cambridge University Press, 1994)

PIPPIN, ROBERT, 'Fichte's Alleged Subjective, Psychological, One-Sided Idealism', in *The Reception of Kant's Critical Philosophy: Fichte, Schelling, and Hegel*, ed. by Sally Sadgwick (Cambridge: Cambridge University Press, 2000), pp. 147–70

―― *Hegel's Idealism : The Satisfactions of Self-Consciousness* (Cambridge ; New York: Cambridge University Press, 1989)

―― 'The Status of Literature in Hegel's *Phenomenology of Spirit*: On the Lives of Concepts', in *Inventions of the Imagination: Romanticism and Beyond*, ed. by Richard T. Gray (Seattle: University of Washington Press, 2011), pp. 102–20

PIROUÉ, GEORGES, *Proust et la musique du devenir* (Paris: Denoël, 1960)
PLATO, *The Republic*, trans. by Paul Shorey, Loeb Classical Library, 2 vols (Cambridge, MA: Harvard University Press, 1930)
—— *Theaetetus. Sophist*, trans. by Harold North Fowler, Loeb Classical Library (Cambridge, MA: Harvard University Press, 1928)
PLESSNER, HELMUTH, *Die Einheit der Sinne: Grundlinien einer Ästhesiologie des Geistes* (1923), in *Gesammelte Schriften*, ed. by Günter Dux and others, 10 vols (Frankfurt am Main: Suhrkamp, 2003), III, 7–315
PÖGGELER, OTTO, 'Hegels Jenaer Systemkonzeption', *Philosophisches Jahrbuch*, 71 (1963), 268–318
POULET, GEORGES, *La conscience critique* (Paris: Corti, 1971)
PRECHTL, PETER, and FRANZ-PETER BURKARD, eds, *Metzler Philosophie Lexikon: Begriffe und Definitionen*, 2nd edn (Stuttgart: Metzler, 1999)
PROUST, MARCEL, *À la recherche du temps perdu*, ed. by Jean-Yves Tadié and others, folio classique, 7 vols (Paris: Gallimard, 1988–90)
—— *Contre Sainte-Beuve: Précédé de pastiches et mélanges et suivi de essais et articles*, ed. by Pierre Clarac (Paris: Gallimard, 1971)
—— *Correspondance*, ed. by Philip Kolb, 21 vols (Paris: Plon, 1970–93)
—— *In Search of Lost Time*, trans. by C. K. Scott Moncrieff, Terence Kilmartin, and Andreas Mayor, revised by D. J. Enright, 6 vols (London: Chatto & Windus, 1992)
—— *Matinée chez la princesse de Guermantes: Cahiers du 'Temps retrouvé'*, ed. by Henri Bonnet and Bernard Brun (Paris: Gallimard, 1982)
PURPUS, WILHELM, *Zur Dialektik des Bewusstseins nach Hegel: Ein Beitrag zur Würdigung der 'Phänomenologie des Geistes'* (Berlin: Trowitzsch, 1908)
RADDATZ, FRITZ J., 'Durs Grünbein — Die dichtende Luftnummer', *Die Welt*, 21 August 2012 <http://www.welt.de/kultur/literarischewelt/article108711083/Durs-Gruenbein-die-dichtende-Luftnummer.html> [accessed 1 April 2019]
RAPIC, SMAIL, 'Husserls Untersuchungen zur Selbstzeitigung der Subjektivität auf dem Hintergrund der Zeittheorien Kants und Hegels', in *Husserl und die klassische deutsche Philosophie*, ed. by Faustino Fabbianelli and Sebastian Luft (Cham: Springer, 2014), pp. 149–60
REUTER, SÖREN, 'Nietzsche und die Sinnesphysiologie und Erkenntniskritik', in *Handbuch Nietzsche und die Wissenschaften: Natur-, geistes- und sozialwissenschaftliche Kontexte*, ed. by Helmut Heit and Lisa Heller (Berlin: De Gruyter, 2014), pp. 79–106
RICOEUR, PAUL, 'Metaphor and the Main Problem of Hermeneutics', *New Literary History*, 6 (1974), 95–110
—— 'Narrative Time', *Critical Inquiry*, 7 (1980), 169–90
RIEDLBAUER, JÖRG, '"Erinnerungsmotive" in Wagner's *Der Ring des Nibelungen*', *The Musical Quarterly*, 74 (1990), 18–30
RILKE, RAINER MARIA, *Gesammelte Briefe*, ed. by Ruth Sieber-Rilke, 6 vols (Leipzig: Insel, 1936–40)
—— *Sämtliche Werke*, ed. by Ernst Zinn, 7 vols (Frankfurt am Main: Insel, 1955–97)
—— *The Notebooks of Malte Laurids Brigge*, trans. by William Needham <http://archive.org/details/TheNotebooksOfMalteLauridsBrigge> [accessed 1 April 2019]
—— *The Notebooks of Malte Laurids Brigge*, trans. by Michael Hulse (London: Penguin, 2009)
—— *Werke: Kommentierte Ausgabe in vier Bänden*, ed. by Manfred Engel and others, 4 vols (Frankfurt am Main: Insel, 1996)
RITTER, JOACHIM, and OTHERS, eds, *Historisches Wörterbuch der Philosophie*, 13 vols (Basle: Schwabe, 1971–2007)
ROSKIES, ADINA L., 'The Binding Problem', *Neuron*, 24 (1999), 7–9

RYAN, JUDITH, *The Vanishing Subject: Early Psychology and Literary Modernism* (Chicago: University of Chicago Press, 1991)
SANDKÜHLER, HANS-JÖRG, ed., *Handbuch Deutscher Idealismus* (Stuttgart: Metzler, 2005)
SAUL, NICHOLAS, ' "Poetisierung d[es] Körpers": Der Poesiebegriff Friedrich von Hardenbergs (Novalis) und die anthropologiche Tradition', in *Novalis: Poesie und Poetik*, ed. by Herbert Uerlings (Tübingen: Niemeyer, 2004), pp. 151–69
SCARANTINO, ANDREA, 'Affordances Explained', *Philosophy of Science*, 70 (2003), 949–61
SCHANK, ROBERT C., and ROBERT P. ABELSON, 'Knowledge and Memory: The Real Story', in *Knowledge and Memory: The Real Story*, ed. by Robert S. Wyer (Hillsdale: Erlbaum, 1995), pp. 1–85 <http://cogprints.org/636/> [accessed 1 April 2019]
SCHEFER, OLIVIER, 'Les *Fichte-Studien* de Novalis et la "Tathandlung": à l'épreuve de la transcendance', *Les études philosophiques*, 1 (2000), 55–74
SCHILLER, FRIEDRICH, *Sämtliche Werke*, ed. by Peter-André Alt and others, 5 vols (Munich: Hanser, 2004), v
SCHILLER, FRIEDRICH, and JOHANN WOLFGANG GOETHE, *Der Briefwechsel: Historisch-kritische Ausgabe*, ed. by Norbert Oellers, 2 vols (Stuttgart: Reclam, 2009)
SCHILLER, FRIEDRICH, and JOHANN WOLFGANG VON GOETHE, *Correspondence between Schiller and Goethe, from 1794 to 1805*, trans. by L. Dora Schmitz, 2 vols (London: Bell, 1877)
SCHIRREN, THOMAS, *Aisthesis vor Platon : Eine semantisch-systematische Untersuchung zum Problem der Wahrnehmung* (Stuttgart: Teubner, 1998)
SCHLEGEL, AUGUST WILHELM VON, *Kritische Ausgabe der Vorlesungen*, ed. by Ernst Behler, 4 vols (Paderborn: Schöningh, 1989–)
SCHLEGEL, FRIEDRICH VON, *Kritische Friedrich-Schlegel-Ausgabe*, ed. by Ernst Behler, and others, 35 vols (Munich: Schöningh, 1958–)
SCHNEIDER, SABINE, *Die schwierige Sprache des Schönen: Moritz' und Schillers Semiotik der Sinnlichkeit* (Würzburg: Königshausen & Neumann, 1998)
——— *Verheißung der Bilder : Das andere Medium in der Literatur um 1900* (Tübingen: Niemeyer, 2006)
SCHÖN, ERICH, *Der Verlust der Sinnlichkeit, oder, Die Verwandlungen des Lesers: Mentalitätswandel um 1800* (Stuttgart: Klett-Cotta, 1987)
SCHOPENHAUER, ARTHUR, *Werke in zehn Bänden*, ed. by Angelika Hübscher(Zurich: Diogenes, 1977)
SCHÜTZEICHEL, RAINER, *Sinn als Grundbegriff bei Niklas Luhmann* (Frankfurt am Main: Campus, 2003)
SEEL, MARTIN, *Ästhetik des Erscheinens* (Frankfurt am Main: Suhrkamp, 2003)
SÉGUIN, PHILIPPE, 'Von der Philosophie zur "ars combinatoria": Novalis' Erwartungen an die Mathematik und die Folgen', in *Zahlen, Zeichen und Figuren: Mathematische Inspirationen in Kunst und Literatur*, ed. by Andrea Albrecht and others (Berlin: De Gruyter, 2011), pp. 248–67
SHAPIRO, LAWRENCE A., ed., *The Routledge Handbook of Embodied Cognition* (New York: Routledge, 2014)
SIMENAUER, ERICH, *Rainer Maria Rilke: Legende und Mythos* (Berne: Haupt, 1953)
SIMON, RALF, *Die Bildlichkeit des lyrischen Textes: Studien zu Hölderlin, Brentano, Eichendorff, Heine, Mörike, George und Rilke* (Munich: Fink, 2011)
——— *Die Idee der Prosa: Zur Ästhetikgeschichte von Baumgarten bis Hegel mit einem Schwerpunkt bei Jean Paul* (Munich: Fink, 2013)
——— *Der poetische Text als Bildkritik* (Munich: Fink, 2009)
SLOTERDIJK, PETER, *Du musst dein Leben ändern: Über Anthropotechnik* (Frankfurt am Main: Suhrkamp, 2009)
SMITH, MARK M., *Sensing the Past: Seeing, Hearing, Smelling, Tasting, and Touching in History* (Berkeley: University of California Press, 2007)

SOKEL, WALTER H., 'The Devolution of the Self in *The Notebooks of Malte Laurids Brigge*', in *Rilke: The Alchemy of Alienation*, ed. by Frank Baron and others (Lawrence: The Regents Press of Kansas, 1980), pp. 171–90

SOUNAC, FRÉDÉRIC, *Modèle musical et composition romanesque: Genèse et visages d'une utopie esthétique* (Paris: Classiques Garnier, 2014)

STADLER, ULRICH, 'Zur Anthropologie Friedrich von Hardenbergs (Novalis)', in *Novalis und die Wissenschaften*, ed. by Herbert Uerlings (Tübingen: Niemeyer, 1997), pp. 87–103

STEINER, UWE C., 'Die Tücken des Subjekts und der Einspruch der Dinge: Romantische Krisen der Objektivität bei Novalis, Eichendorff und Hoffmann', in *Schläft ein Lied in allen Dingen? Romantische Dingpoetik*, ed. by Christiane Holm and Günter Oesterle (Würzburg: Königshausen & Neumann, 2011), pp. 29–42

STEKELER-WEITHOFER, PIRMIN, *Hegels 'Phänomenologie des Geistes': Ein dialogischer Kommentar*, 2 vols (Hamburg: Meiner, 2014)

STERN, ROBERT, *Hegel, Kant and the Structure of the Object* (London: Routledge, 1990)

—— *The Routledge Guide Book to Hegel's Phenomenology of Spirit* (New York: Routledge, 2013)

STEWART, SUSAN, *Poetry and the Fate of the Senses* (Chicago: University of Chicago Press, 2002)

STOLLBERG, ARNE, 'Die Sinnlichkeit des Gedenkens: Aspekte der Leitmotivik bei Wagner und Proust', in *Marcel Proust und die Musik*, ed. by Albert Gier (Berlin: Insel, 2012), pp. 87–103

STONE, ALISON, 'The Romantic Absolute', *British Journal for the History of Philosophy*, 19 (2011), 497–517

STRACK, FRIEDRICH, ' "Fermenta Cognitionis": Zur romantischen Fragmentkonzeption von Friedrich Schlegel und Novalis', in *Subversive Romantik*, ed. by Volker Kapp and others (Berlin: Duncker & Humblot, 2004), pp. 343–64

—— 'Novalis und Fichte: Zur bewußtseinstheoretischen und zur moralphilosophischen Rezeption Friedrich von Hardenbergs', in *Novalis und die Wissenschaften*, ed. by Herbert Uerlings (Tübingen: Niemeyer, 1997), pp. 193–206

STRATHAUSEN, CARSTEN, *The Look of Things: Poetry and Vision around 1900* (Chapel Hill: The University of North Carolina Press, 2003)

SYROTINSKI, MICHAEL, and IAN MACLACHLAN, eds, *Sensual Reading: New Approaches to Reading in its Relations to the Senses* (Lewisburg: Bucknell University Press, 2001)

TADIÉ, JEAN-YVES, *Lectures de Proust* (Paris: Colin, 1971)

TAYLOR, CHARLES, 'The Opening Arguments of the *Phenomenology*', in *Hegel: A Collection of Critical Essays*, ed. by Alasdair MacIntyre (Garden City: Anchor Books, 1972), pp. 151–87

THEISOHN, PHILIPP, *Die kommende Dichtung: Geschichte des literarischen Orakels 1450–2050* (Munich: Fink, 2012)

THORAU, CHRISTIAN, *Semantisierte Sinnlichkeit: Studien zu Rezeption und Zeichenstruktur der Leitmotivtechnik Richard Wagners* (Stuttgart: Steiner, 2003)

TIECK, LUDWIG, *Werke in vier Bänden*, ed. by Marianne Thalmann, 4 vols (Munich: Winkler, 1963–66)

TRAWNY, PETER, *Heidegger und der Mythos der jüdischen Weltverschwörung*, 3rd edn (Frankfurt am Main: Klostermann, 2015)

TURNER, MARK, *The Literary Mind* (New York: Oxford University Press, 1996)

UERLINGS, HERBERT, *Friedrich von Hardenberg, genannt Novalis: Werk und Forschung* (Stuttgart: Metzler, 1991)

UTZ, PETER, *Das Auge und das Ohr im Text: Literarische Sinneswahrnehmung in der Goethezeit* (Munich: Fink, 1990)

VALÉRY, PAUL, 'Poésie et pensée abstraite', in *Œuvres*, ed. by Jean Hytier, 2 vols (Paris: Gallimard, 1957–60)
VAZSONYI, NICHOLAS, ed., *The Cambridge Wagner Encyclopedia* (Cambridge: Cambridge University Press, 2013)
VETTER, HELMUTH, ed., *Wörterbuch der phänomenologischen Begriffe* (Hamburg: Meiner, 2004)
VIETTA, SILVIO, *Ästhetik der Moderne: Literatur und Bild* (Munich: Fink, 2001)
VILLINGER, RAHEL, 'Gedankenstriche: Theorie und Poesie bei Novalis', *Deutsche Vierteljahrsschrift für Literaturwissenschaft und Geistesgeschichte*, 86 (2012), 547–77
VOGL, JOSEPH, *Kalkül und Leidenschaft: Poetik des ökonomischen Menschen* (Zurich: diaphanes, 2004)
DE VRIES, WILLEM A., 'Sense-Certainty and the "This-Such"', in *Hegel's Phenomenology of Spirit: A Critical Guide* (Cambridge: Cambridge University Press, 2008), pp. 63–75
VUKIĆEVIĆ, VLADIMIR, *Cézannes Realisation: Die Malerei und die Aufgabe des Denkens* (Munich: Fink, 1992)
WAGNER, RICHARD, *Sämtliche Schriften und Dichtungen* ('Volks-Ausgabe'), ed. by Richard Sternfeld and others, 16 vols, 6th edn (Leipzig: Breitkopf & Härtel, 1912)
WALDENFELS, BERNHARD, *Das leibliche Selbst: Vorlesungen zur Phänomenologie des Leibes*, ed. by Regula Giuliani (Frankfurt am Main: Suhrkamp, 2000)
—— *Sinnesschwellen: Studien zur Phänomenologie des Fremden 3* (Frankfurt am Main: Suhrkamp, 1999)
WANNING, BERBELI, *Novalis zur Einführung* (Hamburg: Junius, 1996)
WARMINSKI, ANDRZEJ, 'Pre-Positional By-Play', *Glyph*, 3 (1978), 98–117
—— 'Reading for Example: "Sense-Certainty" in Hegel's *Phenomenology of Spirit*', *Diacritics*, 11 (1981), 83–95
WARNOCK, G. J., 'Concepts and Schematism', *Analysis*, 9 (1948), 77–82
WATERS, LINDSAY, and WLAD GODZICH, eds, *Reading de Man Reading* (Minneapolis: University of Minnesota Press, 1989)
WEGMANN, NIKOLAUS, and ULRICH BREUER, 'Editorial', *Athenäum: Jahrbuch der Friedrich Schlegel Gesellschaft*, 23 (2013), 9–18
WEIMAR, KLAUS, *Geschichte der deutschen Literaturwissenschaft bis zum Ende des 19. Jahrhunderts* (Munich: Fink, 1989)
WEINER, MARC A., 'Zwieback and Madeleine: Creative Recall in Wagner and Proust', *MLN*, 95 (1980), 679–84
WELLBERY, DAVID, 'Zur Poetik der Figuration beim mittleren Rilke: "Die Gazelle"', in *Zu Rainer Maria Rilke*, ed. by Egon Schwarz (Stuttgart: Klett, 1983), pp. 125–32
WELLMON, CHAD, 'Lyrical Feeling: Novalis' Anthropology of the Senses', *Studies in Romanticism*, 47 (2008), 453–77
WELSH, CAROLINE, 'Die Grenzen des Menschen: Anthropologie und Ästhetik um 1800. Zum Verhältnis zwischen Physiologie und Autonomieästhetik bei Tieck und Novalis', in *Die Grenzen des Menschen: Anthropologie und Ästhetik um 1800*, ed. by Maximilian Bergengruen and others (Würzburg: Königshausen & Neumann, 2001), pp. 113–34
—— *Hirnhöhlenpoetiken: Theorien zur Wahrnehmung in Wissenschaft, Ästhetik und Literatur um 1800* (Freiburg im Breisgau: Rombach, 2003)
WESTPHAL, KENNETH R., 'Hegel and Hume on Perception and Concept-Empiricism', *Journal of the History of Philosophy*, 36 (1998), 99–123
—— *Hegel, Hume und die Identität wahrnehmbarer Dinge: Historisch-kritische Analyse zum Kapitel Wahrnehmung in der Phänomenologie von 1807* (Frankfurt am Main: Klostermann, 1998)
—— 'Hegel's Phenomenological Method and Analysis of Consciousness', in *The Blackwell Guide to Hegel's 'Phenomenology of Spirit'*, ed. by Kenneth R. Westphal (Oxford: Wiley-Blackwell, 2009), pp. 1–36

WIESING, LAMBERT, 'Einleitung', in *Philosophie der Wahrnehmung: Modelle und Reflexionen*, ed. by Lambert Wiesing (Frankfurt am Main: Suhrkamp, 2002), pp. 9–64
—— *Das Mich der Wahrnehmung: Eine Autopsie* (Frankfurt am Main: Suhrkamp, 2009)
WILSON, EDMUND, 'A Short View of Proust', *The New Republic*, 54 (1928), 140–48
WIMSATT, W. K., and M. C. BEARDSLEY, 'The Affective Fallacy', *The Sewanee Review*, 57 (1949), 31–55
WINKELVOSS, KARINE, *Rilke, la pensée des yeux* (Asnières: PIA, 2004)
WITTE, BERND and OTHERS, eds, *Goethe-Handbuch*, 4 vols (Stuttgart: Metzler, 1996)
WOLZOGEN, HANS VON, *Thematischer Leitfaden durch die Musik zu Rich. Wagner's Festspiel 'Der Ring des Nibelungen'* (Leipzig: Schloemp, 1876)
—— *Thematischer Leitfaden durch die Musik zu Richard Wagner's 'Tristan und Isolde', nebst einem Vorworte über den Sagenstoff des Wagner'schen Dramas* (Leipzig: Feodor Reinboth, 1882)
WORDSWORTH, WILLIAM, and SAMUEL TAYLOR COLERIDGE, *Lyrical Ballads*, ed. by R. L. Brett and A. R. Jones (London: Routledge, 1991)
YOSHIKAWA, KAZUYOSHI, 'Vinteuil ou la genèse du septuor', *Études proustiennes*, 3 (1979), 289–347
ZAHAVI, DAN, *Subjectivity and Selfhood : Investigating the First-Person Perspective* (Cambridge, MA: MIT Press, 2005)
ZAISER, RAINER, *Die Epiphanie in der französischen Literatur: Zur Entmystifizierung eines religiösen Erlebnismusters* (Tübingen: Narr, 1995)
ZYMNER, RÜDIGER, ed., *Handbuch Gattungstheorie* (Stuttgart: Metzler, 2010)

INDEX

Adorno, Theodor W.:
  on Beethoven 23, 40 n. 87, 107 n. 58
  on *Dingkult* in Rilke 169
  on Hegel's style 106 n. 46
  on redemption in Wagner 208
aesthesiology:
  when listening to music 22–23
  when looking at things 23–24
    see also object perception
  as defined by Helmuth Plessner 22, 39 n. 71
  as metaphorology 187–88
  as temporal logic or 'story' of perception x, 20–24
    involving retention and protention 20–22, 149
    combining thoughts with sensations 22
    sensuous force 31–32
aesthesis (perception) 11, 34 n. 26
  in relation to concepts 55, 78, 96–101
  involves form-giving 9–13, 90–92, 96–99, 134–37
    vs passive sensation ix, 9–10, 55, 86, 119–22, 134, 166
  historicity of perception xi, 123–24, 152 n. 12, 162, 163, 229 n. 2
  interplay between aesthesis and diegesis ix–x, 10–11, 229, *et passim*
  as poetic activity 117–23, 150
  as both process and relation, or, (hi)story: 10, 72–73, 98–99
  temporality of perception: 64, 66–67, 70, 78, 126–27
    see also aesthesiology
  as *Wahr-Nehmung* 8, 84, 151 n. 6
aesthetics:
  aesthetic power:
    of literature ix, 8–9, 20, 150
    of works of art 177–78, 179, 213–19
  rooted in *aisthēsis* 7, 47
  as 'coincidence of form, feeling, and intellect' xi, 227
  Romanticism as turning point 121
Andriopoulos, Stefan 110–11 n. 96
Apel, Friedmar 118, 122, 151 n. 4
Aristotle:
  on mimesis 11, 34 n. 27
  on particulars 55, 107 n. 59
  on time 68
Augustine of Hippo 68

Backhaus, Inge 200, 221 n. 30, 223 n. 56
Bal, Mieke 72

Barthes, Roland 18, 208
Baudelaire, Charles:
  on inspiration 219
  on leitmotif technique 199
Beardsley, M. C. ix, 6
Beethoven, Ludwig van 23, 107 n. 58, 222 n. 46, 224 n. 65
Beiser, Frederick 105 n. 32, 127–28
Bernhard, Thomas: 37 n. 50, 228
Blumenberg, Hans 39 n. 68, 187
Böhme, Hartmut 165, 192 n. 45
Bowie, Malcolm 218
Brandom, Robert 109 n. 79
Brodsky, Claudia 7, 12, 223 n. 55
Brooks, Peter 29, 31, 34 n. 5, 211
Burke, Kenneth 41 n. 94
Burnham, Scott 22–23

Celan, Paul 32 n. 6
Cézanne, Paul 167
Chatman, Seymor 35 n. 29, 72, 113 n. 119
Cœuroy, André 195, 196
Coleridge, Samuel T. xi
Corngold, Stanley ix, xi, 33 n. 12, 192 n. 45
Culler, Jonathan 35 n. 29, 161

Dahlhaus, Carl 198, 205
Daube, Uwe 200, 221 n. 29
Davidson, Donald 112 n. 108
De Man, Paul:
  against Hans Robert Jauß 18
  'non-perceptual' (rhetorical) approach to literature 6–8, 36 n. 44, 38 n. 54
  on Rilke 176, 189 n. 8
Debussy, Claude 220 n. 12
Defoe, Daniel 132
Deleuze, Gilles:
  on art as essence of perception 27
  on Bergson 108 n. 63
  on Proust 204
Derrida, Jacques:
  on Hegel 52, 60, 66
  on perception 33 n. 18
  on phenomenology 19
  on time 21, 68, 69
description, *see* diegesis
Dewey, John 13

Di Giovanni, George 62
diegesis (narration, description) 11–12
　as narrative world (Genette) 11, 16–20
　as narrative speech (Plato) 11, 34–35 n. 27
　showing vs telling 228–29
　see also story
Doherty, Brigid 192 n. 49

Eichendorff, Joseph von 15

Fauré, Gabriel 223 n. 52
Fichte, Johann Gottlieb:
　on Hume 112 n. 104
　on perception 92, 111 n. 100
　on *Tathandlung* 125–27
　on *Wechselbestimmung* 130
Flaubert, Gustave 31, 208
Förster, Eckart 112 n. 112
Foucault, Michel 124
Frank, Joseph 203
Frank, Manfred 127
Freud, Sigmund 165
Friedman, Norman 230 n. 3
Frye, Northrop xii n. 4
Fuerst, Norbert 193 n. 54

Gadamer, Hans Georg 19, 192 n. 41
Gebsattel, Viktor Emil von 165
Genette, Gérard:
　on *diégèse* 11–12
　on Proust 199, 204
Gibson, James J. 12–13, 166
Gide, André 216
Goethe, Johan Wolfgang:
　on aesthetic reception 14
　and Hegel 63, 97, 102 n. 6, 112 n. 112
　on interrelation of form and content 106 n. 43
　and Novalis 140
Goodman, Nelson 17
Gregory, Richard L. 10, 23
Grünbein, Durs 8, 45
　poems:
　　'In der Provinz 2', 1–3
　　'Niemands Land Stimmen' 3–6
　writes poems without mystery 32 n. 4
　on remembrance 32–33 n. 6

Haering, Theodor 127, 156 n. 74
Hegel, Georg Wilhelm Friedrich:
　Bericht über eine Alpenwanderung 45–47
　on dialectics:
　　as 'dynamization and confusion' 73
　　as method of development 51
　　of time and space 69–71
　on Fichte 48–49
　against Goethe's empiricism 97

intentionality (*Meinen*) 54–55, 62–63
Jenaer Systementwürfe 67, 69, 71, 88–89
on Kant 48–49, 110 n. 92
on knowledge 55–57, 62–63, 98–10
　absolute concepts 100–01
　sophisms of 'so-called common sense' 48
on perception:
　contradiction (either/or) of perception 48, 77–78,
　　85–86, 97
　as deixis 58–61
　as determinate negation 75–77, 82–84, 94–95
　as both process and relation, or, (hi)story: 10,
　　72–73, 98–99
　temporality of perception 57, 64, 66–69, 70, 78
　as verbalization of property relations 90–92, 95–99
Phänomenologie des Geistes:
　Faust as model 106 n. 49
　mission 50, 52–53
　obscure style 50
　orthographic emendations xv, 105 n. 35 & 37
　'self-perfecting scepticism' as method 51, 56–57
　scenographic mode of presentation 51–52, 63,
　　99–101
on reflection:
　consciousness is self-consciousnesses 48–49, 86–89
　spirit is self-determination 49–50, 62
Schiller as terminological inspiration 105 n. 32
on speculation:
　etymology of speculation 108–09 n. 76
　as sublation (*Aufhebung*) 56–57, 73–74, 76
translation issues:
　beiherspielen 57
　einzeln/besonders/allgemein 103–04 n. 27
　meinen/Meinung 54–55
on truth as intersubjective logos (i.e. language)
　51–52, 61–63, 91–92, 95–97
Heidegger, Martin:
　on anxiety 173
　on Hegel 68, 105–06 n. 41
　on Rilke 191–92 n. 41
　on the concept of 'world' 37 n. 49 & 50
Heinrich von Kleist 31
Helmholtz, Hermann von 33 n. 2
Henrich, Dieter 126, 127, 153 n. 31
Houlgate, Stephen 48, 74
Hume, David 80, 92
Husserl, Edmund:
　on noesis/noema 178, 187
　on perception 137, 168–69, 186–87
　on poetry as phenomenology 163
　on time:
　　retention/protention 20–21, 39 n. 68, 68
　　sense (*Sinn*) as continuity 39 n. 70
　on the concept of 'world' 16–17
Huyssen, Andreas 169

imagination:
    in acts of perception 12–13
    media history thereof 38 n. 66, 110 n. 96, 190 n. 21
        in Romanticism 35 n. 36, 123, 128, 153 n. 23
    as participation and concretization 13–16
    visual (eidetic) character of literature 19–20
immanence:
    of literature 6, 8–9, 16–20, 188
    of perception 24–25, 184–87
    see also scene
Ingarden, Roman 17–18
Iser, Wolfgang 18–20

Jakobson, Romam 141
Jauß, Hans Robert xii n. 3, 18–19

Kafka, Franz 194 n. 68, 229
Kant, Immanuel:
    on *Chiffreschrift* of nature 152 n. 7
    on cognition as narrative representation 12
    on community (*Wechselwirkung*) of substance and
        accidents 82, 84
    on history of reason 99
    on sensuousness as a receptive faculty 55, 104 n. 29
    on synthesis of concepts and intutions 49, 55
    on time 23, 68
        schemata as 'determinations of time' 22
        in relation to space 69, 71
Kaufmann, Walter 73, 105 n. 32, 106 n. 49
Keats, John 151 n. 3
Kilcher, Andreas B. 157 n. 89
Kittler, Friedrich:
    on mimesis 35 n. 27
    on Rilke 162
    on Romanticism 35 n. 36, 110 n. 96, 123
        Hegel 63, 105 n. 36
        Novalis 144, 157 n. 89
Koch, Anton Friedrich 105 n. 33, 109 n. 78, 110 n. 89
Kramer, Andreas 170, 192 n. 42
Krug, Wilhelm Traugott 103 n. 20

Laplanche, Jean 180
Lessing, Gotthold Ephraim:
    Laokoon 25, 47
Locke, John 92–93
Löwith, Karl 61
Luhmann, Niklas:
    on art as communication of perceptions 27
    on perception as 'actualization of distinctions'
        109 n. 79
    on romantic love 211
    on the concept of 'world' 37 n. 49

Mach, Ernst 166
Mallarmé, Stéphane 25, 216
McSweeney, Kerry xii–xiii n. 5, 33 n. 18

Melville, Herman:
    Moby Dick 24
Merleau-Ponty, Maurice 137, 169, 184, 222 n. 32
metaphor:
    in Kafka 194 n. 68
    in philosophy 49, 100–01, 110–11 n. 96
    in scenographies 169–71, 187–88
mimesis 11, 34–35 n. 27
Molde, Klas 35 n. 29
music:
    involves aesthesiological schemata 22–23, 202
    leitmotif, see Wagner *and* Proust
    as medium:
        of passion 211–12
        of revelation 213–14, 217–19
        of negativity (i.e. time) 107 n. 58

narration, see diegesis
narrative, narratology, see story
Nattiez, Jean-Jacques 196, 224 n. 64
Nietzsche, Friedrich:
    on perception as form-giving 9–10
    on reading 30
    on Wagner 198
Novalis (Friedrich von Hardenberg):
    on Fichte:
        critique of absolute foundations 130–34
        familiarity with Fichte's works 124–25
        Wissenschaftslehre as Robinson Crusoe-like
            scenario 132–33
    on fragmentariness 129–30
    Heinrich von Ofterdingen 139–50
        allegorical interpretations 140, 149
        against *Wilhelm Meisters Lehrjahre* 158 n. 92
    on language as 'gentle measure' of all things 62
    Lehrlinge zu Saïs 118–23
        as training of the senses 118–19
    on magic 119–20, 150
    philosophical interpretations of Novalis 127–30,
        133
    on reading 14–16, 123–24
    on *Wechselbestimmung*:
        in comprehension 138–39
        in perception 134–37
        as basis of 'romanticization' 137–38

object perception:
    affordances 12–13
    according to Hegel 75–97
        particularity 80–82
        properties as 'reciprocal relations' 82–84, 93–96
        as recognition process 179
        requires reflection (i.e. apperception) 86–89
        substance (thinghood) 53, 74, 79–80, 92–93
        verbalization 60–61, 90–92, 95–97
    according to Husserl 168–69, 186–87

according to Novalis 136–37
according to Rilke 163–88
　anonymity 168, 181–84
　cathexis (*Besetzung*) 164–65
　Nachträglichkeit 179–80
　objectification (*réalisation*) as challenge 92, 167–69, 173–76, 184–86
　problems of terminology 166–67
Ouellet, Pierre 27

perception, *see* aesthesis
Pessoa, Fernando 190 n. 21
phenomenology:
　of literature 16–20, 37 n. 48
　of perception 19 n. 61, 34 n. 26
　　see also Husserl *and* Merleau-Ponty
　through scenographies x, 29, 51–52, 63, 74, 99–101, 162–63
philosophy:
　and literature 128–30, 132–33, 139–40, 163
　and theology 61
Pierhal, Armand 208
Pinkard, Terry 65
Pippin, Robert 49, 50, 97, 99, 102 n. 12 & 13, 109 n. 85
Plato:
　on *aisthēsis* 34 n. 26
　on *diēgēsis* 11–12, 34–35 n. 27
Plessner, Helmuth:
　on 'aesthesiology' 22, 39 n. 71
Proust, Marcel:
　À la recherche du temps perdu:
　　literary critics on musicality in Proust 195–97, 199–200
　　leitmotif technique 199, 200–09
　　significance of Swann 205–06, 211–12, 214–15, 216–17
　　significance of Vinteuil's music 197, 206, 209–19
　on reading 16, 216, 223 n. 62
　and Wagner 196–97, 203–04, 208–09, 209–10, 218–19
psychology:
　in the nineteenth century 162, 166
　of perception 10, 12–13, 151 n. 4, 166
　of reading ix, 31
Purpus, Wilhelm 71

reader-response theory 17–20, 37 n. 48
reading:
　as 'modern luxury' 123–24
　as perceptual activity (readerly aesthesis) ix, 6, 8–9, 13–16, 26–27, 29–30, *et passim*
　reader as 'extended author' 14–16, 129–30, 140, 150, 216
　reader-oriented approach to literature xii n. 5, 8, 18, 28, 211
Ricoeur, Paul 18, 72

Rilke, Rainer Maria:
　Aufzeichnungen des Malte Laurids Brigge 163–65, 170–76, 181, 185–86
　on Cézanne 167, 185
　in relation to Husserlian phenomenology 163, 178–79, 187
　Neue Gedichte:
　　'Archaischer Torso Apollos' 177–80
　　'Die Fensterrose' 181–83
　　'Schwarze Katze' 183–84
　and photography 190 n. 21
　on psychoanalysis 165
　on Rodin 178
　preoccupation with things (*Dinge*) 160–61
　　personification (anthropomorphisms) 169–71

scene:
　etymology 24
　as spatiotemporal domain of perception 24–25
　vs image 19–20
　in relation to text (signs) 5–9, 24–27, 141–42, 146, 149–50, 161–62, 176–77
scenography ix, 8–9, 28–31
　constrains readerly aesthesis 8–9, 30, 149, 227
　in architecture and exhibition spaces 28
　in relation to other genres 227–29
　vs image xii n. 2, 28–29, 193 n. 56
　as medium of theory x, 29, 63
　of perception 30–31, *et passim*
　in theatre 28
Schiller, Friedrich:
　on the power of form 36 n. 39
　provides Hegel with terminology 56, 105 n. 32
　on perception 111 n. 100
　on reading 13–14
　on words as medium of literature 25–26, 61
Schlegel, Friedrich:
　on 'sympoetry' 15, 36 n. 44
　on perception 111 n. 100 & 102, 118
　on *Wechselbestimmung* 130
Schopenhauer, Arthur 48
sensuousness:
　double sense of 'sense' 134–36
　of literature 225–29, *et passim*
　　see also aesthetics
　as category of literary criticism xi, xii n. 4, 6–9
Simon, Ralf 28–29, 184
Singer Sargent, John:
　sketch after *El Jaleo* xii n. 2
Sounac, Frédéric 224 n. 63 & 65
Steiner, Uwe C. 137
Stern, Robert 55, 82, 109 n. 82
Stollberg, Arne 203
story:
　becomes aesthesiology in the context of a scene 29, 31

ambiguity of 'story' in narratology 72
  as link between narrative discourse and *histoire* 29, 31, 34 n. 5, 211
  as both process and relation, or, (hi)story 10, 72–73, 98–99
  double-layered temporality 10, 11–12, 21–22, 72, 98
Strathausen, Carsten 179

Tadié, Jean-Yes 195
Taylor, Charles, 51
Tieck, Ludwig 15
  on 'romanticization' 157 n. 86
time, temporality:
  concepts of time:
    Augustine of Hippo 68
    Derrida 68, 69
    Husserl 20–21, 39 n. 68, 68
    Kant 68, 69
    Hegel 66–68
    Bergson 68, 107–08 n. 63
  of narration 11–12, 99–101, 203–04, 207, 227
    see also story
  of perception 20–24, 64, 66–69, 70, 77–78, 98–99
    see also aesthesiology

Utz, Peter 31, 118, 152 n. 14

Villinger, Rahel 129

Wagner, Richard:
  on aesthetic labour 218–19
  on the term 'music drama' 220 n. 15
  on leitmotif technique 197–99, 203
  Ring des Nibelungen 198, 205, 209
  Tristan und Isolde 205
Waldenfels, Bernhard 169
Wellbery, David 189 n. 9 & 16
Wellmon, Chad 152 n. 9 & 14, 157 n. 81
Westphal, Kenneth 87, 104 n. 30, 106 n. 51, 109 n. 82, 109–10 n. 89, 111 n. 98
Wiesing, Lambert 79, 169
Wilson, Edmund 199–200
Wimsatt, W. K. xi, 6
Wolzogen, Hans von 207, 220 n. 16, 222 n. 40
Wordsworth, William:
  'Lines Composed a Few Miles above Tintern Abbey' xiii n. 6, 226
  1802 preface to the *Lyrical Ballads* 141, 229, 230 n. 5

www.ingramcontent.com/pod-product-compliance
Lightning Source LLC
LaVergne TN
LVHW061250060426
835507LV00017B/1988